1998

The Renaissance, known primarily for the art and literature that it produced, was also a period in which philosophical thought flourished. This two-volume anthology contains forty new translations of important works on moral and political philosophy written during the Renaissance and hitherto unavailable in English. The anthology is designed to be used in conjunction with *The Cambridge History of Renaissance Philosophy,* in which all of these texts are discussed.

The works, originally written in Latin, Italian, French, Spanish, and Greek, cover such topics as: concepts of man; Aristotelian, Platonic, Stoic, and Epicurean ethics; scholastic political philosophy; theories of princely and republican government in Italy; and northern European political thought. Each text is supplied with an introduction and a guide to further reading.

These readable and fully annotated versions of a wide range of texts will enable serious students of the history of philosophy to gain first-hand access to the ethical and political thought of the Renaissance.

Cambridge Translations of Renaissance Philosophical Texts

Cambridge Translations of Renaissance Philosophical Texts

VOLUME II: POLITICAL PHILOSOPHY

Edited by

JILL KRAYE

The Warburg Institute

CAMBRIDGE
UNIVERSITY PRESS

PUBLISHED BY THE PRESS SYNDICATE OF THE UNIVERSITY OF CAMBRIDGE
The Pitt Building, Trumpington Street, Cambridge CB2 1RP, United Kingdom

CAMBRIDGE UNIVERSITY PRESS
The Edinburgh Building, Cambridge CB2, 2RU, United Kingdom
40 West 20th Street, New York, NY 10011-4211, USA
10 Stamford Road, Oakleigh, Melbourne 3166, Australia

© Cambridge University Press 1997

First published 1997

Printed in the United States of America

Typeset in Times

Library of Congress Cataloging-in-Publication Data
Cambridge translations of Renaissance philosophical texts / edited by
Jill Kraye.
p. cm.
Includes bibliographical references and index.
"Originally written in Latin, Italian, French, Spanish, and
Greek" – p.
Companion vol. to: The Cambridge history of Renaissance
philosophy.
Contents: v. 1. Moral philosophy – v. 2. Political philosophy.
ISBN 0-521-41580-2 (v. 1). – ISBN 0-521-42604-9 (v. 1 : pbk.). –
ISBN 0-521-58295-4 (v. 2). – ISBN 0-521-58757-3 (v. 2 : pbk.)
1. Ethics, Ancient. 2. Man. 3. Political science – Philosophy –
History. I. Kraye, Jill. II. Cambridge history of Renaissance
philosophy.
BJ161.C36   1997
190'.9'031 – dc20   96-35176
                                                 CIP

*A catalog record for this book is available from
the British Library.*

ISBN 0 521 41580 2 hardback (volume 1)
ISBN 0 521 42604 9 paperback (volume 1)
IBSN 0 521 58295 4 hardback (volume 2)
ISBN 0 521 58757 3 paperback (volume 2)
ISBN 0 521 59208 9 hardback (set)
ISBN 0 521 59772 2 paperback (set)

Contents

PART II. THE THEORY OF PRINCELY GOVERNMENT IN RENAISSANCE ITALY

PART III. THE THEORY OF REPUBLICAN GOVERNMENT IN RENAISSANCE VENICE

PART IV. THE THEORY OF REPUBLICAN AND PRINCELY GOVERNMENT IN RENAISSANCE FLORENCE

PART V. POLITICAL THEORY IN NORTHERN EUROPE

Translators

D. Catherine Brown, Late of the Department of History, Queen's University, Kingston, Canada

Brian P. Copenhaver, Department of History, UCLA

Martin Davies, Incunabula, British Library, London

Alison Holcroft, Department of Classics, University of Canterbury, Christchurch, New Zealand

Neil Kenny, Churchill College, Cambridge

A. S. McGrade, Department of Philosophy, University of Connecticut (Storrs)

David Marsh, Department of Italian, Rutgers University, New Brunswick, New Jersey

John Monfasani, Department of History, The University at Albany, SUNY, Albany

Russell Price, Department of Politics and International Relations, University of Lancaster

J. A. Trentman, Huron College, London, Ontario

Nicholas Webb, Open University, Milton Keynes

Ronald G. Witt, Department of History, Duke University, Durham, North Carolina

Preface

The Cambridge History of Renaissance Philosophy (*CHRP*), published in 1988, attempted to draw attention to the richness of philosophical production in the period from the fourteenth to the sixteenth centuries. The editors (Charles B. Schmitt, Quentin Skinner, Eckhard Kessler and myself) made a point of including within the scope of the volume the wide range of disciplines which in the Renaissance were regarded as part of philosophy: not only those fields which still constitute the core of the philosophical curriculum, such as logic and epistemology, but also subjects which are no longer classified as philosophy, such as natural science, psychology and rhetoric. The aim was to document and analyse the contributions made in this era to all these subjects, and in this way to put Renaissance philosophy on the map.

Not all fields of Renaissance philosophy, however, have suffered equally from the general neglect that *CHRP* was designed to remedy. One which has maintained a remarkably high profile is political philosophy. While in histories of Western philosophy the period from 1300 to 1600 is often passed over, or given only perfunctory and superficial treatment, no account of the development of political thought would be considered complete without at least one lengthy chapter devoted to these centuries. Any study of the formation of the modern science of politics must find a place for the contrasting approaches of Niccolò Machiavelli and Thomas More. The centrality of the roles played by the Italian city-states (especially Florence and Venice), the conciliarist movement and the Reformation is also beyond dispute.

Yet, for all the importance assigned to Renaissance political thought, only a small number of texts have been studied intensively. English translations of well-known books such as *The Prince* and *Utopia* have long been available; and these works, together with treatises written in English such as Sir Thomas Elyot's *The Boke Named the Governor,* have received the lion's share of attention from English-speaking scholars and students. The aim of this volume is to make possible a broader and more accurate picture of Renaissance political philosophy by publishing seventeen new translations. The texts have been selected from among those discussed by Quentin Skinner in his chapter on 'Political philosophy' in *CHRP*. An anthology of Renaissance political philosophy which does not include Machiavelli's *The Prince* runs the risk of being compared to a production of *Hamlet* without the prince. It is to be hoped, however, that the benefit provided by a substantial increase in the amount of material available to an Anglophone readership will outweigh any disadvantages caused by the absence of works which can be readily found elsewhere. In order to make it as easy as possible for readers to locate published translations, a bibliography of Renaissance political philosophy texts available in English has been supplied.

As in *CHRP,* a broad view of Renaissance philosophy has been taken in this volume. Scholastic as well as humanist works, vernacular texts as well as Latin ones, have been included. A large proportion of the works derive from an Italian context, but northern European political thought is also well represented. Although many texts have been translated in their entirety, it was not possible, due to constraints of space, to have complete versions of all the works in the volume. Where it has been necessary to translate only part of a particular text, priority has been given to those passages discussed in *CHRP.* Each translation is annotated and has been provided with a brief introduction, as well as a list of further reading, so that the book, although intended primarily as a companion volume to *CHRP,* can also be used on its own.

Given that the aim of this anthology is to make inaccessible texts accessible to a wide public, it would be failing in one of its main duties if the translations, while faithful, were so literal that they did not read well in English. I have therefore encouraged (browbeaten, some might say) the translators to strive for maximum readability. That said, it is by no means possible – or desirable – to translate all Renaissance texts in the same style. An attempt has therefore been made to capture the difference, for instance, between the formulaic and rather stilted Latin of scholastic authors such as Jacques Almain and the fluid and rhetorical Latin of humanists such as Josse Clichtove. Where a particular word or phrase has proved especially difficult to translate or the translation chosen might be regarded as controversial, the original is given afterwards in square brackets. Insertions on the part of the translator are also placed in square brackets; omissions are indicated by an ellipsis. All quotations from the Bible are taken from the Revised Version, and its numeration of chapter and verses has been followed (even when this differs from the original Vulgate citation).

I am immensely grateful to the translators who contributed to this volume. All of them were faced, at one time or another, with awkward textual, philosophical and historical problems. Many, in addition, had to work from uncritical and unannotated Renaissance editions. Collaborating with the various translators, I have acquired some new friends (though in some cases our communication has been conducted entirely through postal, telephonic and electronic channels) and strengthened some old bonds. Despite occasional moments of irritation – both on my part and that of the translators – it has been an enjoyable and, I hope, useful enterprise. I am particularly indebted to one of the translators, Martin Davies. An experienced editor himself, he gave helpful advice on a range of linguistic and stylistic matters, performing with commendable generosity and patience the thankless role of husband of the editor.

Part I.
Scholastic Political Theory

1

Jean Gerson

D. CATHERINE BROWN

Introduction

Jean Gerson (1363–1429) was one of Europe's most influential churchmen of the early fifteenth century. The pupil of Pierre d'Ailly at Paris, he became chancellor of the university in 1395, a position he held until 1429. He wrote numerous pastoral and mystical works and was a preacher of renown, delivering sermons both to clerics (in Latin) and to the laity (in the vernacular). He is probably best known, however, for his efforts to end the Great Schism. The complex and difficult situation created by this schism led Gerson to produce a number of writings in which he strove to define the exact position and power of the papacy in the ecclesiastical hierarchy and its relationship to a general council. His views, in fact, shifted as the concrete situation changed, and it was by almost reluctant stages that he came to embrace a conciliarist position. In the period before and during the Council of Pisa (1409), one of his chief arguments in favour of the power of a general council was based on the principle of *epikeia* (or *aequitas*), according to which, he argued, the law, in cases of necessity, should be interpreted not according to the strict literal sense, but rather according to the underlying intention of the lawgiver. By the time of the Council of Constance (1414–18), Gerson had become a fully committed conciliarist – committed not only to the doctrine that if there was no true pope or if there were rival claimants (a case of necessity), the entire power of the Church could be exercised by a general council, but also ultimately to the doctrine that a council had a part to play even when there was a single true pope. His mature doctrine appears in both *Ambulate*,[1] the sermon he preached in March 1415 after John XXIII's flight from Constance, and in the treatise *Concerning Ecclesiastical Power,* read by Gerson to the council on 6 February 1417. By this time, John XXIII had been deposed by the council (May 1415), Gregory XII had abdicated (July 1415) and preparations were underway for the deposition of the sole remaining pontiff, Benedict XIII. It was with these controversial events in mind that Gerson wrote the treatise, which centres on the relationship of pope to council and of both to the Church.

The Latin text of *De potestate ecclesiastica* is published in Jean Gerson, *Oeuvres complètes,* ed. P. Glorieux, 10 vols. (Paris, 1960–73), VI, pp. 210–50; the passages translated here are at pp. 227–33, 247–8. Catherine Brown, who very sadly died on 17 August 1993, before the final editing of her translation was finished, wanted to express her gratitude to her colleagues A. J. Marshall, W. D. McCready and especially N. J. Brown for their help and advice.

Concerning Ecclesiastical Power: Selections

TENTH CONSIDERATION

Ecclesiastical power in its fullness resides formally and as to its subject in the Roman pontiff alone.[2] Therefore, we may take it for granted in the first place that, although someone who is not a priest can be elected pope, just as such a person can be elected bishop, nevertheless he cannot and should not be called supreme pontiff unless he has been consecrated priest and bishop. And although he can have a certain jurisdiction as a result of election, he cannot enjoy the fullness of ecclesiastical power – whether the power of order or that of either kind of jurisdiction[3] – before consecration to the episcopacy. This is clear from the meaning of the terms employed.

But here a not inconsiderable ambiguity arises, thanks to the master jurists, who, when they speak of the plenitude of papal power, appear to be speaking only of the power of jurisdiction; and from this way of speaking the absurd consequence seems to follow that a mere layman – indeed, even a woman – could become pope and enjoy the plenitude of ecclesiastical power.

We may further take it for granted from what has already been said that, in accordance with the institution of Christ, no one in the Church ought to bestow, or receive, the grades of the hierarchy, which are to purge, illuminate and perfect, unless the authority of the supreme pontiff or sole ruler [*monarcha*] in the Holy Church of God plays a part either expressly or by implication. This is so that confusion may be avoided in the Church and that it may be ruled by the best form of government according to the model of the Church triumphant. For this reason John says in Revelation [21:2] that he had seen the new city of Jerusalem descend from heaven; and to Moses it was said: 'As it hath been shewed thee in the mount, so shall they make it.'[4] Again, we may take as true the doctrine of Aristotle that all actions are the actions of individuals.[5] And finally, from these and the preceding arguments, we can offer the following discursive definition: the fullness of ecclesiastical power is the power of order and of jurisdiction which was supernaturally conferred by Christ on Peter as his vicar and first monarch, to be used by him and his legitimate successors until the end of time for the building up [*aedificatio*] of the Church militant towards the goal of eternal happiness.

The term 'supernaturally' in this definition is used to distinguish this power from the power and jurisdiction which may well have accrued to Peter's successors in accordance with the civil and political laws of human society; or from that dictate of the natural law which decrees that the head of every society should enjoy many honours and privileges denied to others; or by special endowment or gift from princes and other laymen; or, finally, by favourable concessions from the Church itself or its general councils such as any perfect society[6] might naturally grant to its head. There was one reason for such a concession which had merit insofar as it arose from the need for interpretation of the laws and from day-to-day problems about Church government: recourse to the pope and his Curia is easier than to a general council. This was the motive for setting up kings in the first place and giving them the power to establish and interpret laws.

But some people have disregarded this distinction and have fancied that every privilege which is now accorded to supreme pontiffs belongs to them by virtue of Christ's original institution and is of immutable divine ordinance. But this is quite false, since it would remain the case that a man was a true and perfect pope even if he actually lacked many such privileges and honours; for it is not these which constitute the plenitude of ecclesiastical power, such as we have described as vested in Peter, and which no human being except Christ – and hence not even the whole Church – could confer, or, by the same token, remove, as we noted already in the ninth consideration.[7]

There are some learned scholars who now maintain that, after rules about the holding of elections and the conferment of benefices by ordinaries were introduced by general councils, according to the intention of the founders (a principle observed in the case of the law of patronage among the laity), it was by no means legitimate for the pope to annul such rules, especially so generally and indiscriminately, by reservations and other means, as has been seen this past century and more. It was not legitimate, moreover, for him to issue the number and type of waivers about matters decreed by general councils as has been customary in papal bulls – to the point, indeed, where Alexander V was led in certain of his supposed bulls to allow waivers with respect to that very salutary and widely observed statute *Omnis utriusque sexus*. . . .[8]

But others reply to the above argument not by addressing the question of the origin of ecclesiastical power as it was established by divine law, but rather by confining their considerations to decretals with the glosses, arguments and countless concordances of doctors, one following the other like a flock of sheep. They answer, in point of fact, with this single argument: that general councils have always understood that an exception was made of the authority of the supreme pontiff in all their decrees of whatever sort because, doubtless, they held papal authority to be above the council, or at least not beneath it; and it is obvious to them that equals have no authority over equals or lower ranks over their superiors.

But blessed be God, who, by means of this sacred Council of Constance, enlightened by the light of divine law, which gave it understanding through the trial of the present schism, has freed his Church from this dangerous and most pernicious doctrine whose persistence would have perpetuated the schism which it had nurtured. Indeed, it has been declared and decreed that a general council can be convened without the pope and that in certain cases a pope can be judged by a council and, moreover, that a general council has the authority to prescribe laws or rules according to which the plenitude of papal power is to be restrained and regulated – not, to be sure, in itself, for in itself it remains always the same, but in its use. Furthermore, it should not be thought that general councils have exempted papal authority from their decrees in such a way as to permit the pope an unbridled liberty to destroy so lightly what has been established so weightily and with the seasoned maturity of the wise. The exception made for papal authority, then, is understood to have been provided to the extent that temporary necessity or evident utility demanded it, on occasions when recourse to a general council was not open; under any other circumstances it would constitute not a use of the plenitude of papal power but a gross abuse of it. Whether anything which resulted from such an abuse would be valid or lawful, I do not presume to determine under any single generalization. I do know that many things are wrongly done, many inexpediently and many to the disfigurement of the Church, which nevertheless, once done, retain their force. It seems, however, that some declaration should be added by this sacred general council through which it may become clear in what sense, and to what extent, papal authority is recognized as exempt either from decrees already issued or, since (as they say) the law does not address itself to the past, from decrees to be issued in the future. And finally, the quashing or annulment of every ill-conceived act of past times would seem plainly to be difficult, of questionable validity and inexpedient.

The following rules should be noted as an aid to understanding what has been said here about the interpretation of laws and decrees.

First rule. Human laws are framed with a view to what happens in the majority of cases. It would be impossible for a human legislator to enumerate all particular cases or to offer the remedy of a special law for them, since they are infinitely variable. Indeed, it would not be desirable, for the outcome of such a multiplicity would be a disorder as distasteful as it would be confusing. On the other hand, according to Isidore, a law should be worthy of respect, just, capable of being observed and appropriate to the place and time in the light of the customs of the country; furthermore, it should be necessary, useful and clearly expressed, so that it contains nothing which misleads through obscurity; and it should be framed not for private advantage but for the common benefit of the citizens.[9]

Second rule. Human laws which are construed generally can and should admit of exceptions when the reason for the law does not apply in a particular case, when, that is, the legislator if present, or any prudent man if asked, would except from the general rule a particular case which might arise under such and such circumstances. This sort of exception is given a variety of names: sometimes it is called 'equity' [*epikeia*], as by Aristotle; sometimes 'interpretation of the law', as by jurists; sometimes 'dispensation', as by canonists; sometimes 'good faith', as by statesmen who say that it is good faith when one does not pretend to do one thing while in fact doing another; and sometimes it is called 'equity' [*aequitas*], as when the prophet says to the Lord: 'thy commandments are equity'[10] – that is, equity demands their performance.[11]

Third rule. We find three types of interpretation of or exception to a law. One belongs to the judicial power and is the province of the legislator and the judges, according to the well-known saying: 'The person who is responsible for establishing legislation is also the one responsible for interpreting it.' A second type belongs to doctrinal authority and is the province of those who, by authority of the supreme pontiff, have received a licence to give scholarly interpretations of the law. It is also the province of those who are well equipped, by skill or experience, with the knowledge of interpretation in these matters, on the principle: 'The expert in his field should be believed'; and again: 'Each person judges well in the area of his experience.' A third type of interpretation is based on unavoidable necessity. It can fall to anyone at all who sees with certainty an imminent danger to himself if he does not repel force with force and act in opposition to the general letter of the law. In this case a man is blameless before God, although he ought to regret that he has fallen into such a necessity. And provided he is able to make his case with legitimate witnesses before a human judge, he will be acquitted – though not otherwise; for what is not apparent before the judge in these matters is no different from what is not the case.

Fourth rule. The interpretation, dispensation or exception which belongs to judicial power operates in such a way that someone who disobeys the letter of the law is not punished before men in the external forum. But before God, in the forum of conscience, both the person who dispenses and the person to whom the dispensation is given will sin, unless the one who dispenses fits the description given by Christ: 'faithful and wise'.[12] Faithful, so that he does not abandon the divine or the common good and seek personal advantage, favour or honour; and wise, so that he may consider from all angles the reasoning behind the law and the intention of the legislator; for a dispensation is a fair distribution of the common good – as indeed is the law itself – to individuals in accordance with the law's intention, taking into account the variety of circumstances which arise. A dispensation which is not faithfully and wisely made is said by Bernard to be a dissipation [*dissipatio*] of the common good rather than a dispensation [*dispensatio*][13] – that is, as far as God and conscience are concerned, if it is a case about which there is, or should be, general agreement. But very often, in the eyes of men who judge according to externals, such a dispensation holds, unless it contains a glaring error or is prohibited by a higher law. This latter point is added because of the statutes that can be made by a general council about the use of papal power.

Fifth rule. The interpretation of law, or exception to it, which belongs to doctrinal authority affords most relief to those not obeying the bare letter of the law, in that it applies both to external judgements, insofar as it frees [those who break the law] from penalties, and also to divine judgements in the forum of conscience. This is especially the case when the majority of doctors are men of repute, experienced in their craft and of proven integrity; otherwise iniquity will often betray a man under the influence of entreaty or reward, for 'a gift doth blind the eyes of the wise'.[14] And if we are to believe Aristotle, speaking the words of experience, malice can cause error not only in conclusions far removed from first principles but at the very threshold of moral principles themselves.[15] Thus, theft was formerly thought to be licit among the Germans, as Julius Caesar bears witness in his *Gallic War* [VI.23.6]; and foul and unnatural sins were thought to be licit among the Romans, as the apostle records in his epistle to them.[16] The same is true with many men given over to pernicious ideas on account of the variety of faults encompassed by their depravity.

Sixth rule. The interpretation of law, and exceptions and dispensations, when they occur in either of the previously mentioned modes, judicial or doctrinal, demand that we adopt a double point of view: one which looks to the divine and public good, the other to the particular advantage of the person on whose behalf the interpretation or dispensation is granted. Therefore, it quite often happens that when the rigour of the law is indiscriminately relaxed, out of a certain compassion (so it is imagined) and merciful condescension towards particular individuals subject to the law, the stability and strength of discipline decays correspondingly – strength which should especially be preserved in all law. The Romans taught us this lesson when they put even their own sons to death and turned the rigour of the law against themselves in order that military discipline and obedience to the law should remain inviolate. The Carthusian brethren teach us the same lesson. They never, or very rarely, receive a dispensation for the eating of meat, and accordingly monastic discipline flourishes among them;[17] whereas one would be amazed and saddened to see how much it has deteriorated among certain other orders which make indiscriminate use of dispensations. It was about this very thing, happening even in his own time, that Bernard's complaint arose.[18] What then are we to say about the dispensations, as they call them, so easily granted by pope and prelates, from lawful oaths and reasonable vows? What shall we say about the unlimited plurality of benefices, about the modifications of the decrees of general councils or about the granting of privileges and exemptions which weaken the common law? Could anyone count up all the acts by which at present the strength of ecclesiastical – and, indeed, evangelical – discipline has almost universally weakened, withered and disappeared? May this holy Council of Constance give attention to all these things.

The stability of the laws is based upon this root principle: that custom is the best interpreter of positive law – provided that it is contrary neither to divine nor to natural law. The same principle is the basis of Aristotle's view, presented in his political treatise, that no reward should be given to those who introduce new laws, even though these may in themselves be improvements, since frequent change to the laws causes instability and does not allow them to grow strong upon the firm root of custom.[19] Note should be taken of this by those who, when any notion comes into their heads, or when they imagine that anything might be worth doing, busy themselves with the making of new laws, piling penalties on penalties, as if it would be good and expedient to enforce by a penal law anything at all which, if it were done, would be a good thing. But this is no way to govern a state.

Based on the same principle is the reasonableness of quashing or repealing certain positive laws where they conflict with those customs of the subjects which depend on nature. The reasonableness of permitting certain evils, not for the sake of approving them, but so that their punishment does not make matters worse, is based on a similar foundation. The same applies to the law of prescription, which, in order to prevent titles becoming uncertain, punishes those who neglect their own property by rightly – even in the sight of God and conscience – transferring such titles to possessors who are in good faith and have a legitimate prescriptive claim.

Eleventh Consideration

Ecclesiastical power in its fullness resides in the Church as its end, and also as the body which regulates the application and use of this sort of plenitude of ecclesiastical power, either through its own agency or through a general council adequately and legitimately representing it. And so it is established that the plenitude of ecclesiastical power was given by Christ to Peter for the building up of his Church, just as the definition, in conformity with the apostle,[20] lays down. Moreover, Augustine, with certain others, says that the keys of the Church were given not to one man but to the community, and in fact to the Church itself.[21] And this can be appropriately understood in the ways that this consideration explains, since the keys were given for the sake of the Church and its unity. And so this plenitude of ecclesiastical power may be said to reside in the Church or a council, not so much merely formally and of itself, as in two other ways: namely, with regard to its application to this or that person and with regard to the regulation of its use, in case there was an attempt to abuse it.

It is agreed that in these three ways the plenitude of ecclesiastical power resides in the Church and in a general council acting in its stead. There is to be sure no difficulty about the first and second ways, and likewise not about the third either, if we consider the definition of the plenitude of ecclesiastical power at the point where it lays down that it is given for the building up of the Church. Since therefore the supreme pontiff, who possesses this power as its proper subject, is capable of sin and could want to use it for the destruction of the Church, and if similarly the sacred college, which was given to him so that it could work together with him as an aristocratic body, is not strong in grace and faith, the only alternative is that there should be some other standard [*regula*], incapable of deviation or error, set up by Christ, the best of all legislators, by which abuses of this sort of power can be restrained, directed and controlled. But this standard is precisely the Church or the general council. And so, since the mean of virtue can only be found in the judgement of the wise, the final appeal will be to this wisdom, to the Church, where there is wisdom incapable of error, or to a general council. This is the basis of the many decrees and resolutions of this holy council, as for example that the pope may be judged and deposed by the council, that he is subject to the council for the regulation of his power as far as its use is concerned and that he is open to question about the motive for his actions. And so on with regard to the many matters that are discussed in the sermon 'Prosperum iter'.[22] . . .

THIRTEENTH CONSIDERATION

. . . Finally, now that we have discussed justice, right, law, jurisdiction and authority, let us say something about the polity. It may be defined as a community organized with a view to some perfect end. Organization or order, however, is an arrangement of like and unlike elements which accords to each his due. And so order is thoroughly in accord with justice, which gives to each his own; hence the divinely inspired utterance of the prophet that the work of justice is peace.[23] Why is this so? Clearly because peace is nothing other than the tranquillity which comes from order. But justice creates this tranquillity of order by according to each his due; on which subject it is said: 'Justice and peace have kissed each other'.[24]

One sort of polity is celestial, about which we shall say nothing at present, while the other is human, the polity of wayfarers upon earth. And this latter is of two types, one of which, to use the usual and proper term, is called 'ecclesiastical', the other 'secular'. Now, the secular polity is divided by Aristotle in his political treatise into three. The first he calls 'kingship', the second 'aristocracy', and for the third he uses in a specific sense the general term 'polity',[25] which we may refer to as 'timocracy'. Kingship is defined as a community under one good man, or more explicitly, as the gathering of a perfect community under one man, in accordance with his laws which are for the good of the commonwealth. This one good man is called 'king' or 'emperor' or 'monarch', and in his dominion he strives principally not for his own but for the common good. Aristocracy is defined as a polity under a few good men, or more explicitly as the gathering of a perfect community under a few men, whose principal aim through their laws is the good of the commonwealth; a senate would be an example. What is called in a specific sense a polity, or a timocracy, is defined as a polity under many good men, or more explicitly as the gathering of a perfect community under many good men, whose principal aim through their laws is the benefit of the commonwealth.

The community here is called 'perfect' to distinguish it from the domestic way of life, which is not perfectly self-sufficient. We say 'in accordance with his laws' since the sovereignty of the ruler is seen to consist in this: that he is found to rule the polity on his own initiative under his own laws, without the constraint of foreign laws.

Every ecclesiastical polity, therefore, whether the ruler is one good man or a few or many, is properly called 'divine', because, whichever type it is, it is bound to accept regulation according to supernatural law. And so it is clear that the three types of polity we have spoken of are united in the Church, as they are not in a civil polity, by the unity of divine law. It is quite clear also, as a consequence, that the question of whether in the ecclesiastical realm theology ought to be preferred to another science, natural or human, smacks of blasphemy and the Pelagian heresy.[26] The Church is not to be taken as a material temple, which a stonemason would better know how to build than a theologian or jurist; nor should discussion about the Church be only for the sake of revenues and rents and ecclesiastical jurisdictions oriented to temporal rights and the secular life. This would be to think just like the heathen.

But this is just the way in which brutish people generally conceive of the Church, at least as far as their words and deeds imply. They praise to the skies any bishop or abbot who labours to see walls and estates well established along with his jurisdictions, while letting his subjects go to perdition down the byways of error with regard to the Catholic faith and good morals. This is why, moreover, one expert secular manager might frequently be judged of more use in the government of the Church than a theologian or jurist. Therefore, we should reflect on the Church as it was instituted by Christ on the firm rock of faith to pursue its supernatural end, according to the law of the Gospel and of the divinely revealed Holy Scriptures. It is by this law that judgement about the faith and morals of subjects should be regulated, since what is upright is the judge both of itself and of what is awry. And if, for the preservation of this faith, judges who are highly skilled in theology and free of moral corruption ought to be appointed in the Roman Curia to hear those cases concerning the faith which everyone says should be referred to the Apostolic See (though this is usually interpreted too widely), we should see if this could be done in as reasonable a way as judges in secular cases are appointed, in an orderly and collegial fashion.

Corresponding to Aristotle's threefold distinction of types of polity in the natural order which we mentioned earlier,[27] we may also divide the ecclesiastical polity into three types: the papal, the collegial and the synodal or conciliar. The papal constitution is modelled on the kingly; the collegial, embodied in the college of cardinals, on the aristocratic; and the general council is modelled on the polity or timocracy. But the perfect constitution is instead that which involves a combination of all three. By contrast, we have those polities, if they deserve special names, which, unlike the foregoing, are not led by a free and, so to speak, fatherly regime but are instead dragged along under a despotic and servile yoke, either because, through their own fault, it is permitted by God, who makes 'the godless man reign', according to Job

[34:30], to 'ensnare the people', or for some other reason by a just judgement of the same God. Aristotle calls the first of these 'tyranny', the second 'oligarchy' and the third 'democracy'.[28] In a tyranny, one man rules, seeking only his own good, wishing his subjects to be powerless, ignorant and divided among themselves; in an oligarchy, a few men of similar character rule over the others; while in a democracy the corrupt multitude rules itself, each man seeking his own ends and not those of the community. The attentive reader will recognize for himself from these remarks whether any such phenomenon, with analogous threefold distinction, can be found in the ecclesiastical polity. . . .

Translator's Notes

1. Translated in C. M. D. Crowder, *Unity, Heresy and Reform 1378–1460: The Conciliar Response to the Great Schism* (London, 1977), pp. 76–82; see also the translation of the decree 'Haec sancta' (p. 83), fully supported by Gerson, which declared that councils were superior in authority to popes.
2. Gerson is thinking in terms of the four Aristotelian causes. In the first section of the treatise he states (p. 211) that 'ecclesiastical power is the power which has been supernaturally and specially granted by Christ to his apostles and disciples and to their legitimate successors until the end of the world, for the building up of the Church militant in accordance with the evangelical laws, for the sake of the achievement of eternal happiness'. He then notes that the efficient cause is denoted by the words 'granted by Christ', the material or subjective cause by 'to his apostles etc.', the formal cause by 'in accordance with the evangelical laws, for these laws provide the model or form for the exercise of the power', and the final cause or end by 'for the building up of the Church militant for the sake of the achievement of eternal happiness'.
3. Earlier in the treatise Gerson defined the power of order as that of consecrating the real body of Christ and administering the sacraments. The power of jurisdiction he divides in two. The first operates in the external forum and is coercive, that is, it can be exercised against subjects even against their will, as in the cases of excommunication, the decreeing of laws and the punishment of those who disobey these laws. The second aspect of the power of jurisdiction, which is based on the power of priestly and episcopal order, operates in the internal forum of conscience and is not coercive, but rather voluntary on the part of those who subject themselves to it – for example, the power of absolution – for no one, as Gerson says, can be absolved against his will.
4. Exodus 27:8.
5. For Aristotle's doctrine of the individual see, e.g., *Metaphysics* VII.13.
6. That is, 'self-sufficient' as opposed to domestic societies, as Gerson explains in the thirteenth consideration.
7. Jean Gerson, *Oeuvres complètes,* ed. P. Glorieux, 10 vols. (Paris, 1960–73), VI, pp. 225–7.
8. This decree of the Fourth Lateran Council in 1215 commanded yearly confession to 'one's own priest'. Gerson is here probably referring to *Regnans in excelsis,* a bull issued by the antipope Alexander V (1409–10), which affirmed the right of the Mendicants to hear confessions. He saw this as an infringement of the rights of parish priests: see Gerson, *Oeuvres,* VII, pp. 985–6.
9. Isidore of Seville, *Etymologiae* II.10.6.
10. Psalms 119:172. The Revised Version has 'righteousness' instead of 'equity'.
11. Gerson, like Thomas Aquinas (in *Summa theologiae* IaIIae, q. 96, art. 6; IIaIIae, q. 120, art. 1), uses the terms *epikeia* (the Latinized spelling of the Greek word *epieikeia*) and *aequitas* interchangeably. *Epikeia,* in Aristotle, involves an alteration of the law in cases where the circumstances are different from those for which the law was originally in-

stituted: see, e.g., *Nicomachean Ethics* V.10. *Aequitas,* a term drawn from Roman law, strictly means the justness of law, but it can also refer to an interpretation of a law that corrects whatever in that law is contrary to justice, and in this sense it is close in meaning to *epikeia.*

12. Luke 12:42.
13. St Bernard, *De consideratione libri V* III.18.
14. Deuteronomy 16:19.
15. For Aristotle's views on malice see, e.g., *Nicomachean Ethics* II.6 (1107ª8–27).
16. Romans 1:18–32.
17. The Carthusian Order was founded by St Bruno in 1084. A strictly contemplative order, known for the austerity and self-denial of its monks, it was not seriously affected by the late medieval decline of monasticism.
18. See n. 13.
19. Aristotle, *Politics* II.5 (1268ᵇ22–5).
20. Cf. Ephesians 2:19–22; I Corinthians 14:12.
21. See, e.g., Augustine, *De doctrina Christiana* I.18.
22. This sermon was delivered by Gerson at Constance on 21 July 1415, on the occasion of the Emperor Sigismund's departure for Aragon to negotiate for the abdication of Benedict XIII. In it he argues that the pope must obey the council in all matters pertaining to faith, extirpation of schism and reformation in head and members; that he can be deposed for the good of the church; that his decrees can be annulled by conciliar authority; and that his power can be limited, though not abolished, by a general council. For the text see Gerson, *Oeuvres,* V, pp. 471–80. See also J. B. Morrall, *Gerson and the Great Schism* (Manchester, 1960), pp. 97–100.
23. Isaiah 32:17.
24. Psalms 85:10. The Revised Version has 'righteousness' instead of 'justice'.
25. Aristotle, *Politics* III.5 (1279ª32–9).
26. Pelagius (c. 354–c. 419) was accused of exalting human free will at the expense of divine grace. The Pelagian heresy holds that man can take the first steps towards salvation by means of his own unaided efforts.
27. See n. 25.
28. Aristotle, *Politics* III.5 (1279ᵇ4–6).

Further Reading

Brown, D. C., *Pastor and Laity in the Theology of Jean Gerson* (Cambridge, 1987)

CHRP, pp. 379, 402–3, 596–7, 820

Combes, A., *La Théologie mystique de Gerson: profil de son évolution,* 2 vols. (Rome, 1963–4)

Conolly, J. L., *John Gerson, Reformer and Mystic* (Louvain, 1928)

Monahan, A. P., *From Personal Duties towards Personal Rights: Late Medieval and Early Modern Political Thought 1300–1600* (Montreal, 1994), pp. 90–5

Morrall, J. B., *Gerson and the Great Schism* (Manchester, 1960)

Pascoe, L. B., *Jean Gerson: Principles of Church Reform* (Leiden, 1973)

Posthumus Meyges, G. H. M., *Jean Gerson et l'Assemblé de Vincennes (1329): ses conceptions de la jurisdiction temporelle de l'Eglise* (Leiden, 1978)

2

Jacques Almain

ARTHUR STEPHEN MCGRADE

Introduction

In his long teaching career at the University of Paris, the Scottish theologian, philosopher and historian John Mair (1467/9–1550) had many illustrious pupils, including Pierre Crockaert (in his own right and as Francisco de Vitoria's teacher at Paris, a pioneer of the 'second Thomism'), the humanist George Buchanan and the reformers Jean Calvin and John Knox. But the most brilliant of Mair's students by contemporary estimates, to judge from his sobriquet, was Jacques Almain (c. 1480–1515), 'Splendor Academiae'. Before his untimely death, Almain, whose own teaching inspired poetry, had written on logic and natural philosophy, commented acutely on the last two books of the *Sentences* of Peter Lombard and produced a probing and widely read treatise on ethics. Both in his *Moralia* (five editions between 1510 and 1525) and in an *Expositio* of William of Ockham's *Octo questiones de potestate pape,* Almain engaged Ockham closely and with evident respect; but, as in the work translated here, he did not hesitate to disagree with the 'Invincible Doctor' even on matters of substance.

The *Question at Vespers* represents Almain's contribution to an academic exercise presided over by his fellow licentiate in theology, Louis Ber, in connection with Ber's reception of the doctorate in March 1512.[1] The initial question (*questio exspectativa*) proposed from the masters in theology at the beginning of the disputation must have been a broad one, for the three multi-part conclusions Almain defends in response to it cover an extraordinary range of topics in natural, civil and ecclesiastical 'dominion' or 'lordship' (*dominium*), including the once again critical issue of conciliar authority in the Church as compared with that of the papacy.

Of special significance for early modern political thought is Almain's appeal to God-given, inalienable natural rights (arising from the duty of self-preservation) as a basis for overriding positive legal titles. He holds that such rights justify not only an individual's use of another's property in case of extreme need but also a community's deposition of a duly constituted ruler whose actions are a menace to its safety. Almain argues for such rights in his first conclusion, on natural and civil dominion. His most pointed assertion, however, is of the right of the Church – or a general council representing it – to take action against a destructively reigning pope. In the month after Louis Ber's Vespers a putatively general council of the Church called by Louis XII of France formally (albeit ineffectually) suspended Pope Julius II from all spiritual or temporal administration. Two weeks later the Fifth Lateran Council, called by Julius, met in Rome. Almain's defence in the *Question at Vespers* of conciliar power in general and of the authority of the Council of Pisa-Milan (1511–12) in particular, in comparison with the pope's impending counter-conclave, made him the natural choice to compose the theological faculty's official response, demanded by the king, to *De auctoritate papae et concilii utraque invicem comparata* by Cardinal Cajetan (Tommaso de Vio), of the preceding year. Almain's *Tractatus de auctoritate ecclesiae et conciliorum generalium adversus Thomam de Vio* did not prevail against Julius II, but it was sufficiently cogent to elicit a reply from Cajetan. In the present work, besides vividly condensing the leading conciliarist ideas of the preceding century, Almain cites more than a score of theological, legal and philosophical authorities to illustrate the diversity of late medieval and contemporary opinion concerning the extent of divinely ordained ecclesiastical power, by whomever exercised, in relation to the natural dominion of individuals and communities and the civil dominion of their rulers. This survey, together with his doctrine of individual and communal rights (which he also fortifies with copious references to earlier writers), makes Almain's *Question at Vespers* an exceptionally valuable example of Parisian scholasticism on the eve of the Reformation.

The *Questio in vesperiis habita* was first published in a collection of Almain's works put together by his student Vincent Doesmier: *Opuscula omnibus theologis perquam utilia non ante hac impressa* (Paris, 1518), ff. 62ʳ–67ᵛ. L. E. du Pin's edition of the work (under the title *Quaestio resumptiva, de dominio naturali, civili et ecclesiastico*), printed in Jean Gerson, *Opera omnia,* 5 vols. (Antwerp, 1706), II, pp. 961–76, has also been consulted and used to correct the text of the earlier printed version; readings taken from this edition are cited in the notes.

In the following translation the Latin *ius* is consistently rendered as 'right', even where 'law' is standard. Thus, *ius naturale* and *ius humanum* are given here as 'natural right' and 'human right' rather than 'natural law' and 'human law'. This policy preserves variations in Almain, who sometimes speaks of *lex naturalis* and sometimes of *ius naturale;* but the main reason for adopting it is to underline the easy allowance made in Latin for both an 'objective' and a 'subjective' conception of right/s. Medieval students of canon law and civil law as *ius canonicum* and *ius civile* could naturally think of *ius* as an objectively right ordering of things. Almain's references to *ius naturale* and *civile* accord with this usage; but his formal definition, near the beginning of his discourse, of dominion as a faculty or power clearly expresses a different conception of *iura*. We must now think of rights as capacities for action possessed by individuals or groups, rather than as their due in an impartial distribution (made, perhaps, entirely by others). The historical and philosophical grounds and implications of this subjective conception of a right are controversial.[2] Almain apparently saw no conflict between it and the objective view.

Question at Vespers

After the apt determination of the initial question by our masters [of theology] and the elegant exposition of the meaning of its terms by our most outstanding master [Louis Ber], it falls to me, according to my abilities, to answer the question proposed. Taking for granted, therefore, the protestations I have made elsewhere, I put forward three conclusions.

FIRST CONCLUSION

The natural dominion belonging to man from God's gift cannot be abdicated absolutely with regard to all things or, similarly, with regard (in every eventuality) to a specific kind of food and drink. After Adam's sin it was fitting to add over and above this dominion the civil dominion of property and, similarly, that of jurisdiction, by which those exercising it have execution of the material sword and from which ecclesiastics are not in the least exempt by divine right.

The first part of this conclusion is that a natural dominion pertains to men from God's gift. As proof of this, it is assumed that natural dominion is a faculty or immediate [*propinquus*] power of taking up inferior things for one's sustenance, according to the dictate of natural law. Now by natural law everyone is bound to conserve himself in existence. From this obligation there arises in everyone a power of taking inferior things to use for their own sustenance; this power is called natural dominion. Its title is necessity. It is said of this dominion: 'In necessity, all things are common', and this dominion is compatible with there being any number of lords [*domini*] at once. To this dominion, according to some, there pertains the power of killing another person who is an invader – observing due measures for protection of the innocent. No human right can derogate from this dominion, since the right of a superior law is not abrogated by an inferior right. From these points there follow some corollaries:

[1] The first is that, notwithstanding any appropriation made by positive right to Sortes, if something is necessary for Sortes's preservation and similarly for Plato's, and Plato has occupied it first, he can legitimately use it; because, setting aside the appropriation made to Sortes by positive right, Plato would have been obliged to this by the right of nature. (Nor do I consider probable what Armachanus says: that Plato would be obliged to give half to Sortes although the death of both would follow.)[3] But positive right, by which the appropriation has been made to Sortes, does not derogate from natural right. Therefore, Plato can legitimately use the item in question. And Pierre de la Palu is of this opinion in Book IV, distinction 15 [of his commentary on the *Sentences* of Peter Lombard], where he says: 'The position of the possessor is better.'[4] Scotus holds the opposite in the same distinction.[5]

[2] A second corollary against Armachanus:[6] that dominion is not based on charity. For it would be absurd to say that anyone using food and drink for relief of his necessities incurs a new crime. Otherwise, as great an examination of conscience would be required for taking physical drink or food as for taking the blessed body of Christ [that is, the sacrament].

[3] Third corollary: no one can be deprived of this dominion by the sentence of any judge whatever on account of any fault whatever, so that he could not legitimately use for his preservation food and drink which was supplied to him. St Thomas is of this opinion, IIaIIae, question 69, last article, *ad* 2 [of his *Summa theologiae*], where he says: 'No one is condemned to inflict death on himself, only to suffer it; and hence he is not bound to do that from which death follows.' And he immediately adds: 'Even if someone is condemned to perish of hunger, he does not sin if he takes food secretly supplied to him, because not to take it would be to kill himself.'[7]

[4] Fourth corollary: whoever has an abundance with respect to nature, although not with respect to his status, acts against natural right in not sharing with another whom he knows to suffer need with respect to nature. That corollary seems to be against St Thomas, IIaIIae, question 32, article 6;[8] similarly, in Book IV, distinction 15 on the *Sentences*.[9] The argument for the corollary is that all status is based on positive right, which cannot derogate from natural right. Durandus is of this opinion in Book IV, distinction 15.[10]

Now that these points have been set forth, the first part of the first conclusion is proved by what is written in Genesis 1[:29]: 'Behold, I give you all plants that bear seed everywhere on earth, and every tree bearing fruit which yields seed of its own kind, that they may be yours for food.' From which it follows correlatively:

[1] That God can deprive man of this dominion. For whatever God gives outside himself he gives purely contingently. Just as he commanded Samson by inner revelation to make the house collapse by pulling down the columns, although his own death would follow,[11] by the same reasoning he can command us not to eat and drink, although death should follow.

[2] Second, the likelihood of Durandus's opinion in his treatise on laws follows: if there are two men, one who is better and another who is worse, for whom there is precisely enough at hand to sustain either of them, the worse man ought to yield to the better one, even though that sufficiency has been acquired by the industry of the worse man, because the better one has more of the goodness of the true supreme lord, since God loves him more.[12] Also, since inferior things were made for man as the less perfect for the more perfect, they will be made more for the more perfect man than for the less perfect one. And there follows consequently the likelihood of St Thomas's opinion that someone can take from himself what is absolutely necessary for his preservation to give to a great person on whom the civil or ecclesiastical *res publica* depends.[13]

The second part of the first conclusion is that natural dominion cannot be abdicated absolutely with regard to all things or, similarly, with regard (in every eventuality) to a specific kind of food and drink. It is not legitimate for a man to kill himself, either positively or negatively, namely, by omitting that which is necessary for his preservation. But if he could renounce such dominion as to a specific kind of food and drink in every eventuality, there is a case in which this means he would kill himself — if, namely, he were in utter need of food, and nothing was at hand except that [particular] comestible. The lord Armachanus is of this opinion in Book II, chapter [23], of his *On the Poverty of Christ*.[14] From this it follows that a Carthusian can eat meat, if nothing else is at hand and he needs food. And Panormitanus deduces this, commenting on the canon *Si vero* in *De iureiurando*.[15] Nevertheless, I do not want to deny that, if it would cause scandal, he ought rather to suffer death, according to Paul's declaration: 'Wherefore if meat maketh my brother to stumble, I will eat no flesh for evermore.'[16] A second corollary is that those who give themselves over to such abstinence that they noticeably shorten their lives act against the law of nature.

The third part of the first conclusion is that it was suitable for both the civil dominion of property and that of jurisdiction to be added over and above natural dominion. As proof of this: any community of persons living with one another is like a single body, of which the individuals are members one of another, according to St Paul in Romans 12[:5]. Second, it must be assumed that by natural right there is in that community a certain power by which those whose life disrupts it can be cut away from the body, even by death. And that is deduced a priori by St Thomas's argument, IIaIIae, question 64, [article 2]: 'Every part', he says, 'is ordered to the whole of which it is a part as the imperfect to the perfect, and if cutting off one member should be beneficial to the health of the whole body — say, because it is putrid or corruptive of the rest — it is praiseworthy to cut it off. Since, therefore, every individual person is compared to the whole community as part to whole, then, if someone is harmful to the community and corruptive of it, it is praiseworthy that he be killed' by the community.[17] And the same conclusion is proved a posteriori, because, since the community gives the authority of killing to the prince, it follows that it is more primarily [*prius*] in the community, and not from the gift of anyone else, unless it be said that it is from the gift of God. Therefore, that power in it is natural. The first step in the preceding argument holds through the principle: no one gives what he does not have. And if it be said that a curate who is not a presbyter gives his vicar the power to absolve, which he does not have, that is denied, because he only gives jurisdiction, which he does have. From this it follows correlatively:

[1] First, that the power of killing is not positive as to its institution, although it is positive as to its communication to a certain person – as, say, to a king – or to certain persons of the community, whether few or many, who may rule it aristocratically or timocratically; because, since this commandment 'Thou shalt not kill'[18] belongs to natural right, then, unless some case were excepted from it by natural right, exception could not be made by any positive right whatever – at least a human one – since there is no human power above natural right (as is certain with regard to individuals). About divine positive right, however, there is doubt among the doctors.[19]

[2] A second corollary: no perfect whole community can renounce this power, just as no individual man can renounce the power he has for preserving himself in existence.

[3] A third corollary: a ruler [*princeps*] does not kill by his own authority, nor can the *res publica* confer that power on him. Hence, William of Paris says that the jurisdictional dominion of princes is solely ministerial in relation to the community, just as the dominion of the priest with respect to the remission of sins is solely ministerial in relation to God.[20]

[4] A fourth corollary: a community cannot renounce its power over the ruler it has established; by this power it can depose him if he does not rule constructively but destructively, since such power is natural. And the gloss to 23, question 3, canon *Ostendit* is of this opinion, where it says: 'A people has jurisdiction, although the law may say that it has transferred it to the emperor.'[21] For if a city or people did not have jurisdiction, why would it be punished for the wrongdoing of a judge? See 23, question 2, the canon *Dominus,* where it says: 'A people [*genus*] and a city that neglect to prosecute what has been done wrongly by those who belong to it or to restore what it has unrightfully taken should be attacked.'[22] Now the city would not be punishable unless it had compulsory jurisdiction. And again it follows that a purely regal monarchy is not to be posited [*non est dabilis*] naturally in any case, taking purely regal monarchy as a certain author has seemed to take it these days, when a single individual rules and is not subject to any others [*unicus preest et nullis subest*]. But the Philosopher does not take a timocratic polity as this author was taking it.[23]

[5] A fifth corollary: Scotus's assertion in question 3 of distinction 15 is quite false,[24] that it is not legitimate for anyone whatever to kill by public authority other than in the cases excepted by God from the commandment 'Thou shalt not kill'[25] – if he means exemption made by divine positive right, such as the judicial provisions of the Old Testament (as he seems to intend) – because then it would not have been legitimate to execute anyone before the Mosaic law, since at that time there was not yet any positive right, and it would not be legitimate to execute anyone in the law of

the Gospel (at least not other than for homicide), because the judicial provisions of the Old Law have been revoked, and no case seems to be excepted in the law of the Gospel (unless it be said that homicide has been excepted in Matthew 26[:52], where it is said: 'for all they that take the sword shall perish with the sword'). If, though, he means exemptions by God through natural right, I make no difficulty – but then his proof is of no value for proving that it is not legitimate to execute anyone for simple theft.

These points being assumed, that second part of the first conclusion is proved. If the things shared among individuals were not appropriated but remained common, their cultivation would be neglected, because what is common is neglected; and the stronger in body would take everything away from the weaker. Therefore, it was fitting to add over and above natural dominion the civil dominion of property. It is proved concerning jurisdictional dominion: since the community – in which the natural authority resides of restraining the bad and of determining right for each particular individual with a view to living together peacefully – cannot easily be regularly assembled, it was fitting that it should delegate it to someone or to several people who could be easily assembled.

I propose the last part of the first conclusion, not assertively, but only probably and for the sake of enquiring after the truth; also for the sake of conferring with that very learned man, Master Robert Jacquinot,[26] most deservedly licensed in the sacred faculty of theology and also principal of the venerable college of Beauvais: ecclesiastics are not exempted by divine law from coercive civil jurisdiction.

[1] And first it is proved from the letter of Paul to the Romans 13[:1]: 'Let every soul be in subjection to the higher powers.' And that by higher[27] powers he means secular rulers appears manifestly from what follows: 'For rulers are not a terror to the good work, but to the evil' [v. 3]. And again: 'for he beareth not the sword in vain' [v. 4]. And that this subjection is not only for the sake of avoiding scandal is plain again from what follows: 'Wherefore ye must needs be in subjection, not only because of the wrath, but also for conscience sake' [v. 5].

[2] It is also proved, in the second place and with clarity, by the example of most blessed Paul in Acts 25[:10–11], where, shunning the coercive judgement of the priests, he says: 'I stand before Caesar's judgement seat, where I ought to be judged: to the Jews have I done no wrong. . . . If then I am a wrongdoer, and have committed anything worthy of death, I refuse not to die.' And again: 'I appeal unto Caesar.' The interlinear gloss says there: 'Because there is the place of judgement.'[28] Therefore, shunning the judgement of the priests, he confessed himself to be subject to the coercive jurisdiction of Caesar. But it is not credible that the Apostle would have said 'by whom I ought to be judged' feignedly or from fear of death, because he had already chosen to die for the truth, as he attested when he said: 'for I am ready, not to be bound only, but also to die at Jerusalem for the name the lord Jesus'.[29] There are many other authorities, which I omit for the sake of brevity, and I prove my thesis by reason, as follows:

[1] If by being consecrated to the priesthood (I raise no difficulty about someone being simply tonsured) a man by divine right became no longer subject to his ruler, it would follow that no one would come to be ordained except by licence of the ruler.

The consequent is false and absurd. The implication is clear. The ruler has some right in a man before ordination, of which he would be deprived by ordination, according to the opposite view, even against his will. But no one ought to be deprived of his right except by his own consent (or fault, for which he can be deprived by a superior). Hence it is that a bishop ordaining a bondsman [*servus despoticus*] without the consent of his lord is bound to make restitution to the lord.

[2] Second, if a presbyter as such is exempt by divine law, he therefore cannot by any degradation be made subject to a lay ruler, and consequently neither can he be justly judged by a layman when subjection to a just judgement is required. The implication is clear. Since he is exempt by divine right, the use of the sword against a priest will also be prohibited to a ruler. But the whole Church cannot change divine right. Therefore, he cannot be subjected to lay judgement by any degradation or human sentence, just as he cannot become a non-priest. Innocent III seems to be of the opposite opinion in the canon *Solite* in *De maioritate et obedientia*.[30] He says: 'Now what is said about punishment of evildoers and praise of the good is not to be understood as meaning that a king or emperor may have the power of the sword over the good and the bad but as meaning that he has power only over those who themselves use the sword and are committed to his jurisdiction.' And Panormitanus is of the same opinion as Innocent in note 6 on the same canon.[31] Similarly, in commenting on the last chapter of *De foro competenti*,[32] he says that the privilege given to ecclesiastics was not a granting of something new but only a declaration of right.[33] The gloss to the canon *Si imperator* of distinction 96 holds the same, where it is said that: 'Before there was any constitution, clerics were not under lay jurisdiction, whence all the constitutions which have been issued were only a declaration of right.'[34] And Carlerius published a copious treatise against the Bohemians.[35] Nevertheless, William of Ockham, Marsilius of Padua and John of Paris say that this was given as a privilege and that it was given in the time of Julius I, while Constantine the Great was still living.[36] Whence Platina refers to him as the first to prohibit ecclesiastics from litigating before lay judges.[37] It should nevertheless be noted about this part of my first conclusion that lay rulers cannot now deprive ecclesiastics of this privilege, because no one can deprive another for any fault whatever of a freedom pertaining to him, unless he has jurisdiction over him, because such deprivation is an act of jurisdiction. But lay rulers now have no jurisdiction over ecclesiastics, at least as to their person, since they have abdicated that which they previously had. Therefore, they cannot deprive ecclesiastics of the freedom given them. Similarly, ecclesiastics were never subject to lay rulers regarding those things which pertain to them by divine right, such as the administration of sacraments and the receiving of tithes. This material would require a very ample tract.

SECOND CONCLUSION

Ecclesiastical or Gospel dominion – by which all believers can be restrained and from which none but unbelievers can be exempted – cannot be instituted by a mere man or changed from royal to aristocratic or timocratic; from divine institution, it has no jurisdiction in temporal matters annexed to it.

The first part of the conclusion is that supreme Gospel or ecclesiastical dominion cannot be instituted by a mere man or men. As proof of this, it is assumed that we are not speaking here of the dominion over sins which ecclesiastics have in the secret, penitential forum, which cannot be exercised on the unwilling; we are instead speaking of dominion respecting the external and public forum. And it is a power immediately instituted by Christ for restraining believers to live according to Gospel laws in order to attain eternal happiness. And this power can be exercised on the unwilling. Now to what acts this power extends is a matter of such controversy among the doctors that the matter is exceedingly confused, so that in these times, as William of Ockham says, it would be of the greatest necessity that those who are wise – compelled by oaths and horrible threats [*iuramentis et horribilibus comminationibus*] to tell the truth – should make clear what pertains to the plenitude of power which the Church is acknowledged to possess.[38] For certain authors so enlarge it, perhaps for the sake of flattery, in order to obtain benefices and privileges, that it seems to absorb all the power of rulers. Others indeed, on the opposing side, perhaps to flatter rulers, so restrict it as to subject it to the will of secular rulers, as does Marsilius of Padua when he says that no one can be excommunicated by an ecclesiastical judge unless with the ruler's consent, as can be seen in his book entitled *The Defender of Peace*.[39]

Some extend it to the dissolution of a marriage which is pledged but not consummated, as the gloss on the chapter *Quod votum, De voto et voti redemptione* of the *Liber sextus*.[40] Similarly, in the gloss on the chapter *Ex publico, De conversione conjugatorum*,[41] where it puts forward this proposition – in my judgement most dangerous and to be condemned – that the supreme pontiff can decree that a first marriage is annulled by a second. Panormitanus, on the same chapter, is of the same opinion.[42] Similarly, Master Tommaso de Vio Cajetan, in his recently printed *Opuscula*.[43] But this is against Christ's word in Matthew 19[:6, 9]: 'What therefore God hath joined together, let not man put asunder . . . except for fornication.' Moreover, it is against the substance of the sacrament of matrimony, which is an indissoluble bond. Nor is it plausible, if it could be dissolved by man, that this could not be ascertained from sacred letters, as is the case concerning marriage between unbelievers when one of the parties has been converted to the faith. Nor does marriage pledged but not consummated signify only the union of God with the soul, [which is separable], but also the union of Christ with the Church, which is inseparable. And if someone alleges that such matrimony is dissolved from purely positive right by a solemn vow of chastity or at least by entering a religious order, de la Palu denies this, in distinction 27 of Book IV, saying this is done from divine right, which we have from the tradition of the Church.[44]

Some extend it to dispensation against natural right, as the gloss on the chapter *Auctoritatem*, 15, question 6.[45] Others say it can dispense against divine prohibition, as Angelus in his *Summa*, on the word 'pope'; but this is with regard to things which do not belong to the primary principles of the law of nature – such indeed are the degrees of consanguinity prohibited by divine law – and he alleges from a Florentine archdeacon an action of Martin V.[46] Panormitanus is of the same opinion, on the chapter *Per venerabilem, Qui filii sunt legitimi*.[47] And that this is false is manifestly clear, because someone subject to a law does not have power over that law, nor does an inferior [have power] over the law of a superior, such as the pope is in relation to the law of God and the law of nature – and it is a wonder that such authors do not absolve him from those laws! Some indeed extend this power to removing minor prelates without reasonable cause and without observing due process, so that the sentence now holds as if it were just, and from the fact that it pleases the supreme pontiff that the prelate is deposed, although the pope sins in so doing. Thus, in articles 5 and 6 of his treatise on ecclesiastical power, Pierre de la Palu says something amazing: that a king cannot depose a vassal to install another (indeed, if he should depose him, he not only sins but what he does is null and void), but that if the pope deprives someone who is better of his position without cause and puts someone worse in his place, although he sins, the institution nevertheless holds; if, however, he deprives someone who is worse of his position in order to put in someone who is better, the institution holds, and he does not sin.[48] This opinion deserves to be burned, since it is clear that prelates and others with benefices also have a true right, of which no one can be deprived against his will without reasonable cause. Nevertheless, the present most holy father seems to use that absolute power over our prelates, as will be made plain here.

Some indeed stretch it to apply to unbelievers, so that they can be compelled by it at least[49] to obey the precepts of the law of nature, as does Panormitanus on the canon *Novit, De iudiciis.*[50] The opposite of this is sufficiently established from the canon *Gaudemus, De divortiis,*[51] where they are said not to be restrained by canonical constitutions,[52] according to the Apostle: 'For what have I to do with judging them that are without?'[53]

Sometimes it is said to extend to the most secret sins, say, sins of the heart, so that men can be bound by excommunication for them, as the gloss on [the canon *Multorum*], *De hereticis* in the *Clementinae.*[54] But this is against almost all the doctors, who say that those sins are reserved to God's judgement, *De penitentia,* distinction 1, canon *Cogitationis.*[55] No one suffers punishment from man for such sins, says the gloss,[56] but certainly from God. And this is clear from the chapter *Mandata, De simonia,*[57] and from the chapter *Tua nos,*[58] and from the saviour's parable in Matthew 13[:24–30]: it is forbidden to use the censure of excommunication to eradicate crimes as tares when they cannot be distinguished from wheat. And the Church cannot do this, according to Durandus on distinction 13 of Book IV, not only on account of lack of knowledge but also on account of lack of jurisdiction.[59]

It does not seem to me, furthermore, that this power is to be extended to those who are in purgatory, for everywhere in the Gospel when promises or grants are made, it is said: 'whatsoever thou shalt bind on earth' and 'whatsoever thou shalt loose on earth';[60] 'what things soever ye shall bind on earth' and 'what things soever ye shall loose on earth';[61] and mention is never made of those who have departed from this life. From this it follows that souls dwelling in purgatory cannot be released from punishment by the granting of indulgences, but can well be by means of prayers. Carlerius shows this most effectively in his treatise on the subject.[62]

Others indeed seem to restrict this power too much. For they say it extends only to sins committed in purely spiritual matters – matters proper to the Gospel – and joined with contumacy, as, say, sins committed against articles of the faith and the sacraments, and not to sins which are against the law of nature. William of Ockham seems to be of this opinion towards the end of his *Dialogue,*[63] as is Jean Gerson in Lectio IV of *On the Spiritual Life of the Soul.*[64] Yet it seems to me to conform better with the Gospel text for this power to extend to all manifest mortal sins to which contumacy is joined, so that those who are contumacious can be bound by it. For in Matthew 18[:15], where this power is instituted, it is said: 'If thy brother sin against thee.' Christ does not distinguish here between one type of sin and another but rather speaks universally of individual mortal sins. And he immediately adds that the Church is to be told if a person is unwilling to make amends on being charitably corrected; and again: 'if he refuse to hear the Church',[65] he is to be excommunicated. Durandus is of this opinion in the treatise he wrote on this subject,[66] where he says that ecclesiastical jurisdiction extends to all the actions of Christians, not only of clerics but also of laymen, especially if they are considered with regard to injustice or any other sin[67] whatever. And to prove this he adduces an argument which he calls irrefutable. But the previously alleged text is more cogent than his argument.

[1] It follows correlatively that this power extends to compelling someone who sells something for more than the just price to make restitution, although not so that he should return half of the just price.

[2] It follows secondly that it extends to compelling a pure layman to pay a debt or to make a settlement with goods. Does anyone doubt that a person who is unwilling to pay his brother sins against him? The process in Matthew 18 should therefore be invoked upon him. And Carlerius posits that corollary in a treatise addressed to the archbishop of Besançon against certain persons who judge wrongly about the keys of the Church.[68] Yet an ecclesiastic ought not to obtrude himself where the lay judge is ready to compel, so that it does not seem that Christ instituted this power as a hindrance to rulers. But when the lay judge is absent, or if not absent is unwilling, or is willing but unable to act, then one should have recourse to the ecclesiastical power – see the canon *Licet, De foro competenti.*[69] The corollary put forward here is in agreement with the view of Panormitanus, on the canon *In civitate, De usuris,*[70] where he says that a cleric can be compelled in court to restore what he has over and above the just price.[71] I think the same holds for laymen, at least in the ecclesiastical court. And this should be noted carefully, since it appears to be expressly against the chapter *Cum dilecti, De emptione et venditione,*[72] and the gloss on the same chapter.[73] But what the gloss says in that chapter is false: that it is legitimate for parties contracting with one another to practise deception this side of half the just price, nor would such a contract be approved by canon law (but it might well be approved by civil law), since it is not likely that canon law, made by instigation of the Holy Spirit, should approve fraudulent deception.

These things being assumed, the first part of the conclusion is proved: a power which includes something that exceeds every human faculty cannot be instituted by a man or by a community. But ecclesiastical power includes something that exceeds all human power, namely, being able to relax the punishment due in purgatory and being able to exclude someone from the prayers of the Church. Similarly, being able to consecrate and to absolve from sins, which particulars exceed human ability. And the doctors use this argument to prove that the Church cannot institute a sacrament. It follows as a consequence that it cannot institute anything which, in virtue of the act performed, remits venial sin, as some imagine about holy water.

The second part of the conclusion is that all believers can be restrained by that power and that no one can be exempted from it. This is proved sufficiently from what has been said about that process 'If thy brother sin against thee'[74] and from what was said to Peter when this power was promised to him: 'whatsoever thou shalt bind'.[75] For if anyone were exempted, this proposition would be false. Furthermore, since all believers are subject to that power, not from human institution but divine, and since, when anyone is subjected to another by someone else's authority and not from his own consent, he cannot be exempted from that subjection except by the authority of the one who subjected him (or by the authority of his superior, if he has a superior) — hence it is that prescription[76] cannot be pleaded against the obedience due the Church. And many emperors and kings have been excommunicated by this power. For example, Innocent [I] excommunicated the emperor Arcadius for consenting to John Chrysostom's expulsion from his see,[77] and blessed Ambrose (though holy, yet not a bishop of the Universal Church) excommunicated the emperor Theodosius the Great,[78] as is reported in the chapter *Duo sunt,* distinction 96.[79]

The third part of the conclusion is that that dominion is not changeable to an aristocratic or timocratic form, so that, apart from a general council, supreme ecclesiastical power might be shared by several persons, whether a great number or a few. And in support of this part [of the conclusion] is the gloss to 7,[80] question 1, in the chapter *Non autem.*[81] William of Ockham regards the opposite as probable in the third part of the *Dialogue.*[82] I prove this part of the conclusion as follows. If it were shared by many, it would be shared by them either jointly or separately. If the first, let us assume that it is shared by two, so that neither of them has it separately. Then, if one of them is captured, since the other[83] does not have supreme jurisdiction, that power[84] can be bound, and consequently it does not then reside in them conjointly. If the power resides in several separately, therefore none of them can bind or loose another, since an equal does not have command of an equal, and so the proposition 'whatsoever thou shalt bind'[85] will be falsified. The gloss on the chapter *Non autem,* 7, question 1,[86] is of this opinion, as is Armachanus, in Book VII of *The Questions of the Armenians,* chapter 15.[87]

The last part of the conclusion is that, from Christ's institution, no lay power is annexed to ecclesiastical power. That proposition is plain:

[1] From the authority of Bernard, who says: 'Your power is not over possessions but over crimes';[88] and *Extra,* canon *Novit, De judiciis,*[89] where Innocent [III] writes to the prelates of France: 'For we do not intend to judge concerning a fief[90] — judgement of which pertains to the king — but to exercise discernment about sin, the censuring of which without doubt pertains to us and which we can and ought to exercise on anyone.'

[2] The same proposition is proved in the second place: it is of the nature of lay power to be able to inflict civil punishment, such as death, exile, deprivation of

goods. But ecclesiastical power can inflict no such punishment from divine institution (not even imprisonment, as it pleases many doctors to say), but it extends solely to spiritual punishment, as for example excommunication. The remaining punishments it uses are by purely positive right. And if someone should say that it pertains to ecclesiastical power to annul civil law, as is clear from the last [canon, *Quoniam*] of *De prescriptionibus*,[91] where the law permitting prescription to be made in bad faith is abrogated, it is said briefly in reply, as we find in the gloss on the rule *Posssessor, De regulis iuris* in the *Liber sextus*,[92] that one functioning with supreme ecclesiastical power can annul no civil law unless it contains a sin, as was the case with that law of prescription; and that act is not an act of civil jurisdiction but ecclesiastical, to which it pertains to restrain individual sins.

And from that proposition I infer the following corollaries:

[1] The first is: if Constantine the Great gave the western empire to the supreme pontiff,[93] it was a true gift and not merely the rendering of what was owed. Note that I say 'if he gave', since in the particular chapters in which it is asserted that he gave [it], *palea*[94] is set down, as is clear in both the chapters *Constantinus* in distinction 96.[95] And if he had given it, it is a wonder that Platina should have kept silent about it. The donation of certain churches in Rome is well reported, but nothing is said about the empire.[96]

[2] There is a second corollary: Constantine the Great could not have transferred the western empire to the supreme pontiff in opposition to the people, since every civil power, especially a supreme one (unless you call tyranny a power), is introduced by the free consent of the people. Nor would consent 'from fear falling on a steadfast man' [*ex metu cadente in constantem virum*] suffice, since it does not suffice for the transfer of a particular thing, as the doctors commonly say in the fourteenth distinction of Book IV of the *Sentences*. The jurists, however (namely, the gloss and Panormitanus on the chapter *Abbas, De his que vi metus ve causa fiunt*),[97] judge the opposite, and especially about things concerning which there can be an action 'because of fear' [*quod metus causa*].[98] (They say that the matrimonial transfer of a body cannot take place on this basis, since there cannot be an action 'because of fear', since those whom God has joined, man may not separate.)[99] But the opinion of the theologians is more probable, and from that again one would deduce that the most Christian kingdom of the Gauls was never subject to the Roman Empire. For it is manifest that the empire forced its way in upon them tyrannically and that the people never freely consented to be in subjection afterwards. But if they consented, this was 'from fear falling on a steadfast man'. And again it follows correlatively that the most Christian king of the Franks is now subject to no one in temporal matters. We find this in the chapter *Per venerabilem, Qui filii sunt legitimi*,[100] where it is said that the king of France recognizes no superior in temporal matters. The gloss says that: 'This is de facto and not de iure, because de iure he is subject to the emperor';[101] but the gloss destroys the text, since it is immediately added [in the canon]: 'And hence without injuring another he could subject himself to our judgement.' For if he had another as superior de iure, as, say, the emperor, it is manifest that injury would be done to that superior by his subjecting himself to another.

THIRD CONCLUSION

Supreme ecclesiastical dominion is prior in time and perfection and greater in extent[102] in the Church than in the supreme pontiff. In exercising it, a general council, which could be convened without the pope's authority, can exercise every act of this dominion over every one of Christ's faithful.

The first part of this conclusion is that ecclesiastical dominion is in the Church prior to being in the supreme pontiff. It is proved thus: that power was conferred on the Church in Matthew 18[:17], where the power of taking cognizance of sin in the external forum was first given with the command: 'tell it unto the Church'. For it would be futile to command that the Church be told unless authority of taking cognizance resided in it. Second, there is a power of the Church to give sentence on the basis of what it has heard and a power of inflicting penalties on those who do not submit to the sentence (which power is proper to coercive jurisdiction), when it was said: 'if he refuse to hear the Church, let him be unto thee as the Gentile and the publican'.[103] And that this should be understood of the Church as it is a collection of many is clear, because it is immediately added in the plural: 'What things soever ye shall loose', and 'what things sover ye shall bind etc.' [v. 18], in which words, according to the doctors, the Church is given the authority of establishing general ordinances from a sentence passed [*sententie late*],[104] regarding not only a sentence of excommunication, but of suspension from fruits and, indeed, of deposition from an office. (So now it is extremely likely that there is a canon of sentence passed on heretics and those who are not installed within a year after acquiring a benefice; [Godfrey] of Fontaines holds this in his *Quodlibeta*.)[105] But at that time no supreme pontiff had as yet been instituted, until after the resurrection, in the last chapter of John [21:16], precisely when it was said to Peter: 'Tend my sheep.' This is held[106] [to be the time of the actual conferring of power on Peter] even by adversaries of the present thesis, although it had previously been promised to him in Matthew 16[:19]: 'I will give unto thee the keys of the kingdom of heaven.' Therefore, it was conferred on the Church before it was conferred on a supreme pontiff. Whence, just as coercive civil power, the goal of which is political happiness (namely, of those having civil intercourse with one another), is in a political body before it is in any of its members, so Christ conferred ecclesiastical power on his mystical body, the goal of which is celestial happiness, before conferring it on any member at all.

From this I infer as a probable corollary that if Christ had not instituted a supreme pontiff or his own general vicar after his resurrection, the Church could have instituted such an office in an equally perfect degree. This is proved by the fact that even if he had instituted no one, supreme coercive ecclesiastical power had already been instituted and communicated to the Church. Therefore, the Church could also have committed it to some individual, just as a multitude of citizens commits power to its prince. It is proved in the second place and in my judgement decisively because when Christ instituted Peter as supreme pontiff in the last chapter of John, he conferred no power de novo on the Church but only on Peter, nor do we ever read that anything was conferred de novo afterwards, and yet it is clearly to be noted that after

Peter died, the power of instituting someone as supreme pontiff was in the Church. Therefore, it was also in the Church before the institution of Peter. Consequently, if Christ had not instituted a supreme pontiff, the Church could have done so.

The second part of this conclusion is that that power is greater in perfection and extent in the Church than in the supreme pontiff. That it is greater in perfection is proved as follows.

[1] It is in the Church in such a way that it never goes astray [*indeviabiliter*], so that the Church cannot err in matters of faith or good morals, nor can it err in judging [*sententiandi*] so that it judges badly, since the Holy Spirit, teacher of truth and infallible guide, always assists it, and it neither judges [*iudicat*] nor establishes anything except at its instigation, according to what is written in Acts 15[:28]: 'For it seemed good to the Holy Spirit and to us.' But it is in the supreme pontiff in such a way that it is liable to go astray [*deviabiliter*]. Therefore, that power is in the Church more perfectly than in the supreme pontiff. From this part [of the conclusion] it is proved correlatively that things determined by the supreme pontiff are not necessarily to be believed, although the opposite is not to be dogmatically asserted in public unless it is manifest from Holy Writ, from revelation or by the determination of a council. Things determined by a council, however,[107] are necessarily to be believed. Because of this it seemed to William of Ockham, in chapter 9 of his first question on the power of the supreme pontiff,[108] that many things contained in decretals smack of heresy, and he tries to show this from several passages. First from the chapter *Per venerabilem, Qui filii sunt legitimi,*[109] where it is said that: '"Deuteronomy" means second law. In virtue of the meaning of the term it is proved that what is determined there ought to be observed in the New Testament.' But it is manifest that many things are set forth in Deuteronomy which it is heretical to assert should be observed in the New Testament. If it be said they should be observed in a mystical sense, so also should those which are set forth in Leviticus and other books, and so no difference would be set forth. And Ockham finds heresy in a great many other places which, nevertheless, I would prefer to lay aside out of reverence.

[2] Second, it is in the Church irremovably [*inauferibiliter*] but in the supreme pontiff removably [*auferibiliter*].

It is proved now that the power of ecclesiastical dominion is in the Church more extensively than it is in the supreme pontiff. For it is in the Church as regards instituting a supreme pontiff or committing his institution to certain persons, as the Church commits it to the lord cardinals. It is not thus in the supreme pontiff, however. Second, it is in the Church as regards restricting the supreme pontiff's use of this power, if he does not use it for the building up of the Church (according to the saviour's saying: 'if thy right eye causeth thee to stumble, pluck it out'[110] – 'as to use', says the gloss), as when it restricts his use of this power in mandates and reservations. But it is not in the supreme pontiff to restrict the use of that power in one of his successors, since an equal does not have command over an equal. Third, it is in the Church above the supreme pontiff not only in matters of faith but in particulars, as John the Patriarch of Antioch holds in a treatise on that matter.[111] The gloss also concedes this in the chapter *Se papa,* distinction 40,[112] in relation to sins scandalizing the whole Church.

The third part of this conclusion is that a general council which could be assembled without the pope's authority functions with that power. For a fuller explanation of this part, I say first that by divine right ordinary and regular authority to convene a general council belongs to the pope and to no one else. Therefore, by divine right other prelates are regularly and ordinarily subject to the supreme pontiff, so that at his command they are bound to assemble at a certain place. Concerning the college of cardinals, however, according to those who say that they are of a hierarchical status succeeding the apostles inasmuch as they assisted Christ and also Peter, before their division, it is probable enough that by divine right this authority belongs to that college, since the twelve apostles, and not Peter alone, convened the multitude of disciples in Acts 6. From which again it follows that those with a deliberative voice in a council should be called not only from the rank [*status*] of bishops, who are the successors of the apostles, but also from the rank of curates, who are the successors of the disciples.

Second, I say that when both pope and cardinals are obstinate and are unwilling to convene a council, even when there is urgent need, we should not believe that the Church has been left by the Lord without any opportune means for conserving, guarding and protecting itself. Otherwise a purely civil polity would be better ordered than the ecclesiastical one, since a people can defend itself from adversaries when its rulers neglect to protect it. Accordingly, in such a case, in my judgement, when the necessity for assembling a general council (and the obstinate malice of the person or persons to whom it ordinarily pertains to convene one) comes to the notice of a particular church, that church ought to make this manifest to others – not in the manner of a command but as counsel – and should name a certain place or places to which there is safe access, just as the eye, when it foresees dangers bearing down on the body, makes this manifest to the other members and indicates a place where they can take refuge and the means by which they may protect themselves. And after these things have been made manifest, the other churches ought to assemble at some safe place, not by human but by divine command – just as, after an expert physician has told someone that a certain food is necessary for his sustenance, he is bound to take it, not by a command of the physician but by a command of the law of nature. It follows correlatively that the prelates of certain provinces who are sufficiently instructed of the necessity of a council and are not otherwise labouring for the peace of the church will not be safe in their conscience if they do not attend such an assembly.

Third, I say that if individual particular churches come together at a certain place on this basis, the authority of the Church resides with that group, as it would indeed if they came together by chance, as Jean Gerson says. Does anyone doubt that the gathering of the apostles who came together by chance (as he says)[113] at the Assumption of the Virgin had as much authority as [it would have had] if they had come together at Peter's command?

Fourth, I say probably, asserting nothing rashly, that if, after such an explanation of the grounds making an assembly necessary, some particular churches come together at a certain place while the rest are perniciously negligent, the whole authority resides in them. For if the right hand cannot or will not, if we can imagine it [*per imaginationem*], stir itself to defend the body, will not the power of defending the body reside in the left? And if neither hand will or can, it will reside in the other members. This fits well with the saying of Christ: 'where two or three are gathered together in my name, there I am in the midst of them'.[114] And he says, 'in my name', and not, 'in Peter's name'. And that is proved again, for it is possible for the supreme pontiff to be obstinate with one church and to be unwilling to occupy himself with the building up of the church but rather with its destruction; in which case would anyone dare to assert that there was not power in the remaining part? How I wish that zeal for the house of the Lord consumed the prelates of our time as it did the royal prophet,[115] and that they were more zealous for the safety of Christ's faithful than for money! Let them not delay! Let them hasten to the Council of Pisa,[116] or whatever other safe place they like and stop the spilling of so much Christian blood and the loss (as seems likely) of countless souls committed to their care! They see the French church entirely ready to meet in any safe place whatever. But will anyone regard Rome as a safe place for them, when the spirit of the most holy father rages so much against them that he judges his own Romans to be a council, and, not waiting for the arrival of the fathers, notwithstanding that a legitimate appeal has been made, and not observing the order of right, they proceed against the fathers – deposing, excommunicating – so that now he calls them *formerly* bishops of Lyons and Sens and so of others, and when the fathers arrive, he will say that they have been deposed? How does it look to you? Can anyone doubt that these times are more dangerous than the times of the schism? For the head seems to rage against those who intend the safety of the body as if power were given him for destruction, not for building up, and when they duly object, he inflicts penalties on them. But it is certain from what the doctors say (namely, Durandus) in Book IV, distinction [18], question 4,[117] that those censures should not be feared: when a sentence contains manifest error, as if, say, it were to be said, 'I excommunicate you because you believe in God',[118] it is in no way to be feared or observed, either in secret or in public. But enough about these matters.

The last part of this conclusion is that a general council can exercise all the acts of ecclesiastical jurisdiction in relation to any of Christ's faithful. That it can dispense is clear from the chapter *Presbyter,* distinction 82.[119] That it can lay down binding canons is clear from chapter 18 of Acts and the chapter *Si quis de clericis,* 12, question 2.[120] That it can give indulgences is clear, since indulgences are given from the treasury of the Church, of whom the pope is a servant [*minister*]. For if the servant can disburse something from the Lord's [*domini*] treasury, a fortiori Lady Church [*ecclesia domina*] can do so. That it can excommunicate is clear from the chapter[s] *Episcopi* and *Placuit,* 11, question 3,[121] and the chapter *Omnis utriusque sexus, De penitentiis et remissionibus.*[122]

Concerning this part [of the conclusion], the lord of the Vespers, Master Louis Ber, has put forward a proposition together with me: that the supreme pontiff can be excommunicated while remaining supreme pontiff. I am unwilling to contradict this proposition, because it has been determined by councils of old and is now recalled by the sacred council at Pisa that the supreme pontiff is subject to the precept 'If thy brother sin against thee etc.'[123] not only actively but passively. This is true; neverthe-less, his proposition is not so certain as to have prevented the greatest zealots for the power of those councils[124] from doubting it, not because of the powerlessness of a council but on account of the contradiction of the thing. This is clear from Nicholas of Cusa in the book he compiled at the Council of Basel, which is entitled *On Ecclesiastical Concord* (an outstandingly useful work in which he brilliantly delimits the power of councils and of the supreme pontiff and of kings and the emperor), in chapter 18 of the second tract, since the papacy seems to be 'a free power of administration', and it seems to be 'nothing other than a free power over all of binding and loosing'.[125] And Jean Gerson, having considered the papal status, says that: 'The papal status, although it exempts the pope from purely positive civil or canon laws in such a way that he cannot be coercively punished according to them etc.'[126] And that he is speaking of the canons of general councils is clear enough from the same consideration. To prove this, I shall adduce reasons which seem to me rather evident, leaving aside the authorities, which vary.

[1] First thus: the pope cannot be separated from the communion of the faithful. Therefore, he cannot be excommunicated. The consequence holds, because any excommunication involves that separation. And the antecedent is proved, because when anyone is excommunicated, his subjects can legitimately communicate with him, as is noted in all the doctors.[127] But every one of the faithful is subject to the supreme pontiff. Therefore, he can in no way be separated from the legitimate communion of the faithful. And that argument is confirmed by the fact that he is bound by divine right to tend every believer of Christ, and every believer of Christ is bound to accept his shepherding, because the care of every believer whatever is assigned to him when Christ says: 'Tend my sheep.'[128] But a general council cannot release anyone from a divine command.

[2] Second, if the supreme pontiff could be excommunicated by a council without being deposed, he would therefore be able to remain an excommunicate supreme pontiff when the council had been dissolved. The consequence holds, because the council could be dissolved after such a sentence without deposition and absolution. But I ask, who will then absolve him? And it is apparent that no one will be able to absolve him except at the approach of death, because no one can absolve anyone from a censure passed by a man or men except the person, precisely, who passed it, or the persons, if it is passed by a community, or someone superior to him or them. Then, second, absolution from such a censure is an act of jurisdiction of the external forum, which neither any person nor any group, except for a general council, is recognized as having over the pope. For this reason, the doctors say – even Gerson[129] – that he can submit himself to no one else who could excommunicate him, although he could submit himself to someone who could absolve him from sin.

[3] Third, if the supreme pontiff could be excommunicated by a council, he could therefore incur a sentence of automatic excommunication by the canon 'of a sentence passed'[130] on the basis of a conciliar canon, such as the canon *De semel confitendo in anno* [*Omnis utriusque sexus, De penitentiis et remissionibus*],[131] and so the supreme pontiff would be excommunicate ipso facto if he did not confess once a year. This, however, would be extremely dangerous, because then all his acts of jurisdiction, such as excommunications, dispensations, conferring of benefices would be null and void, since an excommunicate cannot exercise jurisdiction. Moreover, then it would

not be the case that there should be prayers for the supreme pontiff. Similarly, the head would then be separated from the body and so would not be a head any more. And Nicholas of Cusa says in reply to all the canons of the councils of Constance, Basel and Lateran concerning the penalty of suspension for the supreme pontiff that they should be understood to concern suspension from exercise of jurisdiction of the external forum.[132] And to the argument that a curate can be excommunicated while remaining a curate, it is answered that the case is not similar, because to every curate there are assigned by purely positive right these or those particular sheep, but to the supreme pontiff all believers of Christ are assigned as sheep by divine right. For this reason, he cannot be deprived of their communion while remaining pope.

Translator's Notes

1. R. García Villoslada, *La Universidad de Paris durante los estudios de Francisco Vitoria, O.P. (1507–1522)* (Rome, 1938), p. 168.
2. See B. Tierney, 'Origins of natural rights language: texts and contexts, 1150–1250', *History of Political Thought,* 10 (1989), 615–46.
3. Armachanus (Richard Fitzralph), *De pauperie salvatoris,* Book III, chapter 10, imagines Adam and Eve reduced to a sufficiency for one. The first four books of Fitzralph's work are printed with John Wyclif's *De dominio divino* in the Wyclif Society's edition of Wyclif's Latin works, 35 vols. (London, 1883–1914), X; for the passage cited see p. 396. Fitzralph (c. 1295–1360) was archbishop of Armagh from 1347. 'Sortes' is the usual medieval form of the name Socrates.
4. Pierre de la Palu (Petrus de Palude), *Quartus Sententiarum liber* (Paris, 1514), f. 64vb (dist. 15, q. 2, art 1). De la Palu (d. 1342) was a Dominican theologian; he was consecrated patriarch of Jerusalem in 1329.
5. John Duns Scotus, *Quaestiones in quartum librum Sententiarum,* in his *Opera omnia,* 26 vols. (Paris, 1891–5; reprinted Westmead, Farnborough, Hants., 1969), XVIII, pp. 345–6 (dist. 15, q. 2, *ad argumenta*). Duns Scotus (c. 1265–1308), known as the 'Subtle Doctor', was a leading Franciscan theologian and philosopher.
6. Armachanus, *De pauperie salvatoris,* p. 348 (Book II, ch. 8).
7. Thomas Aquinas, *Summa theologiae,* 5 vols. (Ottawa, 1953), III, p. 1787^b. The Dominican Thomas Aquinas (c. 1225–74), known as the 'Angelic Doctor', was to prove the most influential theologian and philosopher of the late Middle Ages, although Duns Scotus and Ockham had wider followings in the fourteenth and fifteenth centuries.
8. Thomas Aquinas, *Summa theologiae,* III, p. 1595^a.
9. Thomas Aquinas, *Scriptum super libros Sententiarum,* ed. R. P. Mandonnet, 5 vols. (Paris, 1929–47), V, p. 691 (Book IV, dist. 15, q. 2, art. 4).
10. Durandus of Saint-Pourçain, *In quattuor Sententiarum libros* (Paris, 1508), f. 378ra (Book IV, dist. 15, q. 6). Durandus (c. 1275–1334), although a nominalist, was the leading Dominican theologian of his day.
11. Judges 16:28–30.
12. Durandus, *Tractatus de legibus,* in the collection of texts edited by J. Barbier (Paris, 1506), sig. a5^r.
13. Thomas Aquinas, *Summa theologiae,* III, p. 1595^a (IIaIIae, q. 32, art. 6).
14. Armachanus, *De pauperie salvatoris,* pp. 366–7; Almain mistakenly cites ch. 25.
15. Panormitanus, *Commentaria . . . in primum[– quintum] Decretalium librum,* 7 vols. (Venice, 1578), IV, f. 163rb. For the canon *Si vero* see *Corpus iuris canonici,* ed. A. Friedberg, 2 vols. (Leipzig, 1879; reprinted Graz, 1959), II, p. 361. Panormitanus (Nicolaus de Tudeschis, 1386–1453/5) was a Sicilian canonist and member of the Benedictine Order.

16. I Corinthians 8:13.
17. Thomas Aquinas, *Summa theologiae,* III, p. 1757[ab].
18. Exodus 20:13.
19. Scholastic teachers of high reputation were known as 'doctors' (*doctores*), that is, learned men; and the most eminent were given distinguishing epithets, such as the 'Seraphic Doctor' (St Bonaventura) or the 'Irrefutable Doctor' (Alexander of Hales).
20. William of Auvergne, *De sacramento ordinis,* in his *Opera,* 2 vols. (Paris, 1674; reprinted Frankfurt am Main, 1963), I, p. 543 (ch. 10). The scholastic philosopher and theologian William of Auvergne (c. 1180–1249) was bishop of Paris from 1228.
21. *Corpus iuris canonici* (1879 ed.), I, p. 898. Almain cites the *glossa ordinaria* to the *Decretum* by Joannes Teutonicus (d. 1246), which is printed in the margins of early editions of Gratian's work, e.g., *Corpus iuris canonici,* 3 vols. (Turin, 1588), I, p. 1530.
22. *Corpus iuris canonici* (1879 ed.), I, p. 894.
23. Aristotle, *Nicomachean Ethics* VIII.10, describes a timocratic polity as a state in which honours are distributed according to a rating of property.
24. Duns Scotus, *Quaestiones in quartum librum Sententiarum,* XVIII, p. 374.
25. Exodus 20:13.
26. Jacquinot followed Louis Ber and Almain himself in the 1512 list of licentiates in theology.
27. Correcting *seculares* to *sublimiores.*
28. The interlinear and marginal glosses making up the standard medieval commentary on the Bible were completed by about the middle of the twelfth century.
29. Acts 21:13.
30. *Corpus iuris canonici* (1879 ed.), II, p. 197. Innocent III (1160–1216) became pope in 1198.
31. Panormitanus, *Commentaria,* II, f. 161[vb].
32. *Corpus iuris canonici* (1879 ed.), II, p. 255.
33. This is implied, rather, by the assertion that the clerical privilege in question is held by divine right: Panormitanus, *Commentaria,* III, f. 112[vb].
34. *Corpus iuris canonici* (1879 ed.), I, p. 341; the gloss at *Corpus iuris canonici* (1588 ed.), I, pp. 553–4, *v. Et discuti.*
35. Aegidius Carlerius (c. 1390–1472), dean of Cambrai, was active at the Council of Basel. His lengthy account of legations from the council to the Bohemians was first published, from a Paris manuscript, in 1857: *Liber de legationibus concilii Basiliensis pro reductione Bohemorum,* ed. E. Birk, Monumenta conciliorum generalium seculi decimi quinti, 1 (Vienna, 1857), pp. 359–700.
36. William of Ockham, *Dialogus,* in his *Opera plurima,* ed. J. Trechsel (Lyons, c. 1494), ff. 50[ra] (Part I, Book V, ch. 31), 80[ra] (Part I, Book VI, ch. 62), 274[vab] (Part III, Tract II, Book III, ch. 21); Marsilius of Padua, *Defensor pacis,* trans. A. Gewirth (New York, 1956), p. 271 (Discourse II, ch. 18, sect. 7); John of Paris, *On Royal and Papal Power,* trans. J. A. Watt (Toronto, 1971), p. 158 (ch. 13). The Franciscan theologian and nominalist philosopher William of Ockham (c. 1285–1347) wrote various polemical works against Pope John XXII (1249–1334). The Italian political thinker Marsilius of Padua (c. 1275–1342) maintained in the *Defensor pacis* (1324) that the Church must be completely subordinated to the state with regard to coercive authority; the work was placed on the Index in 1559. In the controversy over temporal and spiritual power between Philip the Fair and Boniface VIII, the Dominican theologian and controversialist John of Paris (d. 1306) sided with the king against the pope. Julius I (d. 352) became pope in 337, the year in which Emperor Constantine the Great died.
37. The Italian humanist Bartolomeo Sacchi, known as il Platina (1421–81), wrote his *Lives of the Popes* while serving as Vatican librarian under Sixtus IV. Platina notes that Julius I issued such a prohibition: see the translation by P. Rycaut (London, 1688), p. 57; but earlier in the work (p. 52) he had ascribed the same prohibition to Pope Sylvester I (d. 335). For Platina's *On the Prince* see Chapter 6.

38. Ockham indeed came to regard the correct delimitation of papal *plenitudo potestatis* as a major problem demanding consideration from the theological experts of his time. Almain seems, however, to have in mind here a passage in Ockham's massive earlier general discussion of papal heresy, where it is suggested that if kings or other public powers wish to extract the truth about the teaching of a heretical pope from the experts, they will have to constrain them *per iuramenta et per horribilissima comminationes:* see his *Dialogus,* f. 152va (Part I, Book VII, ch. 56).

39. Marsilius of Padua, *Defensor pacis,* pp. 147–52, 292–3 (Discourse II, ch. 6, sect. 11–13 and ch. 21, sect. 8).

40. An additional book of decretals (*Liber sextus*) was added by Boniface VIII in 1298 to supplement the five of Gregory IX (c. 1155–1241). Almain cites the gloss by Joannes Andreae (c. 1270–1348). The canon glossed is at *Corpus iuris canonici* (1879 ed.), II, p. 1053, the gloss at *Corpus iuris canonici* (1588 ed.) III, p. 601.

41. *Corpus iuris canonici* (1879 ed.), II, pp. 580–1; gloss at *Corpus iuris canonici* (1588 ed.), II, p. 1409, *v. Consummatum.*

42. Panormitanus, *Commentaria,* VI, f. 210va–211va.

43. Tommaso de Vio Cajetan, *Opuscula* (Paris, 1511), sig. f7^{va}. The Thomist theologian and philosopher Tommaso de Vio (1469–1534, called 'Cajetan' from his birthplace, Gaeta) became general of the Dominican Order in 1508, cardinal in 1517 and bishop of Gaeta in 1519.

44. Pierre de la Palu, *Quartus Sententiarum liber* (1514), ff. 148rb–150ra (dist. 27, q. 3, arts. 2–3), asserts here that some aspects of marriage are *iure divino* but does not allege Church tradition as a source.

45. *Corpus iuris canonici* (1879 ed.), I, pp. 755–6; gloss at *Corpus iuris canonici* (1588 ed.), I, p. 1281, *v. Absolvimus, ad fin.*

46. In his *Summa Angelica de casibus conscientie,* Angelus Carletus de Clavasio (1411–c. 1495) refers to an archdeacon of Florence who reported that Pope Martin V (1368–1431) gave a dispensation permitting a man to marry his sister [*germana*] (Venice, 1499), f. 329va. More accurately, Archbishop Antoninus of Florence (1389–1459) reported that Martin V had allowed a man to marry a woman with whose sister he had previously fornicated: see his *Summa sacrae theologiae iuris pontifici et caesarei,* 4 vols. (Venice, 1581–2), III, f. 11va. I am grateful to Brian Tierney for the information in this note.

47. Panormitanus, *Commentaria,* VII, f. 53rb; *Corpus iuris canonici* (1879 ed.), II, pp. 714–16.

48. W. D. McCready, ed., *The Theory of Papal Monarchy in the Fourteenth Century: Guillaume de Pierre Godin,* Tractatus de causa immediata ecclesiastice potestatis (Toronto, 1982), pp. 243–4, 287–8. The treatise cited has traditionally been ascribed to Pierre de la Palu, as in the collection of texts published in Paris by Barbier in 1506 (see n. 12).

49. Reading (with du Pin) *saltem* instead of *talem.*

50. Panormitanus, *Commentaria,* III, f. 39vb; *Corpus iuris canonici* (1879 ed.), II, pp. 242–4.

51. *Corpus iuris canonici* (1879 ed.), II, p. 723.

52. Reading (with du Pin) *constitutionibus* instead of *questionibus.*

53. I Corinthians 5:12.

54. The *Clementinae,* embodying the canons of the Council of Vienne, were issued by John XXII in 1317, following the order of his predecessor Clement V. Almain cites the gloss by Joannes Andreae to the phrase *Eo ipso incurrant* in the canon *Multorum:* see *Corpus iuris canonici* (1879 ed.), II, pp. 1181–2, the gloss at *Corpus iuris canonici* (1588 ed.), III, p. 297.

55. *Corpus iuris canonici* (1879 ed.), I, p. 1161.

56. *Corpus iuris canonici* (1588 ed.), I, p. 1966.

57. *Corpus iuris canonici* (1879 ed.), II, p. 767.

58. *Corpus iuris canonici* (1879 ed.), II, p. 763.

59. Durandus, *In quattuor Sententiarum libros* (Paris, 1508), f. 371rb (Book IV, dist. 13, q. 5). Durandus here mentions only lack of knowledge.
60. Matthew 16:19.
61. Matthew 18:18.
62. Aegidius Carlerius, *Super diversis erroribus in materia de sanctitate Beate Virginis, de visione Christi in eucharistia, de indulgentiis* . . . , in his *Sporta et sportula fragmentorum* (Brussels, 1478–9), f. 43^v.
63. William of Ockham, *Dialogus,* f. 248va (Part III, Tract II, Book II, ch. 4).
64. Jean Gerson, *Opera,* ed. P. Glorieux, 10 vols. (Paris, 1960–73), III, pp. 177–8. The French theologian and churchman Jean Gerson (1363–1429), known as the 'Most Christian Doctor', was active in promoting a conciliar resolution of the Great Schism in the papacy.
65. Matthew 18:17.
66. Durandus, *De origine iurisdictionum,* sigs. a5^{vb}–6ra [the signatures are misnumbered and should read a4^{vb}–5ra].
67. Reading (with du Pin) *peccati* instead of *peccata.*
68. Aegidius Carlerius, *Contra certas propositiones et additiones male sonantes in materiis auctoritatis ecclesie iurisdictionis et clavium eius,* in his *Sporta,* f. 35^r.
69. *Corpus iuris canonici* (1879 ed.), II, p. 255.
70. *Corpus iuris canonici* (1879 ed.), II, p. 813.
71. Panormitanus, *Commentaria,* VII, f. 145va.
72. *Corpus iuris canonici* (1879 ed.), II, pp. 518–19.
73. *Corpus iuris canonici* (1588 ed.), II, p. 1256, *v. Deceptione.*
74. Matthew 18:15.
75. Matthew 16:19.
76. That is, previous enjoyment of rights not limited by such obedience.
77. Pope Innocent I (d. 417) excommunicated Arcadius (Roman emperor from 383 to 408) after St John Chrysostom (c. 347–407) was deposed as bishop of Constantinople and exiled in 404.
78. Theodosius I the Great (Roman emperor from 379 to 395) was traditionally thought to have been excommunicated by St Ambrose (c. 339–97) on account of the massacre at Thessalonica in 390.
79. *Corpus iuris canonici* (1879 ed.), I, p. 340.
80. Correcting 2 to 7.
81. *Corpus iuris canonici* (1879 ed.), I, p. 571, the gloss at *Corpus iuris canonici* (1588 ed.), I, pp. 971–2, *v. Ut non succederet.*
82. William of Ockham, *Dialogus,* ff. 198vb–204va (Tract I, Book II, chs. 20–8).
83. Reading (with du Pin) *alter.*
84. Correcting *potestate* to *potestas.*
85. Matthew 16:19.
86. *Corpus iuris canonici* (1879 ed.), I, p. 571, the gloss at *Corpus iuris canonici* (1588 ed.), I, p. 971, *v. Ut non succederet.*
87. Armachanus, *Summa in questionibus Armenorum* . . . (Paris, 1512), ff. 48^v–49^r.
88. St Bernard, *De consideratione ad Eugenium papam,* in his *Opera omnia,* 8 vols. (Rome, 1957–77), III, p. 402 (Book I, ch. 6). St Bernard (1090–1153) was abbot of Clairvaux, one of the chief centres of the Cistercian Order.
89. *Corpus iuris canonici* (1879 ed.), II, p. 243.
90. Reading (with du Pin) *de feudo* instead of *defendo.*
91. *Corpus iuris canonici* (1879 ed.), II, p. 393.
92. *Corpus iuris canonici* (1879 ed.), II, p. 1122, the gloss at *Corpus iuris canonici* (1588 ed.), III, p. 847.
93. The 'Donation of Constantine' was a document (fabricated in the eighth or ninth century) in which the Emperor Constantine purportedly conferred on Pope Sylvester I dominion over the entire western empire. The authenticity of this document had sometimes been

doubted in the Middle Ages: Otto III, for instance, rejected it as a forgery at the beginning of the eleventh century: see B. Pullan, *Sources for the History of Medieval Europe: From the Mid-Eighth to the Mid-Thirteenth Century* (Oxford, 1966), pp. 121–2; and Ockham argued that it was apocryphal: see his *Breviloquium: A Short Discourse on the Tyrannical Government,* ed. A. S. McGrade, trans. J. Kilcullen (Cambridge, 1992), pp. 166–8; for a summary of the range of opinions in the fourteenth century see ch. 13 of Lupold of Bebenberg's *De iure regni et imperii romani,* in S. Schardius, ed., *Sylloge historico-politico-ecclesiastica* (Strasbourg, 1618), pp. 198–9. Its authenticity was decisively challenged in 1440 by the Italian humanist Lorenzo Valla in his *Treatise on the Donation of Constantine,* trans. C. B. Coleman (New Haven, Conn. 1922).

94. 'Palea' is a term of uncertain etymology used from the second half of the twelfth century to indicate additions to the *Decretum.* The meaning may be 'straw', in contrast with the good grain of Gratian's original collection. The two canons cited here are indeed inauthentic.

95. Reading (with du Pin) 96 instead of 76. See *Corpus iuris canonici* (1879 ed.), I, pp. 342–3.

96. Much of Platina's life of Pope Sylvester is concerned with Constantine's erection of churches in Rome: see his *Lives of the Popes,* pp. 51–4.

97. *Corpus iuris canonici* (1879 ed.), II, p. 219; the gloss at *Corpus iuris canonici* (1588 ed.), II, pp. 541–2; Panormitanus, *Commentaria,* II, f. 193vab.

98. 'The fear that falls on a steadfast man' was a stock canonist phrase to describe the degree of fear that could invalidate an act, such as the yielding of property or a vow of marriage. An action 'because of fear' could be brought to abrogate a contract on this basis. The canonists cited by Almain held that as a rule such an action, before a competent judge, was indeed necessary to reverse the effects of the coercion, but marriage contracts were among the exceptions they allowed to this rule – a coerced marriage vow was void of itself.

99. Matthew 19:6.

100. *Corpus iuris canonici* (1879 ed.), II, p. 715.

101. *Corpus iuris canonici* (1588 ed.), II, p. 1716, *v. Minime recognoscat.*

102. Reading (with du Pin) *extensione* instead of *intentione.*

103. Matthew 18:17.

104. Excommunication or other punishment *sententie late* is incurred immediately, from the fact that the relevant offence (previously defined) has been committed, in contrast with punishment inflicted *per sententiam,* by particular sentence of a competent authority.

105. Not identified; Godfrey of Fontaines (c. 1250–1306/9), in *Quodlibet* I, q. 17, defends the thesis that at the pope's command (but at his command alone) rulers are obliged to punish with the secular arm those who remain excommunicate for a year: see *Les Quatre Premiers Quodlibets de Godefroid de Fontaines,* ed. M. de Wulf and A. Pelzer (Louvain, 1904), pp. 39–40.

106. Reading (with du Pin) *tenetur.*

107. Correcting *aut* to *autem.*

108. William of Ockham, *Octo quaestiones de potestate papae,* 2nd ed., in his *Opera politica,* ed. H. S. Offler (Manchester, 1974–), I, pp. 39–40.

109. *Corpus iuris canonici* (1879 ed.), II, p. 716.

110. Matthew 5:29.

111. John of Antioch (d. 441), *Epistola* 3; printed as *Epistola* 35 among the epistles of Cyril of Alexandria, in J. P. Migne, ed., *Patrologia Graeca,* 162 vols. (Paris, 1844–55), LXXVII, cols. 163–6.

112. *Corpus iuris canonici* (1879 ed.), I, p. 146; the gloss at *Corpus iuris canonici* (1588 ed.), I, pp. 225–6, *v. A fide devius.*

113. Not identified, but see Gerson's *Propositio facta coram Anglicis,* where he counts among four councils recorded in Acts the gathering of the apostles to consider testimonies to Christ's resurrection: Gerson, *Opera,* VI, p. 133.

114. Matthew 18:20.
115. Psalm 69:9; and see John 2:17.
116. A council had been called at Pisa in 1511 by Louis XII for the purpose of deposing Pope Julius II, who had not fulfilled promises made before his election in 1503 to call a council within two years and to follow the advice of the college of cardinals in important matters – and had in 1510 formed a league against the French after defeating Venice with their help.
117. Durandus, *In quattuor Sententiarum libros,* f. 394[vb]; Almain mistakenly cites dist. 8.
118. Reading (with du Pin) *Deum* instead of *eum.*
119. Reading (with du Pin) 82 instead of 86. See *Corpus iuris canonici* (1879 ed.), I, pp. 292–33.
120. *Corpus iuris canonici* (1879 ed.), I, pp. 700–1.
121. *Corpus iuris canonici* (1879 ed.), I, p. 645.
122. *Corpus iuris canonici* (1879 ed.), II, pp. 887–8.
123. Matthew 18:15.
124. Reading (with du Pin) *zelatores maximi potestatis illorum conciliorum* instead of *multorum potestas conciliorum zelatores maximi.*
125. Nicholas of Cusa, *The Catholic Concordance,* ed. and trans. P. E. Sigmund (Cambridge, 1991), pp. 123–4. Although the German philosopher and theologian Nicholas of Cusa (1401–64) was initially a spokesman for the conciliarist position at the Council of Basel (1431–49), by 1437 he had switched to support for the papal cause; he was created a cardinal in 1448 and was appointed bishop of Brixen in 1450.
126. Jean Gerson, *De statu papae et minorum praelatorum,* in his *Opera* IX, p. 26.
127. For example, in Durandus, *In quattuor Sententiarum libros,* f. 395[vb] (Book IV, dist. 18, q. 5).
128. John 21:16.
129. Jean Gerson, *De potestate ecclesiastica,* in his *Opera,* VI, p. 219; for a translation see Chapter 1.
130. See n. 91.
131. *Corpus iuris canonici* (1879 ed.), II, pp. 887–8.
132. Nicholas of Cusa, *On Catholic Concordance,* pp. 123–4.

Further Reading

Burns, J. H., 'Scholasticism: survival and revival', in J. H. Burns, ed., *The Cambridge History of Political Thought 1450–1700* (Cambridge, 1991), pp. 132–55, esp. 147–51

Burns, J. H., and Izbicki, T. M., eds., *Conciliarism and Papalism 1511–1518: Almain, Cajetan, Mair,* trans. T. M. Izbicki (Cambridge, 1997)

CHRP, pp. 404–5, 807–8

McGrade, A. S., 'Rights, natural rights, and the philosophy of law', in N. Kretzmann, A. Kenny and J. Pinborg, eds., *The Cambridge History of Later Medieval Philosophy* (Cambridge, 1982), pp. 738–56

Monahan, A. P., *From Personal Duties towards Personal Rights: Late Medieval and Early Modern Political Thought 1300–1600* (Montreal, 1994), pp. 114–21

Oakley, F., 'Almain and Major: conciliar theory on the eve of the Reformation', *American Historical Review,* 70 (1965), 673–90

Skinner, Q., *The Foundations of Modern Political Thought,* 2 vols. (Cambridge, 1978), II, pp. 43, 45–7, 117–23, 176–8, 342

3

Francisco Suárez

J. A. Trentman

Introduction

The Spanish philosopher, theologian and jurist Francisco Suárez (1548–1617) was born in Granada and entered the Jesuit Order in 1564. After studying at the University of Salamanca, he taught at Segovia, Valladolid, Avila, Alcalá and the Jesuit Collegio Romano. In 1593 he was nominated to the chair of theology at Coimbra by Philip II, and it was here that he delivered the lectures which were later published as *On the Laws* (1612). A prominent representative of Spanish scholasticism and a key figure in the Counter-Reformation, he wrote treatises on various philosophical, theological and political topics, as well as producing important and influential commentaries on a number of works of Aristotle.

Readers of this selection from Suárez's *On the Laws* might be pardoned for getting the feeling that he wants to have his cake and eat it too. His theory of sovereignty, which is discussed here, shows how willing he was to go at least part way with the Ockhamist and Bartolist tradition in what he allows to the political community or the 'people', while at the same time giving a very high kind of authority to legitimate rulers, both secular and ecclesiastical. Balancing opposing views and attempting to arrive at a new synthesis as a result is very characteristic of Suárez's philosophy. We see the same thing in his metaphysics, which mixes old and new elements, criticizing and responding to positions taken by Ockham and his followers from a point of view that looks at first glance like a sort of Thomist metaphysics but turns out in the end to be something that is quite distinctive and innovative. He does the same thing in his theory of natural law; and, as this selection shows, we see it also in his political theory.

According to Suárez, political power resides directly in the people and is transferred from them to rulers; however, he regards this power in rulers not as delegated but 'ordinary'. As he puts it: 'The transfer of this power from the people to the ruler is not a delegation, but a sort of alienation or an unlimited surrender of the whole power which was in the community.' Quentin Skinner remarks of this theory of sovereignty: 'The idea that the whole body of the people constitutes the original "subject" of sovereignty is . . . rendered compatible with the rising absolutism of early-seventeenth century Europe.'[1] This sort of balancing act, attempting to show the compatibility of apparently conflicting opinions, is seen throughout this selection as Suárez tries to do justice to the claims of God, people and prince in his analysis of civil power.

The Latin text of the selection translated here is printed in Francisco Suárez, *De legibus,* ed. L. Pereña and V. Abril, 7 vols. (Madrid, 1971–81), V, pp. 36–50, and in his *Opera omnia,* ed. M. André and C. Berton, 28 vols. (Paris, 1856–78), V, pp. 184–8. I wish to thank the Reverend Timothy Connor and Dr Charles J. Jago for their helpful suggestions on the translation.

On the Laws

BOOK III, CHAPTER 4

Concerning Civil Power

Conclusions from the preceding doctrines

1. Monarchy is the best form of government.
2. When is civil power derived from the community? In the nature of things power resides directly in the community. The first foundation of royal power is its immediate derivation from God.
3. The second foundation of royal power is hereditary succession.
4. The third foundation of royal power is the just war.
5. Royal power, considered formally, comes from human law.
6. After power has been transferred to the king, natural law obliges one to obey him.
7. No existing universal law extends over the whole world, binding every human being.
8. The ways in which this power plays a role in making laws.
9. Ordinary power and delegated power.
10. Which power can be delegated?
11. Princely power, which is transferred in an absolute sense from the power of the people, is not delegated but ordinary.
12. The kind of power that cannot be delegated.

1. Monarchy is the best form of government

From what has been said in the preceding chapter we can draw some inferences that shed considerable light on all these matters.

First, while civil power in an absolute form comes from natural law, the determination of the particular mode of power and the particular form of government comes from human free will. Plato and Aristotle declare in their teaching that there are three forms of simple political government: monarchy, that is, government by one leader; aristocracy, that is, government by the few and by the best people; democracy, that is, government by the many and by the common people.[2] From these simple forms one can construct various forms of mixed or composite government by combining all or only two of them. This has been copiously and expertly set out by Bellarmine.[3]

So far as natural law is concerned, people are not constrained to choose any one particular form from these various types of government. Among these forms monarchy is the best, as Aristotle amply shows.[4] The same conclusion can also be deduced from the governance and providence of the whole universe, which ought to be the best form of government. Accordingly, Aristotle concludes that the best form of government is monarchy, saying: 'Let there be one ruler.'[5] The same is also shown by the example of Christ our Lord in instituting and governing his Church. Furthermore, the widespread practice of all nations argues in favour of this. Nevertheless, although I would say that this is so, some other forms of government are not bad but can instead be good and useful. For this reason, as far as the pure law of nature is concerned, human beings are not compelled to invest civil power in one person, or in many persons, or in the collectivity as a whole. Therefore, the particular determination of the form of power in a particular case must necessarily come from human free will.

In fact, experience reveals great variety in this matter. For where monarchy exists, it is rarely simple. Owing to the fact that human beings are weak, ignorant and malicious, it is ordinarily appropriate to incorporate an element of common government, which involves the participation of many citizens. This common element is observed, to a greater or lesser degree, in the various customs and opinions of mankind. All this therefore depends on human decision and free choice.

Consequently, it must be understood that individual human beings in the nature of things have a partial faculty, so to speak, for constituting or bringing about a perfect community. When they do constitute such a community, however, power turns out to be placed in the whole of it. Nevertheless, natural law does not dictate either that this power is directly [*immediate*] exercised by the whole community or that it is always maintained in it. But because this is in practice a most difficult thing to do (for there would be infinite confusion and captiousness if all laws were put up for approval by universal suffrage), human beings reduce this power to one of the previously mentioned forms of government, since, as anyone who considers the matter can easily see, it is not possible to think of other forms.

2. When is civil power derived from the community? In the nature of things power resides directly in the community

The first foundation of royal power is its immediate derivation from God. In the second place, it follows from what has been said that civil power, no matter how often it is found in one man or one prince, derives by legitimate and ordinary law from the people or the community, either proximately or remotely, nor can it rightly be otherwise.

This is the common opinion of jurists.[6] It can be deduced from legal texts as well. In addition, it is the view of Panormitanus and other canonists, and also that of Thomas Aquinas, Cajetan, Francisco de Vitoria and other theologians that have been cited.[7] The justification for what has been said is that in the nature of things this power resides directly in the community. Therefore, as it comes to reside legitimately in some one person as in a supreme governor, so necessarily it is granted to him by an agreement of the community.

This can be adequately explicated by recapitulating the foundations of royal power.[8] For this power can be understood as granted to kings directly by God himself. Although such an empowering has sometimes occurred, as in the cases of Saul and David, this way of doing things is extraordinary and supernatural. In the common and ordinary course of providence this kind of thing does not happen, because human beings, as far as the order of nature is concerned, are ruled in civil matters not by revelation but by natural reason. Nor is it an objection that Scripture sometimes says that God appoints and changes rulers by a nod of command (Daniel 4[:31–2]) and that Cyrus was constituted a king by God (Isaiah 45). Whence, in John 19[:11] Christ says: 'Thou wouldest have no power against me, except it were given thee from above.'

In all these cases, however, what is signified is that this sort of thing does not happen without the special providence of God, who either orders or permits it, as Augustine says.[9] Nevertheless, this does not mean that it does not come about through human agency, just as all other effects which are produced by secondary causes are principally attributed to the providence of God.

3. The second foundation of royal power is hereditary succession

Second, this power can be in a king by hereditary succession. It is the opinion of many jurists that this has happened from the beginning. But others rightly note that a succession necessarily presupposes that there is dominion or power in the person from whom one succeeds, and that, tracing this back, we must come eventually to a person who does not succeed from another, because the process cannot go back infinitely.

Consequently, we must first enquire where the rule and power which do not derive from natural law itself come from. Succession cannot be the first source of this power in the king. It necessarily follows that the first king would have supreme power directly from the people, although his successors would have it in an indirect and fundamental way [*mediate et radicaliter*]. And because a thing goes to a successor with its burden of obligations, the conditions with which the first king received his rule from the people are passed on to his successors. Therefore, the reign is held by his successors with the same burden of obligations.

4. The third foundation of royal power is the just war

The third foundation of royal power customarily is war, and this war must be just for a true foundation of power and dominion to be conferred. On this point many believe that kingdoms are originally introduced by tyranny rather than by true power, as we can see in Alvaro Pelayo, Jean Dridoens and Pierre Bertrand.[10] But when a reign is supported only by unjust force, there is no true legislative power in the ruler. It may, however, come about with the passage of time that the people consent and admit the legitimacy of such a sovereignty; in this case, power is brought back to the transmission and gift of the people.

Now and then it can happen that a state, not having been subject to a king, may become subject to him through a just war. But this always happens accidentally, as it were, in punishment for some crime. The people are then obliged to obey and consent to their subjection. Thus even this way of establishing sovereignty in some manner involves the consent of the people – either in the publication of a formal legal arrangement or in a kind of moral obligation. In these cases one principally speaks of power that can itself be publicly introduced and granted to one particular person.

So, finally, if the issue has been considered correctly, this subjection to a king comes about by a just war when the royal power in him by which he can declare war is already presupposed, and this power only exists as a just extension of his rule. Therefore, such royal power ought always to be brought back to the person who acquires it, not by war, but by a just election or by popular consent. It follows from this adequate account of the matter that one ought rightly to conclude that this power flows from the people to the sovereign.

5. *Royal power, considered formally, comes from human law*

The objection might be raised, however, that royal power is derived from human law alone, which appears to be contrary to the way in which Scripture speaks: 'By me kings reign' (Proverbs 8[:15]), and: 'For he is a minister of God . . . ' (Romans 13[:4]). Likewise, it would follow that the kingdom is superior to the king, because it gives him power. From which it could further be the case that, if it wished, the kingdom could depose him or change him, which is completely false. On account of this, Vitoria thinks (as stated earlier) that one ought to affirm absolutely that, presupposing an election by human beings, royal power derives from divine right and is granted by God.[11]

Bertrand, Dridoens and Castro, however, teach the opposite.[12] Without doubt they are right if one is speaking formally about royal power, insofar as it really is such and exists in one person. This governing power, considered in itself, without doubt comes from God, as I have said. Nevertheless, it exists in the particular person as a gift of the people themselves, as has been shown. In this sense, therefore, it derives from human law.

Such a monarchical system of governing a state or a province is of human institution, as I have shown here. Therefore, the very institution of monarchy derives from human beings. This is indicated by the fact that according to the pact or convention made between the kingdom and the king, his power is greater or lesser. Speaking in an absolute sense, therefore, power comes from human beings.

6. *After power has been transferred to the king, natural law obliges one to obey him*

Divine Scripture signifies two things by these expressions.[13] First, this power, considered in itself, is from God and is just and conforms to the divine will. Second, when this power is transferred to the king, he then takes the place of God, and natural law constrains us to obey him. Likewise, when an individual person is sold and traded as a slave to another person, the master–slave relationship that is established has an entirely human origin. But, this contract having been established, the slave must obey his master by divine and natural law.

And so the response that verifies this point is clear. I deny absolutely the consequence. After power is transferred to the king, the king is superior to his kingdom, because, by granting the power, the kingdom subjects itself to the king and loses its previous liberty, as the example of the slave shows, in spite of the differences between the two cases.

For the same reason, the king cannot be deprived of this power, because he acquires true possession of it, unless he degenerates into a tyrant. If this occurs, a just war can be undertaken against him. I have discussed this matter elsewhere.[14]

7. *No existing universal law extends over the whole world, binding every human being*

Third, it can be concluded from what has been said that in the nature of things or, likewise, in the natural and ordinary course of human events, there are no civil laws that are universally promulgated for the whole world and bind all human beings.

This is evident as well from the terminology itself. For when we speak of human laws, we distinguish them sharply from the law of nations. So what are called civil laws are those that belong to particular individual cities or nations, as is stated in the *Digest* [1.1.9]. We speak in the same way about the laws that are made through natural power, leaving aside for the moment supernatural power. Such laws require as an intrinsic condition that they not be universal.

The reason for this condition is that there is no legislative power which has jurisdiction over the whole globe or over all human beings; therefore, no civil law can possibly be universal. The consequence is clear because law does not go beyond the boundaries of the legislator's jurisdiction. As Paul says: 'Now we know that what things soever the law saith, it speaketh to them that are under the law.'[15] For, as the *Digest* [II.1.20] states: 'law does not hold with impunity outside its territory'. Much less ought it, therefore, to obligate anyone outside the territory for which the law or precept is proposed.

The antecedent is clear from what we have said. This power does not reside in the whole community of human beings, because all persons are not component parts of one state or kingdom, nor does this power reside in some one person. It would have to come from the hands of human beings; but this cannot be imagined, since human beings never come together to confer it on or constitute it in one leader. Nor as a result of war, whether just or unjust, has there ever been any prince who has held temporal dominion over the whole world for a period of time, as history demonstrates. Therefore, because of the way human nature is constituted, there neither is, nor has been, nor can there be imagined a legislative human power which has universal jurisdiction over the whole globe. But a difficulty may arise about this point in relation to the emperor, a matter which I discuss in chapter 3 of the following book.[16]

Therefore, while the whole world may be governed and bound by civil laws, which as a general rule is true of all nations that have some political organization and are not barbarous, the whole world is not governed by any particular laws. Instead, each state, in accordance with its structure, is governed by its own laws. In the same way, power has its place in the Church of Christ, and whether this comes from some particular institution is a matter that I shall discuss in what follows.[17]

8. The ways in which this power plays a role in making laws

Fourth, from what has been said one can briefly account for the ways that this power plays a role in making human laws.

One ought to say first of all that this power comes directly from God, because it cannot have some other origin, as the preceding chapter shows.[18] Furthermore, God is the author of all good and, consequently, of all power and especially of that power which in the highest degree depends on the divine providence which is necessary for the ordering of good human customs and for the preservation and governance of humanity. Therefore, someone must necessarily receive this power directly from God. Because if someone has it indirectly, it must be directly in another person, because the process cannot go back infinitely.

This power can come from God in two ways: naturally, as from the author of nature; or supernaturally, as from the author of grace. I shall speak about the latter in

Book V. Enough has been said, however, about the former. From which it is clear that this power can come directly from human beings and indirectly from God; indeed, this is ordinarily the case when we are speaking of natural power. Since it exists directly in the community, it is diverted by the community to kings or princes or senators. Rarely or never is it retained by the whole community so that it is directly administered by it.

When this power is transferred to a particular person, although it may be passed on to many people through successions or through various elections, it is always understood to be held directly by the community, because it is passed on to others by virtue of its primary institution. Such is the pontifical power: although it passes successively by many elections to various individual persons, all of them receive the power directly from God.

9. Ordinary power and delegated power

Now we ought to distinguish two ways in which power is generally held: as it is held ordinarily or as it is delegated. For what has been said holds for ordinary power, which passes directly from God to the community and in the same way is passed from the community to the prince, so that he exercises it as its particular master and holds it by virtue of his own office.

As for the second sort of power, it can be asked whether it is capable of delegation. The question was raised by Bartolus and Panormitanus.[19] One can trace this in all human legislative power, supernatural as well as natural, and in whatever situation. And so we can see it described in the authors I just mentioned, who teach that this power can in an absolute sense be delegated. Panormitanus concludes in the passage just cited: 'Some citizens of Pisa were delegated by the power of the people to promulgate the laws of the city, etc.' The same conclusion is usually drawn from the first law of the *Code*.[20]

10. Which power can be delegated?

Now we must turn our attention to the two ways in which this commission or delegation can come about. The first method of delegation has to do with the establishment of a law, by which it is determined whether it is just or useful or necessary and in which words it should be stated. The determination in this case does not extend the power of delegation to the establishment of the obligatory force of the law and, consequently, not to the promulgation of it as law. It is clear that such a power is capable of delegation. Nevertheless, in this case we do not really have the delegation of jurisdiction, but only a certain function requiring knowledge and experience. This appears to be rather a certain kind of consultation. And this mode of delegation is an everyday affair. Indeed, princes could scarcely make laws without it, for they themselves do not possess all that is necessary to enact a law. And, if anyone correctly considers the texts that I cited, this is all that they prove.

Real delegation is different from this. It comes about when the promulgation of a law is committed to someone in such a way that he can give it authority and validity according to his own wishes, without any confirmation or approbation on the part of the person who does the delegating. This mode of delegation is not as common or as easy as one might think. This is why Bartolus, in the passage cited earlier, distinguishes between the community and the prince, and says that the community can delegate this power when it holds it as ordinary power and can do with it what it wishes. By contrast, the princes and judges to whom this jurisdiction is entrusted cannot be said to delegate it. In the first place, since their personal diligence is required when this jurisdiction is committed to them, they cannot transfer their responsibility for it to someone else;[21] and second, since this power seems to be in them solely as delegated power, they cannot subdelegate it.[22]

11. Princely power, which is transferred in an absolute sense from the power of the people, is not delegated but ordinary

We may disregard the first term of the distinction, since it is clear. But the second requires an explication. If this doctrine is understood as applying to the emperor and to kings and other rulers, to whom this power of the people is transferred, the doctrine is false, because the power in such rulers is not delegated but ordinary. It is perpetual and applies to them by virtue of their offices. Likewise, because this power is ordinary, these rulers may grant it to other cities and to inferior princes. Why, therefore, can they not also entrust to them the function of delegating? For there is nothing to prevent a power being delegated on the part of the power itself, as Bartolus himself supposes.[23] It is clear that every power of a single jurisdiction can be delegated. And this is such a power.

In consequence, the transfer of this power from the people to the ruler is not a delegation, but a sort of alienation or an unlimited surrender of the whole power which was in the community. Wherefore, just as the community can delegate it, so too can the ruler. It is not committed to him in such a way that his personal diligence is required more than it is required of the community; it is instead granted to him absolutely for his personal use or for his use through his agents in any way that seems to him most suitable. For this same reason, not only the supreme pontiff, but also a bishop, can delegate his legislative power when his legislators have ordinary power. And the same reasoning applies to them.

12. The kind of power that cannot be delegated

Consequently, Bartolus's opinion only holds in the case of those magistrates and judges to whom this power is delegated from the highest sources of power. The arguments of Bartolus are valid solely in these cases. But because he speaks specifically of these communities, his opinion can be said to be true of those states that are in fact free and in which supreme power is retained even though legislative power is entrusted to a senate or to a peer of the realm, either to use on his own or in collaboration with a senate. For they are really only delegates, and so they cannot delegate this power unless it has been expressly declared in the very act of delegation itself that they can do so, or it is an established custom that power is committed to them in this sense. Since this is more a matter of fact than a matter of law, we can affirm nothing more certain about it. For the same reason we can say nothing about the actual delegation of this power, that is, to whom this power is delegated, because this depends on free will, and nothing has been established about this matter in common law.

Translator's Notes

1. *CHRP*, pp. 406–7.
2. Plato, *Statesman* 291D–E and *Republic* IV 445D; Aristotle, *Politics* III.5 (1279ª32–9) and *Nicomachean Ethics* VIII.10 (1160ª30–5).
3. Robert Bellarmine, *Tertia controversia generalis: De summo pontifice* I.1–4, in his *Opera omnia*, 12 vols. (Paris, 1870–4; reprinted Frankfurt am Main, 1965), I, pp. 461–9. Bellarmine (1542–1621), an Italian Jesuit theologian and controversialist, canonized in 1930, was one of the key figures in the Counter-Reformation.
4. Aristotle, *Nicomachean Ethics* VIII.10 (1160ª31–1161ª10).
5. Aristotle, *Metaphysics* XII.10 (1076ª4), quoting Homer, *Iliad* II.204.
6. *Digest* I.4.1.
7. Panormitanus, *Commentaria ad quartum et quintum libros Decretalium* (Turin, 1577), f. 44ᵛª; Thomas Aquinas, *Summa theologiae* IaIIae, q. 90, art. 3 ad 2; q. 97, art. 3; Cajetan, *Opuscula omnia* (Turin, 1582), p. 52; Francisco de Vitoria, *De potestate civili* (Madrid, 1960), pp. 161–4. Nicolaus de Tudeschis (c. 1386–1453), known as Panormitanus, was an Italian Benedictine canonist, bishop of Palermo and cardinal. Thomas Aquinas (c. 1225–74) was one of the leading Dominican theologians of the late Middle Ages. The commentary on his *Summa theologiae* by the Dominican theologian Tommaso de Vio (1469–1534), known as Cajetan, helped to promote the sixteenth-century revival of Thomism. The Spaniard Francisco de Vitoria (c. 1485–1546), also a Dominican theologian, founded the strongly Thomist School of Salamanca.
8. Literally, 'recapitulating the parts'.
9. Augustine, *Tractatus in Ioannis Evangelium* CXVI.5, in J. P. Migne, ed., *Patrologia Latina*, 221 vols. (Paris, 1844–64), XXXV, cols. 1942–3, and *Contra Faustum Manichaeum* XXII.75 in Migne, ed., *Patrologia Latina*, XLII, col. 448.
10. Alvaro Pelayo, *De planctu Ecclesiae* (Venice, 1560), ff. 18ᵛᵇ–20ʳᵇ (I.41); Jean Dridoens, *De libertate christiana* (Louvain, 1546), f. 41ʳ (I.15); Pierre Bertrand, *Tractatus . . . de origine jurisdictionum* (Paris, 1520), sig. +3ʳᵛ (q. 1). Alvaro Pelayo (1275/80–1349), a Spanish Franciscan author and bishop of Silves, wrote on political and religious matters. The Flemish theologian Jean Dridoens (1480–1535) was a professor at Louvain. Pierre Bertrand (1280–1349) was a French professor of canon and civil law at Avignon, Montpellier, Orléans and Paris; after becoming bishop of Nevers and Autun, he was made a cardinal in 1331.
11. See n. 7.
12. Bertrand, *Tractatus . . . de origine jurisdictionum,* f. 2ʳᵛ; Dridoens, *De libertate christiana,* f. 42ʳ; Alfonso de Castro, *De potestate legis poenalis libris duo* (Salmanca, 1550; reprinted Madrid, 1961), ff. 6ᵛ–8ᵛ (I.1). On Bertrand and Dridoens see n. 10. Alfonso de Castro (1495–1558) was a Spanish Franciscan theologian.
13. See the beginning of section 5.
14. Francisco Suárez, *Defensio fidei* III.3.3, in his *Opera omnia,* ed. M. André and C. Berton, 28 vols. (Paris, 1856–78), XXIV, p. 213.
15. Romans 3:19.
16. Suárez, in fact, discusses this matter in *De legibus* III.7.
17. This is discussed in Book IV of *De legibus.*
18. See Suárez, *De legibus* III.3.5.
19. Bartolus of Sassoferrato, *In primam Digesti Veteris partem* (on *Digest* I.1.9), in his *Omnia opera,* 10 vols. (Venice, 1615), I, f. 10ʳᵇ; Panormitanus, *Commentaria,* f. 196ʳª. Bartolus of Sassoferrato (1314–57) was an influential Italian jurist. On Panormitanus see n. 7.

20. See *Corpus iuris civilis,* 3 vols. (Berlin, 1902–15), II: *Codex Iustinianus,* ed. P. Krueger, p. 1 ('Haec quae necessario' ¶ 2).
21. *Digest* I.21.1.
22. Bartolus of Sassoferrato, *In primam Digesti Veteris partem* (on *Digest* I.1.9), in his *Opera omnia,* I, f. 10[rv–va].
23. See the previous note.

Further Reading

Abril, V., 'L'obligation politique chez Suarez: bilan et perspectives', *Archives de philosophie,* 42 (1979), 179–202

Burns, J. H., ed., *The Cambridge History of Political Thought 1450–1700* (Cambridge, 1991), pp. 237–40, 292–7, 697

CHRP, pp. 318–19, 333–4, 405–7, 444, 475, 480, 482, 514–16, 611–17, 627, 669, 837

Hamilton, B., *Political Thought in Sixteenth-Century Spain: A Study of the Political Ideas of Vitoria, De Soto, Suárez and Molina* (Oxford, 1963)

Lohr, C. H., *Latin Aristotle Commentaries* (Florence, 1988–), II, pp. 441–5

Monahan, A. P., *From Personal Duties towards Personal Rights: Late Medieval and Early Modern Political Thought 1300–1600* (Montreal, 1994), pp. 166–84

Simposio Francisco Suárez = Cuadernos salmantinos de filosofía. 7 (1980), 3–394

Trentman, J. A., 'Scholasticism in the seventeenth century', in N. Kretzmann, A. Kenny and J. Pinborg, eds., *The Cambridge History of Later Medieval Philosophy* (Cambridge, 1982), pp. 818–37, at 822–8

4

Tommaso Campanella

BRIAN P. COPENHAVER

Introduction

Tommaso Campanella (1568–1639) was born in Calabria, in the south of Italy. At the age of fourteen he entered the Dominican order; and he soon became interested in the materialist natural philosophy of another Calabrian, Bernardino Telesio (1509–88), who inspired Campanella's lifelong struggle to refute and replace the prevailing Aristotelian system. His pro-Telesian and anti-Peripatetic *Philosophy Demonstrated by the Senses* appeared in 1590, provoking his first imprisonment and trial in 1591–2. Sentenced to restriction in the South, he fled to Rome and points north, to be jailed again by the Inquisition in Padua in 1593. Defending himself, the young monk wrote his first works on politics, *On the Monarchy of Christians* (lost) and *On Church Government,* but they did not save him from being taken to Rome and tortured in 1594. All the while, he continued to write profusely. More trials, sentences and imprisonments followed until 1599, when he went again to Calabria and involved himself in a conspiracy to replace Spanish rule in the South with a priestly government headed by himself. The plot quickly unravelled. In 1601–2, Campanella was arrested, removed to Naples, tried by state and church, tortured and driven to confession and madness, feigned or real, ending in a sentence of life imprisonment for heresy. Another Dominican, Giordano Bruno, had been burned alive in Rome for heresy in 1600.

In 1602, in these harrowing circumstances, Campanella produced his most famous book, the utopian *City of the Sun,* and began his philosophical masterpiece, the *Metaphysics.* He had already finished *The Monarchy of Spain* in 1600, while persuading his jailers that he was mad. In all, he wrote about a hundred works, but less than half survived his painful adventures and less than a quarter saw print in his lifetime. Of those that survived, many – about forty per cent – were on political topics. He composed the first, vernacular version of *The Monarchy of the Messiah* in 1605, in confinement made worse when he was caught practising magic and trying to escape. In 1608 he was moved to the famous Castel dell'Uovo in Naples, where followers sometimes visited him and left with ideas that reached beyond Italy to Germany. Galileo's *Starry Messenger* of 1611 prompted him to study astronomy, and five years later he gave fortune another hostage by issuing an *Apology for Galileo* after the Church had forbidden the great scientist to teach the Copernican system. His confinement again grew more severe, then improved in 1618 as he prepared the Latin version of *The Monarchy of the Messiah.* Hopes brightened in 1621 with a new pope, Gregory XV; but Gregory died in 1623, followed by Urban VIII, who moved Campanella to Rome in 1626, used him to work astrological magic and allowed him some liberty of movement. His enemies had him in prison again by 1633, when *The Monarchy of the Messiah* was published with two *Discourses on Liberty,* then immediately suppressed. Even the pope now advised him to flee Italy, which he did in 1634, arriving in Paris by year's end to be welcomed by Cardinal Richelieu, lionized (briefly) by Gabriel Naudé, Marin Mersenne, Pierre Gassendi and their circle, and received at court in 1635 by Louis XIII, who gave him a pension. Campanella died in Paris in 1639, but not before casting the horoscope of the new Sun King born in the previous year.

Needless to say, the text partially translated here can only be understood in terms of the author's extraordinary career and in relation to his other major statements on the political and moral theory of church and state in *The Monarchy of Spain, The Triumph over Atheism* and elsewhere. Much of his belligerent case for papal power could have been made – indeed was made – by Bernard of Clairvaux, Innocent III and Bridget of Sweden in the Middle Ages, but other aspects of his argument reply to more recent opponents such as Diego Covarruvias, Domingo de Soto and Niccolò Machiavelli, the last not named in the chapters translated here. In keeping with Campanella's messianic self-conception, the most important background to *The Monarchy of the Messiah* is the Bible, especially the Old Testament prophets, but the technicalities of canon law and the struggles of pope against emperor were also prominent in his thinking. In the age of Galileo, his *Metaphysics* did not replace the Peripatetic system as he wished it to do, nor did his vision of papal monarchy prevail as Europe fought the Thirty Years War. Nonetheless, the ideas – sometimes bizarre ideas – of this courageous Dominican have continued to surprise both friends and enemies over the centuries since his death.

For the Latin text, see L. Firpo's facsimile edition, *Monarchia Messiae con due 'Discorsi della libertà e della felice suggezione allo Stato ecclesiastico'* (Turin, 1973), pp. 65–75. The notes that follow are as complete as possible for Campanella's explicit references to sources, some of which, however, seem to have come not from texts but from a prodigious yet fallible memory. Jill Kraye's help in the detective work that led to this conclusion was indispensable.

The Monarchy of the Messiah

CHAPTER 14

All the World's Kingdoms, Spiritual and Temporal, Were Established by Christ, Our God, and after the Incarnation the Pontifical Apostolic Power Was Given Charge of All the Kingdoms of the World, Not to Take Them by Force and Destroy Them, But to Unite, Correct and Reform Them, to Set Them Up or Set Them Aside as the Construction of Christendom Required. And Even in Temporal Affairs All Powers Derive from That Bestowed on the Pope, Not Chiefly from the Commonwealth or from the Community of the Christian Commonwealth. And in Controversies Arising between Peoples and Kings or between Kings and Kings, It Is Better for Kings If They and Their People Depend on the Highest Priest of All Rather than Await Judgement from Commonwealth or Parliament or Any Other Tribunal Whatever, as Experience Shows

[Certain] theologians used to say that the authority of princes does not derive imme-diately from God, in the way that papal authority derives from divine law, but rather that natural law mediates, having been given to the commonwealth so that it can preserve itself. Hence, they say that princely authority derives immediately from the commonwealth, which has the power to rule itself and to confer power on the prince by choice of election and then bestow it on his heirs by succession, as each nation determined from the beginning. But now, they say, a commonwealth cannot take away the power conferred on princes, unless they have been tyrants, and princes can also take possession of other kingdoms through purchase or just war. At no point, however, according to them, do princes depend on the pope. Only when princes stray from heaven's path can the pope correct them; and from princes to pope there can be no appeal. Indeed, Diego Covarruvias claims that in temporal matters the pope depends on the king, and often in spiritual matters as well, as Aaron depended on Moses. He says that priesthood and principate are separate ranks but that clerics have certain prerogatives as a privilege from the laity, and this false theologian says that these are exemption from taxation and from secular jurisdiction. He understands St Thomas to teach this and the first emperors to have proclaimed it; for the empire also was a lay foundation before the coming of Christ.[1]

Against all the aforesaid opinions it has been demonstrated in the discussions preceding that the kingdom of the Messiah is one and that it has one head, the lordship of all in things temporal and spiritual, and that all the titles of lords, whether by choice of election or succession or purchase or just war, derive from the pope as vicar of Christ, our God.

In the first place, Christ is the Word of God, Wisdom and Eternal Reason. Even in the law of nature, then, all titles of lordship conforming to reason derive from Christ, the first Reason and Wisdom, who said: 'By me kings reign',[2] and 'Your dominion was given you from the Lord.'[3] Moreover, this Reason, when he became flesh and lowered himself to us who could not approach him, did not lose the lordship that he had but rather enlarged it by right of redemption. St Leo says that this great act of humility did not, in fact, decrease his majesty.[4] Hence, all power depends on Christ more truly, more plainly and to a greater degree now than before the incarnation, as he himself said in Matthew 28[:18]: 'All authority hath been given unto me in heaven and on earth.' And St Thomas demonstrates this in *Opusculum* 20, Book III.[5] For this reason, when Peter was made vicar of this incarnate Wisdom, he received all the powers which Christ had and which were needed to govern humans, according to the figure in Jeremiah: 'That he might pluck out and destroy, build and plant and reform.'[6] Otherwise his kingdom would not be adequate and universal; but clearly it is, because Christ always gives this power universally, saying 'Feed', 'Strengthen' and 'Whatsoever'.[7] Therefore, all titles derive from Peter's authority, which is God's. And surely, if this were not so, Peter could not correct human authorities – for the very reasons given by my opponents – because they are unwilling. And so they destroy themselves.

Indeed, if you look in the prophets ('There shall be the root of Jesse, and he that ariseth to rule over the Gentiles';[8] 'Kings shall shut their mouths at him';[9] 'He shall have dominion also from sea to sea';[10] 'All kings shall fall down before him, all nations shall serve him';[11] 'Thou shalt break them with a rod of iron';[12] 'And kings shall minister unto thee';[13] 'And one king shall be king to them all';[14] 'And all the kings shall rejoice in it, and they shall adore the king of Israel';[15] and innumerable other prophecies cited in the previous chapters), you will understand very well that all the titles of those having lordship depend, in keeping with reason, on the lordship of the Messiah himself and that all powers come from his original power, which, on his behalf, was increased in heaven and earth, and in addition by the merit of the passion, as he himself testifies.

To say that human powers derive from the commonwealth is a kind of Peripateticism, but legists, if they are resolute, know better and say so, more than some theologians. For the Christian commonwealth has only one head, from which the whole body has been put together, as the Apostle says;[16] thus, all powers derive from this head, or else it is a monster. Aristotle also has proved this in *Metaphysics* XII.[17] Likewise, for the same reason, St Thomas in Book III of *De regimine principum* teaches that all princes depend on the pope, not the contrary, because the pope holds power from God and princes hold it from the commonwealth, which God makes subject to the pope.[18]

Also, this commonwealth has its law from Christ. But among Christians there is no law save that of the Gospel. Therefore, all election, succession, purchase and right of war must be regulated by the Gospel. Since the pope is the Gospel's first minister, he will also be the lord, the model and the judge of all Christian governments. Although other civil and practical laws may be devised, they do not endure because they derive from another head at a time before the Messiah became flesh, but only insofar as the Messiah and his vicar approve them. Or at least they are permitted until he purges all principalities and powers.

Besides, if those holding the contrary view do not regard Christ as God-become-man and as first Reason, architect of all laws, but as a human leader, founder of a particular, non-universal lordship, and if they bind him by the rules of Aristotle, who was unaware of God's providence, the life to come, the power of religion or the universal kingdom, what will seem unthinkable to them? How can those who are steeped in prejudice of this sort possibly make correct judgements?

Therefore, the fourth chapter of the Fifth Ecumenical Council condemned those who say with Theodore of Mopsuestia that Christians are named after Christ, as Platonists after Plato.[19] Yet it is not the language that can be condemned here, for Christians really are named in this way. One condemns the fact instead: that insofar as one thinks of Christ by way of this nomenclature, he is the prince only of those known to be Christians, not universally of all nations, princes and laws; and among Christians he is merely a prince limited to spiritual affairs, in prescribed ways, as Plato is master only of Platonists. Much more to be condemned, then, are those who make Christ subject to temporal princes and, as a consequence, subject his vicar to the same princes.

They are incorrect to say that there is a law of nature different from Gospel law, for the Gospel contains the pure law of nature, with the sole addition of the sacraments, which enable us to keep the law. De Soto teaches this in his first and second books, along with St Thomas; Gratian in the first *distinctio* from Isidore's testimony; Jerome; Augustine's book *De vera religione;* and all the leaders of the Church.[20]

Moreover, Christ is not a partial but a universal lawgiver and thus the lawgiver for all of nature.

Moreover, any prince, so long as he is Christian, enters the Church, which is the kingdom of heaven. But for the sake of this kingdom – the pearl of great price celebrated in the Gospel[21] – he should forsake all power, everything he has that conflicts with the Gospel and unjustly acquired temporal goods. He should put these things at the disposal of the law, the lawgiver and his vicar. From this point of view, then, he examines these things. For if by the unerring power of the keys (a destructive power, but aimed at constructive ends and for the sake of the truth, for otherwise it could not do anything) the pope were to decree that a prince could not keep what he had before he became a Christian, without question the prince must obey, just as Jews converted to Christianity give up all their goods because the pope assumes that they were unjustly acquired. This is what Constantine did, of course, and all wise princes, although at that time the obligation was less rigorous so as not to create difficulty for the strength of the young Gospel.

Truly, grace does not destroy nature, but it does correct and perfect corrupted nature. Grace cannot do this, however, unless all things are placed under the control of the one who has the power to correct. And a Christian will retain these things only insofar as the head of Christianity judges them good for him and for the common-wealth; therefore, the head strengthens and improves princely powers.

Moreover, when Christ redeemed the world, he redeemed these powers as well; he was their lord and so too is the pope.

Moreover, the Christian commonwealth is one, just like a body, a family, a ship, a flock or a bride, and the blood of Christ has redeemed it. Therefore, it depends on him entirely and likewise on his vicar. So when commonwealth and people transfer their power to a prince by choice of election, in doing so they transfer it according to the law that gives the commonwealth its power. Because the commonwealth is the Church, therefore, the commonwealth is the bride of the highest pontiff. But a bride, in divine and human law, can give only to the degree and in the way that the husband permits. And those who say that Christ alone, and not the pope, is the spouse of the Church are mistaken; for this would mean that no bishop was the spouse of his church, only a caretaker – not a shepherd, but a mercenary, because Christ alone is the shepherd. The heretic is deceived, however: in all the teachings of the canons and of theology [the pope] is called the spouse, but, as it were, the vicar of the spouse. He is a shepherd in the same manner, taking the place of the greatest shepherd. Christ transferred to his own not only these titles but also the untransferable title of god-hood, saying: 'I said, ye are gods'.[22] Wherefore, although the prince may depend on Paul through choice of election, so much more must he depend on the pope, who can void the people's choice and that of his bride and has every right to vex, correct and forgive. Much less can the sheep do what the shepherd neither wants nor approves.

This is clearly so, seeing that [the pope] deposed King Childeric of Gaul not on account of schism or heresy but simply because he was unfit to govern.[23] He also conferred the electorship of the empire on seven German princes in order to abolish wars and conflicts among nations and to stabilize the defence of Christendom; and he can still make other arrangements for the empire, as I have argued here, along with St Thomas.[24] He also divided the western empire from the eastern, and when the German emperor was disobedient, the pope was asked to unite the empire by the emperor in Constantinople, who promised to defend him, but the pope did not want to go along.[25] He imposed tribute on the king of England;[26] he deposed several em-perors;[27] he voided many elections; he divided the New World between the Castilians and the Portuguese;[28] he deposed the king of Navarre.[29] He granted many imperial, territorial and ducal titles all over the earth, and he always did whatever he wanted to build the Church.[30] As Christ promised, he prospered in the midst of persecution. In addition, he confirms all anointings and the swords of princes and emperors. Therefore, all the power, lordship and might of Christians derive from him.

Now, when Innocent III says that a king has no superior on earth, he means a *lay* superior; and on this canon De Soto defends himself in vain, for his own Peripateticism requires him to acknowledge the commonwealth from which the king takes his power.[31] But the commonwealth acknowledges the pope, of whom it is the bride, flock, daughter and so forth. While De Soto exempts princes from the power of the pope, he subjects them to the commonwealth without appeal to the pope, to the detriment of both, for without this remedy kings cannot avoid the insurrections of the people nor can the people avoid the tyranny of the king.[32] Admittedly, they can use arbiters or a new tribunal set up over both parties, as the kingdom of Aragon did, or they can send abroad for an authority, like the Genoese and the Florentines.[33] But this is a feeble remedy, always worthless for one party or the other.

The kings of France think that Innocent's canon refers to them alone, stating that they have no superior and that Pope John XXII aggravated the *Extravagantes* of Boniface VIII,[34] who subjected everyone except them to the will of the pope; but they are mistaken.[35] For when Pope Zacharias transferred kingdom, title and royal power from the Merovingian family to the line of Charlemagne, and then it passed from the race of Charlemagne into the Capetian family, it could not have been their right. Hence, from Charlemagne's time and later since Hugh Capet, there has so far been no legitimate king in France because none of them came from the stock of Pepin, whom the pope enthroned.[36] Thus, more than all others, the kings of France are subordinate to the Lord Christ, father of kings. Also, Charlemagne received the empire from the pope, and he sent the will that made his sons heirs of France, Germany and Italy to the pope for corroboration.[37]

All kings have depended so much on the pope that they do nothing without his authority, as history shows. It is deplorable, then, that so many of today's authors and critics wish to be seen as bent on decreasing the pope's authority in order to provide an extremely useful service to a favourite son and his people all at once by resolving quarrels, confirming kings, protecting them from vassals and outsiders, and protecting vassals against either sort of enemy – so quick are these critics to take care to confer authority instead on meetings held by subjects. All the fortunes of a most flourishing kingdom have declined because secular authority has waxed as that of the pope has waned. Plainly, once the heresy that shatters the pope's authority entered into France, the French have been fighting among themselves constantly and have been incapable of preserving or extending their principate outside France or of exalting the head [of their kingdom]. A mockery and a victim, they have yielded to hostile nations. Those who read will understand.

And now, kings, understand and be instructed, so that you do not stray from the just path when the Lord, your God, grows angry. When Louis the Pious was deprived of his kingdom, by a decree of the national Council of Lyons urging the Parlement to do so, did not Pope Gregory IV rescind the decree and restore the kingdom to him?[38] Stephen, bishop of Paris, excommunicated King Louis the Fat because he wished to preside over elections of bishops, and Pope Honorius absolved him.[39] In insurrections kings have often come for help to the pope, who also aided them against heresies, as did Pius V and Gregory XIV.[40] Certainly, kings have ever been quick to accuse vassals of insurrection and vassals to accuse kings of tyranny, which is why a judge seems to be needed between them. For this purpose the kingdom of Aragon has a tribunal of justice to judge between king and kingdom. Florence and Genoa once borrowed an authority from foreign parts in order to prevent one person from harrying another or vice versa.[41] But God has provided for this evil, setting over all nations a common father, the pontiff, who has preserved this benefit for one and all, especially the people and princes of France. And this is contained in the canon *Omnis oppressus* and in Constantine's decree.[42] Hence, to overthrow this power is to encourage constant strife, rivalry, plots and counter-plots between kings and their kingdoms. As the one applies the reins, the others scurry to shake them off with flimsy excuses. Arbiters cannot use force, and, whether from home or abroad, they are influenced by one of the parties. Judges are the same. No remedy is safe but to resort to the most powerful father, who can provide well from the counsel of cardinals and laws and who can be far more resolute than any other judge you like. And his judgement is more potent by far in recognizing that necessity has often forced kings to act. Let them see, then, how bitter it is to have abandoned God in the person of his vicar, as the Jews rejected him in Samuel. And because they had rejected God, God himself testified concerning the tyrant's law. Although they were seeking a king on account of wrongs done by the priests who were sons of Samuel, they took it that it was the priests who had incurred this threat.[43]

In addition, all kings are called sons of the pope, so their power comes from their father.

The fraud perpetrated by these theologians derives from the view that before the Messiah there had been founded a lay empire which, as a result, they regard as independent of the pope. Yet they do not see that the founder of these empires was Christ, the Eternal Wisdom, through whom kings rule and so on, by means of natural law, and that this same Christ later corrected these empires by means of the law of grace. Over all these powers – which even if they existed before his time still always derived from him – he also founded a new supreme power, which as chief power contains them all in itself, and a universal head of the world containing the particular heads, on account of which the Apostle says: 'Know ye not that we shall judge angels? How much more, things that pertain to this life?'.[44] St Thomas's *De regimine principum* also teaches that at God's command in imperial times Augustus became vicar of the newborn Christ.[45] Therefore, kings indeed depend on a commonwealth, but it is the commonwealth of Christ, who lived yesterday, lives today and will live forever.

Moreover, we say that it was not Christ incarnate who gave us the power to eat and walk, for these powers he had given us already. He only taught us how we should perform these actions reasonably according to the law of God and not be shut out of the kingdom of heaven. So too he did not give the sword, election and succession because he had already given them before. He only corrected and put one head over them all; and on this head, not on the people, they must be said to depend. Nor are they exempt from his power because their relation to it is not immediate. For the justiciary of Naples depends directly on the viceroy, and only indirectly on the king; but this does not exempt him from the king's power.[46]

What Christ told St Bridget in Book II, chapter 7, and in Book VIII, chapter 1, impresses me more: that he had established two powers in the earth, the one clerical in Peter, the other lay in Paul. And elsewhere he says that he set up the clergy as judges of the Church, signified by 'Peter', and princes as its defenders, signified by 'Paul', in a mystical sense. And he says that the common people who are ruled also supply the whole body of the Church with its temporal food.[47]

This doctrine is most reasonable. Plato, in his *Republic,* which was praised by St Clement, also made this distinction, on the model of the human body, in which there is a power of reason (the judges), a power of anger (the guardians) and a power of desire (the craftsmen and farmers), though all should share in reason.[48] And I too have shown this when I first wrote *On the Monarchy of Christians.* As I have explained already, all are enlivened by religion.[49]

St Peter, united in death with St Paul and hallowing the Roman soil on which they founded a heavenly tribunal, as Arator says, certainly indicates that the imperial and pontifical powers were united in the Apostolic See of Rome and that all lay power derives from them.[50] Thus it is said in the Apocalypse: 'Thou madest them to be unto our God a kingdom and priests'.[51] Both powers, then, were given by Christ.

Paul, in fact, was a defender of the Church. Even though he was a cleric, he still signifies lay empire in a mystical sense for St Bridget because princes are laymen held to be foolish on account of their belief in warfare. And by the same token kings and emperors are consecrated and brought into the clergy. A traditional image teaches this truth by always depicting Peter holding the keys that he received when he was made prince of the apostles. But Paul is shown with a sword – not with the sword that persecuted the apostles but with the one that signifies the imperial power added to the apostolate, according to Bridget.[52] Otherwise he was to be painted with keys or a book or a shepherd's crook or in some other way.

Moreover, if Christ founded the lay power when he made a whip of cords and when he entered in triumph, as the canonists suppose, it is quite reasonable that after the ascension he would have shown this power in Paul. For empire comes after priesthood in dignity and time – in Christ and in Adam. In fact, Paul testifies that when he ascended into heaven, he left behind apostles, evangelists, teachers and finally governors, and this will be the lay power of which he speaks to St Bridget.[53] This most holy woman speaks as God's witness, not to offer conjectures or to flatter, as these theologians do; for in other revelations when the need arises she calls an unjust pope 'Lucifer', 'Pilate' and 'Judas.'[54] So she ought to be trusted.

Hence it is true that both powers exist in the papacy, and all cases can be referred to it, according to Deuteronomy 17 and Constantine's decree.[55] But at present we do not do this, except perhaps in special circumstances – for good cause, though in some situations the cause is wrong. Not every case should be appealed unless it affects the whole community of Christendom or its vassals and, as St Thomas advises, unless it is for the good of the faith or because of some heinous crime.[56] To do otherwise would produce conflict and reduce the Apostolic See to trivialities. Let Moses judge the graver cases, priests the common ones: this was St Bernard's advice to Eugenius, and it is current practice.[57]

I add a prophetic doctrine besides: that all Christendom, since it is the kingdom of the Messiah, the son of David, holds no temporal authority or power of the sword from the people (and in this I agree with Bridget) but only from the Messiah, David and God – though not all hold it directly, but some (as they say) by the mediation of the people; for when he made kings of Saul and David, he wished them also to be chosen by the people.[58] So they depend on God through this medium of election. Now, however, Christ has grafted all Christians onto the stock of David, as the wild olive to the cultivated tree (as Paul wrote to the Romans); David has been king long since and has been installed as priest in the manner of Melchizedek, as I mentioned earlier;[59] and the Apocalypse says: 'Thou didst ransom us' and 'thou madest them to be unto our God a kingdom and priests'.[60] So it seems obvious that all Christians are Davidic kings and priests – each on his own part but not, as Calvin thinks, as belonging to the commonwealth.[61] For this reason, as some suppose, Peter called them 'a royal priesthood';[62] but I refer this instead to the head of Christ's body in which the royal priesthood exists, just as in Mosaic law the kingdom was called priestly with respect to Moses, because he possessed the better parts of the kingdom, or with respect to both of them – Moses and Aaron. But let us say that all Christians are called priests morally and figuratively, inasmuch as they sacrifice the fruits of good works to God and submit to the law for direction, as kings submit, but not for compulsion, except those who make themselves beasts and slaves of sin. For coercive law was not imposed on the just, says the Apostle, but on the unjust.[63]

Historically, the kings of the whole community are lay princes and bishops, and in respect to both the supreme pontiff is called king of kings and god of gods. These kings are also priests who bring Christ to the commonwealth, and the pope is also priest of priests, uniting them in one body and kingdom. Hence we see all Christians anointed in baptism as if they were kings and priests, each one individually in his own right, according to Hrabanus as cited by Gratian, *De consecratione,* and Innocent I, *De sacra unctione.*[64] But there are these differences among those consecrated to govern the commonwealth: lay princes are anointed on the shoulders and arms because they are defenders whose strong arms must wield David's sword and represent Christ; bishops, on the other hand, are anointed on the head because they better represent the greater power of Christ's head, which is the Reason and Eternal Wisdom, whose command moves the arms; yet the pope's anointing is all over, as if the head of them all were Peter through the apostolate and Christ through the anointing, according to Bernard.[65] Therefore, the Church has a material sword; it is, however, to be wielded by the hand of lay princes, who perform this role but do not have priority in it simply because they perform it. Not the head but the arm has been appointed to do this job, except where pressing hostilities require even the arm's job to pass to the head, as when Leo IV moved against the Saracens, as did other pontiffs when arms were lacking.[66]

Now I assert that princes, if they wish to be Christians, must recognize that this power and sword come from the Messiah in whose kingdom they have been incorporated, because all of them are Davids and their swords belong to David reborn. But these are not the powers they had before from the pagan people, except insofar as those people came from Christ – author of nature, Wisdom and First Reason – in keeping with reason. But to the extent that people conform to reason, they are all Christian, since Christ is the highest Reason. Zacharias 12[:8–10] explains this:

In that day shall the Lord defend the inhabitants of Jerusalem; and he that is feeble among them at that day shall be as David; and the house of David shall be as God, as the angel of the Lord before them. And it shall come to pass in that day, that I will seek to destroy all the nations that come against Jerusalem. And I will pour upon the house of David, and upon the inhabitants of Jerusalem, the spirit of grace and of supplication; and they shall look unto me whom they have pierced: and they shall mourn for him, as one mourneth for his only son. . . .

These verses show, of course, that Christ was crucified and that many mourn him every year, especially in Holy Week, because he was pierced for our sins. They also show how every Christian is like David and David like God: because priests are David mystically, they are like God; and they are like angels because a priest is 'the messenger of the Lord of hosts', says Malachi [2:7]. Wherefore, although all princes are called gods when compared with the people, the pope is still their God for princes, as is clear from Psalm 81, wrongly cited by the false theologian.[67] But here, where the Holy Spirit calls princes Davids, he also calls priests gods and angels. So it is foolish to infer from the fact that they are called gods that the laity can judge the clergy and show its strength by any authority independent of the pope. For the pope is god of gods.

Also, if Ezekiel was right to say that 'one king shall be king unto them all; and neither shall they be divided into kingdoms any more at all',[68] doubtless there can be no king in the world who does not depend on that one. This division between temporal and spiritual overturns the whole Bible and the whole commonwealth. It creates another head independent of the first one, as Dante made two suns rather than make the emperor the moon and thereby the recipient of light and strength — of knowledge, law and sword — from the pope.[69] Taking the world as his pattern, he clumsily tore apart the hierarchy of the Church. And De Soto is wrong to think that in the night of temporal affairs the moon takes precedence even over the sun; for the moon has no power at night except from the sun, from which it gets its light.[70] Thus, in temporal matters the emperor depends on the pope. It is better that Dante makes two suns, though falsely, in order to protect his opinion.

Finally, I conclude that the sword of Christian princes is David's sword taken from the pagan Goliath and hence the sword of the Messiah.[71] Princes cannot wield it except according to the law of the Messiah, of whose Church Micah 4[:13] says: 'I will make thine horn iron, and I will make thy hoofs bronze.' Princes are the hoofs of the feet and hands, but the horn is on the head, which is the pope. So the head has a horn of iron. For that reason David said of his Messiah: 'my horn will be exalted like the horn of a unicorn',[72] and 'All the horns of the wicked also will I cut off; but the horns of the righteous shall be lifted up',[73] and Isaiah 51[:5], 'my righteousness', that is, the Messiah, 'is near, and mine arms shall judge the people'. These arms are the Christian princes. And elsewhere he says: 'the isles shall wait for me, and on mine arm shall they trust'.[74] The isles are the New World, which has waited behind us until now for the law of the Messiah. But the king of Spain is the arm of Christ which is trusted — the arm, in other words, of the mystical body. And Isaiah had already said in the same place: 'He shall not fail nor be discouraged, till he have set judgement in the earth; and the isles shall wait for his law.'[75]

Jeremiah 30[:18], which refers to Rome, rightly and clearly shows that the papacy was rebuilt on high. And later he says: 'and their prince shall be of themselves, and their ruler shall proceed from the midst of them; and I will cause him to draw near, and he shall approach unto me: for who is he . . . '.[76] This clearly shows that election produces the pope whom God brings near to him and directs by his Spirit, for man by himself cannot rise so high. Then he declares him head of the whole world, according to Ezekiel, Isaiah, David and all the prophets already cited.

The rest of my opponents' arguments are based on acts of people who have wrongly assumed a position above the Church, and they must soon be put in their place according to the rule of Constantine, as promised to St Bridget.[77] But these arguments are not based on any prophecy or the truth of reason.

Moreover, those words, 'unto Caesar the things that are Caesar's, and unto God the things that are God's',[78] do not cause a division of the princely power in the kingdom of Christ. They were said so that the false questioners who wanted to accuse Christ of being a rebel against Caesar would be trapped by their own cleverness. So say it in an evasive manner: 'render unto Caesar the things that are Caesar's and unto God the things that are God's'. But all things are God's, and nothing is Caesar's except to the extent that he depends on God. Therefore, since the pope represents God, all things are under the pope's authority, not Caesar's, except as the pope's teaching allows, in conformity with God. For what does Caesar have that he did not receive? De Soto ridicules this opinion of his opponents while conveying another absurd view; and the emperor Basil says: if the pope is a shepherd and every emperor a sheep, it follows necessarily that the sheep can do nothing against the shepherd; furthermore, the sheep can do nothing but follow the law laid down by the shepherd.[79]

What soldier engaged in another's service says, once he has enlisted, that he must use the sword he had before entering service? What monk, professed and assuming the habit, wears clothing that he brought from home to be his own? Would they insist on their own wishes and disregard the new superior to whom they have subjected themselves? These are like the choices and powers that Christians have before they become Christians, which are always to be recognized as actually dependent on the supreme prince of Christianity to whom they have dedicated themselves.

In the end they keep repeating that he who gives heavenly kingdoms does not take away mortal kingdoms, from which they also conclude that the pope has no power over kingdoms of the laity, nor can he take them away since Christ did not take them away but left them as they were. I respond with this conclusion.

Christ, the Reason of God, did not establish new lay powers by force of arms because, where they were reasonable, he had already established them through the law of nature, and elsewhere he permitted them. He only gave them a superior and a single head over the whole group, and he protected them with every power. But he takes away no head that anyone has, although he incorporates it into his Christian principate; that is, he unifies all principates, only correcting, reforming and directing them to the eternal kingdom. Thus, no form of principate nor any reasonable form of commonwealth is incompatible with the apostolic principate because all were established by Christ, the highest Reason. Division alone is incompatible; and for this reason he united all under one apostolic prince, who has been obliged to accept no limits at all on his universal power, except constructively, so that he can unite and direct so many forms of commonwealth and principate. And thus was it said: 'Feed my lambs',[80] in a universal sense. But since human powers have been incorporated, they are reformed and made Davidic, as it were, and united in one commonwealth whose head is the pope. Thus, under a single pope they are unvanquished by enemies and peaceful among themselves. But I do not think that princes are feudatories of the pope (as someone wrote after me), unless they accept office from him on new terms. They are, however, sons subject to a father, students subject to a teacher, sheep subject to a shepherd guiding from above.

Christ acted like a man who has a ship that is wrecked at sea: it is shattered, worn out and split among several steersmen; one of them takes the ship here, another there. Accordingly, the owner goes to sea, finds the ship and restores order, so that he can sail to the port that he selects. He appoints masters to teach the sailors, and he puts one captain over all, letting the better sort remain, if any can guide the ship well, correcting others, but bestowing authority on one, a captain for all, able to direct everyone and to get rid of those who stray from the homeward course, that is, from God. This is a paramount advantage in politics as well, for all evils in the commonwealth arise when a prince makes himself and his own welfare the purpose of the commonwealth; the result is that insurrections and tyrannies run riot, as Plato also knew. But if God is the purpose, all this ceases, as Christ said: 'Seek ye his kingdom'.[81] He provided supplies to repair the ship, also rations, meat, oil and everything needed for the journey. And to administer these things he appointed new teachers and a head to lead them. The supplies for repairing and steering the ship of Peter are the sacraments and the law of the Gospel; those who administer the supplies are the clergy; the seamen are the laity. And princes have a role in government as before, but according to the new rules of the Gospel, which is the good news, the safe port; and Peter is made prince over all. Therefore, it must not be thought that princes are independent of Peter as a result of their being chosen, as before, by the people. They most certainly are dependent, and for constructive purposes. But knowing whether a purpose is constructive or destructive falls within the competence not of lay princes but of a council of the pope and his shepherds, just as it is not given to the flock to judge the laws and acts of their shepherds. St Augustine holds the same view in *Contra Faustum*.[82]

At this point, one must also insist that when princes bestow goods on the Church, it is not really a matter of *giving*. In the first place, we give nothing to God because everything, including ourselves, is his, as David says in II Chronicles;[83] we only signify our simple goodwill towards God. Second, there is no giving to the Church, only a kind of providing for the community and a yielding to the good of all, just as the hands do not give food to the stomach but provide it to be shared in common among all the bodily parts; for the giver does not rob himself and his heirs by his gifts. Indeed, through the practice of virtue any prince can become a cleric – bishop, pope, monk, friar and so on. Such a contribution, then, is meant to produce a community of goods serving the whole body.

But when a prince bestows some fief or makes a cleric his viceregent, he does not thereby become the cleric's superior but makes him his partner in ruling. Also, many things are given to a person and not to that person's office. Thus, indirectly he has power over the cleric, inasmuch as he has power over the performance of his administration.

Moreover, when a king makes a bishop viceroy, episcopal rank does not diminish while he assists in ruling; submission to the king in temporal affairs is submission of viceregal rank, not of episcopal rank. It is a partnership whereby the parts of the Church's body aid one other. The hands serve the feet by putting shoes on them, although they are of higher rank than the feet. For this reason, the Apostle says that Christ set up in the Church, 'first apostles; secondly prophets, thirdly teachers, then miracles, then gifts of healings, helps, governments'.[84] Last mentioned are the lay powers that help shepherds and apostles to rule, according to the words of Isaiah [61:5–6]: 'strangers shall stand and feed your flocks; . . . but ye shall be named the priests of the Lord'. But then the Apostle teaches that all the parts of the body aid, help and maintain one another. And thus are they blended in order to prevent schism among the parts of Christ.[85]

Never will you see the pope become viceroy or vice-emperor since he is the head of all, even in jurisdiction; the bishop, however, in jurisdiction, is a part. For this reason, we see that deacons can excommunicate, imprison and condemn bishops, not on their own authority but on the pope's; this does not make a deacon superior to a bishop. Likewise, the king is not superior to a viceregent bishop except indirectly, as mentioned already, insofar as he is superior in ruling and lordship. And a man acts in the same way with respect to an angel when he is in charge of the angel's activity.

CHAPTER 15

On the Emperor's Authority over the Whole World and That of Other Princes

Following all this, I maintain that insofar as the emperor is defender of the Church – the master of the whole world in spiritual and temporal matters – he is himself the master of the whole world, but in temporal matters, since the Church is dispersed, or is to be dispersed, through the whole world, as it is written: 'Preach the Gospel to the whole creation'.[86] Therefore, not for the reasons given by Baldus or Bartolus, which De Soto ridicules, nor perhaps for the reasons of Hostiensis, though these are stronger, but only inasmuch as he is defender of the Church can the emperor act universally as the main arm of the Messiah's body.[87] But now, since the emperor's might has diminished, every prince has this power, in those places and instances where the Church has authorized it, as St Thomas teaches in *Opusculum* 20.[88]

Therefore, the king of Spain holds the New World as the arm of the Messiah, having no right there except as he defends the Gospel faith and spreads God's Gospel, as will be clear from the prophets in the following chapters, where we shall see that the pope also divided the earth, not as arbiter but as judge and lord, because as vicar of the Messiah he rules from sea to sea and takes possession of the ends of the earth. And all kingdoms, insofar as they conform to reason, are Christian from Christ, the first Reason, either explicitly and completely or at least implicitly and incompletely. To the extent that they do not conform to reason, they must be forced to keep the natural law, as Aristotle teaches in the first book of the *Politics*.[89] On this basis the Romans and Aleander have posited a right to dominate barbarians, for whom it is better to be subject than to lead – a happy necessity that compels to the good, according to Augustine.[90] One must not push the Gospel in by force, though it may be defended by arms. But one uses force to push out the barbarity of those who eat human flesh and practise sodomy and the most bestial idolatry. No one denies that the pope has the right to do so except those who do not know Christ, the Word and Reason of God, and do not know that he is the universal Messiah, not the head of a sect.

Wherefore it is clear that as a matter of right all depend on one head in the body of Christendom, and Christians will be happy when they understand this well and order it done, for wars, schisms, heresies, plagues, famines, losses of government and alarms from the infidel will then cease among them. But as long as the teaching of Christ is neglected, everything will decline from bad to worse.

Those canons of Gelasius I, *Duo sunt* and *Cum ad verum ventum est,* seem to divide the powers of the Church into kingship and priesthood and to say that the devil introduced the union of these powers before the Messiah, apart from the case of Melchizedek, but I do not find that they prejudice a kingdom of the Messiah in the manner of Melchizedek.[91] They suppose that a lay prince cannot assume the papacy, as previously the Roman emperors were pontiffs and kings simultaneously, not however that a Christian pontiff cannot – like Melchizedek – be judge over a lay empire. True, the devil united priesthood with kingship in pagan principalities subservient to him, to arrogate to himself the glory of both ranks and the divine worship owed to God, so that emperor and king rather than any common priest would offer him idolatrous sacrifices. The devil is jealous of God's honours, as if he were the ape of God, who had united kingship with priesthood in the natural law for his glory. But the canons do not deny that the same person can be king and priest naturally. Indeed, every opinion and effort of these pontiffs was directed towards persuading the emperors not to take pontifical rights for themselves again, as they had before Constantine. This is not, however, to deny the natural law of ancient standing in Adam, Noah, Abraham, Moses, Samuel, Matthias, Judas Maccabaeus, Melchizedek and Peter, and in other princes listed in chapter 2, who were priests and kings at the same time and were appointed not by the devil but by God, as mentioned earlier.[92]

Other canons say that the pope should not intrude himself into secular government and that he should observe imperial laws in temporal affairs; however, they say that the pope *ought not,* not actually that he *cannot,* do so, as Bernard carefully notes, so as not to confuse the duties of the parts or have the greater rank perform lesser tasks, as the king performing those of the tribune, but that they should help one another.[93] Yet the right of the head over all parts and acts of the body of Christendom persists continuously. And if such canons of Gelasius prove anything else when they are twisted by my opponents, I counter them with the *Extravagantes* of Boniface VIII and the canon of Nicholas I in *distinctio* 97 and *distinctio* 21, from the letter to Michael, which are later than Gelasius.[94]

Surely, if the union of these powers with one another were impossible, the pope could not have any temporal lordship; but it has been proved that for the stability of the apostolic power it is necessary to have temporal lordships so that they do not become the prey of heretics and secular tyrannies, and so forth, from which our conclusions follow.

Therefore, it greatly pleases God that such goods are given to the Church – that they are shared in common. For the apostles were concerned about this, and thus it will happen, but only so that all things might revert to the community as it was in the law of nature and began to be again with the apostles, as I explain elsewhere, in the section concerning prophecy.[95]

Also, the most learned saints Sylvester, Augustine, Urban, Ambrose and other learned men never condemned but rather praised the acts of Constantine and the transfer of empire and goods to the Church.[96] Chrysostom, however, sometimes complains that secular authorities, to relieve themselves of the burden of supporting the clergy, gave them property and busied them with harvesting grapes and embezzlement.[97] Having been dragged from their books, they wanted these things all the more because worldly people cared for them. And thus the most holy saints Bernard and Romuald accepted properties and worked on them as part of their activities; but since in doing so they were hindered in their sacred duties, they used laymen as servants, as is clear, and thus provided for this evil.[98] Bishops and popes should make use of this warning.

Translator's Notes

1. Diego Covarruvias, *Opera omnia,* 2 vols. (Frankfurt am Main, 1592), I, pp. 545–6. The jurist Covarruvias (1512–77) was one of many influential students of the great Dominican teacher, Francisco de Vitoria, who died in 1546, after having excited new interest in Thomism at Paris and then at Salamanca. See Q. Skinner, *The Foundations of Modern Political Thought,* 2 vols. (Cambridge, 1978), II, pp. 135–6; B. P. Copenhaver and C. B. Schmitt, *A History of Western Philosophy,* III: *Renaissance Philosophy* (Oxford, 1992), pp. 112–16.
2. Proverbs 8:15.
3. Wisdom of Solomon 6:3.
4. Leo I, *Sermo* XXXVII, in J. P. Migne, ed., *Patrologia Latina,* 221 vols. (Paris, 1844–64), LIV, cols. 136–9. St Leo I the Great (440–61) was a major early theoretician of the papal monarchy as founded on Christ's having conferred leadership on Peter alone, who then transmitted it to his successors; W. Ullmann, *The Growth of Papal Government in the Middle Ages* (London, 1955), pp. 7–14; J. N. D. Kelly, *The Oxford Dictionary of Popes* (Oxford, 1986), pp. 43–5.
5. Thomas Aquinas, *De regimine principum* III.13–15.
6. Not an exact quotation; cf. Jeremiah 1:10, 24:6, 42:10.
7. John 21:15; Luke 22:32; Matthew 16:19.
8. Isaiah 11:1, 10; Romans 15:12.
9. Isaiah 52:15.
10. Psalms 72:8.
11. Psalms 72:11.
12. Psalms 2:9.
13. Isaiah 60:10.
14. Ezekiel 37:22.
15. Tobias 14:9.
16. Ephesians 4:10–16; I Corinthians 12:12–27.
17. Aristotle, *Metaphysics* XII.7–8 (1072^a19–1074^b14).

18. Thomas Aquinas, *De regimine principum* III.10, 19.
19. Theodore, bishop of Mopsuestia from 392 to 428, was unjustly condemned as a Nestorian after his death when his pupil, Nestorius, was accused – also wrongly, it seems – of claiming that divine and human persons (not just natures) were distinct in Christ. The Fourth Ecumenical Council of Chalcedon condemned the Nestorian heresy in 451, but the monk Eutyches had already bred the Monophysite counter-heresy by seeming to exaggerate the unity of Christ's nature. Justinian called the Fifth Ecumenical Council in Constantinople in 553 to settle the quarrel, having previously issued the controversial 'Three Chapters' that defamed Theodore. Here, Campanella cites the Council's twelfth anathema: G. Alberigo, ed., *Conciliorum oecumenicorum decreta* (Basel, 1962), p. 95; D. Christie-Murray, *A History of Heresy* (Oxford, 1976), pp. 59–74; Kelly, *Popes,* pp. 60–2.
20. Gratian, *Decretum,* I.i.7; Thomas Aquinas, *Commentarium in quartum librum Sententiarum* XVII.3.1.2; Isidore, *Etymolgiae* V.4. For Jerome, Campanella may be thinking of his *Commentary* on Paul's letter to Titus (Migne, ed., *Patrologia Latina,* XXVI, col. 617 B–C). Nothing in Augustine's *De vera religione* seems directly relevant, but Campanella may have had in mind chapters 30–1 (Migne, ed., *Patrologia Latina,* XXXIV, cols. 145–8). Like Covarruvias, the Dominican theologian and philosopher Domingo De Soto (1495–1560) was a student of Vitoria. He played a major role at the Council of Trent, in the preparation of its Index, in debates on the status of Spain's American possessions and in discussions of natural philosophy and scientific method; for his views on natural and biblical law, see his *De justitia et jure* I.i–vi, I.i–iii, discussing Thomas Aquinas, *Summa theologiae* IaIIae, q. 90–100; on De Soto, see B. Hamilton, *Political Thought in Sixteenth-Century Spain: A Study of the Political Ideas of Vitoria, De Soto, Suárez, and Molina* (Oxford, 1963), pp. 14–17, 27–8, 176–80; on Gratian, see n. 94; on the canons ascribed to Isidore, see Migne, ed., *Patrologia Latina,* LXXXIV, cols. 25–92; and for the orders of grace and nature in Thomas Aquinas, see W. Ullmann, *Principles of Government and Politics in the Middle Ages* (London, 1966), pp. 243–58.
21. Matthew 13:46.
22. John 10:34.
23. St Zacharias, pope from 741 to 752, was on the papal throne in 751 when Pepin the Short ended the Merovingian dynasty by deposing Childeric III. Later advocates of papal power exaggerated the role of Zacharias, which was to support Pepin's claim that the throne should go to the person who held effective power. See C. W. Previté-Orton, *The Shorter Cambridge Medieval History,* 2 vols. (Cambridge, 1953), I, p. 298; Ullmann, *Papal Government,* pp. 53, 301; J. R. Strayer, ed., *Dictionary of the Middle Ages,* 12 vols. (New York, 1982–9), IV, pp. 157–60; Kelly, *Popes,* pp. 89–90.
24. In 1356, Charles IV, Holy Roman Emperor, issued the Golden Bull that regularized the rights and duties of the seven imperial electors; but their role had been evolving since the late twelfth century, when Innocent III, pope from 1198 to 1216, intervened after the double election of Otto IV and Philip of Swabia led to conflicting claims on the empire. Innocent IV, the fifth pope to rule from Avignon (1352–62), had good relations with Charles IV but was no match for his namesake in power politics, staying quiet when the Golden Bull gave him no voice in approving the choice of the electors: Previté-Orton, *Medieval History,* II, pp. 648–51, 847–9; *Dictionary of the Middle Ages,* IV, pp. 425–9; Kelly, *Popes,* pp. 187, 222; see n. 5.
25. Between 843 and 870 the Carolingian Empire split into eastern and western halves as the heirs of Charlemagne quarrelled. Towards the end of this period St Nicholas I, pope from 858 to 867, enlarged papal authority over the empire; but Hadrian II, pope from 867 to 872, and John VIII, pope from 872 to 882, were less successful. Although the Byzantine emperor Basil I, who reigned from 867 to 886, tried to become reconciled with the pope, the Council of Constantinople ended in 870 without attaining the goal of reuniting east and west, whose bad relations had worsened when Nicholas excommunicated the patriarch Photius in 863: Previté-Orton, *Medieval History,* I, pp. 254–5, 342–54; Ullmann, *Papal Government,* pp. 190–225; Kelly, *Popes,* pp. 107–11.

26. The English Peter's Pence originated in the Anglo-Saxon period, but the papacy treated it as a compulsory tax only after the Norman conquest. Under severe pressure from Innocent III, King John recognized the pope's right to the payment in 1213, and it lasted until Henry VIII abolished it in 1534. See Ullmann, *Papal Government,* pp. 334–5; *Dictionary of the Middle Ages,* IX, p. 526; Kelly, *Popes,* p. 187.

27. Gregory VII, pope from 1073 to 1085, excommunicated and deposed Henry IV in 1076, referring to the precedent of Childeric's deposition (see n. 23): Previté-Orton, *Medieval History,* I, pp. 490–1; Ullmann, *Papal Government,* pp. 299–303; Kelly, *Popes,* p. 155; see also n. 38.

28. The Treaty of Tordesillas of 1494 modified the initial division in 1493 of Spanish and Portuguese territories in the New World determined by Alexander VI, pope from 1492 to 1503. See *The New Cambridge Modern History,* 14 vols. (Cambridge, 1957–79), I, pp. 424–31; Kelly, *Popes,* p. 255.

29. Sixtus V, pope from 1585 to 1590, excommunicated Henry of Navarre (later Henry IV of France) in 1585. See *New Cambridge Modern History,* III, pp. 303–7; Kelly, *Popes,* p. 272.

30. Particularly important was Innocent III's explicit conferral of the kingship on Joannitza of Bulgaria in 1204. See Ullmann, *Principles of Government,* pp. 82–3; Kelly, *Popes,* p. 187.

31. Gregory IX, *Decretals* I.33.6, citing a letter to the Byzantine emperor from Innocent III, whose enormous legislative programme put into practice the theory of papal supremacy over the lay ruler. The sixteenth-century Thomist school of which De Soto was a prominent member taught that God gives the power of government to the commonwealth, from which the ruler receives it indirectly. See Hamilton, *Political Thought,* pp. 30–8; W. Ullmann, *Law and Politics in the Middle Ages* (Cambridge, 1975), pp. 144–5; Ullmann, *Principles of Government,* pp. 50–6, 80–3; also see nn. 24, 26, 30 and 94.

32. See n. 31.

33. See n. 41.

34. See n. 94.

35. The influential canon lawyer Boniface VIII, pope from 1294 to 1303, aimed to enlarge the role of the papacy in international politics, but his quarrel with Philip IV of France over clerical taxation led him to take a strong but practically indefensible stand in the bull *Clericis laicos* (1296). Nonetheless, intrigue in Rome and the ongoing contest with Philip caused Boniface to make even bolder claims in *Ausculta fili* (1301), *Unam sanctam* (1302) and *Super Petri solio* (1303), provoking Philip to send his agents to Italy to arrest the pope. After the brief reign of Benedict XI (1303–4), the bishop of Bordeaux was elected as Clement V and reigned from 1305 to 1314; under relentless pressure from Philip, he moved his court to Avignon in 1309. His successor, John XXII, pope from 1316 to 1334, was also French and another effective canon lawyer; his most memorable disputes were with Emperor Louis the Bavarian and the Franciscans about the concept of property. After Louis gave protection to William of Ockham and other prominent Franciscans whom John had condemned, the pope excommunicated the emperor in 1327 – along with Marsilius of Padua, an important theorist of secular power; but Louis replied by deposing John and moving militarily on Rome. See Kelly, *Popes,* pp. 208–16; n. 31 on Innocent III; n. 94 on Boniface VIII, John XXII and canon law; and nn. 97 and 98 on property.

36. When Louis V, the last Carolingian king of France, died childless in 987, Hugh Capet, the duke of the Franks, was preferred to Charles, the Carolingian duke of Lorraine, because his effectiveness seemed greater. For Pope Zacharias and the Merovingians, see n. 23; *The Cambridge Medieval History,* 8 vols. (Cambridge, 1911–36), IV, pp. 82–4.

37. Leo III crowned Charlemagne 'Emperor of the Romans' on Christmas Day of the year 800. In 806, when Charlemagne decided to divide the empire among his three sons at his death, he sent the will to Leo for his signature. See *Cambridge Medieval History,* II, p. 265; Previté-Orton, *Medieval History,* I, p. 315; Kelly, *Popes,* p. 98.

38. After 829, Gregory IV, pope from 827 to 844, sided with Lothar I, Louis the German and Pepin in revolt against their father, the Emperor Louis I the Pious, leading to Louis's

capture by his son Lothar at the 'Field of Lies' in 833. Gregory was angered at Louis's (temporary) deposition, perhaps seeing how this imperial family quarrel would erode earlier gains in papal power, so the emperor's restoration in 834 pleased him; during this unsettled period there were regional councils in Lyons in 829 and 834. See Previté-Orton, *Medieval History,* I, pp. 340–2; Kelly, *Popes,* pp. 102–3.

39. Around 1126 the bishop of Paris excommunicated Louis VI, 'the Fat', who reigned from 1108 to 1137, in a quarrel over benefices. Honorius II, pope from 1124 to 1130, lifted the sentence, but his efforts to end the breach between king and clergy in France displeased Bernard of Clairvaux. See Kelly, *Popes,* pp. 165–6.

40. Pius V, pope from 1566 to 1572, helped Catherine de' Medici against the Huguenots; and Gregory XIV, pope from 1590 to 1591, opposed Henry IV before his conversion. See *New Cambridge Modern History,* III, p. 304; Kelly, *Popes,* pp. 268–9, 273–4.

41. By the end of the twelfth century, Florence, Genoa and other towns in northern and central Italy appointed citizens of other towns to the office of *podestà,* or chief executive, in order to remove the business of governing from incessant internal strife. *Cortes,* or representative estates of nobles, clergy and townspeople, developed in Aragon and other parts of the Iberian peninsula around the same time. See *Dictionary of the Middle Ages,* III, pp. 610–12; IX, pp. 711–12.

42. Gratian, *Decretum* I.96.13–14; II.2.6.3, in Migne, ed., *Patrologia Latina,* CLXXXVII, cols. 460–5, 618.

43. I Samuel 8.

44. I Corinthians 6:3.

45. Thomas Aquinas, *De regimine principum* III.13.

46. King Roger II of Sicily, whose kingdom included Naples, created the office of justiciary in 1136 as a royal office, but feudal lords soon controlled it in their own domains. See *Dictionary of the Middle Ages,* XI, pp. 268–9.

47. Bridget, in *Revelationes* II.7 and VIII.1, severely criticized the fifth and sixth Avignon popes, Innocent VI, who reigned from 1352 to 1362, and Urban V, who reigned from 1362 to 1370, for staying away from Rome. See Kelly, *Popes,* pp. 221–5.

48. See Plato, *Republic* 435B–441D. St Clement, who followed Saints Linus and Anacletus as the third bishop of Rome (c. 91–c. 101) after St Peter, may have written the *First Epistle of Clement,* dated in the late first century, but not the later pseudo-Clementine documents of the second through fourth century called the *Second Epistle, Homilies, Recognitions* and *Apostolic Constitutions; Recognitions* X.5–6 cites Plato, *Republic* 457, but not the passage on the tripartite soul. Without specific ascription to Plato, however, this idea appears in *Paedagogus* III.1 of Clement of Alexandria, on whom Plato's influence was strong. See E. J. Goodspeed, *A History of Early Christian Literature,* ed. R. M. Grant (Chicago, 1966), pp. 7–13, 83, 87–90; Kelly, *Popes,* pp. 7–8.

49. Campanella wrote *On the Monarchy of Christians* in prison in 1593. It was lost when he was arrested in Calabria in 1599, but its content emerged in the work translated here and in others. See L. Firpo, *Bibliografia degli scritti di Tommaso Campanella* (Turin, 1940), pp. 24, 177–8.

50. Arator, *De actibus apostolorum,* ed. A. P. McKinlay (Vienna, 1951), pp. 146–8 (II.1214–39). In 544 the poet Arator presented his two-book epic version of the Acts of the Apostles to Pope Vigilius. See M. L. W. Laistner, *Thought and Letters in Western Europe,* 2nd ed. (Ithaca, N.Y., 1966), p. 112.

51. Revelation 5:10.

52. Bridget, *Revelationes* II.7, IV.74; but the symbolism is much older. When Stephen IV, pope from 816 to 817, crowned Louis the Pious as emperor in 816, Stephen added an important new element to the coronation rite, bestowing a sword on Louis as a symbol of the duty of the secular arm to defend the Church. The key Pauline text mentioning the sword is Romans 13:4. For Peter's keys, see Matthew 16:19. See also Ullmann, *Papal Government,* pp. 157–9; Kelly, *Popes,* p. 99.

53. Cf. Bridget, *Revelationes* IV.7, VIII.1; John 2:14–15; Ephesians 4:8–13.

54. Bridget, *Revelationes* I.12.
55. Deuteronomy 17:8–12; and n. 42.
56. The reference to Thomas Aquinas has not been identified.
57. Eugenius III, pope from 1145 to 1153, had been a student of St Bernard of Clairvaux and headed a Cistercian monastery at the time of his election. Bernard preached the Second Crusade that Eugenius declared in 1146, but when it failed Eugenius lost his teacher's enthusiasm for international adventure. Bernard addressed to Eugenius his *De consideratione,* which Ullmann calls a 'mirror for popes', setting forth the grand themes of hierocratic papal monarchy in a Christocentric cosmos. See Bernard, *De consideratione* III.2.12; Ullmann, *Papal Government,* pp. 426–37; Kelly, *Popes,* pp. 172–3; and n. 65.
58. Cf. Bridget, *Revelationes* II.8, 15, III.26; I Samuel 10:17–11:15; II Samuel 5:1–3.
59. Psalms 110:4; Romans 11:17–18; Hebrews 5:4–6.
60. Revelation 5:9–10.
61. For Calvin on David as a model for Christians, see E. Gosselin, *The King's Progress to Jerusalem: Some Interpretations of David during the Reformation Period and Their Patristic and Medieval Background* (Malibu, Calif., 1976), pp. 82–97.
62. I Peter 2:9.
63. Romans 7:21–5.
64. Gratian, *Decretum,* III.4.70, in Migne, ed., *Patrologia Latina,* CLXXXVII, col. 1821, citing Hrabanus Maurus, *De institutione clericorum* I.27. St Innocent I, pope from 401 to 417, was a strong and early proponent of papal primacy in teaching and of Rome's leadership of the Church. His letter of 416, *Si instituta,* approves the anointing of the laity in baptism, confirmation and extreme unction; see R. Cabié, ed., *La Lettre du Pape Innocent Ier à Décentius de Gubbio (19 Mars 416): texte critique et commentaire* (Louvain, 1973), pp. 22–5, 30–33. Hrabanus Maurus (d. 856) was a student of Alcuin and a leading Carolingian author of biblical commentaries based on patristic sources; his work *De institutione clericorum* imitated Augustine's treatise *De doctrina Christiana,* just as his *De rerum naturis* followed Isidore of Seville; see R. McKitterick, ed., *Carolingian Culture: Emulation and Innovation* (Cambridge, 1994), pp. 40–3.
65. Bernard, *De consideratione* II.8.15.
66. Leo IV, pope from 847 to 855, won a major naval battle against the Saracens in 849, having previously strengthened Rome's land defences. St Bernard strongly advocated the pope's *possession* both of the spiritual sword and of the material sword; the latter, however, was to be *used* by lay authority at the behest of the clergy: see Bernard, *De consideratione* IV.3.7; Ullmann, *Papal Government,* pp. 430–3; Kelly, *Popes,* p. 104.
67. Psalms 82:6–7; see n. 1 on Covarruvias.
68. Ezekiel 37:22.
69. In making the case in his *De monarchia* for the autonomous power of a Roman lay world monarchy, Dante denied that temporal authority depends on the spiritual in the way that the moon takes light from the sun. In fact, he maintained that the moon produces some of its own light, which the sun then magnifies, and that in like manner divine grace strengthens the independent authority of the lay ruler: see *De monarchia* III.4.
70. De Soto, *De justitia et jure* I.4.1.
71. I Samuel 21:8–9, 22:10.
72. Psalms 92:10.
73. Psalms 75:10.
74. Isaiah 51:5.
75. Isaiah 42:4.
76. Jeremiah 30:21.
77. Bridget's *Revelationes* VIII contains much in the way of promised retribution but nothing that corresponds precisely to Campanella's point.
78. Matthew 22:21; Mark 12:17; Luke 20:25.
79. See n. 70 for a related passage from De Soto and n. 25 for Emperor Basil. A letter of 869

from Basil refers to the pope as pastor, speaking of 'a flock following one shepherd' in allusion to John 10:16: see G. D. Mansi, ed., *Sacrorum conciliorum nova et amplissima collectio* . . . , 31 vols. (Venice, 1759–98), XVI, p. 47.
80. John 21:15.
81. Luke 12:31.
82. Nothing relevant has been found in Augustine, *Contra Faustum.*
83. The correct reference is I Chronicles 29:14.
84. I Corinthians 12:28.
85. I Corinthians 12:12–31.
86. Mark 16:15.
87. The Perugian postglossator Bartolus of Sassoferrato (d. 1357) was one of the great teachers of Roman law of the later Middle Ages. Baldus de Ubaldis (d. 1400) was his student and a major authority in civil and canon law. The important canonist Cardinal Henricus of Segusia (d. 1271) was called Hostiensis because he was bishop of Ostia. See Ullmann, *Law and Politics,* pp. 108–12, 173. Like other Thomists of his school, De Soto held that the emperor could not be the ruler of the world because there was no global commonwealth capable of bestowing this authority; see Hamilton, *Political Thought,* p. 95.
88. Thomas Aquinas, *De regimine principum* III.19–22.
89. Aristotle, *Politics* I.2 (1254^{b}15–25).
90. Cf. Augustine, *Epistulae* CXXVII.8. On Cardinal Aleander (1480–1542), who in 1521 represented Leo X, pope from 1513 to 1521, at the Diet of Worms which led to the imperial ban on Luther, see F. Gaeta, *Un nunzio pontificio a Venezia nel Cinquecento (Girolamo Aleandro)* (Venice, 1960).
91. Gratian, *Decretum,* I.96.6–10, in Migne, ed., *Patrologia Latina,* CLXXXVII, cols. 456–9; but note that *Cum ad verum* actually belongs to Nicholas I. St Gelasius I, pope from 492 to 496, helped lay the foundations for the theory of papal and Roman supremacy, recognizing the distinction between temporal and spiritual authority but subordinating the former to the latter; see M. Fornasari, ed., *Initia canonum a primaevis collectionibus usque ad Decretum Gratiani* (Rome, 1972–), I, pp. 169, 311; Ullmann, *Papal Government,* pp. 14–28; Kelly, *Popes,* pp. 47–9.
92. Campanella, *Monarchia Messiae,* pp. 11–13.
93. Bernard, *De consideratione* III.4.14.
94. Gratian, *Decretum,* I.21.6–9, 96.5–7, 97.3, in Migne, ed., *Patrologia Latina,* CLXXXVII, cols. 120–2, 455–6, 467. In 1139–40 in Bologna, the monk Gratian produced the fundamental medieval textbook of canon law, called the *Concordia discordantium canonum* because it aimed to settle conflicts among earlier rulings on Church law, as set forth in the many 'decretal letters' or 'decretals' of the popes who established the 'canons' or norms of Christian conduct. Hence, Gratian's work was often called the *Decretum.* Popes after Gratian's time added decretals called *extravagantes* because they 'went beyond' ('extra vagantes') Gratian's collection. The first of these was the *Liber extra* issued by Gregory IX, pope from 1227 to 1241, in 1234. Boniface VIII was responsible for the collection called *Liber sextus* because it was the sixth such book of additions; the *Liber septimus* or *Clementinae* added by Clement V and the *Extravagantes* of John XXII completed the *Corpus iuris canonici* as it stood until 1918. Nicholas I wrote his letter (cited in Gratian, *Decretum,* I.96.4–7) to the Byzantine Emperor Michael III, who reigned from 846 to 867, in 865. The medieval canon law is now read in E. A. Friedberg, ed., *Corpus iuris canonici,* 2 vols. (Leipzig, 1879–81; reprinted Graz, 1959). See Ullmann, *Law and Politics,* pp. 120–1, 139–43, 165–9; Kelly, *Popes,* pp. 108, 189–91.
95. Probably a reference to chapter 9: Campanella, *Monarchia Messiae,* pp. 27–35.
96. St Sylvester I, pope from 314 to 335, reigned during most of the period when Constantine was emperor but had little to do with Constantine's promotion of Christianity. Nonetheless, later hagiography inflated his role, preparing the way for the notorious eighth-century

forgery (exposed by Lorenzo Valla) called the 'Donation of Constantine', which claimed that the emperor offered his crown to Sylvester, donated lands to him in the West and recognized his authority over other Church leaders. See Kelly, *Popes,* pp. 27–8.

97. John Chrysostom, *Homilia,* 85.3–4, in J. P. Migne, ed., *Patrologia Graeca,* 162 vols. (Paris, 1857–66), XXXI, cols. 760–4. See also R. A. Krupp, *Shepherding the Flock of God: The Pastoral Theology of John Chrysostom* (New York, 1991), pp. 189–94.

98. St Romuald was one of the founders of the eleventh-century Italian eremitical movement of Camaldoli. It drew ascetic solitaries to lives of extreme austerity, which were lived separately but within a territory near a more or less conventional monastery governed by the Benedictine rule. St Bernard (1090–1153) entered the new monastery at Cîteaux in 1112, moving three years later to Clairvaux, one of the wellsprings of the Cistercian movement. The wish to shun the world led the Cistercians to locate their houses in unsettled places; but, as they tamed the wilderness, economic success overwhelmed their early devotion to apostolic poverty and bred accusations of greed. Their prosperity came in part from the *conversi* or lay brothers recruited from the peasantry, who held a lower place in the monastic hierarchy and formed a powerful agrarian labour force. See *Dictionary of the Middle Ages,* II, pp. 190–4; III, pp. 403–5; X, p. 527; C. H. Lawrence, *Medieval Monasticism: Forms of Religious Life in Western Europe in the Middle Ages,* 2nd ed. (London, 1989), pp. 152–5, 174–89, 197–202; on St Bernard, see also n. 57.

Further Reading

Amabile, L., *Fra Tommaso Campanella, la sua congiuria, i suoi processi, la sua pazzia* (Naples, 1882)

Fra Tommaso Campanella ne' castelli di Napoli, in Roma, in Parigi (Naples, 1887)

Amerio, R., *Il sistema teologico di Tommaso Campanella* (Milan, 1972)

Badaloni, N., *Tommaso Campanella* (Milan, 1965)

Burns, J. H., ed., *The Cambridge History of Political Thought 1450–1700* (Cambridge, 1991), pp. 25, 335–6, 666

Cassaro, A., *L'*Atheismus triumphatus *di Tommaso Campanella: genesi, sviluppo e valore dell'opera* (Naples, 1983)

CHRP, pp. 236, 245, 252–3, 257–62, 292, 294–5, 407, 410, 444, 484, 746, 754, 812

Di Napoli, G., *Studi sul rinascimento* (Naples, 1973)

Tommaso Campanella, filosofo della restaurazione cattolica (Padua, 1947)

Ernst, G., *Religione, ragione e natura: ricerche su Tommaso Campanella e il tardo Rinascimento* (Milan, 1991)

Firpo, L., *Bibliografia degli scritti di Tommaso Campanella* (Turin, 1940)

Headley, J., 'On the rearming of heaven: the Machiavellism of Tommaso Campanella', *Journal of the History of Ideas,* 49 (1988), 387–404

'Tommaso Campanella and the end of the Renaissance', *Journal of Medieval and Renaissance Studies,* 20 (1990), 157–74

Negri, L., *Fede e ragione in Tommaso Campanella* (Milan, 1990)

Part II.
The Theory of Princely Government in Renaissance Italy

Giovanni Pontano

Nicholas Webb

Introduction

The humanist Giovanni Pontano (c. 1426/9–1503) was born in Cerreto (Umbria) and entered the service of Alfonso I of Naples in 1447. He pursued a successful career as a diplomat and, from 1486, as secretary or first minister to Alfonso's successor Ferrante. He left the Aragonese court in 1495, after recognizing Charles VIII of France as king of Naples. He was head of the Neapolitan academy from 1471 and had a wide circle of literary friends throughout Italy. Primarily a Neo-Latin poet, his prose writings include a history of the wars of King Ferrante, dialogues on literary subjects and a series of ethical treatises.

Pontano's treatise *On the Prince* (1468) is cast in the form of a practical letter of advice for the twenty-year-old duke of Calabria, the future Alfonso II, whom he tutored between circa 1468 and 1475. Pontano dedicated another ethical treatise, *On Courage,* to the duke after his expulsion of the Turks from Otranto in 1481; and he continued to be closely associated with him as a personal secretary up to the time of his forced abdication in 1494. Some fifteenth-century Neapolitan manuscripts containing *On the Prince* also have Pontano's *On Obedience* (c. 1470), thus forming a combined guide for both ruler and ruled. His later ethical works develop a number of themes raised in *On the Prince,* but they are less directly prescriptive and devote more space to the theoretical discussion of ethical terminology.

Justice, piety, generosity and clemency are extolled as princely virtues at the start of the work. The usefulness of book-learning is defended against the criticism that it is irrelevant for the active life. In the second half of the treatise Pontano outlines what the prince must do in order to proclaim the majesty of his office to the best effect, both in terms of his conduct of public administration and of his private behaviour – down to his dress, gait and speech. The distinction between the public and private bodies of the prince is not clearly demarcated: the appointment of public officials seems to be an extension of the prince's personal conduct towards others. There is a detailed discussion of decorum, which Pontano claims is a supplement to Cicero's *De officiis.* Along with Alfonso II's own forebears, Xenophon's Cyrus is the recommended model of exemplary behaviour. The quotations and sayings which pepper the treatise come from a range of sources, including two of Pontano's own relations: Ludovico (Alfonso I's representative at the Council of Basel) and Tommaso (the chancellor of Perugia in 1450).

For the Latin text of *De principe* see E. Garin, ed., *Prosatori latini del Quattrocento* (Milan, 1952), pp. 1021–63. I wish to thank Robert Goulding and Silvia Fazzo for their assistance with this translation.

On the Prince

Duke Alfonso, Publius Cornelius Scipio, later nicknamed Africanus because of his prowess, having noticed, while canvassing for election to the aedileship, that the tribunes of the people were complaining that he was not yet of the legal age for entering the competition, said: 'I am old enough if the citizens of Rome want to consider me eligible.'[1] Even though he was a precocious young man, he was still sufficiently confident of his virtue to be prepared to seek the magistracy from the people. Your father made you a sovereign regent and has assigned to you the province of Calabria, even though you have hardly left behind the years of childhood, nor were you seeking the post. This is a tribute not to your years or to your youth, but to your virtue. Everyone has so much optimism about your virtue that you have turned the eyes of the people and the nobles alike onto you alone. Scipio so conducted himself as aedile that the citizens did not regret having run around with such enthusiasm to cast votes for him in their constituencies. In your case, it is appropriate that you strive to go beyond your father's estimate and the general expectation of you. You will certainly surpass this with ease, provided you are not neglectful of yourself. Nor shall you be, if you are prepared to obey sensible instructions and honourable advice, and if both your own subjects and everyone else perceives in you justice, piety, generosity and clemency.

Nothing is more valuable for winning the minds of subjects than a reputation for justice and piety. Therefore, with the following words Virgil prudently introduces his character Phlegyas, acclaiming justice and religion in one and the same breath: 'Be warned: learn to be just and not to scorn the gods.'[2] A person will be considered to have justice when everyone bears his authority patiently and when they even submit themselves to his restraint willingly. This is what we read about Cyrus, who is thought to have been an example not only of justice but of all the royal virtues.[3] Alexander of Macedon has taught us how valuable a reputation for religion is for increasing public goodwill. He was even given to praising superstition, as though by that means leaders could insinuate themselves into the minds of the people.[4] The aforementioned Cyrus, as well as Camillus,[5] Scipio Africanus and all very eminent men have been distinguished in this virtue, and your grandfather Alfonso surpassed every king of his own age and of many earlier centuries. It is an established fact that he observed the holy offices and the Christian feast days with such devotion that he was not outdone by the popes themselves.[6]

Would-be rulers ought to set themselves two fundamental objectives: first, that they are generous; second, that they are merciful. For the king who makes use of generosity transforms enemies into friends, strangers into intimates, traitors into dutiful subjects. He will even cajole foreigners and those who live in distant lands into loving him. We all respect, revere and take for a god those whom we perceive to be merciful. In fact, through his generosity and mercy the prince is made very much like God, whose nature it is to bless all things and spare the backsliders.

Flattery, on the other hand, is to be shunned completely; for the person who inclines his ears towards flatterers utterly ceases to be his own master. He assesses himself and his affairs on the basis of the blandishments of others rather than by his own conscience. You will also expel and banish self-interested ambition from your court, since it is the mother and grandmother of many and great evils. On this point I recall that my kinsman Tommaso Pontano, a man renowned for both his learning and his broad experience, was in the habit of saying that adulation is the curse of cities and of kingdoms.[7] The Roman emperor, [Severus] Alexander, was quite right to order a man of this type to be tied to the stake for seeking popular favour with such zeal that he placed the supreme good in it. Damp wood was then set alight, so that the man suffocated from smoke inhalation; and Alexander maintained that it was just that smoke should be the cause of his death, since he had been accustomed to buy and sell smoke.[8]

The prince who remembers that he is a man will never be puffed up with pride. He will try to keep a sense of proportion. When he sees that everything happens to him exactly according to his own design, it is at that moment above all that he will believe human affairs to be ordained by God, who is greatly displeased by pride. Take care what you promise and also to whom you make promises. You should be aware not only of opportunities and just deserts but also of circumstances and temperaments. On this subject many other points should be taken into consideration, in particular, that there is nothing more despicable than not keeping faith. This is so important that once you have given your word, even to an enemy, it is still right to keep it. And since faith is defined by the ancients as steadfastness and truth in one's words and agreements, nothing ought to be held in greater veneration by the prince than the truth itself. This is shown by the custom most wisely established by our ancestors that each day the Gospels, in which divine truth is contained, are offered to the prince when he attends the divine service, so that being reminded by this book that the truth is to be worshipped, he will recall that he himself is obliged to be utterly devoted to it.

It is especially right to ensure that your servants find you accommodating. For nothing is more alien to a prince, nor generates so much resentment from others against him, than churlishness and what we call pernicketiness. By contrast, friendliness, tempered by solemnity, is greatly praised in every walk of life. Your grandfather gained the goodwill of men through this one quality in particular, because he allowed no one to go away from him unhappy; and he often used to have that sentence of Titus on his lips: 'It is not right for anyone to go away unhappy from a conversation with a prince.'[9]

A person who sees that you are temperate will never dare to seek to obtain anything ignoble from you. 'You lucky man, Marcus Cato', said Cicero, 'from whom no one ever dared to seek a corrupt favour.'[10] You will without doubt be thought to deserve your principate and be guaranteed a good reign if you harass the corrupt, loathe the dissolute and spurn liars. Flee from the advocates of pleasure as you would from the most dangerous plague. They debauch the mind, however well educated it might be. It is quite impossible for someone who is charmed by these types to maintain any regular pattern of life. His boyhood will be shameless, his youth unmanly, his old age notorious. Nero Claudius used to have many procurers of pleasure, yet what sort of death did he have?[11] The same goes for many others and perhaps all those like him. I am not sure what is more praiseworthy in Scipio: his courage in waging wars or his continence throughout his entire life. By means of the former he vanquished the enemy two or three times; by means of the latter he always conquered himself. He was all the more admirable because while there have been many in the past, and there are many today, who can defeat an enemy, there are very few who conquer themselves, especially since victory makes them arrogant and intemperate.[12]

Someone who governs others ought to be entirely free from the passions. For anger does not permit us to discern what is right; hate drives us to crime; love muddles our judgement; lust leads us to violence; anguish incites us to vengeance; envy propels us headlong into disaster.[13]

It is particularly advantageous for a man, and above all one who governs a principality, to keep a clear head in adversity and not to give up in the face of deteriorating fortune. Your father King Ferrante did not show the slightest flicker of emotion when, at the beginning of his reign, he was told about the defection of many nobles, common people and even whole provinces to Jean d'Anjou; still less did he show that he was distraught. Not once did he refer to the traitors with an unkind word. When the rebellion of a certain noble (whom I do not name out of respect, even if he has hardly looked after his own reputation) was announced, Ferrante was affected to the extent of saying that he grieved because such a man from so great a family had made himself unworthy of his forebears. Yet he gave thanks to Christ that he had provided the miscreant with no pretext at all for such criminal action.[14] What does this prove, if not that his mind was unconquered, reviving itself even from adversity? After the news of the defeat at Sarno, when all but a few towns in the entire kingdom had deserted the king, Enneco Guevara, the count of Ariano, and Count Onorato Fundano convened a meeting in response to this grave and dire turn of events. Ferrante spoke to the full council in such a rousing manner about his circumstances that not only did he fortify their spirits, but in addition he asserted that the enemy would be driven out very soon and the kingdom would be handed over to his own children much more securely than it had been left to him by his father.[15] The thought that no summit is reached without the greatest trials and dangers should strengthen us even in our adversities.

Moreover, how many people are so keen to be treated mildly and leniently by their father, teacher or master that they never want to be reprimanded by that person? Therefore, wisely was it said that those whom God loves, he rebukes and chastises.[16] You must take that to heart, because it is by this means most of all that God, the governor of human affairs and the controller of our weakness, curbs our rashness. We see it every day: success brings many to the brink of disaster who would have fared much better if they had not always travelled at full sail but had instead been held back for a time by a contrary wind. Why? Because we often see that difficult circumstances have been the occasion of great good. Alfonso, about whom I have already spoken and shall have more to say, was defeated in a naval battle and captured by the Genoese, as if he were destined to get possession of the kingdom of Naples – which eventually he did – by means of his captivity and would not at length have become the victor if he had not previously been defeated.[17] Furthermore, those things which we have obtained and held on to with effort somehow please us more and we value them more highly than if they had come to us by chance, or if it were not necessary to take any trouble to hold on to them.

Our successes are like a mirror of our selves. As we are accustomed to say with regard to political office, success makes it abundantly clear what sort of person someone is.[18] For this reason self-control is needed most of all when someone can do exactly as he likes. His mind has to be disciplined in order to prevent it getting carried away or becoming arrogant or forgetful of itself; and it has to be trained in such a way that he constantly considers the possibility that one day he may be cast from freedom into slavery, from wealth into poverty and from a high and illustrious position into dismal ignominy. According to the fable, after Bellerophon was borne up by that winged horse and reached the heavens, he plummeted headlong downwards. On account of this fall, as the ancient verse has it: 'wretched and sorrowful he wandered through strange lands'.[19] This is liable to happen very often to people who, swollen-headed on account of their good fortune, behave in an arrogant and unrestrained manner.

Plato says, in a passage quoted by Cicero: 'Happy the man who, even in old age, is able to attain wisdom and true judgements.'[20] Excellently put; yet, in order for us to be fit to attain wisdom in old age, the foundations must be laid in youth. When these are well laid, as in a well-built house, there will be no worry that we will give way. The best foundation for young men consists in striving after wisdom, even if someone of that age cannot actually be wise on account of his immaturity and lack of knowledge. A person at this time of life is not capable of perceiving or accomplishing the best things. But what he certainly can do is adopt the manner of life of those who are considered wise. Cicero says as much when he tells how, after he had assumed the toga of manhood, he was taken by his father to Quintus Mucius Scaevola, so that, as far as he was able and the old man would permit, he should never leave his side.[21] For the first priority is that the child gets into the habit of respecting old men. The second is that he willingly listens to their words. The third is that he strives to make himself as similar to them as possible, not only in words but also in deeds. By following these basic principles, he gradually strives towards the wisdom he will triumphantly attain.

Your father has chosen men who are high-ranking and entirely praiseworthy, by whose advice and instructions you are to be directed. This is not because you are incapable of guiding yourself, but rather because young trees usually need to be propped up by some sort of staves. When these men discuss weighty matters, you should listen to them, no less than to the philosophers themselves. For what better masters could you have in order to prepare yourself for action than those men who have achieved many great things? Your grandfather Alfonso (to stay with examples from your own family) habitually listened with incredible pleasure to the poet Antonio Panormita recounting stories from the annals of the ancients.[22] And furthermore he made a point of hearing literary readings by Panormita every day. Although he was sometimes occupied with a great many concerns, he never let these affairs interfere with the time set aside for books.

It is remarkable how much careful and thorough reading helps to train us for the best manner of life. For if, as Sallust records that Scipio was in the habit of saying about himself, the portraits of ancestors have a remarkable power to inspire their viewers to virtue,[23] their words and those deeds of theirs which are worthy of imitation, when repeatedly recalled to mind and set before our eyes, ought to provide much greater inspiration. Your grandfather never set out on a campaign without books. He would order a tent to be set up in which they were readily to hand. And since he had no other portraits of the Fabii, the Marcelli, the Scipios, the Alexanders and the Caesars to gaze upon, he used to pore over the books in which their deeds were contained.[24] It is proper that you, his namesake, should in this, as in many other things, particularly follow his example. For although it would not be unseemly for a grandfather to be outdone by his grandson in learned pursuits, it would be unseemly and shameful for you, the grandson, not to live up to his glory.

Assent should not be given to those people who decry learned pursuits. If they think learning should be scorned on the grounds that it is not necessary to acquire it, I fail to see what sort of knowledge they think should be acquired. What is more necessary, by Christ, than knowing a great deal both about those things based on a knowledge of nature and of recondite matters, and about those founded on the memory of past events and the example set by famous men? Unless they think that it is not necessary to know whether something is fair or foul, good or bad, to be sought after or avoided, whether it heals people who are sick or harms those who are healthy; and that the only thing necessary to know is how to deck out a sumptuous feast.

But if perhaps they decry learning because they regard it as unworthy, they are completely mistaken and, as the expression goes, are on entirely the wrong track. For what is more worthy of a man than to be a paragon among other men? The fact that people who are considered learned always take first place in accomplishing the greatest exploits and arriving at decisive plans proves that those endowed with learning are outstanding.[25] There would not be unanimous agreement that boys should be immediately handed over to schoolmasters, by whom they are instructed in learned matters, if such instruction were going to be unworthy of them later on, when they had grown up.

There are some who, given over to indolence and idle leisure, hold a bad opinion both of learning and of learned men simply in order to justify their own ignorance, about which they even have the nerve to boast. Of course, nobody claims that all those who are ranked among the learned are without blemish. Yet vice reflects on the characters of those who are depraved by it, not on learning, even though learning, on account of its renown, makes that fault more noticeable. But they themselves are forced to admit that even among those commonly called idiots, who are unlettered, there are many who are soiled and defiled with the stains of repulsive vices, and that even if they lack other faults, they are certainly not free from the vice of ignorance and stupidity. What can be more abject and unworthy of a man than that?

When the city of Rome was terrified and uncertain as to what action to take, on account of fear of Catiline and the other conspirators, after the most eminent citizens had been passed over, by the common consent of the city fathers and of the people it was agreed to ask Marcus Tullius Cicero to be consul, even though he was a new man and was not a native of Rome.[26] Apparently, it was not his home-town of Arpinum nor the portraits of his ancestors that had secured such high hopes for him, but rather the distinguished reputation of his literary efforts and the eloquence which he brought to the forum and the senate from the schools of the rhetoricians.

I heard from Marino Tomacello, who was in Rome at the time, that after the death of Pope Nicholas V, his successor Calixtus III, afraid that war would immediately be declared by Jacopo Piccinino,[27] advanced against him; at this point a certain great man, who was nevertheless terrified by the prospect of a new war, said: 'There is no cause to fear Piccinino. The Church of Christ has three thousand or more learned men; with their counsels and wisdom, all the exertions of all the leaders of Europe put together could be easily repelled and overthrown.'[28]

There is no need at present for me to dispute any further with these people. Learning is hardly in need of my protection, especially where you are concerned. It was only necessary to touch on the issue here, not to sing the praises of learning. I therefore come to the end of listing its merits, in case by applauding these things I should seem to be vaunting my own studies. But there is something I simply cannot omit. After Antonio Caldora had been defeated and captured,[29] your grandfather advanced with his army into the land of the Peligni.[30] Having reached a position from which he could reconnoitre Sulmona, he enquired about the area, since it was said that this had been the homeland of Ovid. When those who were present had confirmed this, he spared the city and gave thanks to the spirit of the place in which in former times such a great poet had been born. After a lengthy discussion of Ovid's merits, Alfonso, moved by the greatness of his fame, said: 'I would gladly give up this region, which is no small nor insignificant part of the kingdom of Naples, if this poet had been alive in my day; I value him, even dead, more than the lordship of all Abruzzo.'

As we cannot always be actively pursuing our affairs, and sometimes we need a respite from books, we must have intervals when we seek recreation for both mind and body. Nevertheless, it is right to ensure that every break is without idleness, so that in seeking relaxation we do not make ourselves indolent and unmanly. Our leisure should be equally without business and without sloth. The prudent farmer allows a field to lie fallow, however rich its soil; but if he leaves it untilled for too long, it becomes overgrown with brambles and weeds. Similarly, when we allow our mind to lounge in excessive idleness, phrases such as 'the feather-down of Sardanapalus'[31] or 'a pig from the herd of Epicurus'[32] are justly used to describe us, together with still more demeaning insults, if any exist or can be imagined.

In this rest period some provision is to be made for the renewal of the mind through games and pastimes. Laberius says that a convivial companion on a journey serves as a carriage, a remark which should be applied as well to the recreation I am talking about.[33] Musicians who divert the mind and soothe our cares with both song and instrumental music are also to be employed. Some time, too, is to be given to actors. Your grandfather would spend the noon hour practising archery with the young men; Augustus played pass-the-ball and balloon-ball.[34] Hunting and bird-catching greatly refresh the mind and body as well. Your father at your age devoted himself to horsemanship. As a boy at the court of his grandfather, Astyages, Cyrus rode horses; and, having learned how to spear wild animals enclosed in a park, as a young man he used to hunt lions or boars in the woods.[35] Virgil was therefore right to praise Picus for having been a 'horse-tamer and subduer of wild steeds'.[36]

First and foremost, however, it is necessary to see to it that you are loved most devotedly by those to whom you entrust the care of your person and private life. By so doing you will live in greater security. When this same love has extended its roots more deeply among your household and afterwards has spread over a larger area, it will be disseminated not only among your subjects and your own nation, but even among foreigners. Whoever loves someone wishes that person to live forever; and although a person who is well loved has less need than anyone else for an army, I am inclined to think that no one is better supplied with troops. Thus, the saying cheerfully repeated by Tommaso Pontano appears to have some justification: 'Love is never for hire.' There is another saying of his which is no less shrewd: 'Love advances unarmed, yet sleeps in a breastplate.' For the sake of preserving and daily increasing the love of your household and your intimate friends, it is particularly important that they appreciate that they are loved by you. It is an old saying and a judicious one that 'if you wish to be loved, love'.[37] They will come to this conclusion above all when they see you rejoice in their good fortune and grieve wholeheartedly over their adversities. Generosity combined with gratitude will captivate their hearts and make them particularly loyal. Generosity cannot exceed a certain limit in princes, although the same rule is not to be applied in every circumstance and in relation to everyone. For when people get used to receiving favours on a daily basis, if you are forced by necessity or persuaded by some valid reason to withdraw your hand, they may change their minds and, reacting as if they had received some injury, look to see how they can take revenge on you.

Kindness also brings many benefits. Since you excel in that virtue, you are not only assured of being loved by your friends, but also by everyone else. Cyrus, whom I particularly want you to imitate, at a time when he was least able to be generous, due to his own poverty, used to try to obtain the goodwill of his followers through kindness, assisting them in their work and sharing their labours. When afterwards he acquired the kingdom of Assyria, he was unstinting in every type of generosity, since it was not money but his friends, to whom he had given considerable wealth, which he regarded as his treasure. He took so much pleasure in the prosperity not only of his friends and household but also of each one of his subjects that he said it was the duty – and in fact a requisite – of a good king to make communities happy as well.[38]

You should make an effort to ensure not so much that you are considered generous and kind as that you avoid the vices which are said to be the opposites of these virtues. Other people should not see you behaving in an avaricious manner or casting longing glances at those things they themselves take delight in or esteem. A lord who is greedy necessarily becomes ravenous, using violence, with or without justification, in order to obtain what he desires; next come interdicts, exiles, tortures, murders; and, afterwards, it turns out to be true that:

> Few kings descend to the underworld without bloodshed and injuries;
> Few tyrants die a bloodless death.[39]

What, for that matter, is more alien to kings – or less conducive to their own safety – than behaving in a proud and surly manner when they ought to appear as paragons of kindness? Hard-heartedness is the mother of hate, as pride is of cruelty, and both are bad guardians of your life and your principate. When I was a lad, Cardinal Angelotti Fosco was strangled by his man-servant because he showed himself to be harsh and excessively stingy towards his own household.[40] What can tyrants expect, when those who are considered sacrosanct fail to escape such an end? Constantly afraid, they are inevitably choked and tortured by anxieties, as if they were suffering torments night and day. They say that Masinissa, who once held sway throughout much of Africa, did not trust his sons and therefore committed the guardianship of his person to his dogs, which he reared in large and ferocious packs.[41] How securely he lived can be readily judged from the fact that he considered his dogs to be more faithful than his sons. No more secure and no less unhappy were Alexander of Pherae and Dionysius of Syracuse. Alexander, as Cicero reports, when he wanted to enter a room in order to be with his wife Thebe, whom he loved to distraction, used to order a barbarian, tattooed like a Thracian, to go in before him with a drawn sword; and he used to send his attendants ahead to sift through her caskets and search them in case some weapon had been hidden amidst the clothing.[42] Dionysius had two wives, Aristomache and Dorida. It is said that he never had intercourse with either of them unless they had been stripped naked beforehand. Moreover, he used to retire to his bedroom, which he had surrounded by a broad ditch, by way of a wooden bridge. And when he saw that his daughters, who used to cut his hair, had become women, he was afraid to trust them with a knife and had his hair singed off with a smouldering charcoal.[43]

It is a venerable adage, lacking neither authority nor proof, that the virtue of others is always intimidating to kings.[44] If kings were as concerned about respecting virtue as they were about the prizes they occasionally bestow on scoundrels, without a doubt their lot would be happier; nor would we see their affairs in disorder or the kingdom itself, as happens all too often, unjustly transferred from its rightful lords to unknown upstarts. Seeing that the succession of the large and rich kingdom of Naples is your responsibility, I beseech and advise you to follow in the footsteps of your father and grandfather. Cultivate this habit from boyhood, so that you become accustomed to value the most upright men and those renowned for their virtue. The nature of virtue is such that it does not lie hidden for long in those who possess it. Antonio Panormita was once sitting, worn out from reading, in the hallway of his Plinian villa, which is not far from Naples on the shore of Resina. When the question of virtue arose among those who were gathered there, Antonio stated that its light was extremely bright. The overseer of the estate, who was passing by, remarked: 'I don't know how brightly that virtue you speak of shines, Antonio; but what I definitely do know is that, even though I've wanted to contemplate virtue for a long time, I've never managed to see it.' To which Antonio replied, smiling, 'You, my good man, would be able to speak quite nicely about an ass, which you have lost due to carelessness and have not yet found. But tell me, please, what do you think the brightest object in the world is?' 'The sun', he said. 'And yet the blind do not see the sun', Antonio responded, 'because their eyes are unseeing. Virtue is therefore much brighter, for even the blind see it very clearly.'

Therefore, the most important expectation with regard to yourself about which you must – and in fact you do – give the people assurance is this: they should realize that you take delight in the type of conduct habitually practised by the most eminent men. Seeing this, they will form the hope that you are going to be the one in whom the rewards for virtue are placed. You will strengthen and augment this conviction daily if those who acquire an increased reputation for virtue are aware that they are held in higher esteem by you for that very reason. Even if the number of such men is tiny (for virtue, like other good things, is rare), the same thing happens with virtue as we generally observe occurs in relation to the liberal arts: thus, just as when an award is announced for poetry or natural philosophy, a large number of people will endeavour to be distinguished in those fields, so too many will compete to obtain virtue if they hope that they can also acquire at the same time the rewards which are assigned to virtue. When Pope Nicholas V asked Lorenzo Valla why he, an old man, already accomplished in Latin literature, was making such an effort to learn Greek, he retorted: 'So that I can get a double stipend from you, your holiness.'[45]

Since the changing fortunes of princes are acted out in a lofty and exposed position, in full view of everyone, you should take care that all your words and deeds are such that they not only earn you praise and increase your authority, but also inspire your servants and subjects to behave virtuously. Nothing will inspire them more than if your own virtue and conduct are seen to be of the utmost probity. That line of Claudian is therefore extremely astute: 'The world is arranged after the king's example.'[46] And then there is the saying: 'Like master, like household',[47] which can surely serve as a proverb.

The virtue which will most enhance your reputation, both with your own subjects and with other men, is nowadays called majesty, even by certain learned men, although the term is somewhat inappropriate. (I am not, however, going to quibble about a word. I follow the crowd in this matter, for which I beg your indulgence.) Majesty is the characteristic quality of princes. It has its origin in nature and is cultivated through practice and great diligence. First of all, therefore, it is needful for you to have self-knowledge and to understand that you are to conduct yourself as befits a prince. Having grasped that point, you will be sober and consistent in all your words and deeds. And since all planning and all action involve taking advice, both in public and private affairs, you should, when taking counsel, listen to many points of view and consider even more, determining the grounds on which each individual case is based. You should neither agree immediately nor always reject matters out of hand, expressing a great deal by means of a glance and a nod, wearing a pensive aspect when weighing up many matters and scrutinizing the opinions of others in such a way that you appear to want to look inside the minds of those who are speaking. You should not reveal your own thoughts at once, or only to a few, and you should be cautious and to the point in speaking. Apply reproach sparingly and in proportion to the nature of the fault. Punish rarely and not without very good cause. Give praise in a dignified manner, restrain your anger, which is the enemy of majesty, and in nothing be so carried away that you step out of line. By following these precepts and others which nature, age, time, circumstances and practice will teach you, and on which no clear guidelines can be imparted, a certain feeling of awe towards you will come into being, without which there can be no majesty.

Public affairs — and by 'public' I mean that which concerns the peacefulness of the populace and the governance of the kingdom — are dealt with by means of another skill. Show yourself to be kind and affable with those ambassadors from towns who seek audience with you; listen to them presenting their petitions with an attentive expression, thereby giving them the confidence to speak. When you dismiss them, do so in such a way that they understand that they will readily obtain those things which are honourable and just from you. Not content with this, you will also reward and compliment them with honours and gifts that you think will please them both now and in the future. If, on the other hand, they have sought things which are lacking in honour or fairness, you should not always refuse them, either openly or by wearing a pained expression or speaking harsh words. Instead it is to be made clear to them that you are not prepared to grant their requests, not because you yourself are unwilling, but because you judge them to be disadvantageous for the petitioners and that, therefore, it is in their own best interests for these requests to be denied.

When it is a matter of law, make no distinction between individuals, but rather assume the role of those very laws, which are always the same for everyone. It is also necessary that you frequently exhort, advise and encourage the people – sometimes through written proclamations, sometimes through emissaries – depending on the time and circumstances. Nor will you always wait until they ask for something but will spontaneously grant a gift which has not been asked for. Prizes, too, should be offered to those professions which you feel to be the most renowned in the city.

Behave towards your citizens in such a way that they regard your presence like that of a head of a family among his dependents, a magistrate passing sentence, an arbitrator in civil disturbances and disagreements – rejoicing in their successes and prosperity, grieving over their difficulties and resisting dangers and violence with all your might. Eventually, whether you are absent or present, they will understand that you have concern for their affairs, so that they fear you as their lord and revere you as their patron. Let them, however, perceive you to be stern in your judgements, sober and cautious in your replies, agreeable in conversation, acute in thought, but not at all argumentative. Your words should be neither superfluous, nor lacking in authority or dignity. In regard to criminals and to those whom the law has sentenced to suffer punishment, be mindful that you are seen to condemn and punish not the man, but the crime. By these and similar means, you will procure for yourself love and reverence, the faithful and daily companions of majesty, even though the poets think that majesty is born out of reverence and honour.[48]

Some instruction should also be given about private affairs; but if I want to cover everything, I'm afraid that I may go beyond the appropriate length. There are several things which are approved of in one context but condemned elsewhere; for many matters change according to the place, the subject and the time. Nature herself will be the best guide to this, combined with that close observation of time, circumstances and character from which expertise derives. Since, therefore, private affairs should be considered either from the outside as they affect the individuals with whom you have private dealings or as they affect you yourself, this is the rule which you should follow in dealing with others: that you welcome those coming from abroad with kindness, listen attentively, deal with them generously and present yourself as affable and well disposed in everything. Also, as far as you can, try to acquaint yourself before they come with their character, the people with whom they have lived, the skills they have cultivated, their opinions, the factions to which they belong, whether they are gloomy or cheerful, urbane or rather surly in conversation, the nature of their instructions, what they hope to accomplish, whether they come in a public or private capacity.

In addition, you should become thoroughly acquainted with national customs and pursuits. From this information you will easily discover how you should behave. Receive guests at banquets lavishly, talk convivially among the diners, show yourself to be greatly amused by their conversation. Try to glean a good deal of information from them about national customs, about geography and about those things which they have seen or heard on their travels which are worth remembering. Also, urge those who are present to speak about light-hearted matters as well as serious ones, which produces both admiration and pleasure. And when they have come to the point in the conversation where they ask a favour of you, it is proper for you at this time to display your generosity and munificence and, when either your dignity or the things sought by them demand it, to make a show of your religion, justice, restraint and kindness. As you send them away, speak in flattering and courteous terms. And rather than being satisfied with those things which you have already given them, promise many further gifts yourself and also offer them ones to be obtained through the services of others.

You will place in charge of the magistracy those citizens whom you have recognized to be outstanding on account of their character, loyalty or wide experience, paying them salaries and assigning some to military affairs, others to civil duties. You will entrust the government of towns and provinces to men who have good judgement and are respectful of justice. You will put men of proven loyalty and steadfast character in control of fortresses, and assign those whom you know to be thrifty, meticulous, hard-working and temperate to oversee financial matters and act as treasurers. You will show yourself to be severe with some, gentle with others, depending on the cause, character, time and situation, knowing that the greatest justice sometimes constitutes the greatest injustice and that it is often better to act out of a spirit of fairness and goodness than according to the letter of the law. Some things are better forgiven than punished, while others should be passed over as if you did not know about them or else postponed to another time.

It would be best if rulers were acquainted with each of their subjects; for then good men would receive positions and benefits, while evil and scurrilous ones would receive punishment. The weakness of human nature does not, however, allow us to attain this ideal, and the fickleness of fortune prevents it, for many things turn out contrary to expectation. Nevertheless, if you cannot become acquainted with all of your subjects, you should at least get to know most of them, keeping in mind that any merchant who takes in and pays out coins is aware how much each one is worth. Take particular care that those whom you have appointed to dispense justice keep their minds unencumbered and uncorrupted by avarice and other evil cravings. Forbid anyone to resort to violence, so that you show yourself to be more vigorous in defending the laws and liberty than in any other matter. Do not demand anything of anyone which is not just and honourable.

Pay attention, also, to the way in which you behave towards your servants; for as Juvenal puts it: 'the worst part of a bad servant is his tongue'.[49] The Neapolitan knight Niccolò Maria Buzzuto used to say: 'A bad servant is an infamy born under the eaves of one's home. As soon as it grows a bit older, it will steal away from home secretly and travel the world over.' On this account, take care that your servants and those who nowadays are called 'courtiers' think most highly of you. You will accomplish this very easily by adopting the following behaviour and techniques: if you show yourself to be affable, courteous, kind and generous towards them, quick both to condone their faults and to praise their good deeds even more highly than they deserve; if everyone understands that, in fulfilling his official capacities, he is valued by you on account of his actions and his character; and if, on the basis of those gifts which you, without prompting, bestow on them, they assure themselves that each day even greater ones will be conferred on them without having to ask you for them and that when they do make a request, they will readily obtain what they seek.

It is a fine observation of Ludovico Pontano, a most dignified man and the foremost judge of his day, that no one is able to gain a reputation for learning unless he reads and listens a great deal and stores the information in his memory.[50] And if we think about the matter more carefully, we will realize that it is also quite impossible to be a king unless one reads a great deal and often, listens to many people recounting many things and consigns to one's memory what one has read and heard. Homer, who wanted Ulysses to represent the image of the wise man, appears to support this view, for right at the start of the work he describes his character by praising him as someone 'who has seen the customs and cities of many men'.[51] If, therefore, you want to be loved by those in your household (which you especially strive to achieve), if you want to promote the expectation that you will be a good king (which you can only pray for from the immortal gods), make sure above all that you do not become enthralled to one favourite apart from everyone else – something which is completely unworthy of a prince. Instead, divide your attention between everyone in turn, making it quite clear that they all must refer to you alone, as that is your wish. Just as God himself would have acted badly in relation to the human race if he had answered only the prayers of one single person or a small group of people, in the same way the servants of kings and princes are badly treated if positions and trust are bestowed on one person or a few among such a large company. Nothing causes more dismay among members of the household than when communication with their own prince has to be conducted via an intermediary. The ruler who wants to be loved by his subjects and to do the least wrong in the state should employ many eyes and ears.[52] Jacopo Caldora, the most illustrious military leader of his age, used to say that he had considerably increased his wealth on the day that he had heard a great deal since, in his opinion, hearing a great deal constituted the greatest treasure.[53] It is unbelievable how effective a cheerful demeanour and, as they say, a sunny expression can be. According to a judicious saying: 'The body gains sustenance by means of the right arm, the mind by means of the face.'

This is the foundation of all majesty: if you live with yourself in a way that entails no inconsistency and if in all your words and deeds you keep faith and constancy; whatever you deem to be reprehensible in others, you will, like a stern judge, correct first in yourself; you will not let your mind succumb at all to immoral desires. Just as you strive to excel in power and authority, you will do the same in relation to justice, piety, steadfastness and moderation. Although you will abhor the name of perfidy and treachery, you will not, in your words or decisions or in other things, keep faith at all times and with all people so rigidly that you do not assume that they can sometimes be deluded, erroneous or mistaken, given that so many uncertain and doubtful things happen in the life of mortals. The truth takes many detours and 'inhabits', as the very astute theologian Narciso was accustomed to say, 'hidden recesses'.[54]

Endurance of heat, cold and hunger is not only recommended in princes, it is a necessary requirement for them. Great moderation is to be observed in food and drink, along with other pleasures of the body. What could be more out of keeping with majesty than someone who is in command of others but is himself at the behest of wine and indulgence? The contrast is monstrous, for if, as Ovid has it, 'majesty and love do not go well together, nor do they linger in the same place',[55] how much less do drunkenness and debauchery go with majesty, since they are regarded as very great vices even among disreputable men? Excessive sleep and those pleasures forbidden to mankind are also to be utterly avoided, for sleep reduces vigour and pleasures undermine manliness. A prince who continually spends his time in the dark, lying on a featherbed, as they say, is necessarily surrounded by many vices, since mattresses are the breeding ground of sensual titillation. The secret conclaves which take place in the bedroom provide much assistance to this particular disease. Horace was therefore right when he said: 'Idleness has before now proved the ruin of kings and of wealthy cities.'[56]

Ample attention should also be paid to deportment. Do not allow your gait to be languid or hurried or uncoordinated: find a happy medium between these ways of walking. All bodily movement should be entirely free from awkwardness and arrogance. Hand-clapping and overly energetic arm-swinging are quite gauche. Is a contorted facial expression anything other than disgusting? Are roaring laughter and guffaws that are practically hiccoughs anything other than vile? Is tossing one's head about (a gesture, I would almost say, more suited to neighing horses than to human beings) anything other than vulgar? Nature places a clear indication of our mental processes in the eyes; for this reason, make sure that when your eyes move they are neither fidgety nor staring. And since no part of the body ought to be lacking in self-restraint, it is particularly needful for a prince to keep his eyes under control. Let nothing disgraceful, shifty, cruel, sinister or unreliable appear in your eye movements or gaze, nor in your eyebrows or forehead.

Your clothing and the decorous and suitable finery which covers your entire body should also help to preserve and increase that quality which I call majesty. Apparel needs to be changed according to the place one is in, the nature of one's business, the issues at stake, one's age, the time at which an event happens (for the same clothing does not suit both the young and the old, both those at war and those at peace, both those suffering from adversity and those enjoying success, both the courtroom and the theatre). You should make an effort to ensure that at all times and places you are appropriately dressed: neither wearing drab clothing in a triumphal procession nor multi-coloured silk in a funeral cortège. How I wish that we had not reached such a degree of brazenness that there is no distinction in dress nor in finery between a merchant and a patrician! But while such licence can be censured, it cannot be prevented. We see fashions change on a daily basis, so that the clothes that delighted us three months ago we now reject and cast aside as old-fashioned. What is insufferable is that no garment gains approval unless it has been imported from France, where frivolous things are generally highly valued – though it must be said that we very often dictate fashions and certain fads to them. Just as not every colour nor every type of cloth or silk is suitable, so not every garment or accessory befits a prince. Certain costumes are only for herdsmen or oarsmen. And in the same way some colours suit boys and others old men; some are appropriate for servants, others for nobles.

Amidst such wide differences and variations, therefore, it is necessary to choose what is most appropriate. Stick to this rule when a doubtful situation arises: give least approval to those things which you think least enhance your dignity as a man and your majesty as a prince. Does anyone doubt that pointed shoes and hair which is brushed from the back of head over the eyes are inappropriate not only for a prince but even for a bashful youth? While it is occasionally permitted to put aside something of your majesty – which should be allowed, although only now and then – you should nonetheless bear in mind this piece of advice from Ovid: 'A masculine appearance takes pleasure in moderate adornment.'[57]

Everyone understands why youths and old men take a womanly concern in their attire and indulge in excessive grooming. So let your attire add to your dignity, not flatter your physique. Admittedly, one's appearance can be greatly helped by clothing, and sometimes even natural defects are diminished or covered up. But does anyone approve of shoulder-length hair twisted in ringlets? Is there anyone who does not shudder at the sight of a beard which flows down to a man's chest, or at tufts of hair which protrude from his collar or are exposed on his arms, even though these fashions are characteristic of certain nations? Seeking beauty through care for one's appearance is for women; seeking to inspire horror is for barbarians. We should instead uphold the manly, Italian regimen, not because worthy foreign customs should not be adopted on principle – we, in fact, adopt them all the time – but rather so that we are apprised of the fact that no nation is more earnestly committed to level-headed seriousness than the Italians. It is difficult to say, however, what sort of finery is especially appropriate or what the limit is in terms of adornment, since nowadays there exists no fixed standard in these matters, nor anything which can be determined sufficiently through rules or precepts, unless perhaps the standard is to observe the mean. I approve of this rule for men in private life; however, since something more exalted is needed and required for a prince, I'm afraid that the mean itself may not be sufficient for you.

I observe, Duke Alfonso, that this theme of maintaining and increasing majesty, which I have been pursuing up to this point, has been entirely neglected by the ancient philosophers. No author whose works survive, as far as I know, lays down anything on this subject. Of the things which were clearly and judiciously stated by Cicero concerning decorum, many applied either to individuals or to magistracies held by private individuals for a set time. In relation to kings, there is not much that can be transferred from that context to this one.[58] If I wanted to discuss this subject more thoroughly (I am well aware how extensive such a tract would be), I would have to be released from affairs from which I cannot be absent, nor would your father permit it. Yet if that leisure which is usually given to writers had been granted to me, I would have omitted nothing which was relevant to instruction in this matter, and I would have fully developed themes which I have now touched on only in passing. I would have explained these matters in many volumes, separately according to their topics and component parts, rather than abridging them in a single letter. I would have indicated what sort of behaviour was suitable for a prince when attending banquets, games, ceremonies and legal proceedings. I would also have had something to say about the type of consort needed by a prince, as well as the finery and other paraphernalia she should be provided with. And since majesty is particularly associated with fame — for princes must not ignore what foreign nations think of them — I would have elaborated this section at great length, which, as I said, my commitments do not allow me to do.

This letter is drawing to a close, but I will nevertheless add to it a section in which I briefly explain what sort of speech is appropriate for a prince. Since there are only two things in which we are markedly superior to other animals, our mind and our power of speech,[59] and since speech is the indicator of those things which we conceive of or perceive in the mind, you should see to it, using all the skill at your disposal, that your speech does not reveal anything lewd, foolish, rash, malevolent, proud, frivolous, greedy, lustful or ruthless in your mind and thoughts. Let your speech instead show you to be solemn in serious matters, witty and urbane in jests, cautious in doubtful affairs, truthful and stern in judgements, brave in adversity and unhappiness, gentle, affable and kind in prosperity and happiness.

Let your words be in accordance with the way things are. This should also be reflected in your face and the fitting and decorous movements of your entire body. You should take care to refrain from using words which come from the lower classes or from foreign parts, and you should also avoid military jargon. Lower-class words are coarse and ridiculous. Although foreign terms are sometimes pleasing on account of their novelty, they are not heard without bringing criticism on the speaker. There is something reckless and uncouth about military slang.

Your speech should be neither rapid nor abrupt. I should like it to be smooth and fluent, suggesting a certain candour and indicating that you say what you want in a few well-chosen words. Sometimes, however, the subject-matter itself compels you to mount an attack through speech: striking at one moment, threatening at the next, like a soldier engaged in hand-to-hand combat. This cannot happen without a certain incitement of anger and vehement agitation of the mind; so, whenever it becomes necessary to speak words of reproach and censure, let your rebuke, as far as possible, be free from anger; for once anger rears its head, there is no way that majesty can be preserved.

Nature herself gave us our voice at birth, yet skill improves it in no small measure. A clear and pleasant-sounding voice, neither weak nor loud, is especially prized. You will need to lower it at times and to raise it at other times, and to inflect or alter it depending on your mood, so that not only your words are in accordance with the way things are, but your voice too is in harmony with both.[60]

I have written to you, Duke Alfonso, at shorter length than instruction on such important matters requires, and I am well aware how much scope there is for discoursing and laying down precepts. But it was not my aim to educate a king. Therefore, read these things, which I have written not with the intention of teaching you anything, but rather so that in reading them you will recognize yourself and those accomplishments of yours which win the highest praise, and you will inspire yourself on towards greater glory each day. Be apprised that someone who teaches a person to do what he is already doing assumes the role not of an instructor but of an encomiast, which is what I have done in this letter (if you prefer to call it a book, I shall not dispute your opinion). And if I perceive that this work does not displease you – for to seek praise would be an act of gross impertinence on the part of someone who flatters his own talent – other treatises which I think you will find useful will soon follow.

Translator's Notes

1. Livy, *Histories* XXV.2.7.1–2. Scipio Africanus (236–184/3 BC) was a Roman general and statesman.
2. Virgil, *Aeneid* VI.620.
3. Xenophon, *Cyropaedia* I.1.3. Cyrus the Great (d. 529 BC) was the founder of the Persian Empire.
4. Quintus Curtius, *History of Alexander* IV.10.1–7. Alexander the Great (356–323 BC) was king of Macedon and perhaps the most famous general of antiquity.
5. The fourth-century BC Roman statesman and general Camillus was regarded as the saviour and second founder of Rome.
6. See *Speculum boni principis,* ed. J. Santes (Amsterdam, 1646), sec. 8, pp. 51–4.
7. See P. Pirri, 'Le notizie e gli scritti di Tommaso Pontano e di Giovanni Gioviano Pontano giovane', *Bolletino della regia deputazione di storia patria per l'Umbria,* 18 (1913), 357–496.
8. *Historia Augusta*: 'Severus Alexander' 35.5–36.3. Severus Alexander was Roman emperor from AD 222 to 235.
9. Suetonius, *Lives of the Caesars* VIII: 'The Deified Titus' 8. Titus was Roman emperor from AD 79 to 81.
10. Not an exact quotation; cf. Sallust, *Bellum Catilinae* 54.3; Cicero, *Pro Murena* 31.65. Marcus Porcius Cato of Utica (95–46 BC) was a Roman statesman renowned for his integrity.
11. See Suetonius, *Lives of the Caesars* VI.26–31. Nero (Nero Claudius Caesar) was Roman emperor from AD 54 to 68.
12. See Seneca, *Epistulae* 86.1.
13. See, e.g., Xenophon, *Cyropaedia* VIII.1.30–2; Isocrates, *Ad Nicoclem* 29; Pliny the Younger, *Panegyricus* 79.
14. See Bartolomeo Facio and Giovanni Pontano, *Rerum suo tempore gestarum libri sexdecim* (Basel, 1566), pp. 432–3 (defection of nobles to Jean d'Anjou), 435 (Ferrante's response to the revolt of Marino Marzano).
15. See Facio and Pontano, *Rerum gestarum libri,* pp. 439–42 (battle of Sarno and aftermath).
16. Revelation 3:19.
17. For these events, which occurred at the battle of Gaeta (1435), see Antonio Panormita, *Facta et dicta Alfonsi* (Naples, 1485), sig. fiv.
18. Aristotle, *Nicomachean Ethics* V.1 (1130a1–2), quoting Bias.
19. Homer, *Iliad* VI.201; quoted in Cicero, *Tusculan Disputations* III.26.63; Pontano's text has *alienis* (strange) instead of *Aleïs* (Aleïan).
20. Cicero, *De finibus* V.21.58, quoting Plato, *Laws* II (653A).
21. Cicero, *De amicitia* I.1. Quintus Mucius Scaevola (d. 82 BC) was an eminent Roman Stoic, lawyer and statesman.

22. See Panormita, *Facta et dicta Alfonsi,* sig. fiv[r]. The annals referred to here are the books of Livy's *History of Rome.* Antonio Panormita (Beccadelli; 1394–1471) was a Sicilian humanist and Neo-Latin poet.
23. Sallust, *Bellum Jurgurthinum* 4.5–6. For Scipio see n. 1.
24. Panormita, *Facta et dicta Alfonsi,* sig. aviii[v]. The Fabii and Marcelli were illustrious Roman clans. Scipio Africanus (see n. 1) had a famous descendant and namesake, who lived from 185/4 to 129 BC.
25. Cf. Pier Paolo Vergerio, *De ingenuis moribus,* ed. C. Miani, *Atti e meorie della Società istriana di archaeologia e storia patria,* 20–1 (1972–3), 185–251, at 218–29.
26. Sallust, *Bellum Catilinae* 23.5–6. The conspiracy organized by the demagogue Catiline was foiled by Cicero in 62 BC.
27. On Jacopo Piccinino, who belonged to the well-known Milanese family of condottieri and who ended up being strangled in a Neapolitan prison on the orders of King Ferrante, see M. Mallet, *Mercenaries and Their Masters: Warfare in Renaissance Italy* (London, 1974), pp. 95, 97, 220. On Calixtus III, pope from 1455 to 1458, see J. N. D. Kelly, *The Oxford Book of Popes* (Oxford, 1986), pp. 245–7.
28. See Platina (Bartolomeo Sacchi), *Liber de vita Christi ac omnium pontificum,* ed. G. Gaida, Rerum Italicarum Scriptores, 3.1 (Città di Castello, 1923), p. 343.
29. See 'Caldora, Antonio', in *Dizionario biografico degli Italiani* (Rome, 1960–), XVI, pp. 633–7.
30. The Peligni were an ancient people of central Italy who inhabited present-day Abruzzo.
31. Juvenal, *Satires* I.159.
32. Horace, *Epistles* I.4.16.
33. Publilius Syrus, *Sententiae* 104. Decimus Laberius was, like Publilius Syrus, a first-century BC author of mimes.
34. Suetonius, *Lives of the Caesars* II: 'The Deified Augustus' 83.
35. Xenophon, *Cyropaedia* I.4.5–17.
36. Virgil, *Aeneid* VII.189, 651.
37. Seneca, *Epistulae* 9.6; the saying is quoted by Petrarch in his *Rerum senilium libri XVIII,* trans. A. S. Bernardo, S. Levin and R. A. Bernardo, 2 vols. (Baltimore, 1992), II, p. 528 (XIV.1).
38. Xenophon, *Cyropaedia* III.3.6–7.
39. Juvenal, *Satires* X.112–13.
40. Platina, *Liber de vita omnium pontificum,* p. 325.
41. Valerius Maximus, *Facta et dicta memorabilia* IX.13, ext. 2. Masinissa (c. 240–148 BC) was king of Numidia.
42. Cicero, *De officiis* II.7.25. Alexander of Pherae (369–358 BC) was a Thessalian tyrant.
43. Cicero, *Tusculan Disputations* V.20.58. Dionysius of Syracuse (c. 430–367 BC) was a Sicilian tyrant.
44. Sallust, *Bellum Catilinae* 7.2–3.
45. The humanist Lorenzo Valla (1407–57) had, in fact, learnt Greek as a young man; see G. Mancini, *Vita di Lorenzo Valla* (Florence, 1891), pp. 6, 131–6, 322.
46. Claudian, *Panegyricus de quarto consulatu Honorii Augusti* (VIII) 299–300.
47. Cf. Petronius, *Satyricon* 58: 'Like master, like servant.'
48. See, e.g., Ovid, *Fasti* V.23–8.
49. Juvenal, *Satires* IX.121.
50. Ludovico Pontano is also called 'Princeps iurisconsultorum' in Panormita, *Facta et dicta Alfonsi,* sig. bviii[r].
51. Homer, *Odyssey* I.3.
52. Cf. Xenophon, *Cyropaedia* VIII.2.10.
53. See Facio and Pontano, *Rerum gestarum libri,* pp. 62–3, 194.
54. On Narciso de Verduno see Vespasiano da Bisticci, *Le vite,* ed. A. Greco, 2 vols. (Florence, 1970), I, pp. 343–7. He was created bishop of Mileto in 1473 and died in 1476. A student

of Platonic philosophy, he took part in a disputation with Giannozzo Manetti at the court of Alfonso.

55. Ovid, *Metamorphoses* II.846–7.
56. The quotation is, in fact, from Catullus, *Carmina* 51.15–16.
57. Ovid, *Heroides* IV.76.
58. See Cicero, *De officiis* I.27.93–42.151.
59. On language as belonging solely to man among the animals see Aristotle, *History of Animals* IV.9 (536^{b}1–2).
60. See Quintilian, *Institutiones oratoriae* XI.3.11–14.

Further Reading

Bentley, J. H., *Politics and Culture in Renaissance Naples* (Princeton, N.J., 1987), pp. 202–22

Burns, J. H., ed., *The Cambridge History of Political Thought 1450–1700* (Cambridge, 1991), pp. 689–90

CHRP, pp. 125, 329, 424–6, 443, 651, 736, 749, 834

Kidwell, C., *Pontano: Poet and Prime Minister* (London, 1991)

Miele, L., 'Tradizione letteraria e realismo politico nel "De principe" del Pontano', *Atti della accademia pontaniana,* n.s., 32 (1983), 301–21

Percopo, E., *Vita di Giovanni Pontano,* ed. M. Manfredi (Naples, 1938)

Sbordone, S., *Saggio di bibliografia delle opere e delle vita di G. Pontano* (Naples, 1982)

Tateo, F., *L'umanesimo etico di Giovanni Pontano* (Lecce, 1972)

Trinkaus, C., 'The astrological cosmos and rhetorical culture of Giovanni Gioviano Pontano', *Renaissance Quarterly,* 38 (1985), 446–72

6

Il Platina (Bartolomeo Sacchi)

NICHOLAS WEBB

Introduction

The humanist Bartolomeo Sacchi (1421–81) was born in Piadena, in the Po Valley; and it is from the Latin form of his birthplace that he gained the name by which he is generally known, 'il Platina'. After a short military career, he studied first in Mantua and then in Florence, attending the lectures of the émigré Byzantine scholar Johannes Argyropulos from around 1457 to 1461. Moving to Rome, he was appointed to the papal Curia in 1464 by Pius II, and he became an active member of Pomponio Leto's Roman Academy, a group of humanists united by their passionate interest in classical antiquity. During the pontificate of Paul II, he was imprisoned for almost a year on charges of conspiracy to overthrow the pope and restore republican rule in Rome. He quickly regained papal favour under Sixtus IV, who appointed him Vatican librarian in 1475, a position he held until his death from plague six years later. Best known for his *Lives of the Popes* (Venice, 1479), Platina also wrote a treatise *On the True and False Good,* a *History of Mantua,* a life of the humanist Vittorino da Feltre (who had founded the famous school in Mantua which he attended) and a cookbook entitled *On Virtuous Pleasure and Health.* In addition, he produced a Latin version of Plutarch's treatise *On the Calming of Anger.*

In 1471 Platina dedicated his treatise *On the Prince,* completed in the previous year, to his former student Federico Gonzaga, who was to become marquis of Mantua in 1478 and whose brother, Cardinal Francesco Gonzaga, was an important patron of Platina. An emended version, couched in the form of a dialogue and entitled *On the Best Citizen,* was dedicated to Lorenzo de' Medici in 1474. While the production of multiple dedicatory copies of the same work was not uncommon,[1] the alteration here represents a different political perspective. Not only is *On the Best Citizen* considerably shorter (lacking any discussion of foreign affairs), it also contains thematic changes, such as the replacement of majesty with liberty, designed to make the work more appropriate to the republican regime of Florence.[2]

On the Prince is divided into three books. The first considers the general principles of princely rule, the second the definition of the cardinal virtues and their application to the prince, the third concerns external matters, comprising public works, hunting and war (which is regarded as the main activity of the prince). Dedicated, like Giovanni Pontano's 1468 treatise of the same name (see Chapter 5), to a future sovereign, the treatise offers philosophical support for monarchical rule. Nevertheless, Platina makes the standard humanist case for the importance of the nobility of virtue over that based on blood; he treats the same subject in a later work, the dialogue *On True Nobility.*[3] He warns of the danger of flatterers and detractors, another frequently discussed political problem. Other repeated targets of abuse are the corrupt clergy, especially monks, and the Turks. He advises the prince to coax love from his subjects, a theme which is developed in the chapters of the second book linking justice with good faith, clemency, generosity and magnificence. Platina attempts to demonstrate the interconnections between the cardinal virtues and to combine them with the Aristotelian virtues.

For the Latin text of *On the Prince* see Bartolomeo Platina, *De principe,* ed. G. Ferraù (Palermo, 1979), pp. 53–6, 72–9, 83, 85–9, 107–16, 119–21, 136–8, 152, 155–9.

On the Prince: Selections

BOOK I

Let There Be One Ruler

The authority of the Spartan Lycurgus in founding laws and establishing a principality was such that nearly all races and nations used his rules in governing their cities; for on account of his divine intelligence, these rules were thought, according to Plato, to have come from Zeus.[4] When asked by someone to turn Sparta into a popular government, Lycurgus replied: 'First introduce this into your own home.'[5] The point of this anecdote is to show that affairs go badly in a state where the many seek to better themselves. This inevitably results in disaster, since avarice and ambition arise directly from the common people and from these vices are spawned countless evils, whether in relation to deliberations at home or to actions abroad. How can it happen that the populace, for whom rashness and desire are virtually allies and bosom companions, governs others or impels them to action with the good judgement it stands in need of itself? The prince, to whom, as Aristotle says, the guardianship of the common good has been entrusted against his own people,[6] can scarcely keep them in place through fear of the laws.

Homer, whose entire poetic output abounds with rules and instruction of this sort, says that this is the view of Ulysses, who was endowed with the greatest wisdom: 'The rule of the many is a bad business; let there be one ruler and one king',[7] whom the greatest and best God has ordained to be a likeness of himself, insofar as this is possible. For one king, who is the father both of the gods and of men, moves this universe (which one may call heaven, using another name) through the ages and governs with such wisdom and constancy that not for a single moment can the heavenly bodies leave their station.[8] Moreover, the story of Phaethon – a fictitious tale, though not without meaning – demonstrates that there ought to be only one ruler, so that all are guided by his command and those who, like inexperienced charioteers, expose so many thousands of people to fire by governing badly on account of their own stupidity may be hurled from the polity into the River Eridanus by his thunderbolt.[9]

All acquisition of political power was founded on the moral probity of an individual, since it was produced either by someone's very dignity, by his own virtue or that of his family or else by the benefits he bestowed on the people through military prowess and sound judgement. What the Athenian Codrus did is plain: sacrificing his life for the safety of his people.[10] Cyrus too earned his kingdom because he delivered the Persians from the Medes through his sound judgement and military prowess.[11] Those who established cities also fall into this category. The founding-father of the city of Rome, Romulus, is with good cause ranked among them. After the title of king was abolished, on account of Tarquinius's lack of self-restraint, emperors were named, so that virtue was not denied its reward; and once the state had been transferred to a single authority because of the corruption of the age, Julius Caesar, Augustus, Vespasian, Titus, Trajan, the two Antoninuses and Aurelius Alexander were deservedly included among their number.[12]

By contrast, we call those rulers tyrants who, riding the breeze of popular favour, have contempt for virtue and nobility, foregoing no form of outrageous and unlawful conduct against anyone from the upper classes: for example, Pheidon in Argos, Panaetius at Leontini, Cypselus at Corinth, Pisistratus at Athens, Dionysius at Syracuse, Phalaris in Agrigentum, Tarquinius Superbus at Rome, Herod in Judaea.[13] Keeping a look out for private, rather than public, advantages, tyrants are the complete opposite of the good father, whom Xenophon, the disciple of Socrates, shows to differ in no way from the prince.[14] Nor should you suggest that this applies only to one or more of the tyrants to be found long ago in many cities, above all Athens – in point of fact, they are seen right now in Bologna and Florence. The overriding concern of these tyrants, since they are entirely lacking in virtue, is to take arms away from the citizenry, to oppress the upper classes or else drive them from the city and to leave it empty of inhabitants, so that, in this desolation and solitude, they themselves may be more secure.

It is no part of my aim to praise either the aristocratic or the popular regime: the former declines readily into tyranny or oligarchy, while the latter slides towards princely rule. I am seeking the best prince, who, as a living law, deservedly commands everyone. According to Pindar, it is rightly held everywhere that just as parents rule over their children, the older over the younger and masters over slaves, so superiors should rule over their inferiors, the prudent over the inexperienced and the noble over the ignoble.[15] I am therefore seeking the wisest and best leader: someone who is not given to leisure but to action, not to sleep but to vigilance; someone who reflects, contemplates and calculates about what pertains to the common benefit of men. For the prince's eyes are not private but public and, like beacons, show the way to those who wander uncertainly. Therefore, it is fitting that the person who stands above the rest in dignity and authority should also be superior to them in prudence, counsel, industry and effort. Nor will it be inappropriate for him to excel, if possible, in every type of virtue and learning. By these means, supported by many advantages and instilling a certain religious sense of awe, he keeps the people under control more easily. . . .

On the Nobles Who Are Worthy of the Friendship of Princes[16]

It is well known that the eminent philosophers Aristotle and Metrodorus each wrote books about the nobility.[17] They set great store by this class of men, which is more outstanding and useful than any other, especially if the title of nobility was established through the discipline and practice of virtue.

I am surprised that Aristotle, an exceptionally wise man, said in his *Politics* that nobles seemed to him to be those whose ancestors were endowed with virtue and with riches;[18] for true nobility is derived solely from an individual himself, that is, from his virtue. If we were to accept Aristotle's argument, then pirates, robbers and usurers, who increase their wealth at the expense of others, not by means of effort, but through plundering, would be nobles – for the rich, as Jerome says, are either wicked themselves or are the heirs of wicked men.[19] Unless they warrant the title of nobility themselves, how can those born from glorious ancestors be noble? Writing to his brother Quintus about his suit for the consulate, Cicero mentions the contenders from the families of Mark Antony and Catiline, and he says: 'By no means do outstanding men arise from this breed but rather those noteworthy for their vices.'[20]

According to the Stoics, nobility is a certain radiance emanating from personal virtue, to which all the glory of a noble spirit is to be attributed.[21] But those who appear to place nobility in idleness, like the Neapolitans who boast about their seats at the theatre or some of our own countrymen who go around with well-groomed hair and a hawk as a badge, so they think, of their nobility – they are seriously mistaken. For the nobility we are seeking is won by dint of effort and hard work, not by a pair of golden spurs and a saffron-coloured belt. In olden times Roman knights were given a ring, a clasp and a golden armlet on account of their illustrious deeds in battle;[22] but those were trophies and symbols of virtue, not of sloth. Why do those appointed to this rank in our own time behave differently, parading the gold which glitters in their clothing and shoulder-bands, so that they seem to be not so much nobles as bankers? The lustre of nobility comes from the mind, not from gold. Bragging about the deeds of one's ancestors, ostentatiously displaying halls stuffed with portraits, porches decorated with devices and paintings and the farms and houses built by them – this smacks more of veneration than of nobility.[23] The theatres, palaces and temples of our forebears will indeed be a help to us if we have imitated their virtue and their excellence of mind; if not, these things will be a discredit and disgrace to us.

Deriding this sort of nobility, from which virtue is absent, Diogenes the Cynic said that it was a mask for wickedness and sloth.[24] Marcus Cato the Elder, known as the Censor, was made famous neither by birth nor wealth (for I believe that he came from an obscure and hard-up family in Tusculum): it was his outstanding and splendid virtues which ennobled him.[25] Similarly, the peasant Gaius Marius of Arpinum, a complete unknown, fighting, as one might expect, among rank-and-file soldiers, obtained nobility through his virtue and deeds alone.[26] The same can be said about Sertorius, Ventidius Bassus and Servius Tullius.[27]

Plato divides the nobility into four parts: the first consists of those who come from illustrious, good and just parents; the second of those whose parents are princes; the third is made up of those whose ancestors were illustrious and renowned on account of the garlands they won by military deeds in war or in public contests for office; the fourth consists of those who excel through some type of outstanding learning and greatness of mind. Because this last group is truly noble, Plato ranks it above the rest.[28] Mithridates, King of Pontus, enjoyed the company of nobles of this sort, as did Ptolemy Philadelphus, who took Demetrius Phalereus into his household and put him in charge of his library.[29] Augustus delighted in the company of Marcus Varro and Tucca,[30] Trajan in that of the philosopher Plutarch,[31] Alexander Aurelius of Ulpian[32] and Scipio Africanus of Posidonius.[33] Antisthenes followed Plato chiefly in this belief, for in many other respects he was at odds with the philosopher; placing nobility in virtue alone, he wrote that those who were devoted to virtue appeared to him to be noble.[34] Cicero maintained the same.[35] And Seneca, a distinguished philosopher of the Stoic sect, declared in a letter to Lucilius that Socrates was no aristocrat, nor was he a Roman knight; yet, philosophy, which did not receive him and Plato as nobles, ennobled them.[36]

Certainly if we return to our earliest origin, that is, to the gods, from whom we descend, no one person is more noble than any another. It is the virtues and vices which make men differ among themselves, since, as Plato says, we see that many kings sprang from slaves and likewise many slaves from kings.[37] It is virtue alone which creates nobles and which preserves their descendants in nobility. Select your friends, therefore, from among those of noble stock whose activity and determination inspire you to virtue and glory.

Against Yes-Men

But no worse plague can afflict those whom fortune has elevated than the adulation, blandishments and flattery of shallow and devious men, who speak all manner of things for the sake of your pleasure but nothing for the sake of truth. So you will be well rid of those who immediately and indiscriminately praise whatever you have said or done and, announcing their agreement, laud it to the skies. As Cicero says, they pay attention to the expression on one's face and the nod of one's head, but not to one's mind and will.[38] A crowd of flatterers stands by: whatever someone says they say, whatever someone denies they deny[39] – it is much the most profitable game to play among certain princes. But this is how flattery becomes destructive, for later on, when the truth is spoken, princes do not want to hear it, to their own great cost. Having been poisoned by that venom, they think that they know more than the rest and despise the deliberations and sound advice of others, thereby offering their eyes – as the saying goes – while they are still alive, as pickings for ravens.[40] They stand by, they flatter, they pay attention and they admire. Every word you utter is weighed up to see whether it can be turned to their advantage. How is it that they manage to twist even emotions to their own gain?

> . . . You laugh, and he falls about
> Guffawing; at the sight of a friend's tears, he weeps.[41]

It is hardly surprising that Aristotle saw fit to say that all flatterers were servile, foul and base.[42]

Withdrawing your mind from these enticements, you, as befits the best of princes, must follow the advice of Thales of Miletus to know yourself.[43] In this way, you will very easily discern whether what is asserted about you is true or false. So send these dangerous men far away and, instead, treasure those who dare to criticize you prudently and modestly when you make a mistake. As a result of this freedom of speech, when some matter comes up for deliberation, you will have close advisers who are prepared to give you a frank and honest opinion. Moreover, if you favour these men with worthy rewards according to their deserts, you will drive away the yes-men, who will be branded with disgrace and come to a bad end, when they realize that you have good and true friends around you.

Against Informers and Slanderers

You are right to use the same methods against informers and slanderers, a noxious and detestable breed of men, who do harm to those who are good. They deprive men not only of their livelihood, but of their life. On this subject I myself am an excellent witness, as someone who has been led into the greatest misfortune through the deceits and slander of those types. Nevertheless, I survived, relying on my innocence and the integrity of my character.[44] These monsters are about as meek as Scylla, Charybdis, the Hydra, the Sphinx, the Cyclopses and the Laestrygones.

The villainous informers insinuate themselves into a crowd of people. They converse amiably and, like bird-catchers, entice men into making speeches from which calumnies can be gathered. They pay attention to whatever anyone says. On some points they ask questions, pretending to be ignorant about the matter in hand, in order to make careful observations of men's minds and plans and then report back to their princes. They accuse whomever they like, on occasion inventing a great deal. They claim that a great conspiracy is being planned against the prince. They cry treason either on rich men, thereby earning a fourfold profit, or on some nobleman or other, so that they are held in higher regard. Here is the source of princely feuds, of hatreds, exiles, tortures, punishments, slaughters and the plundering of the possessions of those who are condemned. Here, finally, is the source of the destruction of cities and the devastation of everything good.

How is it that informers readily pour this poison into the ears of princes, so that they drive even a good man to do evil? Bystanders hear what is said, and since it is not possible for them to see everything, unless they behave circumspectly and cunningly, they believe much of what they hear. This is why, all too often, the greatest misapprehensions are spread by the deceits practised by informers. The utterances of informers were so highly valued by Emperor Hadrian, a good ruler in other respects, that he made enemies out of certain friends he had previously appointed to public office.[45]

But what informers find most unbearable is when men renowned for their erudition and learning are esteemed among princes. They fear the virtue and integrity of these men because they are more alert than others in watching out for anything untoward. It is for this reason that Dionysius the Younger, having summoned Plato [to his court] on account of his learning, was later roused to hatred by slanderers and sold this divine man into slavery.[46] The tyrant Phalaris, using every form of torture, tore apart the philosopher Zeno, when he was very advanced in years.[47] Socrates was forced by his fellow citizens to die on account of the slanders of evil men.[48] Boethius, a most learned and innocent man, was deprived of life on the orders of King Theodoric, due to the urging of informers.[49] Domitian, numbered among the imperial monsters, on this one point appeared to be reasonable, for he despised informers and ejected them from the city, frequently repeating this remark: 'The person who does not curb informers eggs them on.'[50] What, then, are we to think of informers, when even a wicked emperor detested them? . . .

On the Affability and Kindness of the Prince

. . . Just as nothing is more ruinous [for a prince] than to be hated, so nothing is more beneficial than to be adored and loved – something which is produced in a miraculous way by kindness, gentleness and obligingness. While pride undermines kingdoms, kindness strengthens those which have been undermined. Sometimes kindness breaks the stubbornness of men to such an extent that it pushes them in whatever direction it likes. Moses addressed his rebellious and hostile people in a winning manner, even after he had received insults from them. He gave them solace for their hardships, soothed them with prophecies, supported them by his labours. Because of this he has ever since been considered the wisest of men; for he won over the minds of the entire population by means of his skills, so that the people cherished the greatness that arose from his gentleness more than they admired him on account of his achievements. Moses was imitated by King David, a young man who was chosen by everyone to rule the people because of his placable disposition. Since he appeared to have taken on the office of king for the benefit of others rather than out of a desire for power, parents selected him in preference to their own sons, and sons preferred him to their parents. For, when an uproar arose among the people, fearing a slaughter because of the ferocity of Saul, he chose to be exiled in Hebron rather than to reign in Jerusalem, so high was his regard for the safety of the people, for whose sake kingdoms and governments were established.[51] . . .

On the Majesty and Good Fortune of Princes

. . . It is a heavy burden which princes bear on their shoulders: namely, to preserve the flourishing prosperity of their city and, if not to avert mishaps and dangers, at least to reduce them. This is why some people, seeing the dignity, wealth, glory and power of princes, would call them demi-gods. Can anything more useful be given to us? Does anything bring more benefits to the human race? What makes men happier and more like God (insofar as this is possible) than doing everything prudently and modestly, respecting justice, behaving generously, protecting the oppressed, giving hope to the afflicted, comforting the sick, helping one's friends, rewarding virtue and being of use to as many people as possible? Surely the majesty of the prince is everywhere made secure not by walls or ditches or bodyguards, but by his own virtue. . . .

Your ancestors, through their virtue, kindness, clemency and illustrious deeds, founded this principality for you on the goodwill and love of its citizens. And you will very easily preserve it, if you wish to do so – as you ought to – since, by virtue of your self-restraint and gentleness, you will have citizens who are more obedient to you than any well-ordered household is to its head. With due respect to the other towns of our province, I would say that there is no city in which the citizens are gentler and more inclined towards harmony than your own. Their extraordinary goodwill and their proven loyalty in adversity ought to be precious to you; for, by means of these supports, you will easily maintain the dignity and the majesty of the principality.

On the Misfortune of Princes

When Socrates was asked whether he thought the king of Persia was happy, he replied: 'Perhaps; but I would not presume to assert it dogmatically, because I have yet to encounter the mind of a man in which lasting and true happiness consists in mental activity in accordance with virtue over a complete lifetime.'[52] A ruler who promotes the good, cultivates virtue and exercises power in the best way can justifiably be described as happy and blessed not only at one particular instant but permanently. Yet, given that foolishness, which constitutes the greatest part of our misfortune, travels far and wide, it can scarcely come about that those who have acquired the power and licence to do wrong, survive in office.

After the death of Augustus, the friends of Tiberius tried to persuade him to assume the imperial authority offered to him by the senate. Stalling, he replied to them: 'you have no idea what a monster supreme power is.'[53] It is not for me to say whether he spoke from the heart; yet this utterance appeared to issue not from a human being but from some highly esteemed oracle. . . .

I remember having read in some author or other the truism that without virtue, without resourcefulness, without diligence, without vigilance and clear-headedness, the life of princes is a sort of tragedy, full of misery. This is to be expected given that there is a variety of hazards in such a life: the insecurity of government, the instability of fortune, the uncertain outcome of plans, the deceit of flatterers, the self-interest of friends, the treason of servants, the plotting of sons, the adultery of wives, the undependable inclination of brothers, the doubtful loyalty of the mob, the fickleness of the crowd, the unforeseeable result of battles, the doubtful nature of peace – this is how enmities and mutual slaughter begin.[54]

Book II

. . .

On Counsel

. . . I recommend that, if possible, you should choose your counsellors from your own city. I cannot see who will advise you more faithfully than your own citizens: they will stay with you through thick and thin. Those who have lived with you or your ancestors under the same sky and have been born and nurtured on the same soil look more clear-sightedly and more carefully at what you intend to do than those who come from abroad, having left behind them all their love for their homeland.

I recommend that your advisers should be older men, knowledgeable about human affairs. You cannot possibly elicit the best advice from a young man, since the memory of past events, the consideration of present matters and the understanding of future ones fall within the scope of the prudent man; and these cannot be possessed unless they are acquired through learning and experience.[55] So [the good counsel] given by the young men Solomon and Joseph can seem – and indeed is – miraculous, for I think it came about by divine power and not through human wisdom and diligence that those two knew so much beyond their years. So great was her admiration for Solomon's wisdom that the queen of Sheba set out from distant lands to visit him.[56] The whole of Egypt, moreover, was preserved from famine and blight for seven years by Joseph's plan, even though he was in prison.[57] This was certainly accomplished, as I have indicated, by divine command, not by human intelligence. For God wished to show the gentiles that his own people, holding the right beliefs, knew more than the others. Therefore, older men, experienced in human affairs, are to be employed as counsellors. The Roman senate, which the whole world used to consult, took its name from old men [*senes*] not from young ones.

Those whom you appoint should be of good repute: let them have no sham about them, no falsehood, no deceit. They should be open and truthful, for moral integrity is useful both in giving and taking advice. Does anyone look for a spring in a mud-hole or want to take a drink from dirty water? Do you think someone who is unable to manage his own affairs is able to look after other people's concerns? A person who has lived his life in such a way that everyone regards him as evil cannot be a good counsellor. You will get trustworthy advice from a person who disdains pleasures, restrains avarice and, in sum, subdues all passions and emotional disturbances. For someone who regards gold with contempt, who rejects gifts with scorn and who keeps justice alone before his eyes will find it very easy to disregard the desires of men and uphold what is right and just. . . .

Just as I have said that you are to listen to the counsel of wise and good men, so I think you should reject those who are shrewd and cunning: stripped of their reputation for probity, the more they seem to know, the more hateful to you they should be.[58] If, however, justice is combined with prudence and experience, there will be nothing which the prince thinks he is unable to achieve by following the advice of his counsellors. Therefore, sharp practices should be abolished, together with that evil which seeks to look like prudence, even though it is distant – indeed far removed – from it: for evil prefers the bad to the good, while prudence distinguishes the good from the bad. Lying for one's own advantage, slandering, deceiving, stealing – none of this can happen in a good man. The mind of Daniel was maintained in such purity that he reformed the behaviour of the barbarians and soothed the lions by means of his integrity. Supported by the friendship of kings, he did not seek gold, nor did he value the honour he received more highly than his faith. He preferred to face the gravest dangers for the law of God rather than be deflected from the truth for the sake of men.[59] . . .

I would like your advisers to be clever, not shrewd or cunning. Cleverness, according to Aristotle, is a fundamental knowledge of what should be done. He says that cleverness and goodness are one and the same thing: 'if the aim in deliberating is upright, this capacity is praiseworthy; if the aim is unworthy, it should be referred to as cunning'.[60] It is impossible, therefore, for someone to be called prudent unless he is also good. Since virtue is a habit determined by reason, and prudence itself is called right reason, the views of each person should be canvassed; then, after an interval of time has passed and the matter has been scrutinized, cautiously and with a willingness to learn, so that you are not misled, action is to be taken quickly.[61]

The prophet David has taught us to walk to and fro within our heart as if we were in a large house and to be on familiar terms with it, like a good companion, just as he himself speaks and converses with himself.[62] Cicero says the same thing, when writing to Curio: 'Invite yourself to a consultation, have a talk with yourself, listen to yourself: no one will ever be in a better position than you to give yourself counsel.'[63] 'Drink waters', says Solomon, 'out of thine own cistern, and running waters out of thine own well',[64] that is, make use of your own counsel. In this mental activity, foresight must be used in order to ensure that at some time in the future nothing untoward happens, that neither war, rebellions, shortages of goods, floods, fires or plague oppress your people, whose safety and care have been entrusted to you. As Plato indicates, past times supply us with abundant examples that we can draw on for advice: observing what has happened to each nation and why, we either take care to avoid it or else imitate what was done prudently.[65] . . .

On Justice

Not only among the Medes, as Herodotus says, but among all nations, princes appear to be esteemed for the sake of justice.[66] Certain foreigners were even summoned to govern cities because of their outstanding reputation for justice, as we read concerning Numa.[67] Since the poor multitudes might be oppressed by wealthier citizens, it was necessary to have recourse to some one person of conspicuous virtue, who could maintain the highest and the lowest classes in an equality of right. The laws, which speak with one and the same voice to everyone, were established for precisely this reason.[68] The opinion expressed by my teacher Argyropulos must surely seem golden: he used to say that just as a soul was necessary in a living organism, so justice was necessary in human society. If the soul is present, the body is moved by an internal motion; if it departs, the body immediately stiffens, disintegrates and rots. In the same way, society remains firm if it is administered with justice; but if justice is neglected, it wilts and dies.[69]

Everyone looks up to and admires the just man as a sort of god. To him they entrust their possessions, children, wives and all human affairs. And with good reason, too, since, as Aristotle maintains, justice is not a particular part of virtue, but the whole of virtue, in the same way that injustice is the whole of vice.[70] The foundation of perpetual acclaim and fame will therefore be justice, without which nothing can be praiseworthy. . . .

Love [*charitas*] is the foundation on which justice is built. It bears all things and endures all things which concern the society of humankind.[71] Society itself is divided into justice and benevolence, which we also call generosity and kindness. The first office of justice, Cicero says, is to prevent one person from harming another, unless provoked by a wrong; the next is to ensure that men use things held in common for the common good and private property for their own.[72] Both parts are rejected by us because, following the authority and example of our saviour, we must not pay back our enemies an eye for an eye, even when provoked by an offence. We should instead bear the offence with resignation; and if it is our lot to be crowned as martyrs for the sake of truth and justice, we should offer the other cheek to our assailant.[73] Furthermore, they say that it is characteristic of Christians and Stoics to use things held in common for the common good and private property for that of private individuals, but not for their own good. These views have, however, long since died out due to the arrogance and avarice of those who, on account of their vocation and the patrimony of St Peter, should have been an example to others in regard to these tenets as to the rest of the virtues. But, in fact, is there anyone more tenacious than they are in avenging wrongdoings? Is there anyone more obsessive in hoarding money? Is there anyone more extravagant in wantonly pursuing dissipation? Although no one would deny that the teachings of Christ are most holy, everyone knows that, through the fault of priests, his teachings are less respected by his very own, that is, by his avowed followers in the Church militant, than by the laity.

We discard the appearance of beneficence, while we struggle to increase our wealth, to accumulate possessions, to occupy lands. All these things, in nature, were held in common; but after private property came into existence in this way, what is prescribed by the laws is also held to be so in civil justice.[74] Let us have in common, at the very least: correcting the wayward; instructing the uneducated or undertaking to have them educated; not forbidding access to water; permitting fire to be taken from fire; giving counsel in good faith to those requesting advice; and always having in mind what may serve the common good.[75] It seems to me in a sense superfluous to classify the degrees of relationship within this human community; for is there anyone who does not consider himself to owe more to his country, his parents, his children, his neighbours, his fellow citizens and those who speak the same language, than to strangers and outsiders?

Many things belong to fellow citizens in common which, as Cicero says, maintain human society: the forum, temples, colonnades, streets, statutes, laws, courts, voting-rights, in addition to social circles and intimate friends.[76] Moreover, there are marriage ties and neighbourhood connections, which are, one might say, very strong knots by means of which the city binds itself together.[77] From here arise the propagation of progeny and the origin of cities. Having concern for this is not out of place for the best prince: the more citizens are united together by their own accord, the more numerous your people become. There can be no mutual goodwill between you and your citizens unless they perceive that you have embraced all of them with the same love and that you see to it that everybody lives as happily as possible. Since no society is more outstanding or more stable than one which is provided with good men, it will be your responsibility to ensure that they are instructed in learning as well as good morals and refinement. In this way, they will be worthy of your society, and in return for the good deeds you from time to time do for them, they will, unless they are altogether ungrateful, feel equivalent gratitude towards you. . . .

On the City Magistrates

And since the city depends on its magistrates in the same way that the body depends on its limbs, you should make very certain that you select those who are best suited to governing the city. There will unquestionably be no sound basis for the management of a family unless the head of the household performs this function. The same is even more true for the city, since it needs many administrators, who are not to be chosen from just any breed of men, but from the true nobility, about which I have already spoken; for it is reasonable that the children of better parents will themselves be better,[78] both in ruling and obeying. The best governor is in most cases preferable to the laws, because he examines not only generalities but also particulars. Magistrates ought to be good men, who are well versed in law, if that is at all feasible or, at any rate, they ought to be knowledgeable about human affairs. This will not happen unless they are older men. This period of life is most suitable for the magistracy since old men command the respect of the people on account of their years. Besides, no one thinks it improper to defer to old men out of consideration for their age, since they know that they themselves, when they reach this time of life, will receive the same reward. They appreciate that a person who has previously submitted humbly and loyally to someone else's orders will command others correctly.[79]

Therefore, those whom you appoint to the magistracy ('the speaking law', as Cicero says)[80] should be good, modest, temperate, just, courageous, prudent, self-restrained and free from any disgrace; they should be moderate in settling disputes and in giving orders. . . . As Plato says, they ought to look after the advantage of the citizens, considering whatever they do in relation to that, regardless of their own interests.[81] Moreover, they ought to care for the citizenry as whole, so that, while protecting one section of the community, they do not abandon the others. Those who consult the interests of one part of the citizenry, neglecting the other part, bring the very destructive force of sedition and dissent into the city.

It is the duty of a magistrate to understand that he has been appointed for the benefit of the city, that he must maintain its dignity and glory, preserve its laws, establish its rights and protect those things which have been entrusted to him. He will undoubtedly do this as diligently as possible if he perceives that justice and piety are fostered by you and that from time to time he must submit to your censure. But all criticism and reproach of him must be handled without recourse to insulting language. And the person who punishes someone or corrects him verbally should do so with reference to your advantage and that of the city, not to himself. Also take care that the punishment is not greater than the crime and that judgement is not passed by someone who is angry. An angry person is unable to maintain the mean between too little and too much. If possible, those who pass judgement should be very similar to the laws, which are led to punishment not by anger but by equity. Thus, Plato said to Xenocrates, who was coming to see him, or, as others would have it, to Speusippus: 'Strike this boy for me. I am not in a fit state to do so because I am angry.'[82] They say that Archytas of Tarentum employed the same moderation when he was incensed at a peasant who had been careless about tending the fields.[83] . . .

On Generosity and Magnificence

. . . Honours and high-ranking positions are to be awarded to those who . . . deserve well both of you and your city on account of their character, their morals, their diligence, their resourcefulness, their handiwork, their effort. But there should be no rewards for yes-men, panderers and idlers, whose natural inclination is towards pleasure and lust rather than towards eminence and temperateness.

By means, too, of giving counsel and making speeches we can deserve well of men. Someone who puts forward a true opinion and gives useful advice about uncertain and doubtful matters, whether in relation to public or private affairs, should rightly be considered generous as well, the more so because this type of benefit accrues not to one person only but to many. Likewise, a speech made in court on behalf of a defendant (I call the accused party in judicial proceedings the defendant, in the manner of advocates) will belong to this category. Thus, someone who has justly defended a man beset by the calumnies of his enemies has deservedly acquired a reputation for benevolence.

In addition, we can acquire an immortal reputation for generosity through learning and erudition since these qualities impress themselves on men's minds. What can be of greater benefit than to give those things which are never taken away from men and which can never be obliterated from memory? Money can be very easily handed over or lost, honours and rank lose their lustre, advice is forgotten, speeches fade away. Knowledge alone is considered to be durable and stable since, as Aristotle says, it concerns those things which are always the same;[84] it also provides resources for our old age.[85] Consequently, we are right to call ungrateful and to brand with even greater opprobrium those who, heedless of their duty, not only fail to regard their teachers as substitute parents, as would be fitting, but do something far worse: they despise them and treat them as objects of hatred. Plato did not behave like this towards Socrates; for his dialogues are written in the name of Socrates.[86] Nor did Alcibiades, who never abandoned Socrates.[87] Nor did Dion act in this way towards Plato: he bore his exile with a calm mind for the sole reason that he was permitted to live with his teacher.[88] Nor did Alexander ill-treat Aristotle, whose native land he restored after it had been ravaged by enemies.[89] Nor, finally, did your glorious father and uncles behave in this manner towards Vittorino da Feltre: they treated this very saintly man during his life with the respect sons normally show their parents.[90] This is the best sort of munificence: for learning is an embellishment in good times, and in bad times it is a matchless haven.

We now come to that sort of generosity which concerns wealth – by wealth I mean what is measured in monetary terms. In this, your own ancestors were particularly noteworthy, especially your grandfather,[91] who left himself with nothing beyond the goodwill of men; for when he was not permitted to give money from empty coffers, he would give away whole estates and farms, claiming that he had done nothing in his life more gladly and with fewer regrets than that which he had performed out of munificence and generosity. He acquired such a reputation for this that all the nobility from the whole of Italy set out for Mantua, to see him as well as Vittorino, who practised the other sort of generosity.

At that time the city of Mantua was full to bursting with talent, with scholarship, with every form of virtue, thanks to the generosity and authority of its prince and its learned teacher. Later on, many excellent men went forth from here, as is said to be the case with the gymnasium of Isocrates; issuing, so to speak, from the Trojan Horse, some were called to arms, others to letters, bringing the greatest fame and glory to your family and your city.[92] This is why, wherever you travel in Italy, all admire you and, as if you were a god, receive you with every type of munificence and honour. This would certainly not happen if your city and your family had turned their backs on visitors and on the virtue of foreigners.

Therefore, embrace and celebrate this glory established by your forebears in every realm of virtue, following in the footsteps of your illustrious brother, Cardinal Francesco Gonzaga of Mantua. On his own, by means of this excellent virtue [of generosity], he has gained more renown and glory in Rome and wherever else he goes than all his fellow cardinals put together. He does not know the meaning of holding on to gold, silver, gems, rings, garments, cloaks, horses, Corinthian vases, Damascene metal-work, rock-crystals, tapestries, embroideries.[93] He has raised many in his household and among the citizenry to better circumstances, and has left them richer through his generosity. And he will do likewise for many others – such is his greatness of spirit – if he is permitted to go on living, which is in the hands of the gods. Just as the death of a greedy man is to be desired, as if he were a public enemy, so one wishes the life of a generous and munificent man to continue, for it is advantageous and useful to everyone. Observe, I implore you, how dear your brother's life is to us; for whenever the master suffers, the entire household is afflicted by a certain anxiety. We assuredly would not feel like this if he were miserly and tight-fisted, as are nearly all other cardinals, who, after their death, are abandoned in the street like dogs, deserving well of no one on account of their avarice. . . .

BOOK III

What Must Be Done in the Territory Surrounding the City

. . . It will be your responsibility to set out occasionally from the city into the countryside and see that the flooding of the rivers does not cause the banks to weaken and collapse; the entire region, although it is very fertile, is liable to this trouble. More frequently than we might wish, the Po, the king of the rivers, swells up, and as your [Mantuan] poet Virgil says, 'drags cattle, along with their folds, across all the fields'.[94] Often it inflicts such damage on those who live nearby that with a single inundation it snatches away an entire year's crops, just before the farmers, expending enormous effort, have readied them for harvest. Also, the marshes should be drained, if this contributes to the abundance and salubrity of the air. This is what they say Hercules did in Lerna, for cutting off the many, self-renewing heads of the Hydra was nothing other than draining the gushing Lernaean marsh using iron, fire and sewers.[95] Provision should be made, in addition, for bridges, gates and roads, so that travellers, either from your own city or from abroad, do not suffer any inconvenience — to the detriment and the disgrace of your city. Since princes have been created for the benefit of the population, they must ensure that no difficulties arise due to their negligence. . . .

On Hunting

. . . Young men in Rome were instructed in the liberal arts beginning in boyhood; after they assumed the toga of manhood, they moved on to more weighty studies. One needs to cultivate character at an early stage: the more tender it is, the better suited it is to absorbing the habits of wisdom and of civil institutions; as the Mantuan poet says: 'so strong is habit in those of tender years'.[96] And it is of no small moment, in Aristotle's opinion, whether someone becomes accustomed to this or that manner of life.[97] Moreover, as we see in animals, bodily strength is not very effective unless it is governed by discernment and prudence, which are normally born out of learning and experience. Therefore, that prince whom we desire to be the best should be instructed in the liberal arts from youth, following the example of Alexander the Great. His father Philip did not remove Alexander from his teacher Aristotle until he perceived that he excelled in every type of learning, so that from then on he would rule by merit. He was taught by his teacher that the learned differ from the unlearned as much as the living differ from the dead or the sleeping from the waking.[98] Julius Caesar's learning was of the greatest splendour when he was at the peak of power: he won almost more glory for himself through his learning than he did through his military feats. His writings are held in such high esteem that there appears to have been more divinity than humanity in the man. What inspired Scipio Africanus to deserve well of the state? What inspired Pompey? And the two Catos?[99] Their learning, to be sure, and their reading of ancient authors.

When Themistocles was asked why he could not sleep at night, he replied: 'The trophies of Miltiades keep me awake.'[100] Cicero confirms that Scipio was accustomed to keep the *Cyropaedia* of Xenophon constantly to hand; and, having worn out his copy through frequent reading, he exemplified the entire book during his command.[101] Nothing stirs our hearts as much towards virtue, courage, temperateness and true glory than seeing the names of deserving, learned men committed to writing for all time. This incentive is entirely lacking to those who are without knowledge and experience of literary pursuits.

Therefore, when our prince is equipped with the arts and skills which are suited to boyhood and youth, he can at length progress to hunting, which in certain respects resembles fighting a war. Hunting is very similar to the art of war since it is necessary to carry nets that are like a palisade, to travel on foot, to mount and dismount from a horse, to ride, to run, to leap, to hurl the javelin, to practise archery, to withstand savage beasts, to endure heat and cold, to enter harsh and rough places in one's desire to capture the prey. At a distance or hand to hand, as happens in battle, hunters struggle with beasts; and by means of such activities, which are like rehearsals, they toughen their souls for undergoing dangers.[102]

But, as in the army, so in hunting: let the prince be everyone's leader. Let him organize the band, arrange the stalking line, rally the assembled hunters to bravery, and bestow both praise and rewards on those who are deserving. Hunting should be done in mountains, on the plains and in wooded places. It should not be pursued in the manner of the Medes and the Milanese, who do battle with unwarlike animals in gardens and cages as if they were in a stronghold and kill them without any effort or strain. This procedure destroys the pleasure of the pursuit, the ardour of the chase and the concentration needed to hit the mark. It is just like those who make bellicose speeches and, not having been present themselves at the battle, execute back home prisoners captured by others. . . .

On Military Matters

They say that when the musician Timotheus wanted to demonstrate his skill to King Alexander, he deftly and expertly improvised a tune: not a gentle or slow strain, which produces lethargy of the soul and sluggishness, but instead exactly that high-pitched tune which Pallas Athena is reputed to have sung. Those notes roused Alexander of Macedon to arms, as if possessed by a god. The reason for this perhaps lay not so much in the music itself as in the energetic and forceful spirit of Alexander. For neither Timotheus nor Marsyas nor Olympus could have roused Sardanapalus. Even if Pallas herself had sung her warlike song,[103] or if the centaur Chiron had strummed the lyre which he customarily used to incite Achilles to battle and then, playing a different tune, to call him back at will,[104] Sardanapalus would not have been stirred, so powerful is the habit of living well or badly.

According to Xenophon, it is said that Hercules, on entering young manhood (which is the natural time for choosing which course of life one should embark on), went to a deserted place and, sitting there for a long time, debated a good deal with himself about which was the better path to follow, since he could discern two roads: one of pleasure, the other of virtue.[105] Spurning pleasure and embracing virtue, he ruled the world, so the stories tell, wearing the skin of a lion which he had killed; and in battle he employed a club for laying low the monsters which oppressed the human race. As befits a hero, he had no interest in gold or silver – except as something to distribute to his friends. To others he gave cows and cattle, regarding everything as his own and valuing very highly the goodwill of the recipients.[106] He travelled the world, not devoted to pleasure or avarice, but rather to serving virtue and the interests of mankind. This is why afterwards, on account of his merit, he was assumed into the ranks of the gods.[107]

Cities and provinces need princes of the same calibre, who, if necessary and if provoked by neighbouring peoples, will take up arms in earnest. All philosophers who have written on politics always assign part of the citizenry to warfare, so that they can protect their fields and the urban population from enemy raids. War, according to Plato, is to be contemplated for the sake of peace rather than vice versa;[108] for wars should be fought so that one may live in peace without harm. But when victory has been achieved, you should retain those soldiers who fought, not for life and limb, but who competed with you for pre-eminence and glory. It is entirely appropriate to fight wars for just causes.[109] The following causes are regarded as just: if goods stolen in the course of raids and pillaging are sought back according to fetial law and are not returned;[110] if borders are violated; if certain castles or citadels are captured, either by stealth or through treason; if the commerce of your citizens is disrupted. . . .

Translator's Notes

1. For other examples see J. Hankins, 'Humanism and the origins of modern political thought', in J. Kraye, ed., *The Cambridge Companion to Renaissance Humanism* (Cambridge, 1996), pp. 118–141, at 120.
2. See Bartolomeo Sacchi detto il Platina, *De optimo cive*, ed. F. Battaglia (Bologna, 1944).
3. See the English translation in A. Rabil, Jr., ed. and trans., *Knowledge, Goodness, and Power: The Debate over Nobility among Quattrocento Italian Humanists* (Binghamton, N.Y., 1991), pp. 269–98.
4. See Plato, *Laws* I (632D).
5. See Plutarch, *Life of Lycurgus* 19 (52A).
6. Aristotle, *Politics* V.8 (1310^{b}7–14).
7. Homer, *Iliad* II.204–5.
8. See Dante, *De monarchia* I.9–10.
9. In mythology, Phaethon, the offspring of the sun, was allowed by his father to guide the solar chariot for a day. Phaethon, however, was not strong enough to control the immortal horses, who bolted, placing the world in danger of being set on fire. Phaethon was therefore killed by Zeus with a thunderbolt and fell into the Eridanus. The story is recounted at greatest length in Book II of Ovid's *Metamorphoses*.
10. Valerius Maximus, *Facta et dicta memorabilia* V.6.ext.1. Codrus, an early king of Athens, was worshipped as a hero because he invited his own death in order to insure the victory of his people over the Dorians.
11. Xenophon's *Cyropaedia* is the main classical source for Cyrus (d. 529 BC), founder of the Persian Empire.
12. For Tarquinius see n. 13. Julius Caesar (100–44 BC); Augustus (63 BC–AD 14); Vespasian (9–79); Titus (39–81); Trajan (53–117); Antoninus Pius (86–161); Marcus Aurelius Antoninus (121–80); Marcus Aurelius Severus Alexander (208/9–35).
13. For the Greek tyrants Pheidon, Panaetius, Cypselus, Pisistratus and Dionysius see Aristotle, *Politics* V.8 (1310^{b}25–32). Phalaris (c. 570–554 BC) was notorious for the brazen bull in which he roasted his victims alive; Tarquinius Superbus (534–510 BC) was the last king of Rome; Herod the Great (c. 73–4 BC) ruthlessly crushed the old aristocracy and was hated by the Jews on account of his policy of Hellenization.
14. Xenophon, *Cyropaedia* VIII.1.1; Aristotle, *Politics* IV.8 (1295a19–24).
15. The lines from Pindar (part of a poem now largely lost) are quoted in Plato, *Laws* III (690A–B). Platina was acquainted with the circle of Platonic enthusiasts around Cardinal Bessarion, whose funeral oration he delivered in 1472; and he may have known George of Trebizond's Latin translation of the *Laws,* which had been criticized by Bessarion in his *Against the Slanderer of Plato* (1469).
16. This section is heavily indebted to Poggio Bracciolini's dialogue *On Nobility,* trans. in R. N. Watkins, *Humanism and Liberty: Writings on Freedom from Fifteenth-Century Florence* (Columbia, S.C., 1978), pp. 121–48, and in Rabil, *Knowledge, Goodness, and Power,* pp. 53–89.
17. See Diogenes Laertius, *Lives of the Philosophers* V.22 (Aristotle) and X.1 (Metrodorus).
18. Aristotle, *Politics* III.7 (1283a36–7).
19. Jerome, *Commentarii in Michaeam* II.6, in J.-P. Migne, ed., *Patrologia Latina,* 221 vols. (Paris, 1844–64), XXV, col. 1213 B–C.
20. Pseudo-Cicero, *Commentariolum petitionis* 12. Cicero made speeches against both Mark Antony (c. 82–30 BC) and the conspirator Catiline (d. 62 BC).

21. See, e.g., Juvenal, *Satires* VIII.20.
22. See Livy, *History of Rome* X.44.5, on the little silver horns and armlets given to the Roman cavalrymen on account of their distinguished conduct in battle against the Samnites.
23. Seneca, *De beneficiis* III.28.2.
24. Diogenes Laertius, *Lives of the Philosophers* VI.72.
25. Valerius Maximus, *Facta et dicta memorabilia* III.4.6. Marcus Porcius Cato the Censor (234–149 BC) was born of peasant stock but rose to become a distinguished statesman.
26. Gaius Marius (c. 157–86 BC) in fact came from an equestrian family, though one which was not of long standing; his military exploits are described in Sallust, *Bellum Jugurthinum.*
27. See Plutarch, *Life of Sertorius,* for Quintus Sertorius (d. 73/2 BC), a Sabine knight who defeated many Roman generals; Aulus Gellius, *Noctes atticae* XV.4, and Juvenal, *Satires* VII.199–200, for Ventidius Bassus, the proverbial upstart of the Roman revolutionary wars in the first century BC; Livy, *History of Rome* I.39–48, for Servius Tullius (578–535 BC), the sixth king of Rome, who, according to tradition, was the son of a maidservant.
28. Diogenes Laertius, *Lives of the Philosophers* III.88–9.
29. Diogenes Laertius, *Lives of the Philosophers* III.25, for Mithridates (d. c. 220 BC), and V.78–9, for Ptolemy Soter – not Philadelphus – (c. 367/7–283/2 BC), king of Egypt, and Demetrius Phalereus (b. c. 350 BC), an Athenian Peripatetic philosopher.
30. Marcus Terentius Varro (116–27 BC) was the author of various works on grammar, antiquities and agriculture. Plotius Tucca was a friend of Virgil and Horace and a member of the literary circle of Maecenas: see Horace, *Satires* I.5.40, and Donatus, *Life of Virgil* 39.
31. For the legend that the Greek historian and philosopher Plutarch (b. before 50; d. after 120) was the teacher of Emperor Trajan (see n. 12) see John of Salisbury, *Policratici . . . libri VIII,* ed. C. C. I. Webb, 2 vols. (Oxford, 1909), I, pp. 281–4 (V.1–2).
32. For the Roman jurist Ulpian (d. AD 223) and Emperor Marcus Aurelius Severus Alexander (see n. 12) see *Historia Augusta:* 'Severus Alexander' XV.6, XXVI.5–6.
33. The Greek philosopher Posidonius (c. 135–c. 51/50 BC) was the teacher of Cicero and a friend of Pompey; the statesman Scipio Africanus (185/4–129 BC) was at the centre of a literary and intellectual circle in Rome and appears as an interlocutor in several of Cicero's works. For similar lists see Petrarch, *Letters of Old Age: Rerum senilium libri I–XVIII,* trans. A. S. Bernardo, S. Levin and R. A. Bernardo, 2 vols. (Baltimore, 1992), II, p. 550 (XIV.1); Giovanni Conversini da Ravenna, *Two Court Treatises,* ed. and trans. B. Kohl and J. Day (Munich, 1987), p. 220 (*De dilectione regnantium*).
34. For the Greek philosopher Antisthenes (c. 445–360 BC) and his attitude towards Plato (c. 429–347 BC) see Diogenes Laertius, *Lives of the Philosophers* VI.7–8, 10–11.
35. Cicero, *Epistulae ad familiares* III.7.5.
36. Seneca, *Epistulae* XLIV.3.
37. Plato, *Theaetetus* 174E, quoted in Seneca, *Epistulae* XLIV.4.
38. Cf. Cicero, *De amicitia* 25.93: 'the person who changes not only to suit another's thought and will but also the expression on his face and the nod of his head'.
39. See Terence, *The Eunuch* 251, and Cicero, *De amicitia* 25.93.
40. See, e.g., Catullus, *Carmina* 108.5; Proverbs 30:17.
41. Juvenal, *Satires* III.100–1.
42. Aristotle, *Nicomachean Ethics* IV.3 (1125^{a}1–2).
43. On the sixth-century BC Greek philosopher Thales, regarded as one of the Seven Sages, see Diogenes Laertius, *Lives of the Philosophers* I.36; see also Plutarch, *How to Tell a Flatterer* 49B.
44. See the Introduction for the accusations made against Platina and his imprisonment.
45. *Historia Augusta:* 'Hadrian' XV.2. Hadrian was Roman emperor from AD 117 to 138.
46. For Dionysius the Younger, the fourth-century BC tyrant of Syracuse, and his treatment of Plato see Diogenes Laertius, *Lives of the Philosophers* III.18–19.

47. For the story of the tyrant Phalaris and his torture of the Presocratic philosopher Zeno of Elea (b. c. 490 BC) see Valerius Maximus, *Facta et dicta memorabilia* III.3.ext.2.
48. Diogenes Laertius, *Lives of the Philosophers* II.38–42; Plato, *Apology, Crito* and *Phaedo*.
49. For the Roman statesman and philosopher Boethius (c. 480–524) and his treatment by the Ostrogothic king of Italy Theodoric (493–526) see Boethius, *De consolatione philosophiae* I.113–17.
50. Suetonius, *Lives of the Caesars* VIII: 'Domitian' 9.3. Domitian was Roman emperor from AD 81 to 96.
51. See I Samuel 6–II Samuel 2; I Chronicles 11–14.
52. See Plato, *Gorgias* 470E, and Dio Chrysostom, *Third Discourse on Kingship* 1; cf. Aristotle's definition of happiness in *Nicomachean Ethics* I.7 (1097ᵇ23–1098ᵃ20).
53. Suetonius, *Lives of the Caesars* III: 'Tiberius' 25. Tiberius was Roman emperor from AD 14 to 37.
54. See Poggio Bracciolini, *De infelicitate principum,* in his *Opera omnia,* ed. R. Fubini, 4 vols. (Turin, 1964–9), I, pp. 390–419, at 416.
55. Aristotle, *Nicomachean Ethics* VI.8 (1142ᵃ11–20).
56. I Kings 10.
57. Genesis 40–1.
58. Cicero, *De officiis* II.9.34.
59. Daniel 5.
60. Aristotle, *Nicomachean Ethics* VI.12 (1144ᵃ23–7).
61. Aristotle, *Nicomachean Ethics* VI.9 (1142ᵃ34–ᵇ5).
62. Psalms 77:6.
63. Cicero, *Epistulae ad familiares* II.7.2.
64. Proverbs 5:15.
65. Plato, *Laws* III.
66. Cicero, *De officiis* II.12.41.
67. Numa Pompilius (715–673 BC), the second king of Rome, was a Sabine; many religious and political reforms are attributed to him. See Livy, *History of Rome* I.18.
68. Cicero, *De officiis* II.12.41–2.
69. See Johannes Argyropulos, *De institutione eorum qui in dignitate constituti sunt,* partially edited by E. Garin, 'Un trattatello politico inedito dell'Argiropulo', in his *Rinascite e rivoluzioni: movimenti culturali dal XIV al XVIII secolo* (Bari, 1975), pp. 121–9, at 126.
70. Aristotle, *Nicomachean Ethics* V.1 (1130ᵃ8–10).
71. I Corinthians 13:4, 7.
72. Cicero, *De officiis* I.7.20.
73. Matthew 5:38–9.
74. Cicero, *De officiis* I.7.21.
75. Cicero, *De officiis* I.16.52.
76. Cicero, *De officiis* I.17.53.
77. Cicero, *De officiis* I.17.54.
78. Aristotle, *Politics* III.7 (1283ᵃ36).
79. Cicero, *De legibus* III.2.5.
80. Cicero, *De legibus* III.1.3.
81. Plato, *Republic* I (347D).
82. Diogenes Laertius, *Lives of the Philosophers* III.39. The fourth-century BC Greek philosophers Xenocrates and Speusippus were both disciples of Plato; the latter was also his nephew.
83. Valerius Maximus, *Facta et dicta memorabilia* IV.1.ext.2. Archytas of Tarentum was a fourth-century BC philosopher and mathematician; he is regarded as the founder of the science of mechanics.
84. Aristotle, *Nicomachean Ethics* VI.6.
85. Cicero, *De senectute* 1.2.

86. Diogenes Laertius, *Lives of the Philosophers* II.45.
87. Plutarch, *Life of Alcibiades* IV–VII. The Athenian general and statesman Alcibiades (c. 450–404 BC) was a pupil and friend of Socrates; he appears as a speaker in Plato's dialogue the *Symposium.*
88. Plutarch, *Life of Dion* XV–XVII. Dion (c. 408–354 BC), having fallen under the spell of Plato during the latter's sojourn in Syracuse, was exiled from his native land; he then spent time in Athens, where he was closely attached to Plato's Academy.
89. Diogenes Laertius, *Lives of the Philosophers* V.4. From 343 to 342 BC the philosopher Aristotle (384–322 BC), known as the Stagirite from his native town of Stagira in northern Greece, was the teacher of Alexander the Great (356–323 BC), the heir to the throne of Macedon.
90. See Platina, *De vita Victorini Feltrensis commentariolus,* in E. Garin, *Il pensiero pedagogico dello umanesimo* (Florence, 1958), pp. 668–99.
91. Federico's grandfather was Gianfrancesco Gonzaga, marquis of Mantua.
92. Cf. Cicero, *De oratore* II.23.94. The orator Isocrates (436–338 BC) was head of a famous school in Athens.
93. See D. S. Chambers, *A Renaissance Cardinal and His Worldly Goods: The Will and Inventory of Francesco Gonzaga (1444–1483)* (London, 1992).
94. Virgil, *Aeneid* II.498–9.
95. See Servius, *In Vergilii Aeneidos commentarius* VI.287; and Coluccio Salutati, *De laboribus Herculis,* ed. B. L. Ullman, 2 vols. (Zurich, 1951) I, pp. 193–4. Lerna, a marshy district in the Peloponnese, was the haunt of the many-headed Hydra; Hercules, as one of his labours, slayed the monster by applying a burning iron to the wounds as soon as one head was cut off, thus preventing new heads from growing.
96. Virgil, *Georgics* II.272.
97. Aristotle, *Nicomachean Ethics* II.1 (1103^{b}24–5).
98. Diogenes Laertius, *Lives of the Philosophers* V.4–5.
99. For Scipio Africanus see n. 33. Pompey (106–48 BC) was a Roman general and statesman. For Cato the Censor see n. 25; his grandson, Cato of Utica (95–46 BC), was a statesman known for his Stoicism and his adherence to old Roman principles.
100. Valerius Maximus, *Facta et dicta memorabilia* VIII.14.ext.1. Miltiades was the victorious Athenian general at the battle of Marathon; after his death (489 BC), Themistocles attained supremacy in Athens.
101. Cicero, *Tusculan Disputations* II.26.62 and *Epistulae ad familiares* IX.25.1; see also n. 11.
102. See Xenophon, *Cyropaedia* I.6.39–40.
103. Dio Chrysostom, *First Discourse on Kingship* 1. Sardanapalus, the last king of Assyria, was legendary for his wealth and his devotion to sensual pleasure. In mythology, Marsyas was a Phrygian satyr who was defeated by Apollo in a flute-playing contest, and Olympus was his student.
104. See, e.g., Statius, *Achilleid* II.87–91.
105. Cicero, *De officiis* I.32.118.
106. Dio Chrysostom, *First Discourse on Kingship* 62.
107. Cicero, *De officiis* III.5.25.
108. Plato, *Laws* I (628D).
109. See Thomas Aquinas, *Summa theologiae* IIaIIae, q. 40, art. 1.
110. Cicero, *De officiis* I.11.36. The college of *fetiales* was composed of priests who represented the Roman people in their dealings with other nations.

Further Reading

Brown, A., 'Scala, Platina and Lorenzo de' Medici in 1474', in J. Hankind, J. Monfasani and F. Purnell, eds., *Supplement Festivum: Studies in Honor of Paul Oskar Kristeller* (Binghamton, N.Y., 1987), pp. 327–37

Burns, J. H., ed., *The Cambridge History of Political Thought 1450–1700* (Cambridge, 1991), pp. 31–3, 35, 40, 41, 689

Campana, A., and Medioli Masotti, P., eds., *Bartolomeo Sacchi il Platina* (Padua, 1986)

CHRP, pp. 21, 369, 421–2, 424, 832

D'Amico, J., *Renaissance Humanism in Papal Rome: Humanists and Churchmen on the Eve of the Reformation* (Baltimore, 1983), pp. 35–6, 92–7

Grafton, A., ed., *Rome Reborn: The Vatican Library and Renaissance Culture* (Washington, D.C., 1993), pp. 23–4, 35, 37–8, 74

Rubinstein, N., 'The *De optimo cive* and the *De principe* by Bartolomeo Platina', in *Tradizione classica e letteratura umanistica: Per Alessandro Perosa,* 2 vols. (Rome, 1985), I, pp. 375–89

Giuniano Maio

Nicholas Webb

Introduction

The humanist Giuniano Maio (c. 1435–93) was born in Naples. From 1465 to 1488 he taught rhetoric at the Neapolitan *studio*. For most of his career he was closely associated with the Aragonese court, and in 1490 he became tutor to the children of King Ferrante. Maio is best known for his popular etymological dictionary, one of the earliest of such works to be compiled in Italy.[1] He also produced editions of the younger Pliny's letters and selected orations of Cicero. There are poems addressed to him by his literary friends, Giovanni Pontano and Jacopo Sannazaro.[2]

It is probably indicative of the close-knit intellectual circle at Naples that there is so much overlap between the works produced by humanists residing there, notably in historical writing and in the genre of the mirror of princes. Maio's *On Majesty,* which he dedicated to Ferrante in 1492 and which survives in an illuminated presentation copy,[3] has close parallels with the subject-matter of Pontano's treatises on the so-called social virtues (e.g., generosity, magnificence, splendour and beneficence). The work moreover bears some resemblance, in terms of the method of presenting examples, to the *Deeds and Sayings of Alfonso* by the Sicilian humanist Antonio Panormita. Maio's penchant for inserting doses of political realism into his treatise is also characteristic of the writings of both Pontano and Diomede Carafa.[4] In addition, these humanist writers all tended to draw on the same range of earlier sources: Aristotle's *Nicomachean Ethics,* Cicero's *De officiis,* Sallust's *Wars against Catiline and Jugurtha,* Valerius Maximus' *Facta et dicta memorabilia,* Isocrates' *To Nicoclem* and Xenophon's *Cyropaedia.* Most of these works had been used in medieval mirrors of princes; but the last two were only recently translated from Greek. Another distinctive feature in the approach of Maio and his Neapolitan contemporaries was their concern with external behaviour as a reflection of inner virtue.

'On Magnificence' is the penultimate chapter of the treatise (the final one concerns glory). Providing advice and guidelines for his royal addressee rather than strict rules and regulations, Maio begins with various definitions of magnificence, drawn primarily from Aristotle's account in *Nicomachean Ethics* IV.2, supplemented by Valerius Maximus and Cicero. He then treats the characteristics of the magnificent man and the magnificent prince, concluding with specific examples of King Ferrante's magnificence. Maio gives preference to building programmes over ephemeral entertainments, endorses the importance of personal possessions, singles out Ferrante's reputation for horsemanship and hunting and, in general, emphasizes the need for the prince to stand out – a matter of political significance in a kingdom in which there continued to be violent tension between the ruler and his subjects.[5]

For the Italian text see Giuniano Maio, *De maiestate,* ed. F. Gaeta (Bologna, 1956), pp. 223–31. The subheadings (which are otiose and, in one case, misleading) have not been included. I am grateful to Marta Ajmar and Alessandro Scafi for helping me with this translation.

On Majesty

CHAPTER 19

On Magnificence

This most stately majesty, [the subject of the present treatise], when tempered by respectful wisdom and illuminated by radiant justice, is lofty and valuable in its own right. Nevertheless, it is far more exquisite and attractive when adorned by magnificence. Conspicuous and elegant magnificence imparts propriety and visible dignity, complementing majesty with a glorious and honourable beauty. Aristotle defines it in the following terms: magnificence is the beautiful appearance of a thing that has been embellished, arousing admiration in the person who sees it; its power consists in the fact that the work is well executed and in its sumptuous grandeur.[6] Alternatively, if we want to follow the authority of Valerius Maximus, magnificence is an esteemed ornament – sumptuous, lofty and constructed, in an appropriate manner, as a model of virtue. By inspiring another person with respect, it provides a noble heart with exuberance and greatness of spirit, motivating that person to do good by imitation.[7]

Aristotle defines this conspicuous and ornamental virtue in these terms: it is concerned with a lofty and honourable enterprise, like those which pertain to divine and holy things devoted to God, such as temples, vessels, sacrifices and consecrated worship. It also consists in those public benefactions which provide entertainment in the form of spectacles, such as games, sports, triumphs, jousts, funerals and such like.[8] Cicero prides himself a good deal on this virtue, which he exercised in a moderate fashion during his aedileship. He gave much more praise, however, and commended in glowing terms the splendid and sumptuous magnificence involved in raising the walls of cities, building shipyards, making piers and quays for ships, constructing aqueducts, erecting bridges and other similar undertakings related to the common good. On account of the great pleasure they produce, and not so much for reasons of expediency, magnificence also consists in building theatres, porticoes, residences, new temples and similar things, recalling the Propylaea of Pericles, which gave the measure of his greatness.[9]

Aristotle maintains that magnificence is a splendid and conspicuous sumptuousness, which is required on a scale appropriate to the dignity of the individual.[10] Furthermore, he says that the magnificent man is like the learned and knowledgeable one, and that magnificence is a certain science of knowing how to evaluate the greatness and the fineness of a magnificent thing, which is worthy of splendid display in proportion to the dignity of the individual, whose stature and rank should be maintained in it, with no effort and expense spared.[11] This undertaking, accompanied by correctness and virtue, should be worthy of praise and honest repute. Since magnificence requires a personal excellence which does not proceed from riches, but only from the honourable merit of virtue, it cannot be granted to everyone. Indeed, Cicero castigates those who, entirely lacking in honour, dignity and virtue, want to consider themselves on a par with great and famous princes.[12] Aristotle supports this view: in everything we do we ought to have due regard for the individual in terms of his dignity and also of the means he is able to expend and the resources he possesses, so that the magnificence of a thing corresponds to the excellence of its originator.[13]

Moreover, such virtue cannot be present in a poor or middlingly well-off person, nor in anyone lacking the highest dignity and grandeur, so that even some who are well endowed and wealthy ought to have a limit set on their magnificence and pomp – in accordance with their dignity, not their wealth. But when an individual's dignity outstrips that of other men to a very high degree, then the excellence of his lavish display ought to exceed and surpass the norm, so that his noble stature matches the magnificent display which is achieved.[14] For this reason, a more illustrious reputation and more extensive acclaim belong to works accomplished through magnificence than to those achieved through generosity. This is especially true if the one who accomplishes the deed is distinguished by the highest majesty, because to no rank is such a splendid virtue more suitable than to the most exalted princes and kings, for the excellence of the sumptuous achievement corresponds to the loftiness of their stature.

This sort of virtue is usually displayed in all the works of princes, in line with their life-style and culture. A case in point is the building of large palaces, fortified castles, magnificent temples and all holy places, where more than anywhere else magnificence is praised; on top of these, there are walls for the defence of cities, quays or piers, shipyards, cities, fountains.[15] These are not only splendid ornaments; they also represent a public benefit and a permanent utility. Because this sort of enterprise combines perpetual benefit with splendid beauty, it produces all the more glory and long-lasting renown. In addition, there are other feats of magnificence which are more immediately effective for enhancing one's reputation than for practical usefulness – for instance, the many forms of spectacle, such as pleasant games, plays, carnivals, parties, banquets, jousts, weddings, funerals and triumphs – where it is excessive luxury rather than the mean which tends to be praised. These types of endeavours are aimed at producing fleeting pleasure, not future benefit. Indeed, this sort of largesse gains vulgar praise, delighting the ignorant rabble rather than men endowed with more discerning judgement.

Other products of magnificent lavishness are found in the context of domestic life – clothes, tapestries, paintings, sculptures, costly garments, vessels made of gold, silver and other materials – where the elegance of the art is appreciated more than the expense. Then, there are precious gems, where one tends to have regard for their opulence rather than their function, although with the regalia of exalted princes it is not so much the exact amount of their worth which is generally esteemed as their overwhelming abundance and inestimable number. None of your contemporaries outdoes you in the richness and splendour of such accessories.

But certainly, even if you have equals in a number of areas, in as many as five of your distinguished activities you make such an outstanding show of splendid magnificence that you are without peer or superior among today's princes.[16] You have already given the clearest proof not only of the stature of your mind, through the scale of your undertakings, but also of your virtue, through your delightful courtesy.[17]

The first type of magnificence is when, seated majestically on a horse, you are the most stalwart prince, as well as the most powerful rider among all those who handle horses.[18] You take so much delight in the grandeur and the beauty of your many horses, which are of such nobility and which are continually increased in number and maintained with such care and constant attention that not only is terror inspired in your enemies but you are also the envy of everyone. In a brief space of time you can appear, like other wealthy kings, with armed men on horseback, and in larger numbers than many could muster. Thus, in time of war your cavalry renders you powerful and victorious, and in time of peace illustrious and splendid.

The second type of magnificence about which we might speak concerns hunting. If we consider the number and the beauty of your dogs, selected from different breeds and from foreign countries, the falcons and other birds of prey imported from various parts of the world, the enclosed hunting forests, the snares which have been made, the new ways of hunting which have been devised, the coverts and nets which have been prepared, your considerable experience in hunting wild beasts, your indefatigable practice – surely, then, your passion should be regarded as not only remarkable but unbelievable.

Hunting is a worthy training for a noble knight and for a magnanimous and excellent king. By means of it, the health and fitness of your body is preserved, preparing and arming you for any eventuality, while at the same time the enjoyment stimulates and supports your noble mind.[19] Since I have already spoken at great length about hunting in another book, treating its origin, inventors and usefulness at length,[20] I shall refer to that work and remain silent here.

Translator's Notes

1. Giuniano Maio, *De priscorum proprietate verborum* (Naples, 1475).
2. See Antonio de Ferrariis, il Galateo, *Epistole,* ed. A. Altamura (Lecce, 1959), pp. 101–3, where Maio is included among the friends awaiting Pontano in the Elysian Fields.
3. T. De Marinis, *La biblioteca napoletana dei re d' Aragon,* 4 vols. (Milan, 1947–52), II, pp. 103–4.
4. For a translation of Pontano's *On the Prince* see Chapter 6. See also Diomede Carafa, *Dello optimo cortesano,* ed. G. Paparelli (Salerno, 1971).
5. It is interesting to note that Leon Battista Alberti, *I libri della famiglia,* in his *Opere volgari* ed. C. Grayson, 3 vols. (Bari, 1968–73), I, pp. 275–7, has his character 'Giannozzo' express doubts about the usefulness of hunting, regarding it with suspicion as a decadent imperial pastime, in much the same way and for the same republican reasons as Cicero (*Epistolae ad familiares,* VII.1.3).
6. Aristotle, *Nicomachean Ethics* IV.2 (1122^b16–18).
7. Valerius Maximus, *Facta et dicta memorabilia* VIII.15.
8. Aristotle, *Nicomachean Ethics* IV.2 (1122^b19–23).
9. Cicero, *De officiis* II.17.59–60. Cicero informs us that the Athenian statesman Pericles (c. 495–429 BC) was criticized for wasting money on building the Propylaea, a monumental roofed gateway on the west side of the Acropolis.
10. Aristotle, *Nicomachean Ethics* IV.2 (1122^b23–6).
11. Aristotle, *Nicomachean Ethics* IV.2 (1122^a34–$^b10$).
12. Cicero, *De officiis* II.12.43.
13. See n. 10.
14. Cf. Giovanni Pontano, *I trattati delle virtù sociali,* ed. F. Tateo (Rome, 1965), pp. 86–7 ('De magnificentia').

15. On the role of magnificence in Renaissance patronage of architecture, see M. Baxandall, *Painting and Experience in Fifteenth-Century Italy* (Oxford, 1972), pp. 1–27; A. D. Frazer-Jenkins, 'Cosimo de' Medici's patronage of architecture and the theory of magnificence', *Journal of the Warburg and Courtauld Institutes,* 33 (1970), 162–70; G. L. Hersey, *The Aragonese Arch at Naples (1443–1475)* (New Haven, Conn., 1973); C. H. Clough, 'Chivalry and magnificence in the golden age of the Italian Renaissance', in S. Anglo, ed., *Chivalry in the Renaissance* (Woodbridge, Suffolk, 1990), pp. 25–47.
16. Although Maio indicates that he is going to discuss five types of magnificence, the chapter breaks off abruptly after the second. In MS Paris, Bibliothèque nationale, ital. 1711, on which the printed edition is based, there is a lacuna at that point (ff. 58–9); see Maio, *De maiestate,* pp. xl, xlvii–viii.
17. Maio seems to have in mind the sense of the Latin term *commoditas* rather than that of the Italian *commodità.*
18. See Pontano, *Trattati delle virtù sociali,* pp. 52–3 (ch. 37: 'On Generosity'): 'Recently King Ferrante has released from service a horse which had done sterling service against some bandits, and he wished the horse to be entirely free of toil, having entrusted him to the care of a stable-manager.'
19. Cf. Xenophon, *Cyropaedia* I.2.9–10; Pliny the Younger, *Panegyricus* 81.2–3.
20. Only the title of the work, *Inventione della caccia,* is known.

Further Reading

Bentley, J. H., *Politics and Culture in Renaissance Naples* (Princeton, N.J., 1987), pp. 67–8, 77, 99, 199, 207–8, 219, 243, 264, 283, 294

Burns, J. H., ed., *The Cambridge History of Political Thought 1450–1700* (Cambridge, 1991), pp. 32–3

CHRP, pp. 424–5

Percopo, E., 'Nuovi documenti su gli scrittori e gli artisti dei aragonesi', *Archivio storico per le provincie napoletane,* 19 (1894), 740–79, at 740–56

Ricciardi, R., 'Angelo Poliziano, Giuniano Maio, Antonio Calcillo', *Rinascimento,* 8 (1968), 277–309

Santoro, M., 'La cultura umanistica', in *Storia di Napoli,* 10 vols. (Naples, 1975–81), IV.2, pp. 317–498, at 426

Part III.
The Theory of Republican Government in Renaissance Venice

8

Pier Paolo Vergerio

RONALD G. WITT

Introduction

The humanist Pier Paolo Vergerio the Elder (1370–1444) was based in Padua from 1390 to 1403, during which time he made frequent visits to nearby Venice and established contact with humanistic and patrician circles there. His treatise on the Venetian Republic, which is incomplete (the second half is especially fragmentary, consisting of little more than a series of notes and jottings), was probably written between 1400 and 1403. He perhaps hoped to find employment by winning the favour of the Venetians with this treatise. After leaving Padua, Vergerio worked for several years in the papal Curia. From 1413 to 1417 he was in the train of Cardinal Francesco Zabarella,[1] first in Bologna and then at the Council of Constance. In 1417 he entered the service of Emperor Sigismund and never returned to Italy.

The treatise falls into two halves. The first part describes the unique geographical setting of the city and the customs and character of its people, above all their total involvement in trade. The second section provides a sketch of the republic's various political, administrative and judicial institutions. It is the earliest general account of Venice and conforms broadly, in terms of organization and of the information it provides, to the popular medieval genre of city descriptions. At about the same time, Vergerio's friend, Leonardo Bruni, produced an account of Florence which bears a much stronger humanistic imprint, being modelled on the eulogy of Athens by Aelius Aristides, a second-century AD Greek orator.[2] Although Vergerio had studied Greek in Florence along with Bruni from 1398 to 1400, his work follows the more traditional medieval pattern, though it is noteworthy for his unusually even-handed and objective stance: his generally positive view of the city and its inhabitants does not prevent him from criticizing the insularity of the Venetians or from mentioning the stench emanating from the canals.

From the standpoint of political theory, the treatise is an important witness to the relatively early stages of the 'myth of Venice': the belief that the economic success and political stability of the city were due not only to its extraordinary geographical advantages and the upright character of its people but also to its excellent institutions. The notion that Venice embodied the classical ideal of the mixed constitution, which was such an important component in the myth, is present in a somewhat modified form: Vergerio describes the city as essentially an aristocracy, but one which incorporates both monarchical and democratic elements.

The Latin text is edited in D. Robey and J. Law, 'The Venetian myth and the "De republica veneta" of Pier Paolo Vergerio', *Rinascimento,* 15 (1975), 3–59, at 38–49; this article also provides an excellent introduction to the text and useful annotations. The headings in the translation are not found in the original. I am grateful to Stanley Chojnacki of Michigan State University for his assistance in identifying the array of Venetian institutions which Vergerio discusses.

The Venetian Republic: Selections

General Account of Venice and the Venetians

The Venetian Republic is ruled by a government composed of the best men, the type of regime that the Greeks call an 'aristocracy', which takes a middle course between monarchical and democratic rule.[3] It is superior because it partakes of the good aspects of each of these extremes and brings together elements from every type of good government. Thus, the doge, in whose name and authority affairs are conducted, is elected for life; and when the position is vacant, the supreme law-making power rests with the people [*populus*].[4] This arrangement cannot be abrogated by any body of officials or any individual, but only by the people themselves. An account of the customs of the Venetians, certain of their laws and their form of government will make all this clear. First, however, the site of the city and the nature of the region will be described.

The city of Venice is situated in a deep bay of the Adriatic Sea. It cannot be reached by land, nor is there easy access by sea since it is set amidst the shallows and the swamps at a distance from the mainland just sufficient to be out of range of missiles hurled from catapults. On the sea side it has the Lido, a sandy beach exposed to the waves, which only allows ships to enter the port through a few gaps,[5] by which the tides flow in and out.

At one time the entire adjacent region, extending far and wide, was called Venice. Many cities and towns of Cisalpine Gaul were included within it, so that the boundaries of the province apparently extended as far as Bergamo.[6] But later on the term came to be used in a more restricted sense, and only that part of the region which was bordered by the sea, even if it was some distance from the shore, was referred to by that name. In this coastal area there were many 'islands' so to say, and on them clusters of dwellings dotted about here and there: wherever solid earth or a pile of sand happened to emerge from the water, providing stable ground for the inhabitants, one would see the isolated houses of fishermen or sailors. Many of those who lived scattered about in these places then joined together, and they began to live together, along with a number of newcomers, who felt themselves secure in the area. The city, already quite famous on account of its size and power, gradually claimed the title of Venice for itself and, as happened elsewhere, what had previously been the general name of the region became specific to it. Not long after they decided on the rule of a doge, it was agreed that only the territory which was enclosed by the Lido di Grado and Cavarzere, the two extreme boundaries to the north and south, would be regarded as belonging to the *dogado*.[7] All territory which was later acquired by means of military action or treaty is not considered to be part of the *dogado* but rather of the city's empire. We know from the commentaries of Julius Caesar, which were corrected and published by Julius Celsus, that there was once another city with the same name which was similarly situated in the far west.[8] It was perhaps this likeness which led to the name Venice being given to this city. But it is more probable, in my view, that the name derives from the race of the Eneti [of Paphlagonia], whom Antenor, after fleeing from the ruins of Troy, brought with him to Italy, settling them close to the place where the city of Venice now stands.[9]

Although it is surrounded neither by walls nor by a palisaded rampart, it is the best-protected city in the world. This has been a key factor in its growth, in terms of population and also of wealth. During the various times when Italy was under frequent attack by barbarians, who destroyed everything in their path, Venice alone remained a secure place, where men could congregate in safety, whether they were untouched by ruin or had lost everything. This is because the city can be approached only with great difficulty by those attacking it from the outside. Also, it is laid out internally in such a way that just when it is thought to have been captured, the reverse has happened; and the very people who thought that they had captured it have themselves been held captive. For in these lagoons (as they call them) the water rising above the shallow marshes cannot admit large ships; and if by chance it does admit them when the tide is high, the water quickly recedes in the next stage of its cycle and deposits them on dry land. Nor can one walk easily on the soft mud: once bogged down, it is impossible to extract oneself. Approaching the city by foot is therefore out of the question. As for boats, there are only a few waterways, and these, which they call canals, are not very wide. The canals were either dug by men in the first place or have been hollowed out by the perpetual ebb and flow of the water. I am inclined to think that they are not the product of human effort because they are very twisted and have not been made with any obvious design, and also because opposite Venice you occasionally find similar ones, which have no purpose or human function except to carry the lagoon waters out to the port and the open sea. So that sailors do not miss navigable canals, the Venetians mark them with poles fixed on the banks; and when these poles are removed[10] from the canals, one cannot enter the city.

When you *do* get there, you cannot just wander about at will, for it is split up by narrow, curving streets, high buildings and then waterways and canals, so that virtually every neighbourhood has been made into an island, and almost every house can be reached by boat – which not only contributes significantly to the protection of the city, but is also very conducive to the pleasure and convenience of private citizens. The entire city is therefore connected by stone bridges (which are, in fact, largely built of wood and which can easily be disassembled when the need arises), so that one can walk to every place in the city or be taken there by boat. The city is divided almost in half by the Grand Canal, which may be crossed at the Rialto by a single, wooden bridge, the main one in Venice. In this area there are two places in particular which are the most famous in the city: the Piazza San Marco, where almost the entire nobility assembles on feast days; and the doge's palace, which is located there and which is the citadel from which the entire republic is governed. The Rialto [*Rivoaltum*], where on working days men are actively engaged in business, is called by that name, I believe, because the channel [*rivus*] is somewhat deeper [*altior*] there.

Thus, no other city, however well fortified with walls and towers, can be safer from the land side than this one, which is without walls. Scarcely any city located far from the sea is less vulnerable to maritime attacks than this one, which is totally surrounded by the sea. No city, even one constructed on solid ground, has such tall buildings as this one, whose foundations are built on the sea. No city located in the middle of the sea and unapproachable by land is less accessible than this one, which is almost connected to the mainland. And what city, though it has fertile lands, is as plentiful in agricultural produce as this one, which has no nearby fields, and in which it is not so much the expensiveness of the goods as the cheapness of money that raises the price of food? Other cities, whether on the mainland or on islands set in the sea, are all constructed in roughly the same way: they are surrounded by a circle of walls and ditches, but can be penetrated from within by means of the continuous streets. This city, on the other hand, though it is not far from the mainland – indeed, is enclosed by the arms of the bordering land – and is separated from terra firma only by a narrow band of marshland and shallow water, is constructed in such a way that nearly every house can be considered an island. . . .

Outside the city are many inhabited islands in the lagoon. Scattered here and there are churches and monasteries – some for men, others for women – with large and spacious orchards. These are well suited for retreats, during which those engaged in secular affairs can refresh their souls, while clerics can spend all their time in pious studies and sacred devotions.

Because of the water, the air in the city is rather thick; in the summer the climate is intemperate, and it is difficult to breathe. When the tide goes out, there is a foul odour, which is offensive to those who are unaccustomed to it. The place produces tall men and women who are rather plump. It is especially suitable for old people, who flourish there, because the salt vapour inhibits the superfluous humidity associated with ageing – as can be seen from the fact that the stones in the walls are consumed by the saltiness of the sea air. There are many very attractive old people, either for that reason, or because hair turns white earlier here than in other places, due to the foul exhalations, and practically everyone has a moist complexion and blond hair, which normally goes white quite quickly.[11]

There is no agricultural land near the city, and nothing grows or lives within its borders except fish, olives, garden fruits and swamp birds. Other food products must be imported from elsewhere, brought in by sea or river transport. They use rainwater or sometimes, after a long dry spell, water from neighbouring rivers, which is conveyed to their wells. Their dress is sumptuous and splendid, their diet moderate. The youth of the city is well mannered and fond of foreign habits and fashions.

The common pursuit of everyone is trade: merchandise sought in every corner of the globe is brought here, making this city the emporium of the entire world, as Petrarch called it.[12] They sail throughout the Mediterranean, through the Black Sea to the frozen Don, to Syria, Egypt and Libya, and beyond the columns of Hercules over the ocean all the way to the distant British Isles, carrying metals and other items – raw materials or handicrafts – which our part of the world has appropriated for itself. Their ships bring back spices, wool, valuable animal skins and products which other areas have in abundance. They transport these same things by river or over land and sell them to merchants, who in turn carry them to regions where they are in short supply. A severe obstacle for merchants, and one which causes them great losses, is the fact that at the very entrance to the port of Venice the sea is not very deep; and almost every year ships which have travelled all over the high seas are accustomed to risk their safety and cargo just as they reach port. Although no expense has been spared in searching for a solution to this problem, none has yet been found. A huge shipyard, which they call the Arsenal, is located within the city and surrounded on all sides by walls; in it they make new galleys, maintain those they have built and repair those which have been battered by bad weather or are suffering the effects of age. There one finds oars, anchors and other naval equipment, as well as incredible quantities of weaponry and every type of instrument of war, all of which are painstakingly kept ready for use.[13]

On land and sea the Venetians now possess a far-reaching empire and are not particularly eager to acquire further territory either as a state or as private individuals. They are, however, very determined to keep what they have. Their ambition is to attain honour, and what attracts them is glory and good repute.

Venetians are gentle by nature, high-minded and courteous in their behaviour. In private, they display great dignity in their speech and gestures. In public, they act with great firmness: no one can remember a case when a citizen or foreigner [*peregrinus*][14] convicted of a capital crime was ever pardoned; nor, in living memory, has it been heard of for a person condemned to exile to have been recalled to the city. It is all the easier for them to maintain this steadfastness because they do not have any hinterland, which could be plundered by exiles or which they could use as a convenient base, close to the city, from which to stir up internal sedition by starting a war. . . .

Nobility of family is acquired by law: while elsewhere it derives from the antiquity of a family, here it stems from its admission to the Senate.

Although they sail to the ends of the earth, these people seem ignorant of foreign customs. This is because they never leave their own country: travelling aboard a ship, they constantly mix with one another; and they are packed more closely together in a ship than they would be in a city or a neighbourhood since it is that much smaller. They rule the Adriatic, and to keep it from becoming infested with pirates, they patrol it with a regular fleet. In addition, every year on Ascension Day,[15] which is the most important feast of the Venetian calendar, the doge, accompanied by other high officials and the entire nobility, is carried a short distance from the waterfront on a boat specially prepared for this purpose. It is then customary for the doge to take a ring from his finger and throw into the sea, as a sign of Venetian sovereignty [over the Adriatic] and also as a means of ensuring that the republic will continue to possess this sovereignty in the future.[16] . . .

Principal Councils and Offices of the Venetian Republic

. . . There is a council composed of a hundred men who, according to custom, are consulted [*rogari*]; the council takes its name from them, for it is called the Rogati, and in it resides the authority of the Maggior Consiglio and of the city as a whole.[17] When a serious matter arises, which requires secrecy or extended consideration, it is usually committed to a body of four men, who are called the Savi grandi or Capi del consiglio;[18] it is a magistracy which confers very great honour.

The office of the Avogadori di comun is also very powerful. The precise, practical reason for founding this magistracy was so that there would be someone to safeguard the laws and the rights of the people, to indict before the Senate guilty men for whom there is no prosecutor and to act as judges for certain types of crime. Investigating the crimes of treason and conspiracy is the task of the Consiglio dei dieci, which is composed of the doge, his six counsellors and the three members of the Avogadori.[19] There is no appeal from their decisions.

There is also a commission charged with investigating criminal matters. Those engaged in a dispute with each other or caught up in unfriendly relations are ordered to go to the Cinque di pace. If a person condemned by this magistracy does not make amends to the injured party, he may be killed with impunity.

The Senate chooses judges for civil lawsuits from among the senators, for no foreigner or commoner can be a magistrate; commoners fill the position of scribe.[20] There are separate judges for Venetian citizens and for foreigners and different courts for different sorts of cases.

Laws have their own statutes, which determine how sentences are to be passed.[21] If, however, something goes beyond these in its character, so that it cannot be decided by either civil or canon law, it is settled at the will and discretion of the judges, for the Venetians do not want to be constrained by any external laws. They are not willing to use their laws to protect those priests who refuse to live by these same laws; therefore, although it is not legal to kill them, they can be beaten.

There is, besides, the office of the Auditori delle sentenze, who review sentences and complaints about other judges; they are three in number and any one of them can intervene. Consideration of the matter is referred to one of the commissions chosen by the judge.

Those who control the grain supply, which the city takes the greatest care over, also have wide responsibilities. The city is divided into six districts. So that no area of the city is unprotected, they select night patrols, one for each of the six [districts], to assist the magistrates.[22] In addition there is a magistracy with responsibility for coining money.

The office of the Procuratori di San Marco is honourable not so much on account of its impressive administrative functions, as because of the authority of those who are usually elected to it. They have charge of the church of San Marco, which they reckon to be the oldest and richest in Venice, and the care of those minors who have no guardian assigned to them by testament or who have one assigned to them who is unable to fulfil the task. It is customary to elect to this office the leading men in the city: those of advanced age who have already held all the other magistracies. This is right and proper, for matters which demand the greatest integrity should only be entrusted to men of the highest quality. When the office of doge is vacant, a new one is usually chosen, by preference, from their number. And they are not permitted to carry on business affairs in their own name, in case they should appear to be profiting from the money of others.

There is no office which does not bring with it a public salary, so that officials are not forced to carry out their duties badly for lack of funds.

In the city there are four major colleges of laymen which were set up for religious purposes; they are called the Scuole grandi and meet frequently to perform sacred devotions.[23] So that no opportunity for revolution is offered by the creation of colleges of this sort, it has been laid down that only a limited number of commoners should be admitted, while as many nobles who ask to join are permitted to do so.

There are heavy taxes on importing and exporting goods, which contribute considerable revenue to the treasury. But almost all of it is used up in paying interest [on loans] and magistrates' salaries. Because of the many serious wars which the city has started or had to endure over a long period of time, it has contracted an almost incalculable public debt. During each war it ordered citizens to make a loan to the treasury, calculated on the basis of their wealth; and now it gives them twenty per cent interest, while the principal of their loans remains unpaid.[24] This expenditure entails a very large sum of money; and since these revenues are regarded as a substitute for investment in property, they can only be bought or held by citizens or by those who have been granted the right by privilege.

Foreigners are also not allowed to buy imported goods from other foreigners; a Venetian citizen must act as an intermediary. Moreover, in the fleet of galleys which they send out each year, partly to patrol the Gulf of the Adriatic and partly to engage in commerce, trading in commodities can only be carried on with money belonging to citizens. Precious merchandise and spices are transported in these galleys; other goods are put into cargo ships.

The galleys are all owned by the government, and no private person is permitted to arm any of them. They are used for five years only, which seems a decent age for a ship, since after that amount of time they no longer appear to be seaworthy. They are then either sold so that they can be refitted, or the wood from which they are made is recycled for other purposes. In naval wars or in any of their expeditions, no foreigner is permitted to be a captain. They do not claim such positions for themselves rashly: the sea is their life and takes up all their waking hours.

By night or day, with or without a lamp, one can walk through the city without a worry. They are so concerned about domestic peace that they do not permit anyone to carry arms.

In addition to the offices already mentioned, there are three Camerlinghi di comun, who receive goods or anything else which is confiscated. It is their job to reclaim public property from anyone who possesses it illegally. They are allowed to take for themselves a quarter of whatever they succeed in recovering. These officials are appointed annually and are members of the Council of the Rogati.

Three other officials, called the Ufficiali del piovego, are also appointed yearly. Their task is to keep the city free from filth and to make sure that the roads are paved, that the rivers are navigable and that usury is not practised within the city. They want their fellow citizens to get rich by legitimate means, not by illegal profits or contracts. For this reason, if they impose a penalty on those who break the law, they receive half for themselves, and the rest is placed in the public treasury. Responsibility for preventing Jews or any other category of person from practising usury was added to the remit of this magistracy when the Venetians decided to expel the Jews (after whom the Giudecca, a district of the city, is called) because they were lending money at usurious rates.[25]

Responsibility for judicial matters is divided up into many parts. The Giudici del forestier deal with visiting foreigners and resident aliens. They are empowered to make judgements in all cases concerning these people, no matter what sum of money is involved. There are three of them, and they are elected annually. Other judges have jurisdiction over the amount levied in tax and are therefore called the Giudici del gran salario; they are three in number and have only limited jurisdiction. There are also three judges who deal with movable property and who are able to pass judgement in cases which involve no more than half a pound of gold.[26] The Giudici di petizion, on the other hand, decide cases involving any sum of money; they have full authority and very wide powers by virtue of their office. Because they can take trials and pass judgements on the basis of right and equity, the office is given only to experienced men, who are chosen by an electoral procedure involving four stages. The Giudici del esaminador deal exclusively with real property. Thus, real property which is either to be sold or given as a dowry is subject to their judgement. It is their job to investigate whether such property can be legally alienated or whether it is bound by restrictions; they determine this through public hearings.

The Procuratori, because of their extensive administrative responsibilities, have a corresponding need for their own judges, who adjudicate in all cases involving those who present petitions of any sort to the public Procuratori.[27] So that nothing appears to be done illegally, the Procuratori never hand over the goods connected with any guardianship or trust unless it is decreed by a decision of the judges. Since there are three publicly instituted administrative divisions of the Procuratori, the six days of the working week are divided among them, with each division having two days assigned to it for legal argument. All these magistracies are appointed annually. And the three men operate individually in such a way that when there is unanimity, it does not breed excessive licence; when it is one against one, discord does not arise; and when there are several different views, confusion is not created.

Four lawyers chosen from among the younger members of the citizenry are appointed to each court, so that they can learn the public law thoroughly and will be able to administer it when the time comes.[28]

Besides these, there are three supply judges, who do not have their own benches, but can operate in any of the courts.[29] So, if another judge is not able to preside at a trial, either on account of sickness or accident or because he is related to someone involved in the case, one of these judges is selected by lot to substitute for him at the trial. There are likewise six lawyers who can plead cases in any court and before any magistracy except the Consoli dei mercanti.[30] These positions, like those mentioned already, are appointed annually.

The three Consoli dei mercanti act as judges in cases concerning merchants and have the power to make decisions in matters involving any sum of money. They hold office for a year.

Venetians prefer each citizen to defend himself without assistance from lawyers, so that the truth can more easily shine forth and so that trials do not become protracted affairs on account of legal sophistries but are instead settled quickly, equitably and justly.

Sopraconsoli are similar in length of tenure and number to the other judges, but they enjoy greater power, in that they can seize anyone who is suspected of being a fugitive, so that he can either give suitable guarantees to his creditors or else plead his case while in custody. Since the goods and riches of merchants consist for the most part in cash and movable property, it is not easy to know the precise extent of each one's fortune. Therefore, estimating wealth in such cases is particularly subject to error. One must add to this the dangers encountered at sea and the devastation which results from disastrous accidents, when a rich man may be impoverished in a flash. It has therefore been necessary to grant considerable power to this magistracy, so that the other party in the dispute does not incur losses. The task of this office is therefore to reconcile with their creditors those debtors who have taken flight or who have been captured when attempting to do so. But since many people carrying on their trade on borrowed money pretended to have suffered losses elsewhere and took flight, and then increased their fortunes to their creditor's grave loss by paying either less than they owed or over too long a period, a law was passed stating that anyone who took flight not out of necessity but on fraudulent grounds would be exiled forever.

Venetians are eager for glory and seek honour more than profit. . . .

Translator's Notes

1 For Coluccio Salutati's letter to Zabarella see J. Kraye, ed., *Cambridge Translations of Renaissance Philosophical Texts,* 1: *Moral Philosophy* (Cambridge, 1997), ch. 16.
2. For an English translation of Bruni's *Laudatio Florentinae urbis* see B. Kohl and R. Witt, eds., *The Earthly Republic and the Italian Humanists* (Philadelphia, 1976), pp. 135–75; on Bruni's use of the *Panathenaicus* of Aristides see H. Baron, *From Petrarch to Leonardo Bruni* (Chicago, 1967), pp. 155–9; see also pp. 232–63 for the Latin text of Bruni's *Laudatio.*
3. For Aristotle's definitions of the three main forms of government (monarchy, aristocracy and democracy) see *Politics* III.5.
4. By the term 'people' (*populus*) Vergerio means the nobility, who by this time made up the political community: see D. Robey and J. Law, 'The Venetian myth and the "De republica veneta" of Pier Paolo Vergerio', *Rinascimento,* 15 (1975), 3–59, at 16. For an earlier account of Venetian government which also stresses its 'mixed' constitution, placing less emphasis, however, on the aristocratic element, see *De quatuor virtutibus cardinalibus* II.16 by the late thirteenth- and early fourteenth-century Dominican, Henry of Rimini: ibid., pp. 54–6.
5. Reading *ostii* instead of *hostii.*
6. Paulus Diaconus, *De gestis Langobardorum,* in J. P. Migne, ed., *Patrologia Latina,* 221 vols. (Paris, 1844–64), XCV, col. 491 (II.14).
7. The *dogado* refers to the territorial jurisdiction of the doge. Lido di Grado is located in the northeast corner of the Adriatic, while Cavarzere is a small town northeast of Rovigo.
8. Caesar, *De bello Gallico* III.8; Vergerio refers to the city of Vannes in Brittany. The distinction between Caesar the author and Celsus the editor of the text is also made by Coluccio Salutati in a letter of 1392: see his *Epistolario,* ed. F. Novati, 4 vols. (Rome, 1892–1911), II, pp. 299–300.
9. Livy, *History of Rome* I.1. The legend of the Trojan origins of Venice was never as popular as that of the foundation of the city by St Mark or the belief that Venice was the new Rome: see Robey and Law, 'Venetian myth', 19.
10. Reading *abstrusis* instead of *obstrusis.*
11. Cf. Boncompagno da Signa, *De malo senectutis et senii,* ed. F. Novati, *Rendiconti della Reale Accademia dei Lincei, classe di scienze morali, storiche e filologiche,* ser. 5, 1 (1892), 49–67, at 57: 'In the city of Venice old people regain strength on account of the temperate climate and moderate diet, and those of medium complexion look radiant.'

12. In *Familiares* VIII.5.14, Petrarch, directly after praising Venice as the most marvellous city he has ever seen, refers to nearby Treviso as the 'home and emporium of delightful living'; it is possible that Vergerio, perhaps citing the passage from memory, conflated the two statements. Petrarch lived in Venice from 1362 until 1367/8: see E. H. Wilkins, *Petrarch's Later Years* (Cambridge, Mass., 1959). For more of Petrarch's comments about Venice, see *Familiares* XI.8; *Seniles* IV.3 and X.2.

13. Cf. Dante, *Inferno* XXI.7–15.

14. Venetians used the term citizen to refer to those who were not of noble birth but nonetheless enjoyed certain legally defined administrative or economic privileges: D. Chambers and B. Pullan, *Venice: A Documentary History 1450–1630* (Oxford, 1992), p. 261; see also pp. 325–52 for foreign communities in Venice.

15. Ascension Day is celebrated on the sixth Thursday, i.e., the fortieth day, after Easter.

16. Vergerio describes the *sposalizio,* the annual ceremony celebrating Venice's marriage to the sea.

17. In Venetian dialect the Council of the Rogati was called the Pregadi and from early in the 1400s, the Senate. Vergerio uses Rogati and Senate interchangeably. He exaggerates the authority of the Rogati; they shared power over the city with the Maggior Consiglio. And it was not until 1413 that the membership was fixed at one hundred, though for a long time it had been customary for the Council of Forty to meet with the sixty members of the Senate: see Robey and Law, 'Venetian myth', 22.

18. By the time Vergerio was writing the Savi grandi were established as six, not four, in number: Robey and Law, 'Venetian myth', 22.

19. Vergerio is mistaken here: the Dieci was composed of ten officials, but they were often joined in deliberations by the doge, his council of six members and the three Avogadori di comun.

20. Only nobleman admitted to the Maggior Consiglio were entitled to become members of councils, hold magistracies and elect others to these positions. Native-born citizens (*cittadini originari*) were permitted to work in the chancery.

21. Venetian laws were codified in statutes.

22. The Signori di notte.

23. On these religious confraternities see B. Pullan, *Rich and Poor in Renaissance Venice: The Social Institutions of a Catholic State, to 1620* (Oxford, 1971).

24. Heavy borrowing was forced on Venice by the War of Chioggia (1378–81). A more stable period followed, in which interest on loans was regularly paid. See Robey and Law, 'Venetian myth', 27; F. C. Lane, *Venice, a Maritime Republic* (Baltimore, 1973), pp. 190–7.

25. The expulsion of the Jews from Venice was decreed on 3 April 1395: see Robey and Law, 'Venetian myth', 29; and P. Molmenti, *Venice: The Middle Ages* (Bergamo, 1906), p. 194. On the Jews in Venice during this period see R. Calimani, *Storia del Ghetto di Venezia* (Milan, 1985), ch. 1.

26. The Giudici del mobile.

27. The Giudici del procurator.

28. The Avocati pizoli.

29. The Giudici di ogni corte.

30. The Avocati di ogni corte.

Further Reading

CHRP, pp. 416–17, 839

Gilbert, F., 'The Venetian constitution in Florentine political thought', in N. Rubinstein, ed., *Florentine Studies: Politics and Society in Renaissance Florence* (London, 1968), pp. 463–500, esp. 468

Hyde, J. K., 'Medieval descriptions of cities', *Bulletin of the John Rylands Library,* 48 (1966), 308–40

Robey, D., 'Humanism and education in the early Quattrocento: the *De ingenuis moribus* of P. P. Vergerio', *Bibliothèque d'humanisme et Renaissance,* 42 (1980), 27–58

'Pier Paolo Vergerio the Elder: republicanism and civic values in the work of an early humanist', *Past and Present,* 58 (1973), 3–37

9

George of Trebizond

JOHN MONFASANI

Introduction

George of Trebizond (Trapezuntius; 1396–c. 1472) was born in Crete, which was then part of the Venetian empire. In 1417 he moved to Venice, where he was employed as a Greek scribe by the patrician humanist Francesco Barbaro. In addition to his accomplishments as a Greek scholar, George acquired an excellent knowledge of Latin and was the first to present Byzantine rhetorical doctrines to Western scholars. He also produced an introductory textbook on dialectic. Having converted to Roman Catholicism, he began to work in the papal Curia in 1440 and soon embarked on a series of Latin translations of important Greek texts, including Eusebius's *Praeparatio evangelica,* Ptolemy's *Almagest* (on which he also wrote a commentary), several Aristotelian treatises (the *Rhetoric, Physics, Problems, De anima, De generatione et corruptione, De caelo, Historia animalium, De partibus animalium* and *De generatione animalium*), as well as two dialogues of Plato (the *Laws* and *Parmenides*). After landing in prison on account of a brawl with a fellow humanist in the Curia, George moved to Naples in 1452 but returned to Rome three years later.

A bizarre combination of paranoia and delusions of grandeur led George to believe that he was destined to rescue the world from impending doom by converting sultan Mehmed II to Christianity. His self-appointed mission in 1465–6 to Constantinople, which had recently fallen to the Turks, not only ended in failure (he never even met the sultan) but also resulted in his second spell in prison, this time on the charges of apostasy and heresy. The doom which George was attempting to prevent with his ill-fated trip to Constantinople was a revival of paganism, under the guise of the renewed interest in Platonism. His *Comparison of Plato and Aristotle* (1458) was an attempt to unmask the true enemy of Christendom, the paganizing Platonist George Gemistos Plethon and his former student, Cardinal Bessarion. The cardinal replied to George's intemperate polemic with his *Against the Slanderer of Plato* (1469),[1] the fifth book of which was devoted to pointing out 255 mistakes in George's Latin version of Plato's *Laws,* a work he had translated in the early 1450s at the request of Pope Nicholas V.[2] As with his translation of the *Parmenides* (1458–9), which was commissioned by Cardinal Nicholas of Cusa, George was not in the position to refuse the request of a powerful patron, despite his distaste for Plato.[3]

Nor was George beyond exploiting his work as a translator of Plato, however reluctantly undertaken, for his own personal profit. In December 1451 he wrote to his former patron Francesco Barbaro, announcing his discovery that the Venetians must have studied Plato's *Laws,* for they seem to have modelled their constitution on his prescription that a long-lasting and happy government needed to combine elements of one-man rule, aristocracy and democracy. Barbaro, delighted by this notion, told George that he would receive a rich reward from the Venetians if he dedicated the translation to them and further elaborated the comparison between Plato's theories and their own political practice.[4] Soon after his departure from Rome in 1452, George abandoned the dedication he had originally made to Pope Nicholas V (with whom he had now fallen out) and wrote a new one to Barbaro.

At the beginning of the fifteenth century Pier Paolo Vergerio had hinted that the success of Venice was due to the fact that its aristocratic government was tempered by monarchical and democratic elements (see Chapter 8). But it was George, in his dedication to Barbaro, who formulated the notion that Venice was a realization of the classical ideal of the mixed constitution, as set out by Plato in the account of Sparta's government which he gives in Books III (692–3) and IV (712D–E) of the *Laws*.[5] According to George, the Maggior Consiglio was the democratic feature of Venetian government; the Senate represented the aristocratic element; and the doge held the position of monarch. This theory was to prove one of the most powerful and enduring aspects of the myth of Venice.[6]

Unfortunately, however, for George, Barbaro died in 1454, soon after he received the dedication copy of the translation, thus ending George's hopes of immediate remuneration. But, finally, after rededicating the work to the doge, George was appointed by the Senate to the chair of humanities and rhetoric in the School of San Marco, a position he held from 1460 to 1462.

The original Latin text of the preface is published in J. Monfasani, ed., *Collectanea Trapezuntiana: Texts, Documents and Bibliographies of George of Trebizond* (Binghamton, N.Y., 1984), pp. 198–202.

Preface to His Translation of Plato's Laws

The preface of George of Trebizond to his translation from Greek into Latin of Plato's book *The Laws*, dedicated to Francesco Barbaro, the illustrious Senator of the Venetian Republic and the Procurator of San Marco, and through him to the republic herself.

Honourable sir and finest senator of the Venetian Republic, when I finished my recent translation into Latin of Plato's book the *Laws,* the facts of the matter suggested to me – indeed, to tell the truth, impelled me – to offer my labour to your republic and dedicate the translation to the citizens of the very illustrious and celebrated city of Venice. Just as this book eclipses the other works of Plato in the opinion of our forefathers (for in it Plato surpassed and outdid himself in eloquence), so too the Venetian Republic certainly exceeds by far in justice, greatness of spirit and the other virtues, as well as in the arts of war and peace, all the free cities which have existed in the past and, I venture to say, will exist in the future, be they under democratic or aristocratic governments. Furthermore, if anyone carefully and thoroughly examines the laws which Plato ordained for his city in order to ensure its permanence and liberty, he will not be able to deny, I believe, that the original founders of Venetian liberty took from Plato the first glimmerings from which they established the government of their city and that they did so in such a way that from the Platonic rivulets much greater rivers have flowed and far greater splendours have shone forth from their constitution than Plato himself had ever imagined for his own republic or, for that matter, than anyone else had ever thought of.

Plato thinks that the liberty of a city will be neither stable nor permanent unless it bears a resemblance to three seemingly praiseworthy types of city: the city governed by a single ruler, the city governed by an élite or aristocracy and the city governed by the people. But Plato said this in a way which only the Venetians understood and the truth of which only they were able to confirm in actual practice. For the Venetians obey a single ruler.[7] They also have an elected élite, distinguished by its prudence, justice and high reputation, which stands ready to advise the republic on all matters of war and peace.[8] Nor have they neglected to incorporate an element which resembles popular government; in fact, they give real power to the people, for all those who are not part [of the government] of the republic meet in the Council, which is responsible for creating the magistrates.[9]

Plato commands that in his city the guardians of the law constitute the supreme magistrates. The Venetians have availed themselves of these guardians – or, as some would call them, censors – of the law, giving them the specific charge of looking into everything and of observing and listening to everything, in order to prevent anything contrary to the law not only from being approved, but even from being said. The very name of this magistrate seems to me to have been taken from Plato; for is there any real difference between 'guardians of the law' and 'advocates and defenders of the republic'?[10]

Plato creates magistrates by means of popular votes of the utmost refinement, which are removed from all suspicion by their manifold complexity. What about your forefathers? Did they not prudently establish as a tradition for later generations these very procedures which you rightly continue to follow? In point of fact, I would argue that never before Plato nor since his time until today have there been voting procedures for the selection of magistrates of such complexity as those which he discussed and which you yourselves realize in practice.[11] There are many other things which show the Platonic erudition of your forefathers and which make even more patently clear their remarkable practical experience and singular prudence.

I am not at all surprised that they read and understood Plato. In those days almost all of Italy knew Greek, and the men of the higher nobility in Italy, who founded the city of Venice by joining together to fend off the iniquities of the times, were as well versed in Greek literature as they were in Latin. What never ceases to amaze me, however, is that they achieved in practice everything of which they approved and that, in fact, they did so with results better than Plato had drawn up [for his city]. They surely would never have been able to achieve this if they had not been men of truly extraordinary natural ability, learning and practical experience, endowed with every kind of virtue. Many people are able to perceive and approve of what is good and useful, but there are also many who find it incredibly difficult to consent to, and agree upon, what they approve, especially before they are constrained and bound to do so by law. I would say it was impossible if I did not have the example of your republic before my eyes. In the many centuries before and after the founding of Venice did anyone who was even the slightest bit learned fail to understand what Plato wrote in relation to ensuring the permanence of a city? Did anyone, furthermore, who understood it not also approve of it? But it all seemed to be so many fables, fictions and total impossibilities. And why not? Our immoderate desires lead us to pillage each other. We are bursting at the seams to give orders, while being at the same time incapable of obeying them. Consequently, no one before had even tried to establish a republic of this kind.

Plato himself had no hope that his laws could ever be enacted unless the people were forced into using them by some tyrant who would set himself up as a ruler with such self-control that even while he was alive his people would become accustomed to exercising this freedom. Plato openly admits that unless some tyrant were to appear who was willing to do this, his laws would be without a city.[12] The founders of Venice, therefore, surpassed all other men in every virtue and in civil science inasmuch as they turned into reality the ideal of the Platonic city, not coerced by a tyrant, but rather following their own inner convictions. And — what is utterly astounding — they established a city that was far better than the one portrayed by Plato, a man whom the pagans described as more eloquent than Jupiter himself.

Even leaving aside the other proofs, in order not to go on for too long, how stupendous are the items which I have already listed! The ruler of Venice is elected not for a year, but for life, and not merely so that he might be a strong ruler possessed of first-hand knowledge and experience, but also so that the majesty of the republic does not seem to be lowered and debased through an annual changing of leaders. The nobles elected to the Senate are men knowledgeable in divine and human matters, distinguished by their piety and devotion to their creator and recognized for their eloquence and culture. The senators, as their name itself suggests, are men deemed worthy of having their judgement [*sententia*] solicited. As for the people: is it not the case that, though of course when compared to the senators, they are the people, in actual fact, considered as individuals who enter the Council, they are all patricians and senators, not some confused multitude or idle and seditious rabble? All this is new. Why, it is unheard of! It is not even a human invention, but rather a divine gift that has been given to you alone. You are all patricians and senators, and you all in turn flow back, as it were, into the people. This is why you alone know both how to give orders and how to obey them in an upright and kindly manner.

It is obvious that the Venetians, taking the germ of their constitution from Plato, but not disregarding the example of earlier constitutions, conceived[13] and brought into actual existence something so much better and nobler that if one were to construct in one's mind the absolute best republic, one would not imagine anything other than the Republic of Venice. You Venetians have not left any room for improvement!

Spiders' webs and children's games are what I think of when someone starts to go on about the wonderful cities of the ancients. Why is that? Shall we compare the Athenians with the Venetians? I would rather not go into the question of the very brief duration of the Athenian Empire, or I will seem to be talking about what resulted from fortune rather than from a flaw in their republic. I do say this, however: that angry populace did not acquire its empire because of the soundness of its institutions; but rather it ruled because of the uncommon valour of a few men. Yet, after receiving the greatest benefits from these generals, the Athenians so raged against them that their fury has remained as much a subject of discussion as the illustrious deeds of the generals themselves[14] — such was the disorder of this government of the people, which, as Plato says, was nothing more than the people. The liberty of the Spartans lasted much longer; but it included no naval glory, nor did it shine with a dignity worthy of the majesty of empire. Always lusting after victory, the Spartans excelled, as we all know, solely in ground warfare.

The Roman Republic, to be sure, was of vast extent; but its liberty did not last long because the government almost never stayed the same, nor did it ever stand firm in itself. Instead, in the manner of a chameleon, the Roman Republic changed from one thing to another on a daily basis. As a result, its empire was unified not because of the unity of the state, but rather because it had been founded by one city, which occupied one place. Transmuting itself from one day to the next and always divided, it was never one state. For this reason, I myself doubt if it ought even to be called a state. No one could live quietly in his own home. The city was racked so continually by internecine wars and seditions that it often undertook external wars as a substitute for peace. Many Romans entered the military simply to enjoy a more peaceful life.

The Venetian Republic, on the other hand, is the dwelling place of justice and the mistress of peace. She never undertakes war except for the sake of peace. She never exchanges peace for war. For more than ten centuries now she has continually had an empire of vast dimensions extending over land and sea from the utmost recesses of the Adriatic to the furthest extremity of Greece. She has now also extended her empire over a large and celebrated part of Italy. Her wealth, her power, her resources have grown to such an extent, by the grace of God and her own virtue, that it seems that nothing can be added to her. There are no factions, no sedition, no trace of dissension. All these things surpass to such a degree what we can say by way of admiration that the only thing left for us is to stand silently in utter amazement. Therefore, if I may briefly make one point, I shall bring this preface to a close.

Below the level of their ruler, all those who govern the Republic of Venice seem to be distributed into two orders: that of the patriciate and that of the people.[15] They enter into both orders in turn. But to me they all, in fact, seem to be kings; for they live in the manner of kings, and they yield to kings neither in authority nor in dignity. They even surpass kings in their practice and knowledge of divine and human matters. Surely, therefore, no one who has ever seen Venice will deny that this state was established and this city founded in the midst of the sea in a way that was beyond [the capacity of] human wealth and design: it came into being not by human counsel but by the will of God, not by the judgement of men but by divine providence.

I have therefore chosen to offer and dedicate my labour, however insignificant it might be, to this divine republic, which fell to us from heaven. I do so through you; for, since I had to give this work to one person through whom it might also redound to all the others and to the republic itself, to whom better ought it to be inscribed than to Francesco Barbaro, a man distinguished by lineage, by learning and by prudence and also an outstanding senator of the republic? Furthermore – and this is especially important to me – I owe to you my start in mastering Latin; for after God, you were the cause of my coming to Italy from Greece and dedicating myself to the study of Latin literature. Therefore, to the republic in which I was born[16] and educated and to you, through whom I was (as I would put it) reborn, I offer this expression of my thanks, the greatest I am capable of, unworthy though it may be. There is also the fact that your expertise in Latin and Greek not merely requires, but emphatically demands, that whatever I translate from Greek into Latin about a republic, and especially about the Republic of Venice, should not be published until it has received your approval and can thereby escape the lash of critics. And there is yet another reason why I feel impelled to dedicate this work to you: your authority has gained you a place among the first men of the aristocracy and a position of high leadership in this the best of republics.

Therefore, honourable sir, may it please you to accept this work which I dedicate to you and through you to the Venetian Republic. And if in translating your Plato I have not achieved his divine eloquence, may you allow me to hide behind the shield of your authority. This is all the easier for you to do because you excel in both Latin and Greek and because from youth you have discharged most brilliantly the duties of a translator.

Translator's Notes

1. For selections from Book II of Bessarion's treatise see J. Kraye, ed., *Cambridge Translations of Renaissance Philosophical Texts,* I: *Moral Philosophy* (Cambridge, 1997), ch. 12.
2. For his dedicatory preface to Nicholas V see J. Monfasani, *George of Trebizond: A Biography and a Study of His Rhetoric and Logic* (Leiden, 1976), pp. 360–4 (appendix X).
3. For his candid comments on the *Laws* see the annotations to the translation, published in J. Monfasani, ed., *Collectanea Trapezuntiana: Texts, Documents and Bibliographies of George of Trebizond* (Binghamton, N.Y., 1984), pp. 744–7; e.g., he says of Plato: 'Alas, the silly man!' 'The foolish man implies that he is a god'; 'The man ought to be stoned!'
4. For these letters see M. A. Querini, ed., *Francisci Barbari et aliorum ad ipsum epistolae* (Brescia, 1743), pp. 290, 292–5.
5. George also discusses this idea in his *Comparationes phylosophorum Aristotelis et Platonis* (Venice, 1523; reprinted Frankfurt am Main, 1965), sigs. R8^r–S1^v. The classical ideal of the mixed constitution is found as well in the Greek historian Polybius and in Aristotle, *Politics* IV.
6. It was taken up, a century later, by Gasparo Contarini, in his influential *De magistratibus et republica Venetorum* (Paris, 1543); see the extract in D. Chambers and B. Pullan, eds., *Venice: A Documentary History 1450–1630* (Oxford, 1992), pp. 41–3.
7. That is, the doge.
8. That is, the Senate.
9. That is, Maggior Consiglio, in which all adult Venetian noblemen had the right to participate. The Maggior Consiglio elected from its membership the members of the Senate as well as of the various Venetian councils and boards.
10. George is referring to the Venetian officials known as the Avogadori di comun, who acted as the state attorneys.
11. For a brief overview of these procedures see F. C. Lane, *Venice: A Maritime Republic* (Baltimore, 1973), pp. 110–11.
12. See Plato, *Laws* IV (709E–712A); see also IV (835C).
13. Reading *peperisse* instead of *peperissa.*
14. George is referring to the Athenians' treatment of Miltiades, Themistocles, Cimon and Pericles. Book III, chapter 6, of his *Comparationes phylosophorum Platonis et Aristotelis* (Venice, 1523), sigs. O5^r–P2^r, is given over to a discussion of these four Athenian leaders. Valerius Maximus speaks of the Athenian treatment of Miltiades, Cimon and Themistocles in his *Facta et dicta memorabilia* V.3.ext. 3 ('On the ungrateful').
15. The Venetian population was divided between the patriciate class (the two per cent of families who were allowed to enter the Maggior Consiglio) and the *popolani* (itself divided into well-to-do commoners or *popolo grande* and workers or *popolo minuto*).
16. Crete, George's birthplace, belonged to Venice at this time.

Further Reading

CHRP, pp. 71, 77, 82, 88, 93–8, 194, 417, 458, 561–3, 566–7, 728–9, 743, 749, 785, 789, 820
Classen, C. J., 'The rhetorical works of George of Trebizond and their debt to Cicero', *Journal of the Warburg and Courtauld Institutes,* 56 (1993), 75–84

Gaeta, F., 'Giorgio da Trebisonda, le *Leggi* di Platone e la costituzione di Venezia', *Istituto storico italiano per il medio evo e Archivio Muratoriano. Bulletino,* 82 (1970), 479–501

Hankins, J., *Plato in the Italian Renaissance,* 2 vols. (Leiden, 1991), I, pp. 165–92; II, pp. 429–35, 445–8

Klibansky, R., 'Plato's *Parmenides* in the Middle Ages and the Renaissance', in his *The Continuity of the Platonic Tradition during the Middle Ages* (Munich, 1981), pp. 289–304

Monfasani, J., *George of Trebizond: A Biography and a Study of His Rhetoric and Logic* (Leiden, 1976)

10

Poggio Bracciolini

MARTIN DAVIES

Introduction

The ancient lessons were absorbed in modern Latin writings on a wide range of ethical and historical topics, to which the Italian humanist Poggio Bracciolini (1380–1459) devoted the latter half of his scholarly life.[1] Morality and history were not clearly distinguished, since history was always for him moral philosophy teaching by example. The stormy vicissitudes of the fifteenth-century papacy and the many different states, in Italy and beyond, of which Poggio had direct experience, gave ample material for moralizing reflection, usually gloomy. Less highly worked than his treatises, but more immediately accessible nowadays, are the six hundred or so Latin letters which illuminate his daily life as bureaucrat, scholar and author. Even more popular at the time and later were the *Facetiae,* or ribald tales, which he gathered together in old age. He was also known as one of the fiercest polemicists of his day.

The moral basis of Poggio's approach to politics comes across very clearly in his tract on the Venetian constitution here translated. For a Florentine who had spent much of his life in papal service at Rome, it was a surprising topic — we do not know that he ever set foot in Venice. But he had good friends there, and at this time (very near the end of his life, in the late 1450s) little reason to love his home-town. Besides that, he could turn his hand, in good humanist fashion, to praise of the Venetian state as readily as to praise of law or medicine or whatever he was not by temperament totally against.

In so doing he helped to transmit and reinforce what has become known as the 'myth of Venice', previously disseminated by Pier Paolo Vergerio and George of Trebizond (see Chapters 8 and 9). This conception of the city, widely shared beyond the Veneto, arose from its peculiar geographical position and its seemingly unchanging nature from its distant and privileged beginnings. Venice was seen as a uniquely stable state, and it was thought to owe its stability to the special and permanent excellence of its constitutional arrangements. Its supposed freedom from internal disharmony and devotion to justice gave Venice a continuous history of liberty which was, and for centuries to come remained, the envy of all other Italian states. Poggio stresses what became in the fifteenth century a standard element of the myth: the civic cohesion derived from combining the best features of the best constitutions recognized by Aristotle; characteristically, he omits the democratic element which earlier and later writers joined to the obvious monarchical and aristocratic features of the Venetian state.

For the Latin text of *De laude Venetiarum* see Poggio Bracciolini, *Opera omnia,* ed. R. Fubini, 4 vols. (Turin, 1964–9), II, pp. 925–37.

In Praise of the Venetian Republic

I have long desired to praise as best I could the singular excellence in every department of the Venetian Republic, but have hitherto been prevented by my many occupations of an official and domestic sort, as well as by a certain diffidence as to whether I could find eloquence equal to the task. Now that I enjoy greater leisure, however, and bearing in mind that fortune favours the brave, I have resolved to set out in writing what I had long had in mind, with the double aim of celebrating such a magnificent city as it deserves and of encouraging other cities to imitate the institutions of this well-ordered republic by a rehearsal of their merits. If ever there has been a republic that deserved praise and celebration, if ever any held in honour the prescriptions of justice, if any ever through its good customs has maintained dignity and respect in all its dealings both public and private, if there has ever been any where the common good was put before private advantage, that republic is surely Venice, a city whose repute eclipses all others that have ever been, or are or may be in future.

As Aristotle says, there are various sorts of constitution, of which two in particular stand out from the rest, namely monarchy and aristocracy, or what we call government by the best.[2] Indeed, Cicero says in *De legibus* that the best sort of constitution is that in which the best men, as he chooses to call them, are in power:[3] men motivated by desire for praise and esteem, who keep their fatherland safe, true lovers of the republic. Such a constitution, I can say with confidence, has only ever been found in Venice. With the Venetians, only the best govern the state, under constraint of the laws, and intent, everyone of them, on the advantage of the commonwealth without consideration of personal gain.

Aristotle never saw such an aristocracy, nor indeed had he read about the existence of one. For if he had ever had occasion to study this polity, in which one noble is set above the others as head,[4] though himself obedient to the rule of law, while the other aristocrats like the limbs of a body attached to the head follow the dictates of justice as a sure guide to action, he would doubtless have given this form of government preference over all others. Here he would have seen a quasi-king, as it were, and after him the aristocrats acting together with a common mind and a common voice for a common goal: the combination of monarchy and aristocracy in a single constitution. We must necessarily think that this is the best form of government of all. In fact, Aristotle himself says that it is better to be ruled by many good men than by one only.[5] In that case a monarchy must be inferior to an aristocratically governed republic in proportion as the talents of many people are more extensive and abundant and in practice better than that of one man alone, just as the benefits they bring would diffuse more widely than those of a single person; and their wisdom and integrity would carry with them greater advantages than his virtues could by themselves. This was the view of Lampridius in the *Life of Alexander Severus,* where he says:

Your grace is well aware of the saying you will have read with regard to Marius Maximus, that a republic is better, and so to say in safer hands, when the prince alone is bad than when the prince's friends are bad, for one bad man may be set straight by many good ones, but no one man, no matter how good, can possibly prevail over many bad ones.[6]

How then shall we judge a republic which joins to a good leader excellent advisers and bends to one united will the talents of many men? Obviously, it is to be thought a very happy state of affairs and such a republic will be supreme above all others, even if Aristotle never knew it.

I imagine that Plato too, had he been able to examine this remarkable manner of governing a city, would have taken it as the model of his *Republic*.[7] There he sought the best possible form a republic might take, having laid down that it must be based on justice. Justice was in turn secured by reward and punishment, so that the good were encouraged to seek praise by having their virtue rewarded, while the bad were to be deterred from wrongdoing by the prospect of having their misdeeds punished. And this must be the very state that the philosophers were looking for, since it is on their principles that the republic is founded: here justice has mastery over all, and through justice the good are honoured and the evil punished, as each deserves.

To bring out more clearly by comparison the special qualities of Venice in the operation of justice, let us look at some ancient constitutional arrangements and the practices of antiquity. The Spartans come in for great praise for having supposedly lived for almost seven hundred years with the same set of laws and absolutely invariable customs.[8] But their form of government was always changing, and their state never stayed the same for long – now subject to kings, now to tyrants, now torn apart by different factions, now shaken with internecine feuds. All this shows that Sparta was by no means a peaceful and contented state but deeply unhappy and turbulent, given over not so much to the public weal as to private hatreds; and so at length, after many disasters, it passed under Roman sway.

The nature of the constitution enjoyed by the state of Athens is explained by the Greek historians. Power of decision on all questions rested with the common people, and what was agreed by plebiscite was taken to be ratified and binding. When the mob had been roused by these decisions, the leading aristocrats were apt to be expelled from the city, excellent citizens would be condemned to death by sentence of the people, their chief commanders punished by exile or prison. Athens was in turn in thrall to kings or cruel tyrants, or prey to the fickleness of the common people – a perverse city indeed, that rewarded the good service of its military commanders with all sorts of trouble, a city constantly unsettled by discord within or wars abroad, where reprobates were preferred to honest men, and scoundrels were actually summoned to occupy the offices of state. It was accordingly no surprise that their liberty was soon lost.

Similar failings led to the collapse of the state of Thebes, as it fell under the alternating sway of the more powerful citizens and of tyrants, or was troubled by faction within the state: you might say it was more a mass of competing interests than a republic.

It is said that Carthage was a great and powerful republic, which engaged in a struggle for supremacy with the Romans over almost four hundred years.[9] But we also read that it had a variety of administrations, all characterized by cruelty and barbarous savagery. It is certainly true that it either killed or exiled its generals, despite all their great qualities. So it is to be viewed more as a haughty and violent tyranny than as a proper republic.

The Roman Republic was the greatest that has ever been seen and is celebrated above all the rest. In literature and oratory it equalled or surpassed all others, and in the arts of war it was without rival. It had many men of great stature across the whole range of human endeavour. Yet everyone knows the number and nature of the revolutions that took place in the free republic from the very beginning – the sudden reversals of fortune, the quarrels and feuds, the uprisings of a fickle populace, the great and frequent struggles between the fatherland and the mob, the trials of strength between the senators and consuls on one side and the tribunes of the people on the other. Alienation and hatred, wars which went beyond mere civil war,[10] theft and plunder, proscription of citizens and fine men driven into exile – in short, there arose in the republic commotions without number, like a stormy sea whipped up by the constant battering of waves. I shall not rehearse the acts of theft and sacrilege, the rapes and killings, the wrecking of cities, committed by consuls, praetors and other magistrates, nor the lust and greed of the Roman soldiery. I pass over the dreadful despotism showed towards subjects and the terrible crimes perpetrated in the provinces due to the unspeakable passions of our ancestors. Cicero witnesses that more allied cities were destroyed by quartering Roman soldiers than enemy cities by the force of their arms.[11] I shall not mention the various coups launched against the republic and the vast lands that were given over to Roman avarice. Why bring up Verres and Clodius and Catiline and all those other conspirators who were born for the destruction of Rome and her provinces?[12] I think it would be accurate to say that for many centuries Rome was not a republic at all but a den of thieves and a despotism of the cruellest sort. Neither law nor morals nor traditional institutions nor the courts counted for anything. Egged on by the tribunes, the order of the day was might and cold steel, leading to slaughter in the forum and in the temples. Cicero himself complained that the republic no longer existed, nor the courts nor the Senate, but everything was done at Caesar's whim.[13] There was a time with the early Romans when the republic deserved the name; but even then one has to take into account the Secession of the Plebs,[14] the wilfulness of the decemvirs,[15] the exiles of Coriolanus[16] and Camillus.[17]

The Venetian Republic, on the other hand, is very different from those of bygone ages – it is quite without those faults and vices which have been the ruin of other cities and republics. There is no discord or dissent among the Venetians as to how to govern the republic, no feuding between citizens, no factions or quarrelling, no open enmities. All of them take the same view, all of them with one mind rush to the aid of the republic, to which they direct their constant thoughts and on whose welfare they spend all their effort. Their whole aim and object is that their state should be as happy as possible. This may seem a thing very difficult to achieve in such a great city, but it will not surprise anyone who considers their manner of government. There are a great many very ancient noble families with whom the governance of the republic lies. No commoner is granted the opportunity of civic service, public office being reserved for the nobility, and of the nobility only the foremost men. One and all accordingly behave like the limbs of a single body and act together with one mind for the city's safety and well-being, regarding it as if it were their own mother who was to be cherished and cared for.

The virtues of this city, then, are rightly thought to surpass by far all others. The most conclusive proof is the fact that for seven hundred years and more, down to our own day, the Venetians have persisted with the same customs and institutions based on the laws, the doge and magistrates – something which has never occurred in any other republic.

Of all the many qualities to be praised in this marvellous state, the first is perhaps its location, which in my view adds greatly to the credit of the city. It is so situated that although it is has no encircling walls nor ramparts to defend it, the Venetians could not be safer or less fearful of siege engines or machines of war. No sudden charge or unexpected enemy attack holds terrors for them. Surrounded on all sides by sea, Venice is free from external threat, being five miles from the mainland and reachable only by sailing through banked channels, so that there is nothing to fear from that quarter. It is also equipped with only one port, which bigger ships cannot enter when they are laden; and the Venetian galleys and other boats can easily block off the approach of any enemy fleet. In all other parts the water is stagnant and marshy and cannot be used by large vessels. There is therefore nothing to fear either from cavalry attack or enemy ships. There is besides a broad wall of heaped-up boulders some twenty miles long, which is kept stable by great wooden piles:[18] this serves to protect the city from the full force of the waves and keeps the marshy lagoon undisturbed.

What is truly remarkable – the great glory and ornament of Venice – is the vast Arsenal with its magnificent shipyards, which far surpass any others in the world and for whose maintenance special levies are raised. Here are berthed more than 100 galleys, all fitted out with weapons (to say nothing of those used for trade), and a great many cargo ships: they could if need be set to sea with a fully fitted-out fleet of 150 large ships inside a month. As for smaller vessels, they have an almost infinite number, the greatest part of them adapted to the transport of vital supplies. As one would expect, everything that is needed to support such a large city is imported in great abundance, so that the Venetians need fear no scarcity. The great number of ships makes a fine sight as they come and go, now to nearby places, now as far away as Pontus and the Black Sea and other ports of the infidels, besides trading voyages to Spain and France, Flanders and Britain. It is a great spectacle of the city to see them returning laden down with their various cargoes and then transferring their goods for transport to other parts of the Mediterranean or Italy.

I need not describe the splendours of their homes and palaces, the sumptuously built churches, the squares and public places – a whole city packed with craftsmen. Nor need I dwell on the modesty of the young or the dignity of the old, the natural authority of the men or the majesty of the Senate, of which one could truly say what Cineas said of the Roman Senate, that it seems to be made up of kings.[19] Indeed, all the citizens have an air of grandeur about them, with their fine clothes and elegant possessions, on which they lavish a good deal of care. In addition, the whole city is criss-crossed by canals as well as paved streets, and this brings them considerable advantages, since everything that they need for daily life can be brought to their homes in boats. The chief glory of Venice, however, is the size and splendour of the churches, which the Venetians adorn with various objects for religious veneration. But this they have in common with many other places. Where they really stand out from the rest is in the treasure of the church of San Marco, whose opulence and ornament make a marvellous sight. There is a great mass of silver and gold, and of pearls too and the so-called precious stones, which are both rare and highly prized.

I shall turn now to my second theme, the rational and orderly system under which everything is administered and carried out at Venice, and say something of the group of magistrates to whom the government of the republic has been entrusted from the very foundation of the city. From the beginning, the citizens elected a doge to act as their head, a man who was to be set above the rest and who would act in the republic's interests. Yet he is still subject to the rule of law, and though of a higher status he is on a level with all the rest when it comes to observing the laws. If he commits a crime, for example, he is duly punished by a magistrate according to legal prescription. On his own he is without power: he may not act in the name of the republic without being obliged to consult a committee of six men,[20] whose advice is binding; he cannot write state letters, open those brought before him or give any audience or official response. The council of six has the real power in the state, always subject to the laws. It is elected by vote of the Senate and may be removed by its decision, if the need arises, but nearly all members die in office. It may still be brought to trial, all the same, if it should act in any way that deserves censure. But the fact that, as they say, no doge has ever aspired to tyranny, save for one who paid with his life,[21] shows how deeply rooted in the Venetian mentality is the respect for decency and justice, and how modestly the doges have lived over these many centuries. And that unique case is all the more remarkable since ambition and the love of power are such widespread failings among mankind. But with the Venetians patriotism extinguishes all other passions and casts out whatever mad longings men may have.

They realize that they are the guardians, and not the masters, of the laws. They realize that they share with others the responsibility for governing the city and are not entrusted with absolute power. The special merit of their laws is that they are completely solid and stable, and they remain in force as long as they continue to serve the republic. They are not repealed at the whim of individuals nor amended from day to day, but are kept safe by perpetual sanctions. Besides those I have mentioned, there are also ten men selected annually from the leading citizens, to whom is given the power of judgement over wrongdoers of all sorts in proportion to their crimes.[22] There is no appeal from their sentence, and their decisions may not be reopened. There is a special magistracy concerned with administration of the law, before whom cases of citizens and foreigners are tried.[23] The proceedings are not conducted on the basis of allegations written down by notaries or the trickery of professional advocates, but by equity, moderation and reason; this leads to a great saving of both time and expense. Nor do they place any reliance on outsiders to administer or deliver justice. Members of the magistracies themselves deliver the law, and their decisions are so temperate that there is seldom any dissent from them.

To these must be added the so-called Procurators of San Marco, men of probity and authority elected from the entire body of citizens, whose function is to supervise the finances of the church. They disburse for pious purposes any surplus remaining after the religious services and upkeep of the fabric have been seen to. There are also what are called officers of the night,[24] whose task is to mete out appropriate punishment for minor crimes, especially those committed at night.

In addition, there is a smaller assembly of two hundred men, called the Rogati, in whose meetings all those magistrates I have mentioned take part. In these sessions the doge presides on a raised dais, the rest being seated after him according to their status. Here decisions are reached after discussion on all matters concerning the state of the republic, and in particular on matters of war and peace. When the need arises, they convene an additional, larger Council [Maggior Consiglio], of which all nobles over the age of twenty are members. By their votes are elected all the governors and other officials who are entrusted with administering the provinces and towns outside the city, as well as those chosen for some special mission. It is open to all who may chance to be at this meeting to nominate and elect anyone they wish. The nominees who are elected by vote of the Council are obliged by law to give those who nominated them a certain cash sum. In this way two virtuous acts are rewarded: that of the man who nominates someone worthy of office, and that of the nominee if he achieves office. Rivalry and contention among the citizens are thus centred on virtue and not on hatred or violence. All of them strive to become men of such high moral character in the eyes of their fellows that they will get more votes than the other candidates.[25] And votes are not won by campaigning or solicitation; so the path to high office lies open to the very best. Each of them thinks that they too share in the success if they nominate someone who is thought deserving of office by the Senate's vote. I remember that certain persons were once subject to a heavy fine for having solicited votes for a friend. In public affairs, they want men's judgement to be completely free, not bought with cash or entreaties. It therefore seldom happens that anyone is selected to govern others unless his own integrity has been tried and tested. If any governor shows himself greedy and cruel in relation to his subjects beyond what the law allows, severe punishment follows. The victims are allowed to make complaints and seek protection from injustice. The Venetian governors therefore keep their hands free of any stain of wrongful conduct, always acting in accordance with the laws, which are entirely devised with a view to the promotion of justice.

This manner of life, these habits and arrangements have never changed since they came into being. The city is governed with such reverence and equity, political power is so evenly distributed to all in office, honours are so equitably granted to the citizens, that the state appears to be preserved in this marvellous concord not by men's devices but by divine assent, not by an earthly monarchy but by some heavenly kingdom. Their whole concern and object, each and every one of them, is what they think will benefit the republic. If ever there is a diversity of opinion, as sometimes happens when matters of peace and war are being debated, the view of the majority is approved and followed, and even those who dissent will change their vote to conform with the larger party. No one perseveres in obstinate opposition, no hatreds or feuding unsettles the republic. Everyone permits his view to succumb to that of the majority. And so it happens that differing opinions are reduced to unanimity and are not the occasion of faction or conspiracy among the citizens. You would think that they were all of one will, one heart and one mind, one united view. No household with any decent man at its head, no brothers or relations ever seek their own private benefit with such concord and fellow feeling as the Venetians show in maintaining the standing and prestige of their city. No one consults his own interests in their deliberations but all keep the common good in view.

A special merit of the Venetians is that when someone is condemned for a crime, sentence is carried out as soon as he is caught. Justice takes its course without special pleading or mitigation, without evasion or intercession on anyone's part. Exiles are rarely allowed to return to the city without paying the penalty. And though the Venetians are harsh in the administration of justice, they are nevertheless at the same time very reasonable. If a man is deprived of his offices for his sins, or exiled from the city or even put to death, he alone is punished for the crime. They allow the rest of his family or household, whether his sons or his relations, to be elected to magistracies, to take part in committee meetings, to attend the Council and undertake public duties, since they have done no wrong. It often happens that a father is driven into exile, while his son keeps the position and status he had before, in accordance with the biblical prophecy that 'the soul that sinneth, it shall die'.[26] Only the guilty are punished in Venice, the others keep their standing untouched. Nor may anyone rail at another's faults or subject him to verbal attack, in case it leads to vituperation or feuding between citizens. Once they have given their word, they stand by it with the utmost fidelity. Nothing is thought more shameful than to renege on a promise.

One great virtue which sets them apart from the rest is the secrecy with which they treat matters raised in the Council. Discussions of questions of state are regarded as highly confidential. Their decisions are shrouded in such secrecy that they only become known when they are put into effect. They discussed the execution of their general Carmagnola for almost eight months, and yet their deliberations were quite unknown until he was captured and paid the price of his folly.[27]

And what of their wonderful generosity towards those who have served Venice well? Everyone who has benefited the republic receives ample benefits in return. A great many men have been admitted to the ranks of gentry, and even to the nobility, for their good services towards the city. This alone puts it above all other cities past or present as a model of virtue, an exemplar of gratitude, a spur to good deeds.[28]

What shall I say of their upright characters, which they have kept intact and uncorrupted down the ages? They speak with the greatest candour, without sarcastic abuse, snide criticisms or bad language. Their conversations are marred by no odious quarrels or slander of one another, for they hold verbal and physical decency in the greatest respect, cultivating the virtue of decorum so highly praised by Cicero.[29] They pay the utmost honour to old age and adopt the good old Spartan custom of allowing the older citizens to take precedence and have greater prestige the older they get.[30] The young people are given an admirable education: from their earliest years they are so brought up that you would think them born for a life of modesty and decency. They are given no schooling except what will fit them for literature and business. They also spend considerable effort on the pleading of cases, in which they are occupied for a good deal of their time. The older ones among them are particularly respected as they yield to their own elders in a graceful display of their dignified manner of life. This arrangement of their early lives leads to a well-spent youth and the emergence of better men, and ultimately fine and modest senior citizens. A man who has been schooled in decency from his first youth will find no difficulty or labour in following virtuous ways in later life. As Aristotle says, the upbringing and moral education one has received at the outset may well determine the course of the rest of one's life.[31] It rarely happens that an early life which has been coloured by bad morals and nourished on evil ways can turn out a good man and an upright citizen.

How flourishing our Christian religion is among the Venetians, and how highly valued, is demonstrated by the splendidly decorated churches and basilicas. There are a great many religious houses which the citizens go to for prayer and the frequent distribution of alms to the needy. They are very pious, especially in the matter of caring for citizens who have fallen on hard times and lost their livelihood. These they do not oppress or throw into prison, as often happens elsewhere; instead, they lift them up and sustain them with hope of a better future. They reckon that the city's vitality is itself diminished if they abandon citizens who have suffered some disastrous stroke of fortune.

It is marvellous to see the care and effort they put into attracting people to live in the city. They offer a wide variety of employments and ensure a regular food supply, so that life for the common folk may be as convenient as possible. People of modest means are not burdened with taxes, nor are they exposed to injury or disaster, and the city is consequently always well populated. What really preserves the city and binds it together in concord is the scrupulous fairness of the tax system. It is not based on the arbitrary whim of the powerful: all the leading citizens pay tax according to their means as determined by the census. They alone take responsibility for the city's public expenditure; and the more people that pay, the less onerous the taxes appear to individuals, since a burden that falls on everyone equally is borne more easily. And so it happens that when they have to go to war on land or sea, money is always available, nor is an opportunity ever missed to carry out a job properly for want of funds.

In this matter of the control of public expenditure, they are in advance not just of Italian cities but of any country in the world. The census of the citizens and their resources has always been carried out in the old Roman fashion, and that has proved the salvation of the city. In time of war it is not a case of one man being ruined while another is enriched, as we see happening elsewhere, but losses hit everyone equally hard, as if from a single inheritance. For that reason they are very careful about declaring war and prefer to deliberate rather than to decide on a course of action. They are even cautious in their deliberations, bearing in mind the possible expense and danger and giving lengthy consideration to the likely outcome of events.

It is greatly to the Venetians' credit that they keep the northern Mediterranean free of pirates. If any of their citizens do fall prey to robbers on the sea, they make sure the crime does not go unpunished. They will pursue them wherever they go with a fleet of armed ships until they are taken and punished, or the stolen goods returned. But they are as concerned with restraining their citizens while they are in office and punishing those guilty of wrongdoing as they are with pursuing thieves and pirates. A father may castigate a son who occupies a magistracy, or a son a father, according to the nature of the misdeed. There is no place here for mitigation by intercession or pleading or the claims of friendship. The laws are supreme, and no one transgresses them, no one repeals them or bends them to his own interpretation. If someone pillages the treasury or squanders the resources they hold in common or secretly filches from public property or fraudulently tries to divert it to his own private advantage, he is at once convicted and given a stiff sentence. It is considered a great disgrace, and a matter of perpetual ignominy, when the names of such people are annually read out in public in the Council, in order that the stain of this infamy may deter others from such crimes.

Under the doge and these magistrates and by virtue of these laws, institutions, customs and constitution, the Venetian people have for more than seven hundred years not just kept their republic intact but daily extended their empire by land and sea, so that their glory now resounds throughout the whole world. In the time of Charlemagne, the Venetian doge was Maurizio, whose son was captured by the Lombard king Desiderius, and then freed and restored to his father by Charlemagne.[32] I should not deny – in fact, I freely admit – that there were a good many doges before Maurizio. But it is cause enough for praise and honour that an identical form of constitution has endured for so many years, something that has happened in no other city. When I come to consider the causes of the republic's durability, one reason in particular stands out: the justice which Aristotle said was the surest basis of any state has flourished here as nowhere else;[33] here laws, not men, are in charge. That virtue has by itself ensured the stability and durability of the Venetian republic to this day. No other city, no other kingdom, no other republic has existed so long, with such austerity and such integrity. Nowhere else has justice been held in such honour. Nowhere else has the law of the people been so deferred to. We must hope that, if anything in human affairs can last, this republic with its constitution and customs (provided always that faction is absent) may rival eternity.

Translator's Notes

1. For biographical information on Poggio and more bibliography, see the translation of his *On the Misery of the Human Condition* in J. Kraye, ed., *Cambridge Translations of Renaissance Philosophical Texts,* I: *Moral Philosophy* (Cambridge, 1997), ch. 2.
2. See Aristotle, *Politics* IV.2.
3. Cicero, *De legibus* II.10.23.
4. That is, the doge, who is elected for life by a committee of the Maggior Consiglio, composed of the Venetian nobility.
5. Aristotle, *Politics* III.10 (1286ª28–31).
6. *Historia Augusta:* 'Alexander Severus' LXV.4. Aelius Lampridius is one of the six authors of the *Historia Augusta,* a collection of biographies of Roman emperors written in the late third and early fourth centuries AD.
7. See Chapter 9, in which George of Trebizond argues that the Venetians modelled their constitution on Plato's *Laws.*
8. Cicero, *Pro Flacco* 63.
9. Cicero, *Pro Balbo* 34.
10. Lucan, *Pharsalia* I.1.
11. Cicero, *De imperio Cnaei Pompei* 38.
12. Gaius Verres, Publius Clodius and Catiline were all attacked in Cicero's speeches: see the *Verrines, De domo sua* and *Pro Sestio,* and *In Catilinam* respectively.

13. Cicero, *De officiis* II.1.3.
14. The Secession of the Plebs refers to their withdrawal en masse from public life in the middle of the fifth century BC.
15. According to tradition, the Roman constitution was suspended in 451 BC, and ten patricians (*decem viri*) were given the power to prepare a new code of laws. A second group of decemvirs was appointed the next year; but the new laws they proposed were considered unfavourable to the plebs, so they were forced to resign and the ancient constitution was restored.
16. Coriolanus, a legendary figure of the fifth century BC, when charged with tyrannical conduct and with opposition to the distribution of food to the starving plebs, is said to have withdrawn from Rome.
17. According to tradition, Camillus, after being exiled from Rome for appropriating booty, retired to Ardea, where he was appointed dictator at the time of the Gallic invasion of Rome (387/6 BC). He raised an army and defeated the Gauls, for which he was regarded as the saviour and second founder of Rome.
18. The sea wall on the Lido of Venice.
19. Plutarch, *Life of Pyrrhus* 19. Cineas was a Thessalian diplomat of the third century BC.
20. The doge's cabinet was known as the Lesser Council, or Minor Consiglio.
21. Doge Marin Faliero, charged with conspiring against the state, was executed on 17 April 1355.
22. These magistrates were known as the Council of Ten, or Consiglio dei dieci.
23. Members of this magistracy were referred to as the Avogadori di comun.
24. That is, Signori di notte.
25. Reading *caeteros* instead of *caeteris*.
26. Ezekiel 18:20.
27. The condottiere Francesco Bussone, called Carmagnola, was decapitated in May 1432 on a charge of treason in the war against Milan.
28. This paragraph is found as a marginal addition in the original manuscript and evidently represents an afterthought. The text is somewhat garbled.
29. See, e.g., Cicero, *De officiis* I.27.93–6, I.35.126, and *Orator* 21.70.
30. See Cicero, *De senectute* 18.63.
31. Aristotle, *Nicomachean Ethics* X.9 (1180[a]14–16).
32. Desiderius reigned from 756 to 774; Maurizio Galbaio was doge from 764 to 787.
33. Aristotle, *Nicomachean Ethics* V.1 (1129[b]18–19).

Further Reading

CHRP, pp. 49, 63–4, 81, 91, 103, 117, 119, 307, 321, 332, 361, 380, 389, 421–3, 427–8, 434–5, 447, 451, 647–8, 728, 784, 833

Davies, M., 'Poggio Bracciolini as rhetorician and historian: unpublished pieces', *Rinascimento,* 22 (1982), 153–82

Gilbert, F., 'The Venetian constitution in Florentine political thought', in N. Rubinstein, ed., *Florentine Studies: Politics and Society in Renaissance Florence* (London, 1968), pp. 463–500, especially 471–2

Poggio Bracciolini, *On Avarice,* in B. Kohl and R. G. Witt, eds., *The Earthly Republic: Italian Humanists on Government and Society* (Manchester, 1978), pp. 231–89

On Nobility, in R. N. Watkins, trans., *Humanism and Liberty: Writings on Freedom from Fifteenth-Century Florence* (Columbia, S.C., 1978), pp. 121–48, and in A. Rabil, Jr., ed. and trans., *Knowledge, Goodness, and Power: The Debate over Nobility among Quattrocento Humanists* (Binghamton, N.Y., 1991), pp. 53–89

Part IV.
The Theory of Republican and Princely Government in
Renaissance Florence

11

Matteo Palmieri

DAVID MARSH

Introduction

By his combination of classical learning and public service, Matteo Palmieri (1406–75) exemplifies the Florentine tradition of 'civic humanism'. Descended from successful merchants and himself a pharmacist, Palmieri early entered the circle of erudite public officials such as Leonardo Bruni and Carlo Marsuppini. By the late 1430s, after the Medici had consolidated their political power, he served in some of the highest positions of the Florentine commune. Like Bruni, Palmieri studied and imitated the greatest authors in Latin and Italian – above all, Cicero and Dante – and wrote a number of moral and historical works in both languages. His Latin works include a biography of Niccolò Acciaiuoli, a history of the capture in 1406 of Pisa by Florence and a eulogy of Carlo Marsuppini. In Italian, he kept a book of *ricordi* (personal memoirs), assembled notes for a history of Florence in his day (partly written in Latin) and composed a visionary poem in Dantean *terza rima* called *The City of Life*.

Written between 1431 and 1438 and dedicated to Alessandro degli Alessandri, Palmieri's *Civil Life* is contemporary with Leonardo Bruni's *Lives of Dante and Petrarch* (1436) and Leon Battista Alberti's *On the Family* (1433–8). Like the latter, Palmieri's treatise is structured as a dialogue in four books in which distinguished elders offer ethical teaching to attentive young men. The setting of *Civic Life* is a villa outside Florence during the plague of 1430, where the prominent citizen Agnolo Pandolfini (also a speaker in a later dialogue by Alberti) discourses for the youths Franco Sacchetti and Luigi Guicciardini. (Palmieri himself is described as present but remains silent.) Pandolfini's topic is how to live well and happily in the urban society of his day. Book I describes the best sort of upbringing and education; Books II and III treat civil virtues, which are seen as the key to republican liberty; and Book IV discusses *utilità* or what is now called the 'quality of life'.

In his central two books, Palmieri discusses virtues according to the four cardinal categories of classical ethics: prudence, moderation, fortitude and justice. Book II proceeds somewhat woodenly through the first three topics, which emphasize the individual's moral valour, while Book III deals with the larger social questions of justice. Palmieri's Book II owes a special debt to Aristotle's *Nicomachean Ethics* (a work available to him in Leonardo Bruni's 1417 Latin version) and to three works by Cicero: *De inventione, De officiis* and the *Tusculan Disputations*. He also demonstrates his Latin culture by citing Aulus Gellius, Macrobius, Plautus, Sallust, Terence, Valerius Maximus and Virgil. Biblical allusions are limited to the discussion of self-control and the concluding passage in praise of Solomon's moderation.

The translation is based on the critical edition: Matteo Palmieri, *Vita civile,* ed. G. Belloni (Florence, 1982), pp. 59–102, from which I derive most of my source notes. There is another modern edition of the treatise, published together with Platina's *De optimo cive* and edited by F. Battaglia (Bologna, 1944).

Civil Life

Book II

My dearest Alessandro, as our fellow citizens are well aware, your excellent character and the laudable instruction of Ugo and other noble and ancient elders – whose
teaching and praiseworthy example urge you to a life of integrity – have abundantly
endowed you with all the virtues.[1] Still, I believe you found my first book enjoyable;
and unless I am mistaken, it has given you no small pleasure, since the precepts of the
ancient philosophers are highly useful in guiding and confirming all our principles
for living.

Philosophy is the foremost and truest medicine of the mind. It eliminates our
anxieties and turbulent passions, restrains our desires and appetites, and banishes
cowardice from baser spirits. Yet it does not possess equal power in everyone but is
most productive when it meets with a receptive and suitable nature.[2]

God created man elevated above all other creatures, inclined to shun what is
earthly while naturally disposed to follow and emulate what is eternal. But our
different pursuits lead us astray and divert us from the true path, so that one rarely
finds a person whose disposition and moral constancy are such that he seeks learning
and knowledge, not as proof of vain erudition, but as a law for living well, heeding
his own nature and true reason in all his words and deeds. We often see erudite people
so inconstant, obstinate and boastful that it would have been better if they had learned
nothing. Some are misers, others harbour vain ambitions, still others are slaves to lust
and unbridled passions – all traits which are especially repugnant in scholars.

Thus, we see that the study of philosophy and other laudable sciences does not
bear the same fruit in everyone. Just as carefully cultivated fields are not equally
productive, but vary according to the quality of the soil, so carefully educated people
do not all turn out to be good, but improve according to their natural disposition.
Without proper cultivation a fertile field cannot produce good fruit, and just so a good
mind cannot be productive without learning. Those who follow their desires, resist
obeying the yoke of reason and are immoderate and devoted to worldly pleasures will
not find the lessons of this book useful.[3] But those who seek to restrain their desires
and make them obedient to reason under the mind's watchful eye will be certain to
find abundant fruit in our precepts and much that will aid their good intentions.

Let us return to our topic. To summarize, we discussed briefly in the first book how
to raise a child to become an outstanding citizen, and we guided this child through a
liberal education to the ripeness of adulthood. The second book continues our discussion. In it, we shall offer advice on what steps a person must take in civil life to
prepare for worthy deeds and virtuous actions. We shall also show how to live with
prudence, moderation and fortitude – three of the main principles of civic integrity.
We reserve the third book for treating justice, which is the highest and noblest topic
of discussion. I ask the reader to consider these topics carefully, for I am sure that
they will prove pleasant and useful. Some of them will seem new and perhaps
unfamiliar to Italian readers. Give me your attention, then, and you will find advice to
make you happy throughout your life.

Franco:[4] I can hardly say how much your remarks have heartened me. When I consider what we shall learn from your discussion, I feel more eager than ever to put into practice your advice. Please continue, since nothing could be more valuable to us.

Agnolo:[5] Pay close attention, for our undertaking now reaches a higher level as we treat more important topics. Thus far, we have discussed those arts and disciplines which teach one to live well. In what follows, we shall examine how one aspires to praiseworthy words and deeds. Where we were concerned earlier with proper education, we shall now concern ourselves with noble deeds.

The best authors agree that above all we should pursue whatever is most fitting and suited to our nature.[6] In defining these traits, they proceed with natural copiousness, according to the clear and manifest order established by nature herself. They say that by nature every animal from birth tends to seek its own survival and devotes all its efforts to preserving its life. Neglecting no possible source of help, it seeks and gathers everything which is necessary to survival or useful in defending and maintaining its way of life. We also see that it is born not only with a desire for its own welfare, but with an instinct to multiply and increase its species. All animals are born with a common instinct for mating in order to produce offspring, thus enlarging and preserving their species. After their offspring are born, the parents care for them diligently and strive to raise them to attain natural adulthood. Now, the superiority of human beings to animals lies principally in rational intelligence and the ability to express thoughts, for such abilities are shared by no animal. It is true that there are many animals that possess keener senses, instincts and physical strength than human beings, but they act only in response to present sensations and lack any awareness of past or future events. By contrast, a human being possesses reason and by recalling the past can examine and judge the present and foresee the future. Since each person easily perceives the direction of his life, he can seek and obtain whatever he needs to guide and govern it. Such perceptions give rise to the bonds of friendship, family ties and attachments between people, and thus to human customs and interactions which allow people to live in close-knit harmony, unified in large groups. This is the origin of cities, whose civil customs and interactions have proved to offer countless benefits that contribute not only to the necessities of life but to its dignity and distinction as well.

In order to preserve and maintain such customs, human and divine laws were established in a sacred manner, with omnipotent God as their first inventor, common teacher and sole ruler. If anyone disobeys God, he will face severe punishments, even if he escapes the penalties of earthly judges. By living together under the law, we seek two goods above all others: first what is honourable, and second what is useful, which is closely related to it. In fact, more subtle reasoning makes clear that the honourable and the useful are inseparably connected. Still, since we seek to benefit everyone, we shall not talk about imagined virtues but only about those which virtuous people have displayed and display now. We shall proceed, then, using less subtle reasoning and consider virtuous those who are highly praised as constant, trustworthy, equitable and judicious. Such persons must always choose above all what is honourable and then add what is useful insofar as it is compatible with the context of their actions.

Now, since the honourable and the useful provide the material for virtuous living, and since our purpose is to speak about the actions of a praiseworthy civil life, we shall begin suitably by discussing these topics, which we may arrange according to the following division. First, we shall examine what is honourable and its categories and, second, we shall treat what is useful, showing the public and private contexts to which wise men have assigned it.

As we said before, there are four principal kinds of civil virtue, and everything that is honourable must derive from one of them. The first virtue is called prudence, which consists in subtle analysis and the ingenious ability to identify the truth in any matter and to demonstrate it logically. The second virtue is justice; but since I shall discuss it in the third book, I proceed now to define fortitude and moderation. Fortitude calls for mental firmness which is unbending and unshaken in defending duty and reason. Moderation observes due measure in all our words and deeds, restraining irrational desires and preserving with measured restraint the dignity of human life. Justice, as queen and mistress of all the other virtues, subsumes all of them.[7] The proper functions of this empress of the virtues are preserving human bonds and friendships, giving each his due and keeping faith in promises.

These four virtues are all joined and connected at many points, like members of one body, but each has its own particular and proper functions. In this, they resemble human limbs, which are all joined and linked to the same body. While each has its own particular and proper functions, each one often needs the aid or collaboration of the others.

Luigi:[8] I assure you, Agnolo, that our desire to hear you grows every minute, for I perceive that you are beginning to treat a topic supremely suited to teaching us how to live. I should only remind you to proceed according to a clear outline, so that each of us can clearly grasp the proper role of the virtues which you are going to discuss.

Agnolo: I shall endeavour to speak as clearly as I can about the virtues. Let me only propose one rule, if I may. I shall speak as plainly as my subject allows and ask you not to interrupt me, so that I can treat this rich topic as concisely as possible.

Luigi: We wish to obey you in every detail and to follow your advice. So, if you think it best, we urge you to proceed as you wish. We shall interrupt you as little as possible, provided you fulfil your promise and instruct us fully in the best way to govern our lives.

Agnolo: I shall omit nothing I have promised, and the order of topics will, I hope, benefit everyone. Listen carefully to avoid misunderstanding. Foremost among the virtues, as I indicated earlier, is prudence, which strives in all matters to determine the pure truth. It is said that prudence is eminently suited to our nature. For all human beings by nature desire to know and understand completely all things.[9] We desire this in order to avoid making shameful errors out of ignorance. The prudent person wishes to avoid above all such ignorance and therefore devotes much time and care to considering his affairs. He analyses them in detail, and judges and guides them according to true reason, so that he can easily determine and select the best course of action. This 'best course of action' refers not only to simple, well-defined actions – such as the best way to raise children or to maintain one's health – but applies in general to every aspect of human life. That is why we say that it is the mark of the prudent person to recommend whatever is laudable or useful in living a good and just life. Prudence is defined as the true ability to examine and discern by reason what is good or bad for human beings. Prudent persons are considered the best suited for public offices and private ventures, since they understand everything in detail and therefore choose only what is right and honourable.

Now, the proper function of the prudent person is the ability to give good advice, something which can only be done if the mind discerns the truth of a question and accordingly admits or rejects a proposed course of action. We must therefore examine what elements indicate the true nature of things. The four principal elements which lead to true understanding are intuitive reason, scientific knowledge, art and wisdom.[10]

Intuitive reason is the natural ability to perceive the universal principles on which we base our enquiries and judgements. For example, since we perceive that the love of virtue does not deter the wicked from wrongdoing, we find it necessary to curb them by fear of punishment. Similarly, since we perceive that men by nature seek to be virtuous, we conclude that we should encourage everyone to pursue virtue. For subtle reasoning shows that, even if it yields no other benefit, virtue alone is sufficient in order to live the best life. Intuitive reason, they say, most properly concerns principles which have no purpose but whose effects imply certain primary truths, even if their true causes are obscure and undemonstrable – such as the principles that fire is hot, men are rational and beasts irrational.

Scientific knowledge is the true cognition of things that are certain. Things are called certain when they are invariable, and since only eternal things are such, we can only have scientific knowledge of eternal things. As for things which may or may not exist, we can never have scientific knowledge of them, but only a conjecture, opinion or belief. Opinions and conjectures admit error, but scientific knowledge does not, since it is always certain. Hence, it follows that everything about which we have true knowledge at present was the same in the past and will always be the same in the future. If this were not true, no science would possess any certain doctrine, and the labours of ancient writers would clearly have been futile. Today's students would be wasting their time, if the medicines which cured typhoid fever a thousand years ago no longer had the same effect today, or if the true laws which were just in the past were not reverently observed and approved in every age and in every place.[11]

A systematic art produces things which are contingent and variable. The practice of such an art achieves its end through perception rather than cognition. Otherwise, the art will not be systematic and will be called imperfect.

Wisdom is the lofty contemplation of what is celestial, wondrous and divine. It embraces the deep understanding and true knowledge of the most valuable things and is therefore called the supreme knowledge of what is divine, rather than human. When geniuses disdain the world to seek in contemplation what is celestial and divine, we call them wise rather than prudent; for prudence is displayed only in human affairs.

Wisdom consists of three principal elements: memory, intelligence and foresight.[12] Memory records past events and reviews them as the basis for judging present and future ones. Memory begins as a natural gift, but it can be enhanced and made encyclopedic through the assiduous study of ancient history, through attention paid to men of experience and through the frequent discussion, repetition and recording of noteworthy words and deeds. By carefully analysing present events, our intelligence allows us to examine them closely, to understand them completely and to judge them accurately.[13] Foresight predicts how future events will turn out.[14] It makes us experts at judging what may happen, so that we can prudently anticipate any eventuality with nearly divine acumen.

We have now sufficiently defined prudence and the elements associated with it. Since we have said that the proper task of the prudent person is to offer good counsel, we must consider the nature of counsel. Unless counsel concerns things that are possible, practicable and alterable, it is folly. (Suppose, for example, that someone advised us to drain the Mediterranean, or claimed to level mountains singlehandedly or counselled us how many surfaces a cube must have.) The subject of counsel, moreover, must lie within the competence of the counsellor. It would be quite ridiculous for a shoemaker to give counsel on passing laws, governing the state or waging war. Great enterprises require persons who are competent planners by virtue of their wide reading, experience and painstaking analysis. It stands to reason that we ask physicians about medical questions and that cobblers stick to their lasts. A good counsellor will only give counsel concerning matters he knows well; about others, he can in no way offer good counsel.

When we have certain knowledge of a question, counsel is irrelevant and should not be given, since it applies only to matters which are uncertain or open to different interpretations. Counsel is praised when it is deliberate, seasoned and well considered; and when it leads to a decision, we must take swift action. Counsel never addresses the question of the goal, but only the manner and means of achieving it. Thus, physicians do not counsel health, but what restores it. Public officials do not counsel peace, but how to achieve it. To cite a minor guild, cobblers do not counsel the use of shoes, but their materials and construction. Health, peace and shoes are the goals fixed in the mind of anyone who practises these arts. Once the purpose is fixed, counsel no longer addresses it, but rather the ways of achieving it. In any deliberation, the counsellor whose rational arguments achieve the best results is deemed the best. Anyone who chances to offer sound advice for the wrong reasons is a poor counsellor, even if his counsel achieves the desired end.

All counsel should be free, true and open. Counsel must be free in two respects, private and public. Privately, one must be careful that the truth is not hindered by one's particular interests. Publicly, in choosing what is clearly the best course, one must not be swayed by fear of arousing enmity, by hope of winning friendships or by dread of powerful people. Counsel is true when it is based solely on a true understanding, the virtue we have described with its constituent elements. Counsel is open when it offers useful observations expressed in clear and appropriate words and properly organized, without irrelevant figures of speech or obscure and tortured locutions.

In acting prudently, we must avoid two particular mistakes. The first is to believe or accept rashly what is untrue. To avoid doing so, we must examine every aspect of an issue carefully and at length. The second mistake is to trouble oneself unduly about matters which are obscure, tedious, futile or completely unnecessary. We justly deserve to be praised if we avoid these mistakes and devote all our care and effort to honourable and worthy subjects that contribute to the private or public good. Those who waste their time in obscure, difficult or ignorant endeavours merit everyone's blame. There is no profit in demonstrating to someone that he does not exist or is a donkey or has horns. Instead, one should show how that person was born to live virtuously and how people can improve themselves – counsel which will benefit many citizens.

It is said that Alexander the Great of Macedon amply rewarded various human achievements. One day, there appeared before the great ruler an accomplished master of the peashooter, who could shoot chick-peas with such marvellous precision that from a considerable distance he hit a point of a needle with a quart of them, never missing a single shot. Having witnessed this display at length, Alexander praised his industry as a marvel. The master was encouraged to expect a singular prize, as was customary for extraordinary talents. Alexander made a gift to him of ten bushels of chick-peas – a highly appropriate prize for one who had devoted so much industry to such a task![15]

Let this suffice concerning the first part of what is honourable. Of the remaining three parts, the next in order is fortitude. Fortitude allows men to disdain worldly goods with a great and lofty spirit, to confront dangers deliberately and to endure labours and suffering in the knowledge that they benefit others. One element of this virtue is the unshakable loftiness which a constant and invincible mind displays in fighting on reason's behalf. Fortitude benefits humankind most when it exalts them and makes them willing to undertake and carry out great and noble enterprises with the unswerving assurance of a steady, elevated and constant mind. Except for real disgrace, fortitude fears nothing – not poverty, enmity, labours or pains. As long as one acts virtuously, fortitude does not even fear exile or death, unless they are the result of misdeeds. Whenever and wherever necessary, the courageous man deliberately confronts any danger, unshaken and without fear or trembling. Since fortitude fights only for what is honourable, anyone who braves danger unnecessarily is not courageous, but ferocious and bestial.

The mind has two parts, one rational and the other irrational. Man's principal fortitude is that which makes reason the empress and mistress of our desires and courageously masters itself, keeping our sensual impulses subordinated and obedient to our true understanding. Intelligence is a mental power which we share with celestial beings, but desire is a bodily power which we share with beasts.[16] In the power of our minds, we rise above all terrestrial animals. In the power of our bodies, we are surpassed by many of them. There are many animals larger, stronger, bolder, braver, swifter and more specialized than man. Many possess hearing, sight and senses of smell and taste which surpass ours. Countless animals enjoy greater pleasure in mating, eating and congregating.[17] Yet since these are powers of the body which are naturally destined to serve, all animals are in the service of mankind. The powers of the mind have dominion not only over beasts but over men. Hence, celebrated persons have always striven to excel by the virtues of the mind, which command all the faculties of the body. And they have constantly preferred intelligence and learning to any physical or external goods, observing that wealth, health and personal beauty and strength soon pass away, while virtue alone renews itself and makes men immortal.[18]

Let our principal fortitude, then, be self-control. Let us recognize who we are and why we were born, how worldly things are ordered and how quickly they pass away. Let us judge what things are honourable and good, and devote ourselves to them. Let us shun all irrational desires. Let us recognize how fortune bestows her goods as a brief jest, and let us disdain them. Many people consider excellent and important many things which a courageous and constant mind will rightly spurn. They consider harsh, hard, difficult and insurmountable many things which a lofty and courageous mind will rightly overcome with dignity. What is more terrifying than death? What is more painful than blows, gashes and bloody wounds? Although no one could possibly want such things, true fortitude patiently endures all things, when it is virtuous to do so and disgraceful to flee. It is not that a courageous person does not find such adversities harsh, but the more virtuous he is, the happier he is. Indeed, he is more troubled by death because he knows himself worthy to live. But even though he knows this, he chooses death for virtue's sake and places first duty, honour, glory and the general welfare, hoping to be rewarded among the blessed for his good action.

Anyone who is willing to face death for virtue's sake will easily disdain wealth and the goods bestowed by fortune, since to place hope in such goods is incompatible with a great spirit. There is nothing more magnificent than to disdain riches if you are poor; or, if you are rich, to bestow your wealth on others with generosity and charity. An exalted spirit should also possess the firm constancy and deliberate patience which move us to persevere in great and difficult endeavours, and to shun no dangers which honour requires us to face – not even when it is to our advantage, which should always be placed last in our minds.

All virtues are by nature so closely related to vices that it is often difficult to distinguish between them. Hence, virtuous people are often wronged by public opinion, and their actions easily dismissed or misjudged. And the wicked are often thought to act well, unless they openly reveal their dissolution and come to grief.

With extraordinary boldness of spirit, Cato preferred to die in Utica rather than witness a tyrant's victory, and the greatest thinkers have therefore celebrated him with the highest glory.[19] For nature endowed him with incredible gravity, which for many years he displayed with unswerving resolve. Having persevered unflaggingly in his purpose, he is cited as an example of perfect virtue for renouncing life when liberty was lost. Nevertheless, such virtue could be disparaged and decried as a vice. One could argue that, when he saw his good fortune decline, Cato proved cowardly and base by choosing desperate suicide rather than attempting to endure unavoidable misery, just as others who killed themselves out of cowardice are condemned and reviled. But many others who had made a courageous defence together with Cato, being conquered and compelled, surrendered themselves to Caesar. They too deserve to be praised, for in their forced servitude they preferred to endure misfortune with equanimity rather than end their woes by a cowardly death. For these, suicide would have appeared as an abhorrent vice, since their earlier lives did not display the severity of Cato. Yet had they possessed Cato's virtue, they could have chosen death as well.

The truly courageous man endures whatever reason dictates and is bold or fearful as the situation requires. Fortitude lies between rashness and fear. Whoever fears too much commits the vice of timidity, and whoever has no fear when he should is ferocious and bestial.[20] It is a great virtue to choose death when it is honourable, but it is a great vice of the cowardly to choose death in order to escape pain, poverty or other miseries.[21] Weakness of character moves a coward to avoid suffering or harm not from a sense of honour, but to escape ills which a virtuous person would face.

In every human spirit, nature has placed frail and abject fear, coupled with feeble and womanly infirmity, to which it is disgraceful to surrender ourselves. But reason, which rules our senses, is always vigilant and guides us towards higher motives: recognizing perfect virtue, she oversees our weaker parts and makes them obey her. Thus, the virtuous person makes slaves of his desires, subduing them as befits a lord and master. But if reason fails, and weak and womanly impulses master a person, the wretch's weaknesses will increase and multiply day by day. Like slaves, our desires ought to be restrained under our mind's custody. True fortitude is such as we have described it, but there are similar kinds of fortitude which, while lacking truly perfect virtue, often serve and aid the imperfect people with whom we generally live.

Fortitude is more often developed in the course of warfare than in other situations.[22] In battle, a brave man prefers to face dangers rather than disgrace. We stand fast not because we cherish great deeds, but because we see how cowards are shamed and brave men honoured and esteemed, and are driven to act lest we be thought base and cowardly. On other occasions, soldiers are moved by the deeds of lesser men and take heart by saying: 'I don't want someone else to vaunt his superiority or to reproach me.' Many are restrained by fear of punishment. When their commanders order them to hold their positions in battle, they choose to die gloriously rather than to risk ignominious execution by fleeing. Sometimes necessity makes men show spirit and fight bravely; for when all hope of safety is lost, only force of arms and manly strength promise survival. In such necessity, Catiline in Sallust's history exhorts his men to fight boldly, saying:

Each of you, like me, realizes what necessity we face. We find ourselves between two enemy armies. One bars our advance and the other our retreat, but we cannot stay here due to lack of provisions. Whichever way we march, we must clear our path by the sword. Show spirit and fortitude, then, and fight valiantly. Remember this: if you win, you and your families will win honour, wealth, glory, power and freedom; but if you lose, your enemies will seize all your goods, and all that will be left to you is disgrace, miserable death and the destruction of everything you possess. Push yourselves, then, and fight bravely. In this way, victory will be yours. Or if fortune chooses the contrary, you will leave a bloody and sorrowful victory to your enemies, and the fame of courageous men to posterity.[23]

Experience, too, lends us strength and makes men brave. Thus, we see veterans join battle with greater daring than new recruits, for practice has given them an understanding of dangers which the others do not possess. Along these lines, Virgil portrays Aeneas as exhorting his comrades to great and manly deeds, and bidding them take heart from the adversities they have experienced.[24] Sometimes fortitude seems to arise from strong emotions, so that in their anger men find new strength and face new dangers with greater daring. But if an angry person fails to consider and foresee the results of his actions, he shows not fortitude but reckless impetuosity. Still, if the decision to face danger is made from virtue, anger can enhance one's fortitude. Thus, when a second wave of troops sees the first flee, they are sometimes moved by contempt and, more impetuous and haughty than valiant, they renew the assault with greater daring, both inspiring their retreating comrades and terrifying the enemy by their display of valour.

Another kind of fortitude derives from experiencing and being accustomed to many victories, for those who have often prevailed have little fear of defeat. This is why armies place great emphasis on winning consistently: first, because victorious troops face daunting conditions with confidence and no dread of defeat; and second, because they are more formidable to the enemy and inspire greater fear and terror. Many display fortitude out of ignorance and face dangers that they fail to recognize.[25] Thus, if someone moves among enemies, thinking they are friends, and is attacked, he will fight back like a man of fortitude. But since his reaction is involuntary, it cannot be a virtue, for virtue lies only in voluntary actions carried out with honour and constancy.[26]

By now, my esteemed young friends, you cannot fail to distinguish between true fortitude and what merely resembles it. I hope, therefore, that as you reach the age of maturity, you will fortify your mind with counsel and prudence against all of fortune's adversities and all the wrongs of wicked men. Armed thus for any contingency, you will remain firm and resolute as you pursue glory for yourselves, honour and advantage in your affairs and the good and welfare of your beloved homeland.

Franco: We appreciate your orderly discussion of the elements which constitute these two virtues. We feel so encouraged by your words that, unless we fail ourselves, we must bless a thousand times the day we met you, for we owe you as much as sons owe their fathers. But since you yourself have taught us that these two virtues do not suffice to make us live happily, we ask you to proceed to the others as promised, so that we may be instructed fully on every topic.

Agnolo: Every honourable promise is a debt. Since I speak to friends who eagerly imbibe my words, you need not flatter me, for I am myself resolved to proceed to the end. Let us now discuss the third part of what is honourable, which we have called moderation.[27]

Moderation comprises the order and due measure by which we restrain shameful desires and behave appropriately in both words and deeds, observing such dignity as enhances our reputation and elegance. This virtue is defined as the stable and ordered rule of reason, which commands the obedience of any shameful desires while maintaining its own dignity. Moderation may be called the restraint and measure of our desires.[28] Its principal task is the decorous observance of what is honourable and appropriate in every aspect of life. A large body, composed of well-formed and well-fitting members, displays no grace whatsoever unless natural vigour pervades it and gives it distinction. Just so, all the virtues lack grace, distinction and proper dignity, unless moderation teaches them what is appropriate and suitable. What is suitable may be discussed under four categories, namely, words, deeds, activities and leisure.[29]

The disposition of the mind most conducive to self-control is the following. Our rational intellect, while never subject to our irrational emotions, must comply with them in such a way that our excessive desires do not run riot without the guidance of reason. Otherwise, such desires would exceed their proper limits, rebel against reason and abandon true order. Every passion is an irrational emotion which disturbs our discernment and hinders our perception of truth. Now, there are four emotions which assail the intellect and cause human beings to err. An analysis of them will benefit everyone, especially the young. Two of these emotions exceed the bounds of propriety by exaggerating what is good, and two by fearing what is bad.[30]

The first emotion, which we call joy, is simply the unrestrained delight caused by our excessive pleasure in a present good. This emotion causes even sages to err so that they can scarcely control themselves. Aristotle records that on the island of Naxos the noble lady Polycrata died of sudden joy. In Greece, when Diagoras saw his three sons victorious and crowned at the Olympian games, he was overcome by unbearable happiness and died of joy in the midst of an enormous crowd. In Rome, a mother learned of her son's death at the unfortunate defeat which Hannibal inflicted on the Roman people at Cannae and wept miserably for several days. Later, when her son returned alive, she died from the unexpected joy.[31]

The second of these emotions is hope, which is an inordinate belief in a good which one longingly expects. The last two emotions derive from ills, namely, pain and fear. Pain is an uncontrolled emotion aroused by ills which are present; fear is a belief in ills which are foreseen. These four emotions invade our life like Furies, confounding with folly any orderly way of life. Hence, everyone who wishes to lead a moderate life must resist these emotions, so that there is no vice in any of our words and deeds, and we may account for all our actions.

Pleasure, hope, pain and fear are the basic elements from which we derive and by which we define all the goods and ills of life. The pursuit of the former and avoidance of the latter constantly task the minds and actions of all mortals. If a noble mind takes pleasure only in what is good and clearly places its hope in that same pleasure, it follows that the pleasure and desire of a good mind are always linked to what is good. If, on the contrary, the mind, engrossed in evil desires, forgets its true nature and makes carnal pleasures its delight, it always suffers grievous emotions and constantly hears the threats of conscience, which witnesses its vices. Such pleasure is necessarily opposed to the virtue of moderation, since it forces us, without regard for duty or restraint, to pursue inordinate desires and makes us slaves to vice. Who could take moderate pleasure in shameful passion, if Hercules himself, who was so virtuous that sages make him a symbol of virtue, could forget his own dignity and become a woman's slave from love?[32] Who will not slip into vice, if love caused Samson to accept disgraceful misery and the ruin of his countless people?[33]

Pride, anger, greed, gluttony and lust are completely opposed to moderation and a moderate way of life, but they are so gratifying to our desires that we flee them only with the greatest difficulty. Indeed, once we fall prey to them, it seems almost impossible to escape their clutches. Even when we begin to feel their power, it is difficult to resist them. All virtue consists in difficult things, and the more we strive for such things, the more perfect and great our virtue becomes. St Paul writes that perfect virtue is found in infirmity, meaning that a virtuous person is recognized when suffering and adversity reveal his virtue.[34] It is easy to eat and drink, to take pleasure in amusing pastimes and to rest and sleep. But since all human beings, and even sheep, can do this, such acts have no virtue and do not make us more virtuous. Instead, they make us resemble beasts, which nature created only to satisfy their bodily desires and to fill their bellies.

Since man by nature possesses the ability to discern the truth and since free will enables him to follow his personal volition, he should choose only those things that reason shows to be the highest and most honourable. He should excise and eject all irrational desires. As John the Baptist's holy words tell us in Matthew's Gospel, the tree that grows in us must be cut and burned if it bears no fruit.[35] Our life, like that of other animals, is short and leads inexorably to death, but the fame of virtuous deeds extends it and makes it glorious and immortal. True virtue consists only in those things which we achieve by unusual effort and excellence and which, when possible, should serve our common welfare. We are always right to take pleasure in, and hope for, what is honourable, for this is the first impulse towards moderation. What is dishonourable corrupts this virtue and all others. To grieve and fear adversity, complaining and weeping like a woman, runs completely contrary to the moderation of the wise man. Avoiding the base weakness of the ignorant masses, the virtuous man recognizes that he is born subject to human adversities, which he endeavours to prevent and strives to resist by his diligence and prudence. But when such adversities cannot be avoided, wise men urge us to bear them with equanimity.

Clearly, all pain is grievous to our flesh and hostile to our senses. But if we consider the nature of earthly affairs, the vicissitudes of life and the fragility of human life, we shall tolerate any adversity with greater ease. There are three sources of consolation which can mitigate all our pains. First, we should continually consider and anticipate future events. Second, we should realize that we must perforce endure the defects of our nature and tolerate irremediable adversities. Third, we must have a clear conscience, for there can be no evil without guilt.

We have said that there are four emotions which make men immoderate and also that the first task of self-control lies in resisting them successfully. I am sure that these topics, expounded in an orderly fashion, have taught you all you need to practise moderation. Now that you have learned what is honourable, it is up to you to pursue this goal diligently, so that your deeds in no way fall short of the desire you have kindly shown in your questions.

Franco: Your kindly nature encourages me to ask you about something we wish to know urgently. When I review your teachings about moderation, I find all your precepts moral, true and coherent. But since these general observations say little about the particulars of our behaviour, they seem more like reminders for men of experience than beneficial instruction for young novices. Please be more specific, then, in describing how to practise moderation and what is appropriate and approved behaviour, so that we derive even greater benefit from your teaching.

Agnolo. As you wish me to continue, give me your closest attention. Keep firmly in mind that, in all their actions, men must follow the order and example of nature. For nature's perfection neither errs by itself, nor leads into error those who follow her. Hence, we must resolve to follow the true order of nature. For nature has clearly shaped the human body according to a careful design and placed out in the open all its members which serve decent functions, with no display of unseemliness. But the other essential parts of the body, whose appearance and function are in part base or unseemly, nature hid in secret, placing them in remoter parts, so that their appearance would not disturb the beauty of the other members. In order to conceal them even more, nature covers such parts with hair when we reach the age in which our discretion and judgement begin to feel shame. Everyone who wishes to live decently must consider nature's careful arrangement and thus use privately the parts hidden by nature, concealing them from the view of others, as nature bids us.

People of good character will mention these parts as little as possible. If it is necessary to refer to them, they will not call them by their proper names, but will do their best to ennoble them by using expressions which avoid unseemly words. Our language should be honourable, and experience shows us that certain things which are honourable in private become dishonourable when mentioned in public. If we must mention such things, we should dignify them with expressions such as: 'He is relieving himself; she is of marrying age; they are making babies.' There are other things which are evil when done and yet which are not indecent in speech: for instance, theft, murder, adultery and similar acts. Hence, we should follow nature as our perfect guide, always avoiding whatever is unseemly to our eyes and ears, or involves any unpleasant aspect.

Being thus admonished by nature, we must bear in mind what I said earlier, namely, that moderation entails appropriate behaviour in our words and deeds, and in our activity and leisure. Let us then consider what is required in each of these categories. To begin with our words, speech can be divided into two principal kinds — lofty eloquence and familiar discourse. We employ lofty eloquence to sway magistrates, public councils, popular assemblies and other large groups. We use familiar discourse in private conversations, which vary according to their context.

In both kinds of speech, we should make our voice pleasant and flowing, and suit our words to the topic. We desire eloquence by nature, develop it through rhetorical art and precepts, and perfect it through assiduous practice in speaking well. Those who desire eloquence may study with the masters of the art. For our purposes, I remind you that one becomes an accomplished master by studying the precepts of the art and by assiduously practising elegant expression. As for the speech appropriate in private, it should be congenial, neither soft and effeminate nor too haughty. One's words should be clear and flowing, and avoid giving offence. When you have adequately voiced your opinion, you should give others a chance to speak. By listening, you promote the exchange of ideas and avoid the boredom and resentment which loquacity provokes.

We must consider the nature of what is being discussed. When speaking of crucial and important topics, you may add a weightier tone of authority to your moderate style. When speaking of pleasant topics, let your words be humorous, festive and entertaining. Never utter words which betray or suggest dissolute qualities. Speaking ill of anyone – whether present or absent – is odious, reprehensible, dishonourable and blameworthy. When not speaking about your own affairs or matters of personal interest, talk about decorous topics which will prove useful and beneficial, such as how to live well, what things merit praise or blame and how to run a family or a state. Whenever we are at leisure, let us talk about enterprises, talents, teachings and the liberal arts. Should the conversation move to other topics, guide it back to these, making sure that your speech gives pleasure and that it begins and ends reasonably, so that you do not talk too much and become prolix.

In life, we wish to avoid emotional disturbances. In our speech, let us avoid being angry, arrogant or haughty; timid or sluggish; confused or disordered. We should always demonstrate our love and respect for those with whom we speak. Moderate speech lends great beauty to our conversation, since it is neither excessive nor deficient. But there are those who abuse it, especially many who agree with everything you say or do and never object for fear of offending. In Terence, the parasite Gnatho calculates how he can earn a good income with little effort, and says to himself: 'There is a type of people who always wish to seem more important than they are. I join them, freely second their wishes, and both praise and marvel at their deeds. If they say one thing, I praise them; if they deny it, I deny it and praise them. In sum, I have resolved to assent to all they do, and derive from them the best and most abundant profit I have ever earned.'[36]

By contrast, others are contentious and fight about everything. They oppose whatever is said or done, not caring whether they displease or offend someone else.[37] Still others are braggarts who invent and vaunt wondrous deeds, with no regard for the truth. They dislike anyone who shows disbelief, as the boastful Thraso does in Terence's *Eunuch*.[38] There are many of an opposite nature who always show less than they have, denying or diminishing their true worth, as we see most old men do.[39]

Now, in festive and pleasant conversations, we must nevertheless observe decorum, for we invite censure if we overdo humorous remarks, and act in the way that a licentious buffoon clowns, striving to raise laughs rather than to speak decently. Still, an inability to make pleasant remarks, and an intolerance for the jests of others, is a mark of rude and savage churlishness. Someone who knows how to jest moderately at the right time is witty.[40] But the most versatile and consummate conversationalist is the one who acts and speaks decorously and gracefully on any topic. Often one may discuss even the most trivial and unimportant subjects with authority and fine observations. In Macrobius, we read how a group of philosophers mockingly raised the age-old question (often treated in jest), Which came first, the chicken or the egg? When asked his opinion, the philosopher Disarius replied 'the egg', and supported his view with such dignity and solid arguments that all found it remarkable, regardless of their previous opinions.[41]

If on occasion it is necessary to reproach or correct someone, we must use more serious and harsher speech, and words spoken with concise gravity. But one must always bear in mind the reasons, the persons and the circumstances involved, so that one does not forget propriety. In Terence, the father Menedemus is reproved for harshly scolding his philandering son Clinias. 'Clinias', he says, 'do you think you can act this way while I, your father, am still alive, and do you hope to take a wife without my knowledge? If so, you are mistaken and don't know me. I can accept you as my son only if you obey me. If you go too far, I shall treat you as you deserve. This is what comes of having too much leisure. When I was your age, you know how I "philandered". In my poverty, I had to enlist and march to Asia just to earn my bread with honour and become someone! You lie in bed all day. But you won't get away with it, for I'm resolved to change your tune.'42 Hearing such words repeatedly, the youth was moved. He believed that his father lectured him out of love and that in old age he knew more than his son. So he enlisted as a soldier and became corrupt and wicked!

In the same way, we reprove as permissiveness the generosity which Mitio showed his son, who was another philanderer. Mitio's brother told him that his son had broken down the door, carried off a maiden by force, beaten the mother and torn everyone's clothes, causing a general outcry. But Mitio replied: 'You are mistaken. No one can forbid young men to love or to enjoy themselves. If *we* didn't act like them, the reason was our poverty. If we had had the means, we would have done the same. Now if you were wise, you'd leave your own son alone while he is young. Stop pestering me. It's my son, and if he acts badly, it only hurts me. He gives parties, enjoys himself, dresses well and falls in love. He spends my money too, but I shall give him more as long as I can. Perhaps some day I'll throw him out. If he broke the door, we'll fix it. If he tore a gown, we'll have it mended; we have the means, thank God. Thus far he is merely acting like other youths, and if he acts no worse, I'll put up with it. That's what we must do. If you don't believe me, ask anyone else you please, but say no more to me about it.'43

The attitudes of the two fathers embody too little and too much indulgence towards the young. Terence defines the just mean and proper attitude when he describes the life that Pamphilus's father approved of, before he learned that his son had lapsed into vices: 'When my son Pamphilus began to grow up, he didn't waste his time with fowling, horses, hunting hounds or with love and other passions, as most young men do. Instead, he continually studied the noble teachings of the philosophers and pursued his other pleasures with moderation. In conversation, he was affable and friendly to everyone with whom he spoke: he agreed with them and imitated their good conduct. He never fought or tried to dominate, so that he readily won praise and true friendships without arousing envy.'44 It would be impossible here to describe what reproaches are suitable, and what kind of life deserves no reproach. Let these examples suffice to show that, as in other things, in our remonstrations we should be judicious and observe decorum. We must never appear angry when making re-proaches. In this way, we shall seem to be offering disinterested advice, loving rather than loathing the person we reproach. We should make our reproaches with gravity and authority, but without arrogance or rudeness, and we should make it clear that they are offered to benefit the person we reproach.

If on occasion we cannot avoid arguments with people who insult us and use foul language, the best course is self-control. In answering them, we must observe pro-priety and moderation, and avoid anger, which prevents us from acting with modera-tion. Once, when Metellus, an honoured and wise Roman citizen, appeared on the rostrum before the people, he was insulted at length by the tribune Manlius. When it was his turn to speak, he first offered his prudent counsel on the matter at hand and then added: 'As for that other question, let the tribune answer. I myself shall say nothing. Evidently he thinks that he will win esteem by provoking an argument with me. I care little about his friendship and less about his enmity. Indeed, I think it disgraceful to mention him in the presence of so many worthy citizens, for his office makes him immune from punishment. When he returns to private life, I shall answer him as he deserves, for then I believe that he can be punished and purged of his faults.'[45]

We have gained little if we control our words but not our actions. Everyone should bear in mind what the philosopher Proteus often said at Athens, namely, that a man of virtue must never do wrong for any reason, even if he is certain that his sin will always be hidden from God and men. For we should not be deterred from sin by disgrace or fear of punishment, but only by our love of virtue and our complete integrity.[46]

Anyone who is so disposed to virtue will find of greatest benefit the saying of the philosopher Musonius, which is cited in an oration of Marcus Cato and which deserves to be written, as they say, in letters of gold. These are his words: 'Consider this carefully. If you labour to do something good, the labour will soon pass, but the good deed will always remain with you. But if you do something bad for the sake of pleasure, the pleasure will soon pass, and the evil deed will remain with you forever.'[47]

Everyone should strive to behave well and should consider how human beings act either secretly and in private or openly and in public. Hidden actions always involve some imperfection: certain actions are shameful and must be hidden, like theft and adultery. Other actions which are not shameful in themselves become so when witnessed, so that we produce children and empty our bowels in private, not because these actions are shameful, but because it would be unseemly to make them public. A moderate person should not only avoid shameful acts but restrain evil desires which may lead to evil thoughts. Whoever persists in thinking evil thoughts deserves punishment. Whoever resists and opposes them with reason deserves praise and proves himself moderate and courageous. It is a clear sign of folly when, instead of resisting evil thoughts, one pursues them and commits misdeeds, which cannot be undone or discouraged by punishment.

To return to our subject, those things which ought to be secret, even if they are proper, should be done in secret as nature and custom require. Nor should we agree with those who say that what is not evil need not be concealed. There are many good, useful and necessary things which, while in no way evil, it is blameworthy, unseemly and reprehensible to display to others.

Thus, all things require a consideration of the time, place and propriety. Philosophy, our guide in life, gives us two main precepts as a sufficient rule for our actions. First, no one should believe that his actions can be hidden from God. Second, one should never do anything that he is ashamed to confess to others. Whoever follows these precepts can only act with moderation, for the actions of all but the wicked must be decent or at least admissible.

It is pointless to admonish wicked people, for they refrain from evil not out of love of the good, but from fear of penalty. Let them receive the punishment they deserve from the appropriate persons. In any event, our admonitions will prove useful to those who live a virtuous life or one conducive to virtue. There are various aspects to our public actions, and we must be diligent and cautious in judging them, so that we do not inadvertently err in imitating the behaviour of others. The primary consideration is whether or not an action is in itself proper. If it is not, we must not imitate it, even if many others do. If it is proper, but so unusual that people consider it reprehensible, we should not do it publicly except with due restraint. I think outdoor banquets held on public streets may be proper and may even inhibit gluttonous behaviour. In Rome, specific measures were taken to eliminate excessive and wasteful eating. Roman law limited the meal to a main course and a fruit course, and prescribed eating outdoors under colonnades, to discourage secret violations.[48] In Sparta, Lycurgus likewise curbed the excesses of insatiable gluttony, requiring by law that everyone eat in public.[49] Today, however, anyone who holds a banquet outdoors might perhaps be justly reproached. Custom in civil practices exercises great power, condemning things which were formerly approved and then reinstating them, as they were, at will. I have seen how fashions, which were once worn in our city by public prostitutes for their indecent and shameless purposes, were adopted by the best of noble women, who wore them in great and solemn festivals and were considered stylish, merry and elegant. In our city, Florentine women once wore blouses cut so low that they showed their breasts and nipples. But when this extreme seemed incorrect, they began to raise their necklines to the other extreme, even covering their ears. At last, having done too much and too little, they found the proper mean, which still prevails and will prevail as long as custom dictates, until some fashion from the past returns.

Let us take as the best rule in our behaviour whatever is the approved convention of civil customs. In following approved customs, we must act with such moderation and decorum that we deserve no reproach. For time, place and circumstances carry so much weight that they sometimes cause us to blame things which in themselves are decent and good. Thus, virtue and learned thoughts about the arts and sciences are praiseworthy. But a guest at a banquet who was pensive and absorbed in difficult speculations would be considered uncivilized and excessively severe. If during a council someone were to jest about important and serious matters, he would be unworthy of his office. We must always judge carefully the subject at hand. If the topic is serious, we should be grave and attentive; if it is less serious, we should speak informally; if it is amusing, our remarks should be witty and festive.

Let no one be fooled into thinking that, since he has heard Socrates, Diogenes or Democritus praised for their extraordinary severity, he can become a celebrity by aping them.[50] In order to live as they did, one would need to combine their many excellences and to demonstrate their proven and constant integrity over many years. Otherwise, the incredible gravity which won glory and immortal fame for such great thinkers – men born as an example and lesson to others – will appear ridiculous and base in lesser men.

There is little need to caution you against actions which greatly disrupt and depart from accepted behaviour, for they are easily noticed. A person of sound mind avoids behaviour such as continual laughter or singing and dancing in public. People of little wit who close their ears to such advice deserve compassion. But we must guard most diligently against minor faults, first because they are more difficult to notice, and second because good people are blamed more for minor faults than the wicked for major sins. The old proverb says: 'The whiter and brighter the surface, the more we see the stain.' We often see dissolute persons engaging openly in their vices – hedonists, gamblers, adulterers and others full of bad habits. But having seen them, we soon forget and neglect them. Once we have judged them depraved in our minds, we pay them no heed, but merely regard them as plying their trade, no more and no less. Yet when a person of good reputation is seen at the gaming tables, the entire populace murmurs at what seems a serious lapse. We pay more attention to the good man and reproach him more for a small mistake than a bad person who always does wrong.

It is useful to observe carefully the actions of others, imitating what we deem good and avoiding what we recognize as blameworthy. Such observations can greatly benefit our behaviour, for although I am unable to explain it, experience (our teacher in all matters) makes clear that we are better at judging the mistakes of others than our own. However excellent the person we choose to imitate, we shall always find some objectionable trait and shall often feel superior in some respect to our model. We must not adhere so closely to one model, even one of excellent learning and morals, that we cannot strive to adopt what is best in someone else who surpasses our model.

We should imitate the example of the great painter Zeuxis, who was hired for a large sum at Croton, the most prosperous Italian city of his day. For their famous and noble temple, he wanted to paint a likeness of Helen of Troy, the most celebrated beauty on earth. Observing that the women of Croton were more beautiful than all the others in Italy, Zeuxis asked to view the form and delicate features of the fairest virgins of the town while he was painting. The townspeople agreed to let him see naked all the virgins of Croton. Zeuxis chose five of them, whose fame still lives on, for they were the best of the beauties chosen by an expert in beauty. Since he could not find in one body the completely perfect elegance of nature, he took from each the feature which was most excellent. And from all of them, he created an image so completely perfect in every detail that the greatest painters of the entire world came to see the painting as a marvel and declared it more an object sent from heaven than one created on earth.[51]

In like manner, by imitating the moderation, order and laudable habits of praiseworthy living, we shall adopt from each virtuous person that quality in which he excels. Imitating many people, each the best in respect to one quality, we shall strive to become as perfect as we can in every virtue. If we are in doubt, we shall avoid mistakes by consulting older people, whose long years make them experts in the art of living. Whenever several people reproach our behaviour, we must correct and improve it, as is expected of wise persons. We should not imitate anything, no matter how good in itself, so obstinately that we cannot abandon it for something better. In this, let us imitate good painters, who submit their works to the people for judgement and correct whatever the majority criticizes, sometimes giving general opinion preference over their art and acting in accordance with the majority. Above all, we should listen to our elders by imitating, revering and honouring them, by obeying magistrates in public office and by conversing amicably with civic officials in concord and peaceful harmony. It is not our task to counsel in matters prescribed by civic ordinances and statutes, for they constitute the laws by which we must live. Let this conclude our discussion of how to act with moderation.

We must now discuss what is appropriate to our bodies in motion and at rest. To avoid prolixity, we shall treat both subjects together. We must avoid any bodily pose or movement which departs from natural habit or appears unseemly. Such things are easier to perceive when they occur than to define. It often happens that the slightest signs betray the greatest vices and yield a clue to mental attitudes. Thus, an imperious gaze indicates arrogance; a downward gaze indicates humility; favouring one side of the body, pain; an intense gaze, concentration; an oblique glance, hatred; raised eyebrows, mockery; half-closed eyelids, suspicion; and winking, slyness. Sadness, laughter, a trembling voice, hushed speech and similar actions all make it easy to recognize a person's intentions and to see immediately what is appropriate and what is not.

Our hands possess a marvellous power for indicating our intentions, so that they seem not only to demonstrate but even to speak and express all our thoughts, and mute persons in fact use them to make their wishes understood. With our hands, we summon and dismiss or show joy and sorrow. We indicate silence and sound, peace and discord, entreaties and threats, fear and audacity. We say yes and no, we point and count. Our hands discuss, dispute and in fact mediate every intention of our mind. They must therefore be used with propriety, avoiding any strange movement and always appearing appropriate and suited to our needs. They must be neither rough and coarse, nor limp and soft in womanly repose, but kept ready to express decently what they wish.

As for our gait in walking, we must consider our age and rank. We must not walk too stiffly, nor so slowly and solemnly that we seem pompous, like a procession of ecclesiastical dignitaries. We must not fill out our robes and walk so inflatedly that we appear to block the road and warn the populace, like the character in Plautus: 'Out of the way, everyone, while I make my toga billow.'[52] We must not walk so swiftly as to appear frivolous and unstable. Every movement should reflect the measured modesty which maintains our dignity and follows nature as our teacher and guide.

To such proper movements, we must add suitable clothing. The body should be kept clean, avoiding any sort of rustic squalor. Yet in keeping clean, we should not be so fastidiously neat that we resemble a young bride. Suitable grooming will preserve our dignity as worthy of manhood. Appropriate and neat clothing will achieve this effect, as long as we are not censured for excessive finery. We must always maintain our personal dignity and leave delicate finery to women, who are better suited to such things by nature and by custom.

We have shown how moderation consists in the proper measure of what is best suited to a person in any situation. We have discussed in detail what is suitable, and I think you have learnt a great deal from my remarks. Now, as Cicero warns us, the same duties are not suited to different ages and ranks, but vary from the young to the old.[53] Hence, we shall give his views of what is appropriate to each group that he distinguishes.

It is the proper duty of the young to revere their elders, to select the most worthy and laudable of them and to follow their advice and authority. In our youth, we are ignorant and weak, and need to be governed and directed by the wisdom of our elders. Above all, the young must restrain their lusts and carnal pleasures, and strenuously exercise both mind and body quite often. In this way, they will increase their endurance and gain the strength to face the tasks of war and peace. When they choose to indulge in some pleasure for recreation, they must obey the precepts of moderation, fearful of disgrace and afraid of going astray. Such things are easy if their fathers are present, whose authority and judgement they should revere and respect.

As for elderly people, they should limit their physical labours while enhancing and cultivating their mental faculties. As much as possible, they should use their wisdom to aid and assist the young, their friends and especially the state. Above all, they must guard against being immobilized by rest and idleness, so that their bodies, debilitated by too much leisure, do not suffer decline and illness. Lust is unseemly at any age, but it is particularly wicked, abominable and repulsive in old people. In them, lust doubles and multiplies its evils. It makes old age disreputable and cloaks it in shameful infamy, while their example increases the immoderation of the young, who become more dissolute and uncontrolled.

Magistrates in public office should at all times disregard their personal interest. In their public role, they are duty-bound to support and defend the dignity and honour of public office, to observe the law, to provide good ordinances, to preserve the entire city and to bear in mind at all times that the masses they govern rely on their good faith.

The private citizen must abide by the same law as everyone else, neither placing himself beneath or behind the others, nor immoderately raising himself above them. He should always desire peace, tranquillity and decency in the state, and prefer the honour, interest and well-being of the public to his own personal advantage. By contrast, foreigners should pursue nothing in other people's cities but their personal business and should take no interest in someone else's government. They should live honourably and show themselves grateful and generous to others.

This is how Cicero describes the duties of various groups. For each person, we must always see that these duties are suited to his nature, his age and the times. There is nothing more essential in our words and deeds than the observance of order and measure with due moderation. We have said a great deal about this virtue, and I wish only to add one final point. The key function of moderation is restraining the appetites and desires of the flesh, so that by exercising self-control, we avoid lapsing into pleasures and instead obey nature and our reason.

The most important and highest form of human moderation lies in tolerating pain and death with patience and virtue. It is clearly an arduous task to withstand two such terrible evils. Yet many people of virtue have borne them when doing so was required by integrity or attended by glory. When the Spartan Epaminondas felt his blood and his life flowing from his wound, he said: 'I master my pain and depart from my life gladly, for my homeland, which was a slave-woman when I found it, I leave behind an empress.'[54] Scipio Africanus used to say that the exertions of war were not equally harsh to a general and his soldiers, for honour relieves the tribulations of the commander. When the renowned Romans Marcus Fabius, Lucius Paulus and Marcus Cato learned of the deaths of their famous and noble sons, they seemed unmoved and showed no sign of pain.[55] When some strangers asked how they could control themselves at such a loss, they replied that men ought not to grieve over or lament any accident which involves no blame. Others who learnt of the unexpected death of their sons patiently replied: 'From their birth, I knew I had begotten mortal sons.'[56]

On second thought, I am not sure that this is such a great feat for men of virtue, for when a woman named Lacaena was told that her son had died for his country, she replied: 'That is precisely why I bore him, that he might grow to be someone who would not hesitate to die for his homeland.'[57] There are numerous fine and trustworthy authors who have collected examples of how valiant men have always tolerated adversity with equanimity. Even in their last breath, such men never abandoned their unwavering constancy and moderation, nor did they let excessive emotions trouble them unduly or cause their virtue to lapse. There is little need to pursue the topic, since its fame makes it evident to all.

I wish to call your attention to a remarkable lesson which in my opinion is quite useful in restraining and tempering any kind of disruptive appetite in mortals, and I am sure that it will greatly aid you and others in learning self-control. Take note and commit to memory this final precept, which will persuade and move everyone to a life of moderation. If you wish to do so easily, reflect and recognize this fact: all human appetites are boundless, and all desires insatiable.

Our minds fully understand this precept, which all men of wisdom have affirmed and approved. It has been demonstrated especially by those who possessed in greatest abundance all the blessings mortals may enjoy. Although Xerxes, the king of the Persians, was endowed with all the gifts of fortune, he was not content with dominion over most of the earth, nor with limitless and innumerable armies, nor with great hosts of peoples and great multitudes of ships, nor with infinite stores of gold. He offered enormous rewards to anyone who could devise new pleasures for him. But when he tried them, he said he was not content. Alexander the Great, obeyed by every part of the world he conquered, found Diogenes living in poverty, but with great wisdom, in a tiny wooden shack. When Diogenes refused all the great gifts he was offered, Alexander said: 'You are far happier than I am – I who try to possess the whole world.'[58] When Alexander heard Democritus say that there are many worlds, he said: 'I perceive that my hope is in vain, if I believe I can rule over everything.'[59]

Solomon was raised up above all the kings of the earth and endowed by God with the highest wisdom and virtue. His very appearance was envied by all the rulers of the earth, revered with great admiration and honoured with precious gifts. He governed so many people that they are likened in Holy Scripture to the sands of the sea.[60] In his magnificence, he possessed more servants, mules, horses and objects of gold and precious gems than the world had ever seen. He was rich in remarkable, ornate and exceptionally magnificent buildings, and was served by more than a thousand noble and exceedingly beautiful young women. In his temples, there was such an abundance of gold and precious gems that they were used in the masonry the way we use cheap stone. In sum, he lived surrounded by every imaginable magnificence, amplitude, honour, abundance, wealth and majesty; and he was endowed with marvellous wisdom and was obeyed in his every wish by all the lords of the earth. Yet having tasted every pleasure that the earth can offer, he concluded in a cheerful voice that everything in this world is vanity, and all things together are worthless.[61]

Let us remember the laudable judgement of such great men and of others like them who, despite their great achievements, felt that they had fallen short of their ideals and were not in the least content. Let us then reject our vain desires and reconcile ourselves to the moderate ways of the virtuous life.

Translator's Notes

1. The dedicatee is Alessandro degli Alessandri (1391–1460), a Florentine magistrate; see Belloni's introduction to M. Palmieri, *Vita civile,* ed. G. Belloni (Florence, 1982), p. 3, and G. Pampaloni in *Dizionario biografico degli italiani* (Rome, 1960–), II, pp. 161–2.
2. This paragraph (and the next) echo Cicero, *Tusculan Disputations* II.4.11–12.
3. Here and later, Palmieri naïvely destroys the illusion of an actual dialogue by referring to 'books' of discussion.
4. A contemporary of Palmieri, Franco Sacchetti (b. 1400) was noted for his learning and public service and served as gonfalonier in 1450 and 1461: see Palmieri, *Vita civile,* p. 7 n. 4.
5. Agnolo Pandolfini (1360–1446) was a prominent Florentine statesman who retired from politics in 1434 to devote himself to study. He also appears as a didactic speaker in Leon Battista Alberti's Italian dialogue *Profugia ab erumna* (c. 1440).
6. The following paragraph echoes Cicero, *De officiis* I.4.11–12.
7. See Aristotle, *Nicomachean Ethics* V.1 (1129[b]27–30): 'Justice is often thought to be the greatest of virtues . . . and in justice is every virtue comprehended.'
8. Luigi Guicciardini (b. c. 1400) was a member of the Florentine patrician family that later produced the celebrated historian: see Palmieri, *Vita civile,* p. 8 n. 1.
9. See Aristotle, *Metaphysics* I.1 (980[a]22): 'All men by nature desire to know.' Here and elsewhere the redundancies are Palmieri's.
10. These four categories echo Aristotle, *Nicomachean Ethics* VI.6–7.
11. On the doubtful universality of laws, see the selection by Bartolomeo Scala in Chapter 12.
12. See Cicero, *De inventione* II.53.160: 'The parts [of prudence] are memory, intelligence and foresight.' Palmieri confuses intellective and practical prudence.
13. See Cicero, *De inventione* II.53.160: 'By intelligence we perceive present events.'
14. See Cicero, *De inventione* II.53.160: 'By foresight future events are seen before they occur'; and *De officiis* II.9.33: 'We trust those who seem to foresee future events, for people consider this true and useful prudence.'
15. The story is told in Quintilian, *Institutio oratoria* II.20.3, and retold by Julius Victor, *Ars rhetorica* 25.
16. See Sallust, *Catiline* I.2: 'All our power lies in our mind and body; we use the mind as master, and the body as slave, for the former we share with gods, but the latter with beasts.'
17. On this theme see Fernán Pérez de Oliva, *Dialogue on the Dignity of Man,* in J. Kraye, ed., *Cambridge Translations of Renaissance Philosophical Texts,* I: *Moral Philosophy* (Cambridge, 1997), ch. 4.
18. See Sallust, *Catiline* I.4: 'The glory of riches and beauty is transitory and frail, but virtue is considered illustrious and eternal.'
19. Marcus Porcius Cato the Younger (95–46 BC) chose to commit suicide at Utica in northern Africa rather than submit to the victorious Julius Caesar: see Cicero, *De officiis* I.31.112.

20. Aristotle, *Nicomachean Ethics* III.6 (1113a6–7) and III.7 (1115b24–8). Aristotle defines courage as the mean between fear and rashness, and he calls mad or insensible the completely fearless person.
21. See Aristotle, *Nicomachean Ethics* III.6 (1115a16–17): 'One ought not fear poverty or disease.'
22. See Aristotle, *Nicomachean Ethics* III.6 (1115a29–31).
23. Sallust, *Catiline* I.58.6–10. Catiline (d. 62 BC) organized a conspiracy, which was foiled by his great enemy Cicero.
24. Virgil, *Aeneid* I.198–203.
25. See Aristotle, *Nicomachean Ethics* III.8 (1116b22–3).
26. See Aristotle, *Nicomachean Ethics* III.5 (1113b3–6).
27. See Aristotle's discussion of moderation: *Nicomachean Ethics* III.10–12.
28. See Aristotle, *Nicomachean Ethics* III.11.
29. Palmieri discusses these four facets of moderation only after several pages on emotions and self-control.
30. For these four emotions, see Virgil, *Aeneid* VI.733: 'hence people fear and desire, feel pain and joy'; and Cicero, *Tusculan Disputations* V.15.43.
31. All three stories are taken from Aulus Gellius, *Noctes Atticae* III.15.1–4.
32. Hercules was sold as a slave to Omphale, queen of Lydia.
33. Judges 15:4–5.
34. II Corinthians 12:9.
35. Matthew 3:10.
36. Terence, *Eunuch* II.245–50.
37. See Aristotle's account of the opposing vices of obsequiousness and surliness: *Nicomachean Ethics* IV.6 (1127a6–12).
38. Terence, *Eunuch* III.1–2.
39. See Aristotle's account of the opposing vices of boastfulness and self-depreciation: *Nicomachean Ethics* IV.7 (1127b9–32).
40. See Aristotle's account of the virtue of being witty and its opposing vices, buffoonery and boorishness: *Nicomachean Ethics* IV.8.
41. Macrobius, *Saturnalia* VII.16.1–2.
42. Terence, *The Self-Tormentor* I.102–12.
43. Terence, *The Brothers* I.100–23.
44. Terence, *Woman of Andros* I.55–66.
45. Cf. Aulus Gellius, *Noctes Atticae* VII.11. Palmieri retells this anecdote of Quintus Metellus Numidicus (d. c. 91 BC) confusedly.
46. Aulus Gellius, *Noctes Atticae* XII.11.1–4.
47. Aulus Gellius, *Noctes Atticae* XVI.1.1–4. Musonius Rufus (b. before AD 30; d. before 101/2) was a Greek Stoic philosopher; many leading Roman citizens were pupils of his. Aulus Gellius does not state that Marcus Porcius Cato the Censor (234–149 BC) cited this saying of Musonius, but rather that the same sentiment was to be found in one of his speeches.
48. Macrobius, *Saturnalia* III.17, offers a survey of Roman sumptuary laws.
49. Plutarch, *Life of Lycurgus* 10; the work was translated into Latin in 1432 by Francesco Filelfo, then living in Florence. According to tradition, Lycurgus was the founder of the Spartan constitution.
50. The Athenian philosopher Socrates (469–399 BC) was, in fact, known for his geniality and keen sense of humour. For Diogenes see n. 58. Palmieri intends the solemn orator Demosthenes (384–322 BC), not the laughing philosopher Democritus (see n. 59).
51. The anecdote is found in Cicero, *De inventione* II.1.1–3; Pliny, *Natural History* XXXV.36.64; and in Book III of Leon Battista Alberti's 1435 treatise *De pictura:* see *On Painting and On Sculpture,* ed. and trans. C. Grayson (London, 1972), p. 99.
52. Plautus, *Amphitryon* III.4.1 and *Epidicus* III.3.435–6.
53. The next four paragraphs echo Cicero, *De officiis* I.34.122–5.

54. Cicero, *Tusculan Disputations* II.24.59. Epaminondas (d. 362 BC) was a Theban general who achieved renown by defeating the Spartan army.
55. See Valerius Maximus, *Facta et dicta memorabilia* V.10.2; Plutarch, *Aemilius Paulus* 35–6 and his *Marcus Cato* 24. Scipio Africanus (236–184 BC), Marcus Fabius (fourth century BC), Lucius Aemilius Paulus (d. 160 BC) and Marcus Porcius Cato the Censor (see n. 47) were illustrious Roman statesmen and generals.
56. Valerius Maximus, *Facta et dicta memorabilia* V.10.ext.3, attributes the saying to the Greek philosopher Anaxagoras (c. 500–c. 428 BC), as does Diogenes Laertius, *Lives of the Philosophers* II.13; see also Leon Battista Alberti, *I libri della famiglia,* in his *Opere volgare,* ed. C. Grayson, 3 vols. (Bari, 1960–73), I, p. 38. In *Lives of the Philosophers* II.54, however, Diogenes Laertius attributes the saying to the Athenian author Xenophon (c. 428/7–c. 354 BC); it also appears anonymously: see H. R. Breitenbach, 'Xenophon von Athen', *Pauly's Real-Encyclopädie der classischen Altertumswissenschaft,* 2nd ed., ed. G. Wissowa, 10 vols. (Stuttgart, 1894–1972), IX A2, col. 1577.
57. Cf. Cicero, *Tusculan Disputations* I.43.102, where 'Lacaena' simply means 'Spartan woman'.
58. Cf. Valerius Maximus, *Facta et dicta memorabilia* IV.3.ext.4. Diogenes (c. 400–c. 325 BC), founder of the Cynic sect, held that happiness was achieved by satisfying only one's natural needs.
59. Valerius Maximus, *Facta et dicta memorabilia* VIII.13.ext.2. The atomist philosopher Democritus (b. 460/57 BC) believed in the existence of innumerable worlds.
60. I Kings 4:20.
61. Ecclesiastes 12:8.

Further Reading

Baron, H., *The Crisis of the Early Italian Renaissance: Civic Humanism and Republican Liberty in an Age of Classicism and Tyranny,* 2nd ed. (Princeton, N.J., 1966), pp. 332–53

Burns, J. H., ed., *The Cambridge History of Political Thought 1450–1700* (Cambridge, 1991), p. 687

Carpetto, G. M., *The Humanism of Matteo Palmieri* (Rome, 1984)

CHRP, pp. 67, 423, 717, 773, 829

Finzi, C., *Matteo Palmieri: dalla 'Vita civile' alla 'Città di vita'* (Perugia, 1984)

Martines, L., *The Social World of the Italian Humanists 1390–1460* (Princeton, N.J., 1963)

Wilcox, D. J., 'Matteo Palmieri and the *De captivitate Pisarum liber*', in A. Molho and J. A. Tedeschi, eds., *Renaissance Essays in Honor of Hans Baron* (Florence, 1971), pp. 265–81

12

Bartolomeo Scala

DAVID MARSH

Introduction

Bartolomeo Scala (1430–97), the son of a Tuscan miller, was a classic self-made man who, like Leonardo Bruni (c. 1370–1444), rose to become chancellor and historian of Florence. After humanistic and legal studies, he was employed as a secretary by Pierfrancesco de' Medici in 1457. Shrewdly casting his lot with the Medici family, Scala soon won the friendship and patronage of Cosimo and Lorenzo, the de facto rulers of Florence, and served as chancellor of the city from 1465 until his death. Scala dedicated all his major Latin works to Lorenzo de' Medici: the dialogue *De consolatione* (written on the death of Giovanni de' Medici in 1463), the *Collectiones cosmianae* (texts compiled in memory of Cosimo de' Medici in 1464) and two sets of one hundred Latin apologues or fables (1481–6). At his death in 1497, he left incomplete a Latin *History of Florence,* narrating the city's past from its ancient origins to the thirteenth century. As a bookish arriviste and ardent Ciceronian, Scala incurred the enmity of the great philologist Angelo Poliziano, who wrote epistles and a Latin ode against him. But Scala's personal fortune continued to prosper. He built himself a sumptuous palazzo in Borgo Pinti (now Palazzo della Gherardesca), outlived Lorenzo and Poliziano, and survived the fall of the Medici in 1494. The poet Michael Marullus married his daughter Alessandra.

The Latin dialogue *On Laws and Legal Judgements* was written in 1483, soon after the dedicatee, Lorenzo de' Medici, had returned from Cremona. In the work, Scala describes how Bernardo Machiavelli (father of the famous Niccolò) paid him a visit while he lay gout-stricken in his villa. After the two men condemn the riotous excesses of the carnival season, they review a celebrated legal dispute between the famed fourteenth-century jurists Baldus and Bartolus. From this discussion, the question arises: does law transcend historical circumstances, or does it vary from place to place and age to age? Machiavelli observes that in Italy Roman law alone provides ample material for study and adjudication. But Scala counters that other nations, such as the Turks, prosper under different legal systems. As for Roman law, our digests and pandects preserve but a small fragment of ancient jurisprudence. Since lawyers are ready to argue any position, Scala asks, what certainty can there be in our legal system? Scala espouses a form of justice which will observe the spirit rather than the letter of the law. In reply, Machiavelli traces the origins of law, reviewing the mythical legislators and inspired prophets of antiquity. In a peroration worthy of Florentine Neoplatonism, he concludes by praising Plato's ideas about law and celebrating religion and its contribution to human society.

The opposition between Machiavelli, who defends the republican belief in the rule of law, and Scala, who inclines towards a princely government based on the 'judgement of a good man', recalls the model of Cicero's dialogues, which offer arguments on both sides of philosophical questions. The dialogue reflects both Scala's legal training and his wide-ranging studies of classical literature – with a contrast between Roman history and Greek speculation – as well as his personal pride in his expensive Florentine villa. Despite his somewhat turgid prose style, Scala offers a lively balance between erudite citation and contemporary anecdote, and his dialogue avoids the didactic awkwardness of Palmieri's *Civil Life* (see Chapter 11). In enumerating the first legislators of mankind, Scala borrows extensively from the *Historia convivalis* (1450) of Poggio Bracciolini (1380–1459), his predecessor as chancellor and historian of Florence. Scala employs etymologies and is fond of citing historical precedents, including several drawn from Livy, the Roman historian beloved of Bernardo Machiavelli and his son Niccolò. Noteworthy as well in the work is the wider cultural horizon opened to Scala (and other fifteenth-century Europeans) by the lands and peoples newly 'discovered' by Western navigators: in this case, the African landfalls of the Portuguese in 1482 and 1483.

For the Latin text of *De legibus et iudiciis dialogus* see the edition by L. Borghi in *La Bibliofilia,* 42 (1940), 256–82. Alison Brown has included the dialogue in her forthcoming critical edition of Scala's *Humanist and Political Writings,* 2 vols. (Medieval and Renaissance Texts and Studies); she has also translated an excerpt from it in E. Cochrane and J. Kirshner, eds., *University of Chicago Readings in Western Civilization 5: The Renaissance* (Chicago, 1985), pp. 171–4. I am indebted to her for several notes on Scala's sources.

Dialogue on Laws and Legal Judgements

Bartolomeo Scala to Lorenzo de' Medici:

In view of your immense and deserved authority in our republic, Lorenzo de' Medici, and of your clearly superior intellect, gravity and wisdom, I would be imprudent and untrue to myself as a citizen and as your friend, if I failed to consult you – whom our entire city consults and whose prudent counsel even foreign peoples and princes admire and seek – before undertaking any private project, much less an instructive moral treatise of the sort that concerns the republic and practically the entire human race. During the few days that you were in Cremona as our envoy to the war council, your absence gave me some extra time off from my duties as public secretary.[1] So I wrote down, as faithfully I could, a brief discussion concerning laws and judgements which I had with Bernardo Machiavelli.[2] But I resolved not to publish it without first sending it with greetings to you, who are the judge and advisor of all my affairs, so that I might have your valuable opinion on this subject. If you approve of my studies and find them pleasing (as you often say you do), I shall strive to demonstrate in them my diligence and zeal as an author, provided I am given some respite from my public duties, while retaining my position, which affords that peace of mind so necessary to writers. You yourself often compose both elegant lyrics and polished speeches and thus know how much leisure I require. Indeed, your own experience has taught you to appreciate such matters more clearly and more truly than those who, being unfamiliar with our business of writing, content themselves with reading nothing at all or with merely browsing the works of others. Farewell.

While I was confined at home by an attack of gout, my good friend Bernardo Machiavelli came to see me at my house in Borgo Pinti.[3] On entering the room, he greeted me and took a seat by the fire. It was the dead of winter, and the strong gusts of the north wind had lately covered the nearby mountains with snow, freezing everything solid and adding to the severity and discomfort of the cold. Bernardo asked how I was faring with the gout, and as my friend he urged me strongly to do all I could to recover my health. I replied that my feet had given me trouble for several days, and I thanked him for coming to see me and for advising me so sensibly to care for my health.

We fell silent a while, and then he spoke. 'It is carnival season', he said.[4] 'You are well versed in the behaviour of our youths. They beleaguer every street in town by throwing rocks, and when they take a break from rock-throwing, they block off the roads and set planks as barricades in the way of pedestrians, so that no one can pass without paying their toll. It wouldn't be so bad if we could buy safe-conduct by paying one toll, the way they say Charon charged a fee on the river Styx. But wherever you turn, you meet with new traps, and new sums are extorted. Even though it's highly uncivilized, our ancient habit of indulgence lets us laugh at such pranks. In any event, that is the main reason why I arrived later than I wished. Having heard that you were ill, I was eager to come and talk to you.'

'You describe the scene quite wittily', I said. 'The permissiveness of carnival often strikes me as excessive. Cosimo de' Medici, father of our country and our wisest citizen, used to detest the practice as pernicious.[5] He didn't agree with Niccolò da Uzzano, who, they say, often asserted that our city would be in sad shape if our youths had to forego such games.[6] Cosimo wanted them to study the liberal arts and to learn prudence and dignity at an early age, rather than to exacerbate the heat of youth and add fuel, as it were, to a madman's madness. For actions like these shape the conduct of private life and the public state. As in buildings, all our actions rest on firm foundations which are fixed early in our minds.[7] If you lay these soundly[8] and wisely, you prepare a suitable course for the honourable inception and completion of private and public projects, and you pave an open and easy road towards living well and wisely. But that's a topic for another time. The errors of our young men are too numerous to rehearse or redress briefly here. Perhaps we shall find a more suitable opportunity for such a discussion.

'Let me return to the excesses of this holiday. I believe that carnival was instituted by our ancestors to resemble the Saturnalia, just as we have inherited many other customs from the ancients. There is certainly the same licence, although we seem to show greater enthusiasm than they did in pursuing Venus, Bacchus and every form of dissolution. As the name Saturnalia suggests, the ancients sought to imitate the liberty of Saturn's reign – so often sung by poets – and they allowed slaves to mix freely with their masters. Today, we feel boorish and are ashamed unless we stuff our throats with wine and meat (good heavens!), sink to every kind of debauchery and wallow in all manner of squalid sensual desires. The ancients justly named their holiday after the simple and desirable liberty of Saturn. But as in other things, we are less noble and name these days 'carnival' [*carnisprivium*] because in accordance with Christian custom we forego eating meat [*esu privemur carnium*]. You'd think that not eating meat was one of the worst misfortunes. But, as you well know, the Pythagoreans deemed the eating of meat not only uncivilized but even bestial and monstrous.'

'I know', said Bernardo. 'What you say strikes a deep chord within me. Please go on, if you have more to say on this topic.'

'I do indeed', I said. 'I am utterly amazed how humankind habitually perverts all things into vices and corrupts nearly all things from good conceptions to the most

pernicious ends. Some learned men have even dared to write that nearly all evils arise
from good principles. According to sacred sources, the Greek anchorite Telesphorus,
the son of Simon Peter and our ninth pope, was eager in his goodness to increase and
enhance our religion. Among his other papal decrees, he instituted in AD 139 a forty-
day fast in imitation of Christ, following the lunar cycle.[9] (Busy with other matters,
his papal predecessors Peter, Linus, Cletus, Clement, Anacletus, Evaristus, Alexander and Sixtus never referred to fasting.) The fast of the four seasons was instituted
some seventy-nine years later by the Roman pontiff Calixtus, son of Demetrius.[10]
Like the Hebrews, the Christians used to abstain from grain, wine and oil three times
a year – in April, July and October.[11] Calixtus moved the fasts to the two equinoxes
and two solstices. Yet who would have believed then that the practice of fasting
would encourage gluttony? I'm inclined to think that initially the decree on fasting
was observed devoutly for several years. But in the customary way of human nature,
things always decline and deteriorate. As the time of fasting approached, the people
were overcome by wantonness and gorged themselves on those meats which they had
to renounce for the entire fast. The practice soon reached such proportions that it was
considered a fault not to defile oneself with every vice and every sort of pleasure.

'But tell me, what is that paper you are holding? Have you brought me an account
of the recent debate between our two celebrated jurists, about which your research
will enlighten me? I asked you about this some days ago, hoping to learn more.'

'That's precisely what I did', said Bernardo, 'and gladly for your sake. I knew I
would be doing you a welcome favour and also wished to add to the authority of the
Pandects, which are religiously kept with other public documents in the Palazzo
Vecchio. Now it is my belief (although you generally disagree) that, when Justinian
had corrected the confusion of ancient laws,[12] he made sure that the *Pandects* were
copied on thin transparent parchment and written in continuous capitals. In this way,
any addition or cancellation, even the smallest erasure or change, would leave an
obvious mark. This he did so that this code of law, which he had redacted with such
order and distinction that it shed great glory on the imperial majesty, would be
preserved undefiled, incorrupt and everlasting. And from it the true reading could be
sought to correct the errors of all other copies. I think that due to the injustice of
history – for fortune alters and confounds all things – these very books eventually fell
into the hands of conquering barbarians. But the Pisans, who were formerly a great
land and sea power, chanced to find them and bought them back for a small sum,
since the barbarians in their ignorance thought them of little value. When we in turn
defeated the Pisans, our ancestors' first concern was to transfer the fifty books of the
Pandects to our city, where they have been placed in the Palazzo Vecchio, as I
already indicated, and even receive the honour of religious devotions.[13] For by public
decree, it is forbidden to touch these books unless torches have been duly lit, a
practice observed by Christians only in sacred ceremonies. While the Pisans still
possessed the *Pandects,* the work's fame was increased by the celebrated controversy
between Baldus and Bartolus.[14] I urge you to read it now if you like.'

'I shall', I said, and glanced through Bernardo's notes, which were learned, in-
sightful, concise and elegant. Then turning to him, I said, 'Why don't you recount the
case from memory? I would prefer to hear your own words, which are far sweeter to

me than sugar or honey. You mustn't distrust your memory. You are one of few men in our city with a prodigious memory, as you have successfully demonstrated many times.'

'It is well known', he said, 'that in Book XX of the *Pandects* the jurist Marcianus makes this ruling: "The question is put: if the creditor makes it a term that the debtor may not sell the property subject to *pignus* or *hypotheca*,[15] what is the legal position? Is the agreement void as contrary to law, so that the property can be sold? Such a sale is void, so that the agreement holds good."[16] Marcianus's ruling gave rise to a dispute between the two greatest lawyers of the day, who took opposite sides in the case. Bartolus fought for the contract, while Baldus defended the sale, both of them relying on Marcianus's words. With wicked zeal, Baldus sedulously located as many codices as he could find and altered them with a special solvent, substituting the word "agreement" [*conventio*] for "sale" [*venditio*]. When the judge ordered an examination of the codices, they were found to read "agreement" rather than "sale". At Bartolus's request, a number of prominent citizens were sent to Pisa to ascertain finally the truth of the matter from the *Pandects*. Thus Baldus lost the case in disgrace. By decree of the Perugians, the corrupt codices were carefully restored according to the reading of the *Pandects*. Baldus was discharged from the bar and spent his few remaining years in obscurity.'

'Well told, Bernardo', I said. 'Since you've brought up the subject of law and justice, and we are enjoying the leisure of carnival, please state your views on justice and laws, unless you object. I have long been in doubt whether humankind derives more good or more harm from the fierce and incessant debates on justice and law which fill our courtroom disputes. It generally strikes me that the tranquillity of society was better served by the former practice of the Spartans. We read that they had no written laws and lived instead according to customs approved by the consensus of the wealthy citizens. After the Romans had driven out the kings and rescinded their royal decrees, they too lived for twenty years without laws.'

'The question you raise', said Bernardo, 'is by its very nature highly doubtful. Yet the consensus of nearly all humankind makes clear how nations have viewed the matter. How few are the communities nowadays who use no legal system, whether developed by themselves or borrowed from others! Those who have no civil law, or an incomplete or imperfect code, supply their need with Roman civil law, which is therefore known as "common" law. Today's students of civil law examine the problems of interpreting Roman law, rather than that of one city or another, and continually leaf through the *Pandects* and the commentaries on them. Those who master civil law by interpreting Roman laws and precepts are honoured in our society. For the most ambitious scholars not only study and interpret but even memorize the very words of the *Institutes*. And these four books, which Justinian had published under his own name, treat an incredible number and variety of authors and subjects with astonishing gravity and wisdom, covering every aspect of civil law with engaging conciseness and elegance. The contemporaries of Giovanni Buongirolami, the greatest jurist of our century, believed that he had memorized the entire work, since he used only the law of the *Institutes* in arguing cases.[17] Having repeatedly consulted these four books with the closest attention, I daresay that they leave nothing to be desired. By contrast, other works in legal studies, history, philosophy, oratory and in the humanities often leave one unsatisfied. One constantly comes across words and ideas which one would wish to change.'

'Would you maintain, Bernardo', I asked, 'that the consensus of humankind makes clear the preferability of being governed by laws?'

'Yes', Bernardo replied.

'Nevertheless', I said, 'I believe there are many nations which have no written alphabet and for whom the judgement of a prince or a man of high standing substitutes for laws. The empire of the Turk spread far across Asia and Europe, and its military might was recently felt at Otranto in Italy, which was raging with its own internal discords.[18] And some assert that the nation of the Turks relies on custom rather than laws. Yet we have learned the true situation from Italian merchants, many of whom trade profitably in their domains. They say that the emperor places men in charge of legal judgements who are called "pashas", a title given to those who sit in judgement or direct the military. The word, I believe, derives from the Greek noun meaning "king" [*basileus*], with the corruption of some letters, as occurs regularly in other Turkish words.[19] When judgement is to be delivered, the pasha ascends his tribunal; and the creditor and debtor, or the plaintiff and defendant, appear before him to plead their case, expounding the truth of the matter in the simplest terms. The judge is informed solely by the parties to the dispute, with no attorney or advocate present. They may only summon witnesses; all the other instruments of proof and disproof so common in our courtrooms are dispensed with, for these are forbidden as evidence. No one is more cruelly dealt with than a person who intentionally and deceitfully conceals the truth. When the judge has heard and weighed the case, he pronounces sentence without delay, convicting or acquitting as he determines. If the judge pronounces sentence unjustly and is shown to have acted deceitfully, he is condemned to death. The death penalty is administered in the following way. Anyone wrongly convicted at once reports the injustice to the sultan; and if he delays judgement or pardons the offence, the judge must suffer the same penalty. If a pasha, once the judge and now the accused, cannot show that no deceit influenced his judgement, a sharp pole is thrust through his bowels. He is then lifted up, impaled on the ground and shown to the populace as a terrible example and pitiful spectacle.

'How many other primitive and savage peoples do you think there are in the world who are averse to this civil discipline? King John of Portugal has recently explored many new islands and found previously unknown peoples who live completely without laws, like beasts obeying nature.[20] Yet nature has its own special law which surpasses all others.[21] Indeed, in my view, it is the only certain pattern and example for living well, and from it we derive good morals and just laws. It is clear that without nature's law neither households nor cities could be founded or justly governed. Her law never varies because of time, place or any other reason, but is constant and immutable, the same for all peoples, inviolable and eternal. Should anyone neglect it, choosing to abandon his human nature, he must fear God, the source of this law. Even if one escapes what are considered the greatest punishments and torments, as Lactantius says, our minds would be in doubt and human reason would find no stable point of reference, if nature had not set before us a sign to keep us from swerving from what is right and honourable.[22]

'Do nothing to another person, nature says, that you do not wish done to you. Does not Our Saviour teach us the same thing? "Thou shalt love the Lord thy God with all thy heart and with all thy soul," he says, "and thy neighbour as thyself."[23] What could resemble nature more than this precept of Our Saviour? For if you love another person as yourself, you will never do anything to him that you would not wish done to you. Thus, from the different words of Our Saviour and of nature we may infer one and the same view of this law, that is, of the source of our entire system for living well. And what does our Saviour add? "On these two commandments," he says, "hangeth the whole law, and the prophets."[24] All the law, he says, hangs on these commandments. This signifies most clearly that the immutable law of nature forms the basis for all the laws of all peoples and nations.[25] In my view, such laws are grasped more clearly[26] by the minds of good men when nature teaches and advises them than they are gleaned from our briefs, our highly polished speeches or that eloquence which our legal profession today most zealously pursues.

'I don't deny that all ages have produced many great geniuses in our legal discipline, and I would scarcely regard with contempt such men as Accursius, Baldus, Bartolus, Cinus and countless others.[27] You lawyers tell me that these men show astounding diligence in distinguishing, arguing and resolving legal questions. But this diligence entails such immense learning and sophistry that nothing can be decided with certain authority. Where clients are involved, no matter is so clear or self-evident that it is not called into question at once, requiring a legal ruling. We needn't look far afield for examples of this, since we have an abundance of local and personal ones. Practically every case of the slightest consequence finds renowned counsellors who vie for victory on opposite sides of the question. Although Plato writes in his *Hipparchus* that profit is desirable,[28] I can scarcely believe that the desire for gain is strong enough to corrupt the good natures of our jurists to take up unjust and abominable arms against an obvious truth.

'Our city has always had an abundance of men who achieved the highest distinction in jurisprudence. But with all due respect for earlier ages, our own is surely second to none in learning and integrity, and is likewise reckoned superior in the art of speaking and in other branches of knowledge which improve our lives. We have witnessed, and continue to witness daily, the excellence of men who speak not only in courts and trials but also in important embassies, in our Senate and highest public offices. No one should be surprised when several advocates of this calibre disagree with each other. Rather, since we see this happen in nearly every case, we must perforce conclude that the obscurity of events is to blame.

'It is obvious that nature is not at fault, for (as I said earlier) she has lit a light within us and placed within our view the entire basis for living well. But when faced with mountains of books and so many great disputes and struggles on the same questions, is it surprising if a mind with uncertain standards is torn in several directions? With nature leading and pointing the way, everyone could arrive at the truth using his own wits; but when arguments are piled up to prove or refute conflicting claims, no one can distinguish the truth. History records that there were two thousand books on the discipline of Roman law before Justinian revised it. Suppose more were found, and suppose they were more incoherent and perplexing – what then? For what jurist of learning, past or present, has not left some written opinions? Unless I am mistaken, no discipline is more fertile in producing books and fomenting discord than this civil science. As the universal confusion grows daily, entire years and entire lifetimes are often wasted in resolving a single case.

'In this regard, I feel obliged to mention the "defences" which Ulpian discusses in Book XLIV of the *Digest.* They provide a clear indication of the licence which litigators abuse in prolonging and confusing a case. "A defence", he says, "has been described as some kind of bar which used to be raised against the action of any party in order to shut out whatever has been introduced into the accusation [*intentio*] or into the condemnation."[29] This definition pertains to the defendant. He then adds "replications", which are made by the prosecution to counter the defences. To these, the defendant in turn introduces "triplications", and thereafter the names are multiplied according as either the defendant or plaintiff raises a defence.[30] The litigants may continue the exchanges up to "centuplications", I suppose, especially if more than one kind of defence is allowed. But there are several kinds of defence, including those which are apparently introduced not to shed light on the case – which would be more tolerable – but to prolong the suit and to delay sentencing. To the waste of time, you must add the inevitably burdensome expenses, which eventually reduce the litigants to poverty. The so-called *lex Cincia,* which forbade pleaders from accepting money or gifts, was quite necessary, although later an edict of the emperor Claudius made it legal to accept as much as ten sesterces for one's time and effort.[31]

'Today, when we must toil even more because of the perplexing multitude and multiplicity of laws and commentaries, lawyers who take one of the more difficult cases are surely justified in asking higher fees. If there is anything wrong, the fault lies with the practice, not the practitioner. For it is the consensus of all humankind, and clearly in consonance with reason, that compensation for every kind of labour is determined by its nature. Hence it happens that both parties are often reduced to poverty, as our ancient and well-worn proverb has it concerning litigants.[32] By engaging in lengthy civil suits which often consume huge patrimonies, such litigants end by learning a lesson at their own expense. Instead of increasing their wealth as they sought to do, they lose everything in court and regret their mistake too late. Still, when such people say that the present system of cases and judgements is far from perfect, we should believe them as speaking from experience.

'As in many other matters, our ancestors were prudent in assigning different judgements to different circumstances. Thus, when contentions arose in the single guilds, as often happens, master guildsmen would act as judges. Today there are twenty-one guilds in our city, each with its own name, but as a group they are called *capitudini.*[33] Each guild has its own convenient meeting-place with a college of magistrates whom it calls consuls, I suppose because in doubtful matters the other artisans adopt their counsel.[34] An ancient statute prohibits appealing against any of their decisions. I believe that this measure was intended, quite prudently, to prevent decisions from being overturned and cases referred to our system of legal review, whose multiplicity of interpretations would obscure what had previously been clear. Still, a law passed not long ago permits appeals to be made to six men selected from the Merchants' Guild (about which I shall speak later), but only in important cases, and the appellant runs a great risk if he makes a challenge unjustly.[35]

'I recently met a learned and quite ingenious jurist (not a Florentine) who has compiled a handbook listing every sort of case that normally comes to trial. For each case, he diligently collected all the arguments on both sides that would contribute to a favourable decision. In this way, he was prepared to undertake all cases indiscriminately. By striving only to win, rather than to find the truth, he made no small fortune in very little time and won a brilliant reputation among jurists. So great is the power of science and intelligence, where the diversity of opinions and laws confuses us, that it can disguise such moral depravity. There's no need for me to name him, as long as my point is clear. I wish to observe my long-standing principle of naming persons only in an honourable context.'

'I know the man you mean', said Bernardo, 'and I applaud your discretion, especially regarding persons of recent memory. For it often happens that men who are just and principled risk losing their good name and reputation because they are the innocent heirs or relatives of someone in disgrace. We suppose that the habitually corrupt morals of one's forebears, especially the more famous ones, are reborn in their descendants, and we approve the words of the satirist: "It behooves a wicked woman to raise a wicked daughter."[36] Yet even if his words are perceptive, we can see many children whose character is unlike that of their parents.

'Of course, I wouldn't deny that the first lessons learned by children from their parents and others in the home exert great influence on the development and direction of their lives. And there is some sense in the saying that you can easily divine the father from his household. Not only do children reflect their parents' nature, but the servants reflect their masters', so that we may say that the same thing happens in the home that Plato describes in the city.[37] We are born with a strong instinct for imitation, and if we are exposed to vices in those who raise us, they take root with incredible ease. Aristotle thought that virtue is concerned with what is difficult and that the attainment of virtue, being more arduous, is also rarer.[38] What's more, we seem to be born with an instinct, reinforced by habit, which constantly urges us to pattern our character after our parents and those we live among. This is the reason I generally give great weight to nobility of birth and family trees, although some exalt them too highly.[39] It is clearly more difficult to become noble through personal efforts and without the aid of one's ancestors. As a close friend, I congratulate you heartily on having achieved this to your great credit.[40] But please continue. Although I don't agree with all your elegant observations about laws and forensic practice, I still feel an overwhelming desire to hear you discuss this subject with your usual shrewdness.'

'I shall continue as you wish', I said. 'But don't hesitate to tell me if you disagree. From the outset, my remarks have not aimed at proving me a specialist or authority in these matters, which in fact lie beyond my competence, but rather at eliciting your opinion of the truth, which you may find easier to formulate when you have heard my position. I hope no one will think it amiss if I who am the amateur speak first before you who are the expert, in the way that games and songs are preceded by lesser ones.

'Now, I have reproached with utmost moderation any lawyer who devotes all his effort and energy to winning his case rather than trying to discover the truth. For there are some who regard our sacred discipline of jurisprudence and law as the art of winning rather than the pursuit of eliciting and illuminating the truth and of defending justice, and they fill the courts with a great deal of clamorous and dissonant shouting. You should visit the libraries (or should I say, workshops?) of certain lawyers and see the books they have accumulated, some of them displayed on rotating stands, others in wall-mounted cabinets, all kept ready and open for readers to consult. They stand in the middle, now turning to one set of books, now to another, according to the diversity and obscurity of the cases. They think that such a show both facilitates their preparing a case and impresses their clients with their wisdom. You know Pandolfo Collenuccio, a grave and widely learned man who is ambassador here representing the ruler of Pesaro and captain of the Florentine militia.[41] He told me an amusing tale when we met the other day by the archbishop's residence, both on our way to court. As we walked, we broached the subject we are now discussing, and I took the occasion to learn his thoughts on it. He said that he used to frequent the house of a pompous and greedy fellow who wished to be thought an expert on law. In the man's book nook, he found the volumes divided into three groups. When he examined more closely the meaning of this arrangement, he found that there were as many groups of books as there are roles a lawyer may play. Books for proving a case were gathered in one section; books for refuting it were in a second section; and those for suspending a trial as undecidable were in a separate section. Whenever the fellow took a case and had received a gold florin as the customary initial fee, he would usually invite his client to see his three-part library. The sight of the books thus arranged would show that he completely controlled the outcome of the trial, since he could at will refute the opposition, prove his own case or create doubt and uncertainty in the judge's mind.

'Of such a calibre, I would think, were Minos, Aeacus and Rhadamanthus, whom the Greeks charmingly fancied to be the judges of souls brought to trial in the underworld. As Homer says, Minos was the son of Jupiter, and during the nine years when he ruled Crete he often spoke with his father, that is, with reason and nature (which are the same as Jupiter), and learned from him precepts for governing.[42] Hence, he wields a golden sceptre, as Homer says in the *Odyssey,* and judges those who are thought to depart this life to join the shades in the underworld.[43] Seated apart and alone, as Plato says in his *Gorgias* [524A], Minos reviews the sentences of Aeacus and Rhadamanthus. Was such zeal for justice displayed by Aristides, who was nicknamed the Just, or by Cato, whose severity and justice are still legendary?[44] Xenophon writes in his *Education of Cyrus* that Persian boys were sent to teachers to learn justice and spent their days arguing and pleading cases.[45] Whoever was convicted of a crime, say, or made false accusations paid a penalty. The Persians wished to foster the seeds of nature and reason, which are the foundations of justice in our minds, and to instill in their youths mental habits by which they could make better judgements than by our confusing legal texts, which the poet in one of his *Satires* calls the "enigmas of laws".[46]

'The Merchants' Court of our city, which usually tries less complicated cases and judges them speedily, readily distinguishes between judgements of nature and conscience (as they say) and judgements of law. They appoint six men who are not legal experts but who are by nature shrewd and good. These men hear the disputes that frequently arise between merchants and decide what seems just and fair, and their judgements allow no appeal. Above the door to the court is written "The House of Equity and Truth", so that whoever enters will understand that nothing carries more weight with the judges who sit there than their zeal to ascertain the truth. The Merchants' Court at Florence once enjoyed enormous fame among foreign nations. Cases that seemed very complicated were referred to it from nearly the whole world, just as people long ago went to consult the oracles at Dodona, Delphi and Delos when in doubt about their affairs. The rulings of the six men were reported to the enquiring parties and venerated like oracles.

'I think we lost our pre-eminence in judging when the formulas of civil litigation began to creep gradually into this court as well. It often distresses me that not even a syllable of our laws, once passed, can be changed for any reason, case or consideration of justice and fairness. This is the subject of a witty fable I wrote about the laws, which runs as follows:

An illegitimate son of noble parents bitterly attacked the laws by which the wealthy wrongly deprived him of the rich inheritance of his family and the honour of citizenship in his country. He said that the laws had acted wrongly and cruelly in condemning an innocent man without a trial, and had become insolent in their power to govern, with no allowances for motive, circumstance or necessity. While they made a grim display of severity, they never enquired about the goodness and justice of a question. Deaf and inexorable, they had never learned to feel compassion at the pleas and tears of those who suffered misfortune. The laws had even condemned their own authors to the worst penalties and had established terrifying examples for posterity. They had impiously abandoned nature, who had given birth to all things, and degenerated into tyranny, setting up their own laws and (good heavens!) abolishing those of nature. Nature had secretly overheard the illegitimate son's just arguments and could no longer bear to let him complain. She summoned the laws, who had long provoked her wrath, and when they made but a poor defence, she found them guilty and changed them into spider's webs, stipulating that they were to obstruct only the tiniest insects.[47]

'Our courts share this defect, although the laws are not to blame. People with the most power bridle at being subject to the authority of the laws,[48] especially when these tend to be rather severe. People in more abject and miserable circumstances also reprove their severity. In my opinion, they are right, since it seems that severity borders on cruelty and sometimes imitates the spirit of savagery and brutality. Who would praise Brutus,[49] the champion of Roman liberty, for inflicting such a dire and fearful death on his sons?[50] Sitting in judgement with what he may think a great and lofty spirit, he orders the fasces unbound and his wretched sons stripped and tied to the stake by their wrists, and then beaten and battered with the axes. The populace can scarcely bear to witness such a sad and terrifying spectacle, and "pitied the men not more for their punishment than for the crime for which they deserved it", as Livy says.[51] I'm inclined to think that the crowd of onlookers would have been much kinder to the consul's sons than their own father. It is unclear whether he acted out of natural brutality or whether he was compelled by his pledge to defend liberty against tyranny. I would like to think he was compelled, even though I can in no wise condone the fact.

'We are witnesses each day to new events unfolding. Human affairs are shaped by so many chance circumstances, and so many diverse situations arise each day that to face them calls for unrestricted powers and freedom of judgement. It is by nature practically impossible for a legislator to foresee every species of event which may fall within the scope of a single decree. If a law has defects, they will be revealed by time, which philosophers, for this very reason, are accustomed to call most wise. For time lays bare and brings to light many things which you will not discover by any art or study, by any force or striving, unless time assists you. Thus, it becomes necessary, when the unexpected arises, either to depart from a strict observance of the laws (than which nothing is more execrable, according to you lawyers) or else to take actions such as I have described earlier, which the Roman people condemned in Brutus, the author of their liberty. Just as we object to incongruities in buildings, our minds are repelled, with nature's guidance, by cruelty in legal judgements.[52] When we see something inconsonant with reason and nature, which should rule our minds, we decry it as imperfect.

'In short, how much better we could live by following the judgement of a good man and good judge who is guided by nature than we can under the constraint men have imposed on themselves, which they must needs obey willy-nilly, especially in the frequent cases when a different judgement would be more appropriate! For nature is always free and subject to no outside decrees; of herself nature supplies abundant reasons for rendering decisions according to the time, the matter, the causes and the chance circumstances of a question. That is why I generally reject the opinion (which I believe you lawyers formulated and which some regard as a wise and grave utterance) that one must either pass no laws or else observe those passed as inviolable and sacrosanct. It would perhaps be wiser to say that, if laws must be passed, they should be obeyed insofar as they do not contravene nature's laws, which she herself established as immutable and eternal within us. For it is nature alone who correctly instructs us without tutors, resolves dubious questions without contention, perceives the truth without error and judges rightly without contradiction. In sum, if anyone boldly dares depart from her, he forgets himself, or rather betrays himself and his nature, and must inevitably fall into inextricable and pernicious errors.

'Now, if the helmsman is lost, the sailors are driven helplessly this way and that; often they perish, dashed on the rocks or engulfed by waves, or gusting winds drive them so far away that no human power can bring them back. If the shepherd of the flock is slain, the sheep are dispersed. If soldiers lose their commander through some mishap, they are filled with confusion and expose themselves to various dangers and even death. By the same token, if you ignore, despise or reject nature, who is the guide, guardian and leader of all human affairs and actions, you must dread, must expect and must suffer every ill that humankind has wisely feared and fled.'

When I had finished speaking, Bernardo was silent a while, waiting modestly, I think, to hear what further arguments I would make to prove my point. Surmising this from his silence, I said: 'Perhaps I have heaped up more arguments than were needed. I am now in a position to hear you, so that I may embrace what you believe rather than what occurred to me to say. You recall that I agreed to speak only if you explained your view of this entire question.'

'I do',[53] he said, 'and since I must speak in defence of laws, it would be improper if I began by breaking them and violated our agreement. Yet before I respond to what you have so wisely said, it seems necessary to review briefly the origin of justice and laws, as well as their types and designations. I think this will greatly simplify our search. Now, the law of nature, as you have just argued at length, is common to all animals as well as to humankind; and I concede that all laws derive from nature as from a most fertile mother.[54] But this natural law is not the only kind, for there is a difference between this "natural law" and what is called "the law of nations",[55] which nations use between themselves by a tacit agreement which nature herself provides.[56]

'Now, the law of nations does not extend to other species, but applies solely to humankind, embracing all human beings everywhere on earth. It is this law which introduced buying and selling, the observance of verbal agreements and those exchanges of goods, today largely effected through the use of money, which enhance and advance our lives. But since customs differ greatly, practically every city has different statutes. Hence, a third kind of law is called "civil law." Under the laws of Lycurgus, the ancient Spartans admired the ability to steal.[57] In Rome, the Twelve Tables imposed fourfold penalty damages on thieves.[58] Today, when someone is convicted of theft, we condemn him to an ignominious death and hang him by the neck from the gallows.

'In other matters, different peoples have customs which are not only different, but even completely opposite. The women of the Getae till the fields, perform men's work and engage without shame in intercourse with anyone, especially strangers — customs which the Bactrians share.[59] By contrast, the Arabs put adulterous women to death, and women caught in the act are not the only ones to meet this fate, for the men think it proper to deal harshly with any women they suspect. Herodotus writes that the Babylonians had a law banning doctors; instead, they would carry a sick person into the square, and no traveller was allowed to pass until the patient had questioned him at length and learned whether he had ever witnessed a similar disease.[60] The people known as the Padaei, who lived in the Orient, fed on raw meat, killing and devouring anyone who fell sick or grew feeble with age.[61] Yet some nations regard old age as very holy and venerable. There are others who copulate in public, an act which philosophers of the Cynic school also endorse. But it strikes me that such behaviour is more suited to irrational beasts than to the excellence of human beings. Indeed, nature did not place our genitals in the open, like our eyes, brow and ears, but aptly and modestly hid them. This is why we appropriately learn to feel shame, a peculiarly human emotion, which gives us the word "pudenda".

'One could adduce countless such examples. Perhaps these are more than sufficient, since the issue is clear even without the aid of examples. Now, civil law is what individual cities have devised according to their own usage and reason.[62] But cities consist of public and private elements, whence we derive public and private laws.

Public laws pertain to the status of public institutions and are divided into two kinds. When they govern religious rites, holy worship and religion, they are called religious. When they concern public offices, they are called secular.

'Unless I am mistaken, you will agree with me thus far. It is the private law which will cause us to disagree. Private law is also divided in two parts, either written or unwritten; and you seem to approve this view. Concerning the written law, the Romans established six species, and some men of Rome were assigned the task of framing and recording laws. But for regulating events, both many and few, that could occur in other cities as well, the people of Rome appointed officials according to their number and variety. In common parlance, their regulations are called "laws" [*leges*], a word derived from "choosing" [*legendo*], just as "kings" [*reges*] comes from "ruling" [*regendo*], "slaughter" [*neces*] from "killing" [*necando*] and "flocks" [*greges*] from the ancient verb "to gather" [*gregare*], a word no longer current, but which gives us "congregate" and "aggregate". Likewise, "defecation" and "feces" have the same root.

'Now, among the Romans, each law had its own separate status.[63] For when a senatorial official, such as a consul, raised a question, the decree of the people was called a law. A plebiscite was the decree of the plebs when a plebeian official, such as a tribune, raised a question. And a decree of the Senate was whatever was ordained by the Senate, which had assumed the authority for decisions on behalf of the people when the latter grew so large that it could scarcely be convened.[64] Later, by a royal law, all the people's power was transferred to a sole ruler. His decisions had the power of law, and the ruler's decisions were called constitutions. Praetors and curule aediles were allowed to make laws, which were called magistrates' edicts. Laws made by others were called *honoraria,* because they were framed by those who held honours such as public office. Finally, the responses of jurists were observed as binding and were called *responsa prudentum,* in other words, the opinions of those regarded as most learned in law to whom Augustus Caesar granted the power of decision in ambiguous cases. In our day, only the people make laws, unless they temporarily delegate their authority to someone else. While such measures do not have a special name, we sometimes call them "provisions" and sometimes "reformations", whether they are adopted by the people or by a magistracy appointed to represent the people.[65] Both kinds are called by the common name of "laws".

'According to the definition given by jurists, a law is a sacrosanct ordinance prescribing what is right and prohibiting what is not.[66] Could anyone devise or formulate a definition more conducive to living wisely? Could any utterance be more noble, more holy or more divine? Is it conceivable that such a notion could contradict nature and reason? Is anything in life more essential to our living well and wisely than this ordinance? Bias of Priene, a man celebrated for his wisdom, was accustomed to say that cities stand on two feet: from one good citizens, and from the other evil ones, received their just rewards.[67] Isn't this in fact the sole concern of laws? What is the purpose of laws, and what do we expect of them? What do they promise, and what do they deliver? Don't they incite our souls to noble deeds by placing before us honour and rewards?

'Concerning courage, moderation and justice, not even philosophers reason more wisely or offer more valuable precepts. Laws teach you how to act. They not only teach you how to live with yourself but also prescribe how you must deal fairly with others. Laws examine in the greatest detail everything that pertains to one's family, one's city and nearly the entire human race. Do you govern your household justly and deal generously with your wife, children, servants and tenants? Do they in turn love and revere you, fear your command and respect you as husband, father and master? Do they heed and obey you? If so, it is thanks to laws. If you wish to know what befits a good citizen and husband, what better source is there than laws? If you have dealings with foreigners, you must learn your duty from laws. For laws protect the rights of hospitality and win us friendships, which are our most precious possession in life. With neighbours and relatives, they nobly create goodwill and offer us aid in preserving it.

'Laws furnish the victories of our troops and the triumphs at home. They often cause men to forget all else in defence of their city's safety and splendour, so that men's spirits overcome all perils and their hearts swell with courage that serenely routs all human fears. As his close friend, you remember how Cosimo de' Medici used to call our laws the "Citadel of Justice" to which, when attacked, Justice would flee to escape force and violence. The Greeks say that, after nearly every nation had declared war on her, Justice left the earth and ascended into heaven, resolved in her fear of violence never to return, unless laws had been framed to protect her.[68] I am often struck that Cosimo spoke not only with wisdom and gravity, but with the greatest grace and elegance. Indeed, I would readily call his wisdom as refined as that of Socrates, embellished by Plato's mellifluous style.

'As with many other inventions, it is unclear who first created laws. Some ascribe the honour to Ceres and think that she is called the lawgiver for that reason.[69] Others think it was Phoroneus, Inachus's son by Niobe, who was the second king to rule the Argives.[70] As people of faith, we devoutly believe that Moses spoke directly with God, as a friend speaks to a friend, and having spent forty days and forty nights without tasting bread or water, passed on to humankind the tablets which the Lord had dictated as the first laws.[71]

'Others say it was Minos, and some Rhadamanthus, who first framed laws in Crete.[72] According to legend, Minos spoke with his father Jupiter and learned from him what to make into law, as you were saying just now. Minos was a good man and a just king, even though some Athenian poets (presumably avenging the siege of their country) portrayed him as harsh and cruel in their tragedies.[73] But Rhadamanthus did not himself frame the laws, nor learn the art of ruling. Instead, he acted as Minos's agent and ambassador in ruling the city of Cnossus and in promulgating the laws which Minos had framed with the advice of his father Jupiter.[74] In the same way, Talus used bronze tablets in order to publish his laws and bring them to the peoples under his rule.[75]

'In any event, it is certain that the laws of Crete were older than any others in the rest of Greece and lasted a very long time, since they were framed at the instance of Jupiter, greatest of all the gods. Anyone who thinks that Jupiter erred will rightly be reproved by the learned as ignorant of the more arcane mystical senses of ancient theology. How can you explain the fact that each day we frame new laws and rescind old ones – as I fear happens in other cities as well – unless our emotions dominate us, and most human affairs are conducted without God's help and with an inveterate tendency to err? If law is an invention of truth – as Socrates argues in Plato's *Minos* [315A] – and if only the just and honourable decisions of legislators may correctly be called laws, can anyone fail to see that laws so established are immutable? For once something has been found to be true, no cause whatsoever can later render it false. Truth is an inalterable and divine force which, even while involved in mortal affairs, remains immortal and eternal.

'If these things are true, it is also not difficult to explain why different people do not make the same decision about what seems the same issue. For such people either hold different views of the issue, and some of them hold false ones (the truth being often difficult to ascertain); or else different principles, which lawmakers must above all respect, rightly create a difference in the law. There are also laws passed temporarily; since they "expire" with time, some reasonably call them "mortal" laws. Yet if you examine them more closely, you will find that even these laws contain an element of immortality. For unless the lawmaker deviated from reason, the recurrence of the same conditions would require an identical ruling in the matter. The tribune of the people Gaius Oppius moved the Oppian Law in the heat of the Punic War, when the victorious Hannibal was triumphant in Italy and seemed about to lay siege to Rome. Under this law, the Romans set limits to feminine fineries that were suited to the moment, but they abrogated the law twenty years later, when the city's fortune had changed for the better, and reinstated the previous luxuries of women.[76] But can anyone doubt that practically every nation, not merely the Romans, would enact and abrogate the same law about women's luxuries, if it were pressed by the same emergency and had similar legislative principles? Did you have something to add?'

'Nothing', I said. 'You seem to me to have defined correctly two kinds of law. The mortal kind serves the moment, arising and passing away with it, as the poets describe the Hamadryads, each born together with a tree and dying with it.[77] The immortal kind concerns those things which admit of no change, variation or alteration; and since its principles do not change, this type of law cannot be changed. A law founded on immutable and eternal principles remains immutable and eternal.

'It is inappropriate to speak of what people mistakenly consider to be laws, but I would like you to clarify a point. Would you ascribe to Jupiter those temporary laws which you have called mortal? Or to Saturn, whom the Greeks call Chronos, believing him to be in charge of time? Cicero maintains that Saturn takes his name from the fullness [*saturitas*] of years, following the ancients' division of all things into powers and assigning each to a specific divinity.[78] In my view, we would act ignorantly if, in pursuing the truth by every means, we were to confuse things which the ancients so carefully distinguished, especially since the topic of our discussion is an ancient one.'

'Your perplexity strikes me as well-founded', he said. 'The question you raise is very complicated, obscured by many layers of ambiguity and fraught (as I often remark) with illusory and impenetrable mystifications. Since it is hardly suited to our present discussion, I think it will suffice to show that laws had their origin in divinity, whether Jupiter or another god, as in fact the authors of laws have variously demonstrated in different nations. For they not only sought to make the masses more obedient by invoking the authority of the gods but also wished to portray the true origin of laws, which we discussed earlier, by means of fables invented for this purpose.[79]

'Zoroaster, for example, the lawgiver of the Bactrians and Persians, asserted that their great deity Oromasius aided him in framing his laws; and Charondas, lawgiver of the Carthaginians, credited Saturn.[80] The Egyptians, in turn, held in highest awe Trismegistus, who was either Mercury himself or Mercury's scribe, as some have recorded. In any event, he persuaded the people that the laws he gave them had been dictated by Mercury. In this way, Lycurgus named Apollo to the Spartans; and Draco and Solon named Minerva to the Athenians. The Roman king Numa Pompilius took secret counsel with the nymph Egeria;[81] and Zalmoxis, lawgiver of the Scythians, did so with Vesta. Mohammed kept the Arabs under his rule by vaunting his familiarity with Gabriel, whom he said he saw frequently.[82] Thus, through the authority of the angel, that is, of divine communications, he made the barbarous masses submissive to him and obedient to his precepts. He was so successful that the wicked sect of Mohammed has survived to our day and, elated by many victories in recent years, even dares contend with us for the truth of religion and the glory of arms.[83]

'As I said before, all these examples surely suggest that laws have their origin in divinity. I think this view tallies with your proposal that we must obey nature in hearing and deciding cases. For if the lawgivers of nearly every nation have been intimate associates of the gods, we can only interpret this to mean one thing: they called upon nature, which assumes different names in different religions, and decreed what was dictated by right reason, which is the likeness of divinity within us.[84] That is what you apparently meant just now in describing Minos's conversations with Jupiter.

'I know that you often express amazement at the wisdom of Plato, a noble man and a philosopher of nearly divine genius. And I know what pleasure you take in seeing his writings win increasing popularity. This has happened especially through the efforts of Cosimo de' Medici, father of our country, who recently showed the greatest diligence in collecting Plato's works and in making them available to his fellow citizens to read and admire.[85]

'In this context, it is worthwhile to record the views regarding the law held by this philosopher and his followers, who chose to call themselves Platonists: how they define laws, what categories they set and what are the sources of each category. They say that law is the true basis of governing, which directs the governed towards their highest end through appropriate means.[86] Law is harsh to those who resist her and benign to those who obey.[87] They define law as eternal, for they do not regard those which suffer change as true laws. From the *Timaeus,* the *Phaedrus* and the *Gorgias,* they derive four types of laws: divine, celestial, "moving" and human. They locate divine law in the mind of God, which Plato calls providence and which is also called the law of Saturn. They say that celestial law, also called fate, is the law of Jupiter and is located in the upper regions of the world soul. They identify "moving" law with nature and place it in the lower potency of the world soul. They assign this law to the first Venus and assign to the second Venus human law, which is found in the human mind and is called prudence. They derive all the types of law from the highest good and refer them to God, who is the first principle not only of laws, but of all other things, and their immutable and permanent cause.

'You see, then, how everything points to the origin of laws in the immortal gods, for their first principles are ascribed to the gods not only by the lawgivers, but by grave and learned philosophers as well. This is why I regard as mistaken those people who do not worship and venerate the inviolable decrees of the laws, or who do not think that their conduct and all human affairs should be governed and administered according to the holy and divine standard of laws. Indeed, if laws did not moderate our emotions and hold in check avarice, ambition and desire, human affairs would inevitably be confused and utterly chaotic. Without laws, I am inclined to think that the life of beasts and brutes would be preferable to ours, for they are driven by far weaker impulses than ours and seek only food and shelter. Except for the times when they are goaded by Venus, they seldom fight each other or disobey the decrees of nature, which alone inspire them. But when desire overcomes our reason, which the gods generously planted within us to remind us of the bonds of our obligations, the human race is soon thrown off course. This is the source of those wars and conflicts which cause the continual strife and misery of nearly all peoples.

'But laws take up arms against these ills and, with nature and reason to guide them, assail the forces of unrest. By their might, laws rout those who violate the peace and tranquillity of human life and hold fairest sway over it. If those who control our affairs did not interfere with the operations of our laws, they would not obstruct justice, whose glory laws willingly protect. But all too often we see how immoderate desires dominate those who rule and hold the reins of power. This is why human affairs are so tempestuous and tormented, for in disregarding the laws (which are our sole guide for living justly) they abandon nature and truth, and battle for political power, prestige and wealth. As a result, I often strongly approve and admire one of our forebears' wise institutions. Every two months, they convoke the senators, praetors, magistrates and all others charged with legal judgements, to hear a detailed speech about justice. I also laud them for naming their highest officers after that virtue which alone preserves cities, to which is joined the title of standard-bearer.[88] Truly this is a precedent which others who judge and govern should contemplate, imitate, follow and adapt.

'Clearly our forebears were aware what great capacity for misdeeds we harbour in our minds, and what great assistance our reason needs in order to control our appetites. For if reason were not toppled from its citadel but could forever preserve its dignity, as is right, I admit that we would have no need of laws to help us live well and wisely according to nature. But since we are so inclined to misdeeds and we stray so readily from the right path, the judging of our affairs could not be freely left to human minds, despite your arguments to the contrary. Many judges would use their power for their own advantage rather than for the good of those who were entrusted to their care; for we all think well of ourselves, and it is hard to find anyone who would not be led by self-love to overstep the boundaries of propriety. Hence, as ambition gradually intensifies, the power of judging can change to tyranny, as we read in the case of the Thirty Tyrants in Athens.[89] So too, the Roman decemvir Appius Claudius, while avenging the cause of liberty, in his love for it transformed it into servitude and forgot all decorum and honour.[90] The Spartans adopted the laws of Lycurgus, and the Romans used them too, whether (as we read in the *Pandects*) twenty years after expelling the Tarquinii or (as Livy seems to prefer) thirty-eight years later, when the Romans established the laws the people should use.[91] Three envoys were sent to Greece in order to transcribe the famous laws of Solon and to learn about the laws and customs of other cities. At first, they composed ten tables of Roman laws. Later, they added two others, and with the name of the Twelve Tables, they had the completed code engraved on bronze tablets.[92]

'Now, as for your opinion that uncivilized and primitive nations have no written alphabet, not to mention written laws, I am not convinced that this is the case. For we see animals that are incapable of reason and speech, and yet have agreed on signs as a sort of alphabet, which they use to offer each other food or help, or to produce songs or cries expressing their inner joy. It is worthwhile sometimes to listen to the howls of wolves, for their variety suggests that they can speak to each other in this language. At least, it happens that, as far as their howling can be heard, all the wolves in an entire forest will gather together very quickly. Fowlers shut a thrush in a cage and place it in the shrubbery, so that its melodic singing lures its fellows to the bird-lime set for them. They catch turtle-doves in a similar manner. Finding a gathering-place of these birds, they fix one end of a six-foot pole in the ground, leaving the other end free to move. To this end they fasten a net woven of rushes, in which they place a dove with its feet bound. Next, they lift the net holding the dove by a rope; then slackening it, they let the bird fly while the net falls to earth. Other doves flock there, so that you can see that they were summoned by the beating of the bound dove's wings. When storks begin to migrate here or return to their home (a place as yet undiscovered), they gather in the open fields of Asia and murmur to each other. The last stork to arrive is torn apart, and then the others fly off. Further instances of animal communications could be adduced, but they are too numerous to recount here.

'If one bears these examples in mind and reflects that even animals lacking speech and reason can make signs to each other to indicate their intentions, I think it will prove difficult to believe that people anywhere on earth can be found whose wits are so unrefined, dull and leaden that they have not devised those signs for expressing their thoughts which we call letters. Still, suppose there are some people lacking letters and laws. Should we derive our models for living from them because they live according to nature, as they say, without industry, letters, praise or renown? Shouldn't we rather derive our models from those who have surpassed other nations in the glorious achievements of war and peace? Should we, like barbarians, neglect justice when it truly protects, unites and nourishes the human race? Or should we embrace and cultivate it, like those whose wisdom is extolled above others?

'Just as humankind possesses nothing more divine than law, so law has obtained a name, *jus,* which readily reminds us of its distinction and usefulness.[93] Whether the root of *jus* comes from *juvare* [to aid] or from Jupiter, whom some consider the creator of law, as I said earlier, the very derivation of the word lends it authority.[94] What is more glorious than to aid the human race and earn its thanks, as even today Greece boasts of Hercules and other heroes? The planet Jupiter is so named because astronomers think that it is salutary to the earth and aids [*juvare*] the human race. If

Jupiter is indeed the creator of law [*jus*] and took his name from it, there can be nothing more salutary on earth, in practice or in theory, than Jupiter's divinity. And, although I often disagree with the views of astrologers, especially when they profess to possess a knowledge of future events, I think we must lend them some credence in this matter. The term "justice" [*justitia*] contains the meaning of law [*jus*], no matter which noun is derived from the other. Justice alone binds people together in society and renders permanent our cities and kingdoms which, without her, would be nothing but bands of robbers.[95] As an intelligent man, I am sure you'll believe me without my adjurations — another word derived from *jus,* since swearing an oath is, I think, merely calling the laws to witness, and the gods who created them.

'If the principles of law are sometimes obscured by the multiplicity and diversity of their applications or through the fault of their interpreters, we would clearly be wrong to blame the laws and their principles, rather than the peculiar conditions of their interpretation or the perversity of their misguided interpreters. It is quite absurd to fault the discipline for the practitioner's mistakes. In medicine, if a doctor loses sight of health, which it is his aim to restore or preserve, is it the science of medicine we should censure, or isn't it rather its practitioner, the doctor? When the same thing happens in philosophy, oratory or the other liberal arts, won't our answer be the same? All the disciplines which are by their very nature laudable can never lose their intrinsic worth, nor can they be debased by the chance circumstances of a practitioner's fraud or lies.

'I am accustomed to denounce in many ways the proliferation of these ranters and pettifoggers, as they are called, who in defending a case in court exalt not the laws but cunning and crafty legal stratagems. I would likewise censure the astute and arrogant multitudes of juridical authors, who in even the most clear-cut cases seem to produce mountains of material for doubt, while hacking away anything which offers a handle by which to judge.[96] Soon we shall have to raise from the dead a second Justinian who can adjudicate most rigorously between so many thousands of books and finally set limits to the writers on law. Otherwise, the immense and invaluable toils which once emended and clarified Roman law will be rendered useless a second and third time by the effrontery and impudence of these writers. For they are convinced they have mastered jurisprudence, and swollen with vain ambition, they claim for themselves the literary province belonging to the greatest scholars. I daresay that, if they understood the onerous task they are taking on, even such audacious and arrogant men would all be deterred by its magnitude.

'For nothing is so arduous or difficult as the profession of author and writer. To begin with, one must have a vast and profound knowledge of all subjects or at least of the subject at hand. For if you make the slightest error, bad luck will taint all your good points with ruinous charges of ignominy and ignorance. And unless you write what you know with learning, brevity, elegance and eloquence, scarcely anyone will want to read it. If you spent sleepless nights and suffered heat and cold, it was all in vain.[97] Often unpolished poems perish before their poet, and inept and inelegant orations before their orator. But these ranters embrace each other, courting and admiring themselves. During a case, they rely on their own writings, and don't even read Roman law, indifferent to the substance and style of Ulpian, Sulpicius, Paulus,

Marcellus, Scaevola, Africanus and the other learned and eloquent authors of Roman laws.[98] Having mastered the art of those frivolities and sophistries which occupy them day and night, they confound the courts and deafen everyone with their shouting, as if obscuring men's judgements in a dark fog. They strike me as unworthy of entering the guild of jurists.[99] For jurists are a venerable and sacred race who aid us in applying the dignity and majesty of laws not only to our private affairs, but to public and divine ones as well. It is they who best teach us to understand the rites and ceremonies of religion and to separate what is profane from what is sacred.

'I have intentionally saved this subject until now, so that we may conclude our remarks with divine topics. We define religion as part of public law, from which we must derive whatever pertains to the order of rites, the care of temples and the duties of priests. For the part of public law which is called secular is administered by magistrates, and it differs from religion in that the uninitiated are occasionally not admitted to certain rites. Thus Virgil describes the Sibyl when Aeneas is about to sacrifice to the spirits of the dead: "'Far off, stand far off, you uninitiated', the priestess cries, 'Leave all this grove behind.'"[100] There is no one view on the origin of the word "religion". In his work *On the Nature of the Gods,* Cicero thinks it comes from *relego* [to go over again], since it examines what is appropriate to the worship of the gods, and is "gone over again" by men of religion [*religiosi*].[101] Lactantius thinks that we human beings are born in such a condition that we should show devotion and deference to God as the creator of life. Since we know God, we obey God and we deem ourselves naturally obliged and bound [*religatos*] to God, he believes that "religion" takes its name from this fact.[102] This seems to be the view of Lucretius when he says: "Now I proceed to release souls from the tight bonds of religions."[103] In Macrobius, Servius Sulpicius is inclined to believe that, because the excellence of divine things seems far removed from us, "religion" is derived from *relinquo* [to leave behind], as "ceremony" is from *careo* [to lack].[104] Virgil, our greatest poet, seems to ascribe to this view when he writes: "There is a grove near the river of Caere, all hallowed by our fathers' religion; on all sides valleyed hills enclose it, surrounding the wood with dark fir-trees."[105]

'Whatever is true, we must rather address the problem of what religion is and which religion we know to be the true one. The apostle James wrote divinely to the dispersed tribes: "If any man thinketh himself to be religious while he bridleth not his tongue but deceiveth his heart, this man's religion is vain. Pure religion and undefiled before our God and Father is this, to visit the fatherless and widows in their affliction and to keep himself unspotted from the world."[106] Now the rites for worshipping and sacrificing to the gods varied until the age of Ninus, when the worship of idols was first established.[107] In our day, we see the same happen according to the variety of peoples and the diversity of their beliefs concerning the gods. To us who were chosen to inherit the heavenly patrimony, Jesus Christ has shown the true way to offer him sacrifice and worship, and he has embellished it with his lofty name. We may no longer stray from the chaste, immaculate and holy religion which he himself taught us, which he confirmed by his life and which he established as eternal by his death.

'Everything concerning the worship and religion of God the highest and best is covered by our laws and in particular by pontifical laws. All sacred and profane days have been marked, and the observances appropriate to each feast have been set forth. Various orders have been distinguished for those who administer the rites, and certain rules have been set for the mass, so that not only the celebrant and other priests understand fully how to act with piety, but even the masses have clear models for their behaviour during the mass. The priests have different titles and different functions, so that nothing can be omitted, through forgetfulness or negligence, which seems essential to religion and sacred rites. Ostiaries, exorcists, acolytes, cantors, lectors, subdeacons, deacons, elders and bishops all play their parts. And archdeacons, archelders, precentors, superintendents and treasurers perform their functions diligently. Is it surprising if I say little here about the supreme pontiffs, more commonly known as popes, who not only oversee rites and religion but also have the power to bind and to loose?[108]

'Our humble and weak discourse will fear and tremble before the vicar of Christ, especially when, as now, there is no need to say more. It is not our aim to discuss in detail every aspect of divine rites and ceremonies. Rather, we have tried to show that laws supervise not only human affairs but divine matters and holy rites as well. We cannot offer our laws a single and simple expression of gratitude. For if we shape our character to the standard of virtue; if we govern our families and homes correctly; if we organize our family and household properly, so that our wives, children and servants obey us and accept our authority; if we are not harmful or troublesome to our government, our friends, our family and foreigners; if we are agreeable servants to the gods and cultivate their worship; and if we lead a life worthy of man, whom God created in his own image and likeness[109] – for all these things we must render enormous thanks to our laws.

'This is what, at your urging, I had to say concerning laws and legal judgements. I spoke not to contradict your view, but in order to protect and defend their cause. Although we have moved quickly through each aspect of the question, stopping only when necessary, like travellers at a way-station, I believe that anyone who reflects on these matters will now find them less difficult to judge.'

Translator's Notes

1. A. Brown, *Bartolomeo Scala, 1430–1497, Chancellor of Florence: The Humanist As Bureaucrat* (Princeton, N.J., 1979), p. 289 n. 25, notes that Lorenzo left Florence for the Congress of Cremona on 12 February 1483.
2. For Bernardo Machiavelli, father of Niccolò, see F. Gilbert, *Machiavelli and Guicciardini* (Princeton, N.J., 1965), pp. 318–19.
3. For Scala's estate in Borgo Pinti (Florence), see Brown, *Scala,* pp. 227–33; and L. Pellecchia, 'The patron's role in the production of architecture: Bartolomeo Scala and the Scala palace', *Renaissance Quarterly* 42 (1989), 258–91. Scala's palazzo and garden currently house the Italian Metallurgy Union.
4. Carnival in 1483 ran from 3–11 February.
5. Cosimo de' Medici (1389–1464), son of the wealthy banker Giovanni di Bicci, led the Medici domination of Florentine politics in the thirty years from 1434 until his death. See F. Ames-Lewis, ed., *Cosimo il Vecchio de' Medici 1389–1464* (Oxford, 1992).
6. Niccolò da Uzzano (1359–1431) was a wealthy Florentine merchant, financier and three-times gonfalonier of the city. A moderate oligarch, he urged cautious opposition to the

ascendancy of Cosimo de' Medici, as Machiavelli notes in *Discourses* I.33. Donatello's bust of him is in the Bargello in Florence.

7. Brown, *Scala,* p. 295 n. 49, compares this passage to the opening words of Book III, chapter 5 in Leon Battista Alberti's *De re aedificatoria,* ed. G. Orlandi and P. Portoghesi, 2 vols. (Milan, 1966), I, p. 189. See also n. 52.

8. Reading *recte ieceris* instead of *redeieceris.*

9. By modern reckoning, Telesphorus was pope from circa 125 to 136. Scala follows the *Liber Pontificalis,* which says he was an anchorite who instituted a seven-week fast during Lent: see *The Book of the Popes (Liber Pontificalis) to the Pontificate of Gregory I,* trans. L. R. Loomis (New York, 1916; reprinted New York, 1979), pp. 12–13.

10. By Scala's reckoning, Calixtus I, pope from circa 217 to 222, instituted this fast in 218. See *The Book of the Popes,* trans. Loomis, p. 20: 'He instituted a fast from corn, wine and oil upon the Sabbath day thrice in the year, according to the word of the prophet, of a fourth, of a seventh, and of a tenth.' Loomis notes: 'If one adds the fast of Lent, which took place during the first month, March, one has the fasts of the four seasons which are mentioned in early Roman liturgies and in the homilies of St. Leo.'

11. Reading *gratiam faciebant* instead of *gratia faciebant.* For the three Hebrew festivals, see Exodus 23:16; for a tithe of grain, wine and oil, see Deuteronomy 14:23.

12. In the sixth century, Emperor Justinian ordered the codification of Roman law; the resulting body of legislation was known as the *Corpus iuris civilis* and consisted of the *Digest* or *Pandects,* the *Institutions* and the *Novellae.*

13. The so-called Codex Pisanus (or Florentinus) is said to have been acquired by the Pisans after their victory over Amalfi in 1135. When Pisa was defeated by Florence in 1406, the codex was taken to Florence. There it was kept in the Palazzo Vecchio until 1786, when it was transferred to the Laurentian Library.

14. The two most famous Italian jurists of the fourteenth century were Baldus or Baldo degli Ubaldi (c. 1327–1400), a native of Perugia, and Bartolus or Bartolo da Sassoferrato (1314–57): on the latter, see F. Calasso in *Dizionario biografico degli italiani* (Rome, 1960–),VI, pp. 640–69. By Scala's account, the 'recent' controversy must have occurred between 1351 and 1356, when both were teaching in Perugia, but it was Bartolus rather than Baldus who died soon thereafter.

15. Both Latin terms mean a security given for a loan or debt.

16. Justinian, *The Digest,* ed. T. Mommsen and P. Krueger, trans. A. Watson, 4 vols. (Philadelphia, 1985), II, p. 596 (XX.5.7). Active in the period after Caracalla (211–17), the jurist Marcianus was the author of voluminous manuals, including *On the Hypothecary Formula,* which is cited here.

17. A native of Gubbio, Giovanni Buongirolami (1381–1454) moved in 1400 to Florence, where he became a distinguished jurist and diplomat with a pro-Medici bias: see Paolo Mari in the *Dizionario biografico,* XV, pp. 234–6.

18. In August 1480, Ottoman forces sacked the city of Otranto in Apulia.

19. Scala writes 'bassia' for Turkish 'pasha' or 'basha' (formerly Italian 'bascià' and English 'bashaw'). The etymology from Greek *basileus* is erroneous: the root is Turkish *bash* or 'head'.

20. The recent explorations sponsored by King John II of Portugal, who reigned from 1481 to 1495, included Diogo Cão's discovery of the Congo River (1482) and of the 'new islands' Fernando Po (Bioko) and São Tomé (1483).

21. For this discussion of natural law, Brown, *Scala,* p. 290 n. 29, cites Cicero, *De legibus* I.6.18–19.

22. See Lactantius, *Divinae institutiones* VII.4, on God's gift of reason to mankind.

23. Matthew 22:37–9 (abridged by Scala); cf. Mark 12:30–1.

24. Matthew 22:40.

25. For this notion of universal law, Brown, *Scala,* p. 290, quotes sources in Cicero, Gratian, Thomas Aquinas and Coluccio Salutati.

26. Supplying *clarius.*

27. Franciscus Accursius (Francesco Accorso or d'Accursio, 1182–1260), the leading jurist of the thirteenth century, taught at the University of Bologna. On Cinus or Cino da Pistoia (1270–1337), Latin commentator of the *Digest* and celebrated Italian poet, see Gennaro Maria Monti, *Cino da Pistoia giurista* (Città di Castello, 1924).

28. Pseudo-Plato, *Hipparchus* 227E.

29. Justinian, *Digest,* ed. Mommsen and Krueger, IV, p. 620 (XLIV.1.2.1). The third-century jurist Ulpian (Domitius Ulpianus) wrote 280 books on law, from which nearly a third of Justinian's *Digest* derives.

30. Justinian, *Digest,* ed. Mommsen and Krueger, IV, p. 620 (XLIV.1.2.3).

31. Sponsored by the tribune Marcus Cincius Alimentus, the *lex Cincia de donis et muneribus* of 204 BC set a limit on gifts and donations to advocates, who were supposed to plead without pay. Emperor Claudius limited the permissible fee to ten thousand sesterces, more than which constituted extortion: see Tacitus, *Annals* XI.7.

32. Probably: 'Fra i due litiganti, il terzo gode' (Between two parties, it's the third who gains).

33. *Capitudine* was the Florentine word for an assembly of the twenty-one major and minor guilds: see S. Battaglia, *Grande dizionario della lingua italiana* (Turin, 1961–), II, p. 696.

34. Scala correctly links consul and *consilium* (counsel), although the etymology may not have determined the choice of the term by the Florentine guilds.

35. The reference is to the law passed on 14 June 1477, by which important cases could be appealed to the Merchants' Court in Florence: see Brown, *Scala,* pp. 290–1.

36. Juvenal, *Satires* VI.241.

37. See Plato, *Laws* IV (711C), and Cicero, *De legibus* III.14.31.

38. Aristotle, *Nicomachean Ethics* II.3 (1105ᵃ8–10).

39. The debate on nobility was an important issue of Quattrocento humanism: see the texts collected in A. Rabil, Jr., ed. and trans., *Knowledge, Goodness, and Power: The Debate over Nobility among Italian Quattrocento Humanists* (Binghamton, N.Y., 1991). See also the translation of Josse Clichtove's *On True Nobility* in Chapter 15.

40. Presumably a reference (added later?) to Scala's knighthood, conferred on him by Pope Sixtus IV in 1484 and confirmed by the Florentine Council of the People in 1485: see Brown, *Scala,* pp. 98–9, 107–8.

41. A native of Pesaro, Pandolfo Collenuccio (1444–1504) wrote a number of works in both Latin and Italian. The ruler of Pesaro and captain of the Florentine militia mentioned here is Costanzo Sforza (1466–1510), who soon became Collenuccio's enemy and eventually caused his death: see E. Melfi in *Dizionario biografico,* XXVII, pp. 1–5.

42. Homer, *Odyssey* XI.568; cf. Plato, *Laws* I (624B).

43. Homer, *Odyssey* XI.568–71.

44. Aristides (c. 520–c. 468 BC) was an Athenian statesman and solider, whose reputation for honesty became proverbial. Marcus Porcius Cato the Censor (234–149 BC) was a Roman statesman and author, renowned for his stern traditional morality.

45. Xenophon, *Cyropaedia* I.2.6.

46. Juvenal, *Satires* VIII.50.

47. This is Scala's *Leges* (Laws), number XXVI in a collection of one hundred Latin apologues or fables written in 1481; see Bartolomeo Scala, *Apologi centum,* ed. K. Müllner (Vienna, 1896), p. 17; and also Brown, *Scala,* pp. 278–88, 291 n. 34.

48. Reading *earum [sc. legum] . . . imperio* instead of *eorum . . . imperio.*

49. Reading *laudarit* instead of *laudavit.*

50. After freeing Rome from its Etruscan kings in 509 BC, Lucius Junius Brutus is said to have ordered the execution of his sons for treason: see Livy, *History of Rome* II.3–5.

51. Livy, *History of Rome* II.5.6.

52. As in an earlier architectural simile noted by Brown (n. 7), here Scala may be echoing Leon Battista Alberti, *De re aedificatoria,* I, p. 95 (II.1): 'by a natural instinct all of us, whether we are learned or not, immediately grasp what is right or wrong in the theory or execution of things . . . so that if we encounter anything in which there is some element that is mutilated, lame, excessive, superfluous or clumsy, we are immediately unsettled

and desire these things to be more agreeable'. First printed in Florence in 1485, with a dedication by Angelo Poliziano to Lorenzo de' Medici, Alberti's treatise no doubt circulated in Medici circles while Scala was composing his treatise.

53. Reading *memini* instead of *nemini* (a printer's error in Borghi's text?).
54. Reading *inde fateor* instead of *unde fateor.* For the natural law of humankind and animals, see Justinian, *Digest* I.1.1 (Ulpian).
55. Reading *illud quod* instead of *illud quo.*
56. Cf. Gaius, *Institutes,* ed. and trans. F. de Zulueta, 2 vols. (Oxford, 1946), I, p. 2 (I.1, text); II, pp. 12–13 (commentary).
57. Xenophon, *Spartan Constitution* I.7–9. Lycurgus was the traditional founder of the Spartan constitution.
58. Justinian, *Institutes,* ed. P. Krueger, trans. P. Birks and G. McLeod (London, 1987), pp. 120–1 (IV.1.5): 'For manifest theft the penalty is fourfold damages.' The Twelve Tables contained the earliest Roman code of laws.
59. The Getae lived along the southern Danube, and the Bactrians in what is now Afghanistan. Herodotus, *Histories* V.6, describes similar customs among the Thracians, but not among their kinsmen the Getae.
60. Herodotus, *Histories* I.197.
61. Herodotus, *Histories* III.99.
62. See Gaius, *Institutes,* I, p. 2 (I.1, text); II, pp. 12–13 (commentary).
63. As noted in Brown, *Scala,* p. 292 n. 39, this survey of Roman laws is based on Gaius, *Institutes,* I, pp. 2–4 (I.2–7, text); II, pp. 13–23 (commentary).
64. Scala connects the *auctoritas* of the Roman Senate with increased population (*populus . . . auctior*), an etymology not found in Gaius.
65. In Scala's day, the Tuscan terms were *provvisioni* and *riformagioni.*
66. An echo of Cicero, *De legibus* I.6.18.
67. On Bias of Priene (sixth century BC), one of the Seven Sages, see Diogenes Laertius, *Lives of the Philosophers* I.5, and Plutarch, *The Dinner of the Seven Wise Men.*
68. On the flight of Justice, identified with the constellation Astraea or Virgo, see, e.g., Aratus, *Phaenomena* 96–136.
69. Virgil, *Aeneid* IV.58: 'law-giving Ceres'.
70. Scala probably borrows the example of Phoroneus, found in Hyginus, *Fabulae* CXLIII, from Poggio Bracciolini's *Historia convivalis:* see his *Opera omnia,* ed. R. Fubini, 4 vols. (Turin, 1964–9), I, p. 40.
71. See Exodus 24:18 (forty days), 32:15 (tablets).
72. The next two paragraphs rely on Plato's *Minos,* which Marsilio Ficino had recently translated into Latin.
73. According to Greek myth, Minos besieged Athens and demanded an annual tribute of human sacrifice for the Minotaur. The legend may reflect early conflicts between Crete and Attica. On the Athenian portrayal of Minos as a bloodthirsty tyrant see W. H. Roscher, *Ausführliches Lexicon der griechischen und römischen Mythologie,* 6 vols. (Leipzig, 1884–1937), VI.2, cols. 2997–3001.
74. Reading *in urbe Cnosso* instead of *in urbe Noso.*
75. Plato, *Minos* 320C. Talus, in Greek mythology, was the guardian of Crete.
76. On the Oppian Law (enacted in 215 BC and repealed in 195), see Livy, *History of Rome* XXXIV.1–8, esp. 7–8 for Scala's remarks. Scala gives Oppius' praenom as Marcus.
77. According to Greek myth, the Hamadryads were wood-nymphs whose life lasted as long as the tree of which they were the spirits.
78. Cicero, *De natura deorum* II.25.64 and III.24.62.
79. The next paragraph names the lawgivers and divinities cited in Ficino's summary of Plato's *Minos,* in his *Opera omnia,* 2 vols. (Basel, 1576; reprinted Turin, 1959), II, p. 1135, as noted in Brown, *Scala,* p. 293. That work in turn echoes Ficino's *Epistula* I.5, 'Lex et iustitia' of 1462–4: see his *Lettere,* ed. S. Gentile (Florence, 1990–), I, pp. 17–18. The list derives in part from Diodorus Siculus, *Bibliotheca historica* I.94, which Poggio Brac-

ciolini translated in 1449 and paraphrased in his 1450 *Historia convivalis:* see his *Opera omnia,* I, pp. 47–8.

80. On Charondas, see Diodorus Siculus, *Bibliotheca historica* XII.12–21.
81. For Numa (715–673 BC), the second king of Rome, and Egeria, see Livy, *History of Rome* I.19.
82. See *The Koran,* trans. N. J. Dawood, 5th ed. (Harmondsworth, 1990), p. 19 ('The Cow', II.97): 'Gabriel who has by God's grace revealed to you the Koran'.
83. Reading *secta . . . elata victoriis* instead of *elatis victoriis.*
84. I punctuate 'que ratio recta, que simulacrum est divinitatis in nobis, dictaverit'.
85. To encourage the Platonic studies of Marsilio Ficino, Cosimo de' Medici gave him a complete codex of Plato's dialogues in 1462 and a country house in 1463.
86. As noted by Brown, *Scala,* p. 293, this paragraph derives from Ficino's epitome of Plato's *Minos,* in his *Opera omnia,* II, pp. 1134–5.
87. Reading *parentibus* instead of *presentibus* (Borghi) or *perentibus* (manuscript); this echoes Ficino's definition, in his *Opera omnia,* II, p. 1134: 'Law is the true basis of governing . . . , ordaining punishments for those who transgress and rewards for those who obey'.
88. That is, 'standard-bearer of justice' (in Italian, *gonfaloniere della giustizia*).
89. After the defeat of Athens in the Peloponnesian War (404 BC), a group of Athenian oligarchs, led by Critias and dubbed the 'Thirty Tyrants', ruled the city for eight months: see Xenophon, *Hellenica* II.3–4.
90. For the tyrannical Appius Claudius, decemvir from 451 to 449 BC, see Livy, *History of Rome* III.33–58. Scala here echoes Livy's description of citizens who 'rushing to liberty lapsed into servitude' (III.37.2).
91. Justinian, *Digest* I.2.2 (twenty years); Livy, *History of Rome* XXXIII.1 (thirty-two years, not thirty-eight). The Tarquinii were kings of Rome; Tarquinius Superbus, the last king, was expelled in 510 BC.
92. See Livy, *History of Rome* III.32–7; Diodorus Siculus, *Bibliotheca historica* XII.23–5.
93. The etymological arguments of this paragraph pose problems for the translator as well as the reader. As is common in classical and humanistic treatises, Scala relies on dubious etymologies, which are further obscured when translated.
94. Cf. Cicero, *De natura deorum* II.25.64: 'Iuppiter, id est iuvans pater'. For the connection of Jove and *ius,* cf. 'ius iurandum Iovis' in Ennius, *Tragedies: Unassigned Fragment* 389 in E. H. Warmington, ed., *Remains of Old Latin,* 4 vols. (London, 1940), I, pp. 364–5, cited by Cicero, *De officiis* III.29.104, and Apuleius, *De deo Socratis* 5.10.
95. An echo of Augustine, *De civitate Dei* IV.4 (noted in Brown, *Scala,* p. 294 n. 45).
96. Reading *in rebus apertissimis* instead of *in rebus apertissime.*
97. Scala echoes Horace's description of the aspiring poet in *Ars poetica* 413: 'sudavit et alsit' (suffered heat and cold).
98. For Ulpian see n. 29. In 88 BC Sulpicius Rufus passed by force a series of laws known as the *leges Sulpiciae.* Julius Paulus, who lived around 200 AD, was a prominent Roman jurist. Marcellus Ulpius was a Roman jurist of the second half of the second century AD. The jurist Quintus Cervidius Scaevola was a legal adviser of Marcus Aurelius, Roman emperor from AD 161 to 180. Sextus Caecilius Africanus was a Roman jurist of the middle of the second century AD.
99. If Scala is speaking literally, he refers to the *Arte dei Giudici e Notai.*
100. Virgil, *Aeneid* VI.258–9.
101. Cicero, *De natura deorum* II.28.72 (noted in Brown, *Scala,* p. 294 n. 46).
102. Lactantius, *Divinae institutiones* IV.28.3 (noted in Brown, *Scala,* p. 294 n. 46).
103. Lucretius, *De rerum natura* I.931–2 (noted in Brown, *Scala,* p. 294 n. 46).
104. Macrobius, *Saturnalia* III.3.8 (noted in Brown, *Scala,* p. 294 n. 46).
105. Virgil, *Aeneid* VIII. 597–9.
106. James 1:26–7 (noted by Brown, *Scala,* p. 294 n. 46).

107. According to some ancient sources, Ninus was the first king of Assyria and the builder of Nineveh.
108. Papal authority is often derived from Jesus' words to Peter in Matthew 16:19: 'I will give unto thee the keys of the kingdom of heaven: and whatsoever thou shalt bind on earth shall be bound in heaven: and whatsoever thou shalt loose on earth shall be loosed in heaven.'
109. Genesis 26:1.

Further Reading

Brown, A., *Bartolomeo Scala, 1430–1497, Chancellor of Florence: The Humanist As Bureaucrat* (Princeton, N.J., 1979), esp. pp. 288–96, 311–13

CHRP, pp. 319–20, 358, 364, 429–30, 772–3

Garin, E., 'The humanist chancellors of the Florentine Republic from Coluccio Salutati to Bartolomeo Scala', in his *Portraits from the Quattrocento,* trans. V. A. Velen and E. Velen (New York, 1972), pp. 1–29

Martines, L., *The Social World of the Florentine Humanists, 1390–1460* (Princeton, N.J., 1963)

Pellecchia, L., 'The patron's role in the production of architecture: Bartolomeo Scala and the Scala palace', *Renaissance Quarterly,* 42 (1989), 258–91

Wilcox, D. J., *The Development of Florentine Humanist Historiography in the Fifteenth Century* (Cambridge, Mass., 1969), pp. 177–202

13

Francesco Guicciardini

RUSSELL PRICE

Introduction

Francesco Guicciardini (1483–1540) was an eminent historian and moralist, as well as a noted political thinker. His *History of Italy* has for centuries enjoyed a very high reputation, and his *History of Florence* has been much studied by recent historians. His *Ricordi* bears comparison with the work of the best French *moralistes,* such as La Rochefoucauld and Vauvenargues. His strictly political works are mostly fairly short pieces, but have been praised for their grasp and realism. He studied law at the universities of Florence, Ferrara and Padua, and practised law; later, he became an important political figure in Florence, and, especially, in the service of the Medici popes, Leo X and Clement VII, serving as governor of Modena, Reggio Emilia, Parma and Bologna, and as president of Romagna.

Guicciardini wrote the following piece in August 1512, in Logroño, Spain; for several months he had been the Florentine ambassador to the king of Spain. (He gave no title to the piece, and it is sometimes called the *Discorso di Logrogno.*) Like most of his works, it remained unpublished until the late nineteenth century. (None was published during his lifetime; the *History of Italy* was published between 1561 and 1564, and a version of the *Ricordi* in 1576.) Nevertheless, the piece is of considerable interest; Guicciardini was an acute and well-informed young man, and in it he analyses the defects of the Florentine popular regime, which had lasted since 1494 (and was about to collapse), and he puts forward various interesting remedies.

At the beginning of chapter 33 of his *History of Florence* (written 1508–9), Guicciardini discussed the problems inherent in the Florentine system of government. Most public offices were held for very short periods, and he identifies the fundamental problem as the lack of a man or men 'charged with continually looking after public affairs — men authorized to carry out an action once it had been decided. Instead the Signoria changed every two months and the Colleges every three and four months. With such a brief term of office, everyone tended to move cautiously and no one felt personally responsible for public affairs.' It was to remedy this problem that the office of permanent gonfalonier of justice was instituted in September 1502. (The first, and only, holder of this office was Piero Soderini.) Both in the *History of Florence* and in this piece, Guicciardini criticizes Soderini's conduct severely.

The first section discusses in a general way the military and political problems confronting Florence, and the solutions that he proposes. Then he proceeds to a more detailed consideration of the political and constitutional problems. He identifies the weaknesses of the Great Council, composed of over three thousand members (see n. 19); nevertheless, he approves of this Council, which is the supreme popular body. Next, Guicciardini discusses the office of gonfalonier. He thinks that it should be permanent (in order to provide executive continuity and stability) but that some of its powers should be removed (for a too powerful gonfalonier represents a threat to republican institutions and civic freedom). Then he turns to a body intermediate between the gonfalonier and the Great Council, and recommends the setting up of a Senate similar to that existing in Venice. This is the main constitutional innovation recommended by Guicciardini and reflects his concern that the wisest citizens should control the affairs of the republic. He approved of popular government, but he favoured aristocratic control. He opposes the practice of calling 'parliaments' (general assemblies of the people, with open voting), maintaining that, in a well-ordered republic, affairs should be decided by established bodies, in a regular manner, and with secret voting. The last section is concerned with the judicial system, and with punishments and rewards. He concludes that if the reforms that he has recommended are adopted, there would be a notable improvement in the conduct of Florentine affairs. He observes, however, that there are some fundamental social problems that would require more radical solutions (of the kind adopted by Lycurgus in ancient Sparta); but he judges these to be impossible in Florence.

There has been a good deal of discussion about some of the political terms used by Italian Renaissance writers (e.g., *stato, libertà*); many of these have been indicated in the text (in square brackets) both in this piece and in the one that follows by Paolo Vettori (Chapter 14).

Stato has various senses: it denotes 'government' and 'regime', as well as 'territories' or 'dominions'. And the phrase *le cose dello stato* denotes 'affairs of state' or 'political matters', as well as 'political offences' and 'political trials'. (In this piece, Guicciardini does not use the words *la politica* and *politico*.) In the few instances in which 'state' is used without square brackets, I think stato is implied.

Libertà means both 'freedom' and 'independence' (see n. 2). When it has been rendered by terms other than 'freedom' or 'freedoms' (e.g., by 'civic freedom', 'free institutions'), I have added *libertà* in brackets.

The use of *governo* is always indicated in brackets. 'Government', 'governing' and 'to govern' usually, but not always, render *governo* and *governare*. Other terms always explained thus are 'regime', 'constitution' and 'constitutional' (*costituzione,* which had various senses, none of which corresponds to 'constitution', is not used in this piece).

Magistrato is a very common word. It denotes either a person or a body (in modern Italian, the latter is *magistratura*); I have usually rendered the former sense as 'public officer', 'office-holder', 'holder of public office' or 'public office-holder'.

Finally, 'the Great Council' always renders *el consiglio grande,* and 'the Council' *el consiglio,* unless otherwise indicated. Guicciardini often uses *el populo* and *la multitudine* when referring to the Great Council (see n. 19), and these instances are always registered. *Populo,* however, sometimes means the 'people' as a body; for the adjective *populare,* see n. 1.

Guicciardini was a notable stylist, and although it has sometimes been thought that he used imagery very sparingly, similes and metaphors are quite frequent in this piece: many of them relate to food and maladies. I have thought it worthwhile to give indications of most of these images.

For the Italian text see 'Del modo di ordinare il governo popolare', in Francesco Guicciardini, *Dialogo e discorsi del reggimento di Firenze,* ed. R. Palmarocchi (Bari, 1932), pp. 218–59; there are also two annotated editions: Francesco Guicciardini, *Opere,* ed. E. Lugnani Scarano, 3 vols. (Turin, 1970–81), I, pp. 249–96; Francesco Guicciardini, *Scritti scelti,* ed. L. Bonfigli (Florence, 1924), pp. 49–92. I have added various headings and subheadings in order to clarify the structure of Guicciardini's arguments. I wish to express my great indebtedness to Paolo L. Rossi and Jill Kraye for commenting on my translation and suggesting many improvements, and to Nicolai Rubinstein, Alison Brown and Francesco Badolato for valuable advice on many points.

How the Popular[1] Government Should Be Reformed

There are two main reasons that make me think that, within not very many years, our city will lose its freedom [*libertà*][2] and its dominions [*stato*], unless it receives great help from God. The first is that there have been so many disasters in Italy, and because these rulers [*questi principi*][3] have been engaged in many battles, it is to be expected that one of them will emerge as a great power,[4] and will aim at subduing the lesser powers [*e' minori*],[5] and perhaps turn Italy into a monarchy. I find this argument especially cogent, considering how much effort was needed to defend Italian freedom [*la commune libertà*] during the period when there were no foreign rulers in Italy. But now that will be much more difficult, since such great birds of prey are gnawing at her vitals [*nelle viscere*]. And in these circumstances I think Florence will be in great danger, because we do not have enough forces to defend ourselves; instead, we live unarmed and (compared with the past) our city possesses little wealth, because the trades and commerce that often enabled us to survive are in decline.

The second reason is that our civic life [*el vivere . . . civile*] is very different from what is appropriate for a good republic, with regard both to our political constitution [*la forma del governo*] and to our various customs and practices: we have an administration that risks becoming tyrannical or else degenerating into a popular anarchy, for there is a general tendency to injure others, with little respect for, or fear of, the laws and public officers; able and worthy men do not have regular opportunities to demonstrate their qualities, nor are there rewards for those who perform meritorious deeds for our republic; there is an overweening ambition in everyone to seize public offices, and an arrogant desire to interfere in all public matters of any importance; the spirits of men are effeminate and enervated, and dedicated to a way of life that is soft and (considering our means) sumptuous; and there is little love of true glory and honour, but much love of possessions and money. All these things cause me to entertain few hopes for our city, but not altogether to despair, because I believe that it is possible to heal [*sanare*] most of these ills; and even if this would certainly be very difficult, it is by no means impossible.

I certainly cannot envisage one or two individual laws having the desired effect; rather, it is essential to provide an overall solution for our problems, so that everything would be moulded into something appropriate, and to introduce a fundamental reform of our constitution in stages [*riformarla e ridistinguerla tutta*], just as one prepares a dish from dough [*cose da mangiare di pasta*], so that if at the first attempt one does not succeed, one begins again, and works the dough into a new form; or (to use a new simile) do as good physicians do, when they are confronted with the various ills that may afflict a body to such an extent that no one remedy will be effective; they have at hand various medicines for dealing with all the causes of these ills, so as to effect a general recovery of the patient. This is certainly difficult to do and requires a very good physician, but it is by no means impossible. It is indeed true that such remedies are more efficacious with a young man than with an old one, which frightens me, because our city is by now ancient. Nevertheless, I do not despair, provided some magnanimous man applies himself to this task, and wise men were to bring to bear on it the skill and energy that is frequently employed in making money and in evildoing. They should do this with all the more ardour, since great glory will accrue to them precisely because the task is so difficult.

I readily concede that if our city were to be healed [*sanare*] completely,[6] it would be necessary to make many changes that would be almost impossible to persuade our citizens to accept, because they are not used to them and because our men are too soft. And by trying to do all these things, one might very well achieve nothing at all. Therefore, I would praise anyone who concentrates on doing the less difficult things and who limits himself to doing at first only those things that are within the bounds of possibility. It would be no small achievement to raise to a moderately good condition a city that has sunk so low; indeed, it would be a considerable achievement to make a start, because once the right path is taken, eventually, with the passage of time, we would achieve much greater success than such a modest beginning might seem to promise.

Military reforms

First of all, it seems to me essential to bear in mind that our city should have military forces that are at least sufficient for defending itself, and that it should not have to be continually afraid of foreign attacks. It would be of no avail for its internal affairs to be well ordered and rationally conducted, if it could be defeated by foreign forces, and therefore the city must have ample troops to defend it. Here it must be borne in mind that if our city has to be defended by the methods used in the past, it has fewer forces at its disposal than it has ever had, because it has much less wealth than it used to have. The public revenues (of which a great part goes in paying off the public debt) are insufficient; the citizens generally are not wealthy, as they used to be, since the city trades are less flourishing than in the past (for many other places and peoples have developed their commerce and are continuing to do so). And those citizens who *are* wealthy are not used to being required to help their native city,[7] as was the practice in former times. It would be exceedingly difficult to restore these ancient customs in the present popular regime [*questo vivere populare*], and it would be better if the efforts and skills needed to bring about these reforms were to be employed in doing things that are more likely to be successful. Indeed, if our city needed to spend a large sum (say, seventy or eighty thousand ducats a month), it would be impossible to raise it; in fact, it would not be possible to raise a large amount of money quickly.

Consequently, there are no grounds for planning on the assumption that our city could maintain for long a large army of paid soldiers and trained officers, as it has often done in the past. And, since we cannot use external forces, we must recognize the need to depend on those made up of our own citizens. Nor is arming its citizens something incompatible with a republican and popular regime [*uno vivere di republica e populare*], because if there is a good judicial system and there are appropriate laws, such arms bring benefit to a country, not harm. This stands to reason, and the examples of many ancient republics, such as Rome, Athens and Sparta, bear it out, for by using citizen armies they both defended their independence [*libertà*] and extended their territories [*lo imperio*]. Moreover, this practice is by no means unknown in Florence, because we read in our histories that our ancestors, in the period when they had newly gained their freedom, fought all their own battles, and so successfully, that this should uplift the spirits of the men of today rather than depress them. That it should also be easy to persuade and inspire them (if it is done with due diligence) is shown by the start that has been made,[8] which although promoted in the face of widespread disapproval, with very few in favour and not in a very orderly way, has been accepted to such an extent that it is now approved of by everyone.

There are many reasons why using citizen armies is very much more useful than using mercenary armies. Above all, anyone who relies on foreign soldiers risks being deceived by them, and this is especially true of republics, which do not have that affinity with them that a prince has. It is dangerous to confer supreme authority on one man, whereas it causes confusion to confer equal authority on several chiefs: they do not expect to receive the same rewards, and they think that it is right to treat public office as a private business; and even if they should prove loyal, they are not motivated by any real devotion. And apart from achieving a modicum of glory (which some of them value and others do not) their interests are not involved; they fight battles when they have to and without displaying any zeal. This would not happen if fellow citizens and subjects were used, because there is no reason to fear being tricked by them, and they certainly would not fight wars slowly or sluggishly in order to draw them out.[9] And since they will be moved by a burning desire for victory (and not by a mere duty to win), who can have any reason to fear that their devotion will be hollow? If our city should suddenly be attacked or if it wanted to undertake some quick expedition, an army could be raised in a few days. This cannot happen if it has to be recruited from distant places or foreign countries. And if a citizen army happens to be defeated, our government [*lo stato della città*] would not fall; indeed, another army would be raised at once. There is no time to do this if one has to raise another army composed of foreign mercenaries. The great importance of this is obvious.

The Romans were able to defend themselves in many wars (especially against Hannibal) only because, after suffering defeats, they were able to regroup their own armies. Carthage was quickly defeated by Scipio because, when its mercenary soldiers were scattered, it lacked an army. As for our own times, who can doubt that, if the Venetians had been able to raise a citizen army after their defeat at Vailà,[10] they would not have lost all their mainland territories [*stato*] within eight days? Their inability to do this reduced them to such straits that, if the emperor[11] had been a man of different calibre, or if the league of their enemies had held firm, this defeat on a single day, and the negligence of one of their mercenary leaders,[12] would have deprived them not only of their territories [*el dominio*] but also of their freedom.[13]

Dominion [*lo stato e lo imperio*] is nothing else but force [*una violenzia*] exercised over subjects,[14] concealed at times by some honourable name. And wanting to maintain it without armies and without one's own forces, but with the help of others, is tantamount to wanting to carry out a task within a particular profession without having the appropriate tools. In short, a state that does not possess citizen armies has great difficulty in dominating other states and in defending itself from its enemies. Moreover, if a state uses citizen forces, the upkeep of armies is much less expensive, for even though in wartime they are paid in the same way as other soldiers,[15] in peacetime there is no other expense but that of ordinary wages and maintenance; and what is paid is paid to one's own citizens. By acting in this way, there is certainly no reason to fear that our territories [*paesi*] will not be well defended, for Tuscany and our other territories [*dominio*] enjoy a strong geographical position and are very fertile, enabling their inhabitants to be fed. Therefore, after a start has been made by establishing infantry in our territories [*fuori della città*], it would be desirable to establish infantry and light cavalry within the city. There is no need to discuss the details of this now, but it will all be easy to do, especially since our city and dominions [*città . . . e lo stato nostro*] are very populous. In order to avoid the danger of factions and discords becoming rife in the city and the territories [*el paese*], it is certainly necessary for a good system of justice to be provided to restrain them; it is easy enough to pass laws, but ensuring that they are obeyed is harder, as will be explained at length later.[16]

POLITICAL REFORMS: PRELIMINARY DISCUSSION

The Great Council

When this matter,[17] which is of the utmost importance, is taken in hand, much attention should be paid to our system of government [*el governo nostro di drento*], and if the right changes are made, there are grounds for expecting a desirable outcome. It is unnecessary to discuss whether rule by one man or by a few or by the many is the best form of government [*amministrazione*], because freedom is a natural characteristic of our city. Our ancestors lived in freedom, and we have been brought up in it. Moreover, it is not just because our ancestors have bequeathed it to us as a fine tradition that we gladly embrace a free way of life; we are ready to defend it, if necessary, with all the means at our disposal, and even to lay down our lives for it. Freedom consists essentially in the supremacy of the laws [*uno prevalere le legge*] and public institutions over the unruly passions of individual men. But because laws are not living things and are not obeyed automatically, ministers (that is, public officers [*magistrati*]) are needed to ensure that they are obeyed. And if we want to live under the rule of law [*sotto le legge*], and not be subject to the arbitrary desires of individuals, it is essential that these holders of public offices should have no reason to fear any individuals, and should not owe their positions to the favour of any man or small group, so that they will not be under pressure to govern the city according to the dictates of others.[18] Therefore, institutions involving a wider participation of the people [*el vivere populare*] are needed as the foundation of freedom, and the Great Council is the basis and animating spirit of these, because it has the function of appointing men to the main city offices.

If this is definitely established, it will be very difficult for any man to hold sway in our city; because such a man will not be able to confer positions or prestige on anyone, those who hold public offices will have no reason for feeling obliged to obey him, either because of fear or because they hope for favours. Otherwise, ours is not and cannot be a free city, for it is inevitable that sects and factions will flourish, and within a few years one man will seize supreme power. Not only do I approve of the Great Council;[19] I also like the way in which it has been organized, because those who formerly did not participate in governing [*anticamente non participavano nel governo*] have been judiciously excluded from it, so that it would not be a body full of plebeians or men from the countryside; and it was necessary to make it possible for all the other citizens to become members, making them eligible, because restricting their numbers or choosing individuals as members was incompatible with its being a popular body. Although this wide membership brings in some madmen, as well as many who are ignorant or malevolent, nevertheless, on balance, elections that result from the participation of the many are usually sound. And if some are not, one should put up with this as the lesser evil. It is better to arrange matters in this way (despite some problems) than to want to see everything in the hands of one man. For it should be borne in mind that no human arrangements can be perfect, and those that have the fewest defects should be accepted.

The Great Council, then, is well organized, because all those who [formerly] participated in governing [*participavano dello stato*] are members. And I have some-times thought that, in the choosing of holders of public offices, not only all those men who today are eligible to choose should be involved, but also a large number of those who cannot participate in government [*participare del governo*]. Experience has shown that most of the errors that the Council makes in appointments to offices arise from a desire to spread them so widely that all the voters can reasonably entertain hopes of being themselves elected [at some time]. This would not be the case with those ineligible to be elected; since they could not expect to be included in any wide distribution of offices, they would have no reason to choose any men except those whom they genuinely think deserve to be chosen. To support this view, there is the experience of the ancient republics, in which a great many citizens were involved in the choosing of public officers. And it is recorded that, as in other republics, the Romans conferred citizenship with voting rights on many men, which in my opinion was tantamount to granting them the right to participate in the choosing of public officers, but not making them eligible to become public officers themselves. The reason for this, as I have said, is that, because the men who do the choosing will have no personal interest in one man being chosen rather than another, they will naturally support the men who seem to them to be the most meritorious; and in this they will follow the natural inclination of all men, which is to do what is right, except when personal interests lead them to act differently.[20] Nevertheless, since this is a novel proposal, and the matter is extremely important (and there are also some arguments that can be advanced against it), I would not want to insist on it, unless it receives widespread support. But I would certainly say that, if this proposal finds favour, it should be introduced with a limited scope, that is, one should give them the right only with regard to choosing office-holders, and they should not be allowed to intervene in any legislation.

When the Great Council's continuance is confirmed, then, and when the pre-viously mentioned element is added, which is the very basis of freedom – the soul of this body[21] – attention must be paid to important political matters [*cose importanti dello stato*], such as those pertaining to war and peace. The first discussions about the laws that need to be made or renewed at appropriate times should not take place in the Council, because they are too important. If it should be objected that the choosing of public office-holders is also of very great importance and is nevertheless done by the Council, I would reply that there is a different reason, namely, that it is essential mainly for the preservation of freedom, which would not be preserved if office-holders were chosen by one man or by a few. This does not apply in other matters, the deciding of which neither endangers the freedom of our city nor results in any man becoming so important that our civic freedoms [*la commune libertà*] are jeopardized. These matters often need to be decided quickly and secretly, which cannot be done by a large body. Moreover, choosing office-holders, even though it is important, is not such a hard matter to make good decisions about. The decisions of the Council [*el populo*][22] are mainly influenced by the kind of reputation that men have and the judgements that are made about them; this reflects the general opinion held about them rather than a careful appraisal made by each individual. This general opinion is not often mistaken;[23] and even if errors are sometimes made, important consequences do not always follow.

But bad consequences do follow with regard to law-making, for laws need to be made by men who are wise. When the Council [*la multitudine*], many of whose members are swayed by their passions, have a hand in making them, it is clear that the laws that result must almost always have harmful consequences or else prove ineffective. This is even more true of the decisions and policies that frequently have to be made about matters of war, peace treaties and similar things, the real features of which are known only by those men who are very shrewd; here when mistakes are made they may very well have the effect of jeopardizing the government and the territory over which it rules [*lo stato e dominio della città*]. Great difficulties certainly arose in the ancient republics, such as Rome, and especially Athens, which permitted the people to intervene in such matters. It is recorded that many political [*allo stato loro*] disasters occurred because of this. And there was a striking example in our own times, when the gonfalonier, Piero Soderini, asked the Great Council to decide whether to attack Pisa:[24] the policy that was supported by the vast majority, against the view of all the wisest men of the city, resulted in a damaging and shameful defeat.

The Gonfalonier

Such matters, then, must be decided by smaller bodies, by men who are shrewd and experienced. And because one of the surest foundations of freedom is the equality of citizens (that is, no citizen should rise higher than the others, beyond a certain limited extent), and because this equality cannot exist if office-holders rule permanently (that is, if the same men always hold power [*sieno . . . in luogo di governo*]), a change of rulers is essential from time to time. Nevertheless, great affairs of state [*le cose dello stato*] require the assiduous attention of experienced men, and indeed need those who take specific responsibility for them, and it is not undesirable if a special duty to take care of them is assigned to one man, who may deal with certain very important matters without revealing them to others. It is recognized that in nature the number one is perfect,[25] but it is not reasonable that such a duty should be performed by a private citizen; therefore, in our city the choice of a permanent gonfalonier, or at least a gonfalonier appointed for some years, would be very desirable, for many good consequences may result from it. This is confirmed by what is done in the Venetian

Republic, in which the office of permanent doge has been a most valuable source of stability. And there is a contrary example in Florence, eight years after the popular regime [*el vivere populare*] was set up:[26] not having anyone with overriding political responsibility [*cura del governo*] resulted in such dreadful dangers that we often survived through divine favour or luck rather than because of our conduct or wisdom; it is clear that if the former had been lacking, the outcome for us would have been certain ruin.

Therefore, it is desirable to establish a head of state [*uno capo*] of this kind. Yet it is not sufficient to have the Great Council with a gonfalonier,[27] unless there are some other institutions. For a gonfalonier has great powers and prestige, and he would rule arbitrarily, which would result in a kind of tyranny. Therefore, it is essential that he should sit with a body of citizens (similar to the Council of Eighty that we have now), composed of elected men who should be the pick of the city; together, they would discuss and decide all the important affairs of the republic.[28] This would avoid having the Great Council [*la multitudine*] involved in deciding very important matters (which would lead to a popular anarchy), and it would act as a curb on the gonfalonier, so that he would not wield too much power. If this body did not exist, decisions would inevitably be made by the gonfalonier with the Signoria, in short, by an oligarchy [*in uno magistrato di pochi*]. In such a situation, a permanent gonfalonier, or one who holds office for a long time, would have excessive personal power. Either decisions would be made by many inexperienced men who,[29] because of their ignorance, would make many mistakes, or the gonfalonier would have too much power, because experience shows (and it stands to reason) that the Great Council [*la moltitudine*] never does anything on its own initiative, but always follows the lead of weighty men; this is due to its inherent lack of strength. And it is natural that the Council will follow the lead of a man who occupies such a powerful office and has great influence, rather than that of anyone else; hence, the gonfalonier's power will become excessive.

The best way to preserve genuine and full freedom is certainly to have a body that can restrain the ignorant desires of the Great Council [*la multitudine*] and curb any ambitious tendencies in a gonfalonier; therefore, it is essential that this body should be composed of all the most intelligent and respected men. This would also have the effect of keeping men of quality in high positions; thus, they will not become discontented because they are not respected and begin to plot rebellion. At the beginning of the regime of popular government [*del governo populare*], the Council of Eighty was established[30] in order to achieve this purpose; but the ignorant views of the members of the Great Council [*della moltitudine*] resulted in men of little merit being elected to it, and those who should always be members of it are often not elected. Hence, the low quality of its members, and the frequent changes in its membership, have resulted in the Council of Eighty [*quel consiglio*] failing to have the authority it should; consequently, it has not been capable of dealing effectively with important political matters [*el peso della republica*], and many mistakes have been made; moreover, the influence of the gonfalonier has been excessive, causing a great deal of harm to our city. Therefore, if our city is to remain completely free and make sound decisions, it is essential that the Council of Eighty should be reformed, so that it is composed of a better class of men and has more power. I shall discuss this matter in more detail later.[31]

There are, then, three foundations of efficient and free government [*governo*] in our republic: the Great Council, the essential institution for preserving freedom; a permanent gonfalonier, or at least one who holds office for a long period; and a body composed of a sufficient number of citizens, for discussing and deciding all important political matters [*le cose . . . dello stato*]. If all these institutions are properly organised, the government [*el governo*] of our city will, in these respects, be built on solid foundations and will be perfect structurally. Until now I have discussed these matters in a general, almost a confused, way, so I must now distinguish between them more carefully and discuss each of them separately in the order in which I have outlined them.

POLITICAL REFORMS: MORE DETAILED DISCUSSION

The Great Council

All the chief public officers of our city, and all the other public officers, both those concerned with decision-making and those concerned with administration, should be elected by the Great Council, once the principle is accepted that no holder of public office [*lo stato*] should be beholden to one man or to a few. Since the government [*el governo*] would be placed completely in their hands,[32] it is essential that good appointments be made, and suitable men chosen. The Council has caused many evils by giving the offices of our city to men of low calibre, either because of ignorance or through ill-will, and this is a grave defect. Apart from the harm that results from ignorant men holding power [*nel governo*], this giving of offices to everyone indiscriminately, without taking account of individual talents or merits, discourages those who are public-spirited and capable, and it encourages bold spirits and bad men to seek their own advantage without any sense of shame. If it were seen that, when someone holding a public office has not acted well or has in general acquired a bad reputation, the Council [*el populo*] does not choose him again, selecting instead someone of proven merit, this would be a great stimulus to able and good men, as well as a serious warning to bad men. If these different kinds of treatment do not exist, rewards for good conduct are lacking, and this is one of the two things[33] that wise men in ancient times used to say republics were based on.

The root of this evil is a widespread ambition to want to seize public offices and to act with presumptuous licentiousness [*l'usare insolentemente la sua libertà*], which is something found in every country that is not well governed [*timoneggiati*]. What has enormously encouraged this evil is the electoral law, the practice of choosing members of public bodies by lot, from all the men who, in elections, have obtained merely a simple majority; for, in a Council in which there are many men who are ambitious, wicked or ignorant, it is not at all surprising that a great number of them succeed in obtaining that number of votes. Therefore, it would be desirable to require a two-thirds majority for elections, as was done in the early years of the Council, when in most cases good men were elected; and these good choices would have increased steadily in number, if the regime [*lo stato*][34] had become more solidly established, and if the judgements of the members of the Great Council [*del populo*] had not been affected, as sometimes happened, by the many fears that they harboured.

This procedure[35] would be best, and more rational, because it is not right that someone who is endorsed by only 501 persons out of 1,000 should be as entitled to hold a position as someone who wins 800 votes. Moreover, it is not compatible with popular government [*governo populare*], in which the Great Council [*el populo*] should be sovereign [*signore*], not the lot [*la sorte*],[36] and public office-holders should derive their authority from it, not from luck. There are two arguments against abolishing the lot. The first is that it would cause enmities and bad blood between those who consider themselves to be equals, if they see that one man is preferred to another, nor does it seem reasonable to them;[37] furthermore, such preferences are frequently wrong, because it cannot be denied that bizarre choices are sometimes made. The other argument is that it would result in appointments to offices being made on a restrictive basis [*andrebbono stretto*];[38] and it is certainly proper that, in a popular regime [*uno governo populare*], in which everyone pays taxes, everyone should have his proper place in public life and, especially, a proper share of the salaried offices. Nevertheless, I do not think we should deviate from the procedure I have recommended, because it promotes more effectively the goal of distributing well the public offices and administrative posts, which is the most important thing. If the regime [*lo stato*] were so stable that the citizens were agreed on its character and recognized that it could not be changed, I would not want to accept any difference in treatment.[39] But since it is still new and very unstable, for the sake of civil tranquillity it might be a good thing for the more important internal offices (such as those of the Signoria, the Ten[40] and the Eight)[41] to be filled by election, with a simple majority of the votes being required, after nomination. Alternatively, the lot could be used for appointing from those two who had gained the majority of votes. And such a procedure would also need to be used for the more important external public offices (such as the captains of Pisa, Arezzo and Pistoia).[42] The public offices that involve some administrative duties, but which are not so important (such internal offices as the officials of the Tower, the countryside,[43] etc.) and the external ones (such as the vicariates[44] and the more important mayoralties): these are a different matter, and the election procedure could be of a kind that permits a large number of electors; for example, everyone could be entitled to put in four or five names, and in choosing them a mixture of the lot and election could be used. And as for elections to the third kind of public offices, which involve little administration and are essentially honorific or profitable (such as the public treasurers and the less important mayoralties and many other city offices), here the present methods could be retained. And even if this procedure can be criticized because it does not entirely remedy the mistakes caused by the extensive suffrage, and it has not been the practice in other republics (none of which, as far as I know, has ever used the lot), nevertheless it should be tolerated as the lesser evil. It should be borne in mind that almost all human institutions are imperfect, and wise men are satisfied with those that have fewest defects.

The second point to consider about the Great Council concerns the laws. I do not mean whether they should be discussed by the Council in the first instance, because that would result in much confusion and would be incompatible with the procedures of a well-organised republic. I mean rather, after they have been passed by small bodies, whether or not they then need the approval of the Council. I find it easy to decide about this point: since the laws are a general matter and concern every citizen, the final decisions about them should be taken in the Council. I should certainly prefer that they not be discussed there publicly, except by order of the Signoria, and then only in favour of what is proposed, because if every member were free to argue in favour or against, there would be a great deal of confusion. But such discussion would be desirable if these measures have not been subjected to examination in another body. However, if they come to the Council after having been previously discussed thoroughly in smaller bodies, and with their merits already clear, there is no need for them to be discussed there. The ratification of laws by the Council is prescribed, not in order to re-examine them thoroughly, but because the laws bind everyone; thus, it cannot be claimed that they have been made by a few men, without general approval. There will also be a curb on the smaller councils, so that they do not introduce any law that changes the constitution [*in alterazione dello stato*] or has other harmful consequences. Moreover, to ensure that the members of the Council make decisions only after due deliberation, it is highly desirable that proposed laws should be published some days earlier, so that when the Council meets to approve them, they should already be sufficiently well known, and private discussions about them will have already taken place.

Whether taxes and allocations of funds need to be approved by the Council is, I think, more problematical. For one thing, experience shows that the Council [*el populo*] is reluctant to pass them, with the outcome that they are often approved so late that the money is not available in time to achieve the desired purposes. Again, it sometimes happens that funds are needed for carrying out a secret policy, which it is undesirable that the Council [(*el*) *populo*] should know about. And if this expenditure has to be approved by the Council, the reason for it must be made known there, because the measure will never be approved unless it is generally accepted that there is an obvious need for it. Furthermore, when the Council [*el populo*] has to decide such matters, very often unjust and harmful measures are approved, which bear heavily on some people and bring little benefit. And because there are many more poor men than rich in the Council, the burdens will not be spread evenly, and they will want the rich to pay for everything and to get off lightly themselves. This would be unjust and pernicious, because even though wealthy men have a duty to make a contribution to our city, it is highly desirable not to impoverish them, because wealthy men bring honour to our city and adorn it, and also so that they will be in a position to contribute on future occasions. These are the arguments for not having the Council decide such matters.

On the other hand, everyone is very attached to deciding about money matters, and it is (so to speak) almost second nature; consequently, if what everyone has to pay is determined by what a few men want and decide, this could well give rise to some discord and disorder. This procedure would also cause serious trouble if it were used dishonourably, and the poor were taxed more heavily than the wealthy. Having weighed all these arguments, I would say that it is important for as much money as is necessary to be available for governing the state [*al governo dello stato*], because a state that lacks sufficient funds can neither defend itself nor attack other states; therefore, it is essential that these matters should not be decided in the Council, for the reasons given above, which are cogent. Moreover, there have been many occasions on which the Council [*el populo*] did not want to vote funds at the appropriate times, and afterwards 100,000 ducats have not proved enough to achieve something that could have been achieved with less than 10,000.

It is true that trouble can easily occur if decisions, especially about taxes, are taken by a small body; therefore, I consider that the final decision should be taken by an intermediate body,[45] composed of the Signoria, the Ten, the Colleges and the Eight of Ward, and of some of the most important officers, such as the captains of the *parte,*[46] the *conservadori,*[47] the Six of Mercantantia[48] and others like them, so that there should be at least two hundred or even three hundred citizens involved. Such a number would be more likely to approve these measures, because there would be more men who are shrewd and amenable to reasoned arguments. Furthermore, with so many men of every class being involved, opportunities for complaints and for trouble-making would largely disappear, because someone from almost every family would be present, and there would be few persons who would dare to raise matters of private interest.

The Gonfalonier

The second foundation of good government [*buono governo*] is the gonfalonier. The first thing that has to be decided is what kind of authority he should have; the second is whether it should be a permanent office or one held for a limited period. This matter certainly needs to be considered very carefully, because if the gonfalonier is given too free a hand, he could become so powerful that this would harm our city and endanger its freedom. It is difficult to set limits to his authority, for it is desirable to strike the right balance, so that the gonfalonier is not hemmed in to such an extent that the office becomes of little value. The main function of the gonfalonier is to be head of the Signoria in exactly the same way that he has been until now. It follows from this that if the Signoria has the same supreme and unrestricted authority that it has at present, and if the gonfalonier can always dominate it, effective power in our city will be concentrated in his hands. Experience shows that a shrewd gonfalonier who holds power for a long time, and has the reputation that he is likely to acquire, will always be able to dominate the Signoria. This is not surprising, because its members are almost always weak, which cannot be avoided if they are elected under the present procedure. For there are so many personal and family disqualifications, which last for such long periods,[49] both from holding their own offices[50] and from becoming members of the Colleges, that it is inevitable (as it always has been) that over the years a large number of men will become members of the Signoria, very many of whom will be ignorant and worthless. Because of their lack of knowledge, and also because they are men of poor quality, they have neither the intelligence nor the spirit needed to oppose the gonfalonier, and therefore he can persuade them to do what he wants. This would not happen if members of the Signoria were shrewd and men of high reputation, because they would be prepared to argue with him and would do it effectively; they would consider arguments on their merits and not be submissive to his authority. (The doge of Venice, although the office is permanent, does not have very much power, precisely because the leading men of that city sit together with him.) It is this weakness of the Signoria that has given excessive power to the gonfalonier, Piero Soderini, and it is essential to remedy this, because the matter is of the utmost importance.

It needs to be done in one of two ways: either this supreme body [the Signoria] must be elected from a small number of very suitable men; or, if its members continue to be chosen from the present large number, limits must be placed on the authority of the Signoria in those matters that, when under the control of the gonfalonier, make him too powerful. If it were possible, having the members of the Signoria chosen from a small number of well-qualified men would be the better solution; because the Signoria is more important than any other body, it would be very desirable for its members to be men capable of exercising so much power. But it must be borne in mind that since it resides continuously in the Palace,[51] surrounded by so much pomp and so many marks of honour, it has been for a very long time highly visible to all the citizens, and membership of it has become a dish [*pasto*] that everyone desires to feast upon at some time. Consequently, a man who has never succeeded in sitting on it does not really regard himself as a citizen of Florence. This way of thinking is so deeply rooted that it would be difficult to change it, and I do not believe that it is a practical possibility. It would be better to concentrate instead on reducing somewhat its very great powers.

Today the Signoria has great authority, and except for very few matters (such as making peace treaties or alliances, engaging mercenary leaders and electing public officers),[52] it is empowered to do everything, provided there is a two-thirds majority in favour: it has cognizance of and decides without any exceptions any civil cases; it can do the same with criminal cases; it can have citizens executed or exiled, without any controls over it. And although with regard to the latter two, it is possible for a man to appeal against its verdict to the Great Council [*al consiglio*], this matter is inefficiently organized, and the right of appeal is not always allowed. It can do all these things either by its own authority or by acting through other bodies, because when it wants to exert its authority, all the other bodies give way to it. Moreover, with regard to affairs of state [*nelle cose dello stato*], it can reply to letters from rulers [*signori*] and ambassadors; it can seek advice from the Council of Eighty if it wants to about any matter, just as it pleases. No taxes can be imposed, no laws passed or decrees made, unless two-thirds of the Signoria give their consent. In short, it can do almost anything, and those things that it cannot do cannot be done by other bodies without its consent. And even though the public officers are chosen by the Great Council [*in consiglio*], at times the Signoria with regard to certain offices, missions and situations also chooses some chancellors and notaries of the chief public officers, which is also a matter of no little importance. Consequently, since the gonfalonier is ex officio head of the Signoria, and because of his authority and the weakness of his colleagues,[53] he is in effect always in command; the outcome is that his power in a free city and society [*una città e vivere libero*] is excessive, and it is essential that it be curbed.

By far the most important thing is to take away the power of the Signoria, with a two-thirds majority, to decide, or to order the other holders of public office to decide, about cases involving the death penalty or exiling citizens or depriving them of political rights [*sopra lo ammunire*], in short, with regard to imposing penalties of whatever kind on any citizens in any political trial [*per conto delle cose dello stato*]. The most important right [*sicurtà*] that should be enjoyed in a republic is to be able to live and act freely, without fear of being harmed by any individuals. And if it should be urged that it is possible to appeal to the Council (as is granted by the law about appeals made in 1494) against any verdicts of the Signoria in political trials [*per conto dello stato*], I would reply that this right is not sufficient, because it is difficult to win an appeal. To succeed, one has (in effect) to overcome the authority of the Signoria and obtain a two-thirds majority in the Council [*nel populo*] (whose members are naturally suspicious and very ignorant, as well as being hostile to important men of great talent); it is not the right body to judge such grave matters. It would be possible to remedy this by setting up a special court (like the *quarantia*),[54] or commit the case to some other body (I shall discuss this in more detail later).[55] However, in the present context,[56] it is enough to say that it is not right that the Signoria can condemn citizens for political offences [*per stato*]; because it is almost always dominated by the gonfalonier, this power causes him to be feared far too much. It is essential to remove from the gonfalonier this power of controlling citizens through fear, and also to take away the means by which he can win men over through hope of favours. It follows that the Signoria should not have the power to give public offices of any kind to citizens; it should not send ambassadors or commissaries (except in cases of great urgency, and then only for short periods), and any such authority[57] must not be extended, either officially or secretly. Nor should the Signoria send Palace secretaries[58] to undertake similar duties, except by decree of the Council of Eighty or else of that body that represents it (except in cases of great urgency, as mentioned before). This measure would have the desired effects that I have mentioned already, and it would stop the Signoria using such persons to negotiate with foreign rulers [*principi forestieri*]. It is not desirable that, with a two-thirds majority, the Signoria should be able to dismiss any public office-holder for any reason whatever, or dismiss the chancellors and public secretaries. For they realize that they are in the hands of the gonfalonier and become afraid of dismissal; this makes them so submissive to his will that they become, in effect, powerful instruments for perverting legal processes and the institutions of government [*le cose delle legge e dello stato*] in any way that he wants, as we have seen happen during Piero Soderini's period in office.

The procedure for discussing and approving laws also adds greatly to the excessive power of the gonfalonier. Laws cannot be made without the consent of the Signoria, and therefore this is very difficult to achieve if the gonfalonier is opposed to them. New laws can be made to deal with defects and mistakes when they become obvious, and if some feature of the gonfalonier's conduct is improper, this can be dealt with by making a special law applying to him. And it is essential that the procedure for passing a law should not be so restrictive that his consent to it is required. I shall discuss the way to ensure this later,[59] when I return to dealing with how affairs of state [*le cose dello stato*] should be decided so that the gonfalonier's will, because of the various methods he can employ for making proposals and the various bodies in which he is involved, is not dominant.

What has to be discussed now is whether the gonfalonier should have all the powers that were conferred on him by the new law of 1502, namely, to have special responsibility for justice and, consequently, the power of presiding over criminal trials in all the courts. Whether or not it is necessary to discuss this depends on another consideration, that is, whether he should hold office permanently or only for a limited period; if it is for a limited period, giving him this power or not is certainly of no importance, for no gonfalonier who is conscious that he will have to return to being a private citizen will want to use it, provided he is free to act as he wishes and is not obliged by law to intervene. Therefore, this matter needs to be discussed only if the gonfalonier holds office permanently, and, if he does, I would be in favour of granting him this power, except in political trials [*le cose dello stato*]. For if he wishes to exercise it, it could well be a useful power, since when a nobleman or a powerful man acts illegally, the judges often do not dare to punish him, because they are aware that they personally, or their interests, could be harmed by the brothers or relatives of the accused man, and indeed they are frequently afraid of becoming the victims of violence.

Such fears will not exist if the gonfalonier holds office for life.[60] His exercise of this right would benefit our city, and it would not confer on him so much power that he would become feared, because it is likely that those who come before the courts on such charges will not be men who aspire to hold important public offices [*al governo dello stato*], but rather lower-class or young men. Nevertheless, this is not a very important matter because, apart from the fact that there will be few men who are likely to resort to such violence, if the judges in our city are reorganized in the way that I shall explain later,[61] they will not need to have so much pressure on them to do their duty properly as they do now.

The last matter to be considered about the gonfalonier is whether he should hold office for life or for a limited period. There are weighty arguments on both sides, and to consider them properly it must be said that there were two reasons for making the gonfalonier's office permanent: the first was the great political [*nello stato*] disorder that existed; the second was that the system of criminal justice in our city was very badly administered, and it was thought that a permanent gonfalonier, who was given the power to preside in any court, would be very useful. And if he were to exercise this power, it was essential that his post should be permanent, for a man who held office for a limited period would have the same reasons for being timid as the other public officers. Today this argument has less force, if his authority is limited as was suggested earlier,[62] and if the system of justice and the judges are changed in the way that will be suggested later.[63] Consequently, leaving aside questions about the system of justice, the important consideration is whether, with regard to the government of the state [*governo dello stato*], it is more desirable that the gonfalonier should hold office for life or for a limited period.

If the gonfalonier is wise and just, it is undoubtedly more beneficial for our city that he should hold the office permanently, because if he always holds it, he will be more dedicated to affairs of state [*alle cose del governo*], and indeed he will have no other concern or goal but to govern well in any matter that concerns his republic; he will become more expert in every kind of business; he will understand better how to deal with events and problems; he will acquire a steadily improved understanding of the characters of the citizens with whom he has to deal and that of the people generally. In short, he will become increasingly effective and capable of accomplishing well all the duties of his office; he will be able to act in ways that benefit our city, with less fear of anyone than if he had a limited term of office. Knowing that he will finish his life in that office will strengthen his resolve and remove any temptation to favour one faction in our city more than another, which might happen if he needed to be re-appointed or (on becoming qualified to hold office again) re-elected. These are very strong reasons for favouring a permanent gonfalonier.

On the other hand, if one wants him to be a gonfalonier and not an absolute ruler [*principe assoluto*], there is no doubt that the best security possible is that his tenure of office should not be permanent. This should discourage him from scheming to usurp more power than the laws permit, because he would be aware that, eventually, he would have to give up his office. And even if he were to scheme in this way, he would lack devoted supporters and that power and influence over the citizens that he would have if his tenure were permanent. Moreover, if it should happen that he is not a good gonfalonier, either through wickedness or through ignorance, which can easily happen, it would be better that our city would eventually be rid of him rather than that his rule should be permanent. Nor should much reliance be placed on the view that he[64] would be driven from office, because this is something that just does not happen, partly because of the favours at his disposal and the friends that he has, and partly because he would not be universally unpopular – everyone would not be aware of his defects. Another consideration of some weight is that having a gonfalonier for a limited period provides opportunities for more men to reach that office [*si dà pasto a più*];[65] and the hopes that the leading citizens have of being elevated to that high office conduce greatly to our city being at peace rather than rent by discords, for they will be less discontented and will also be more devoted to the public good. These are the arguments for the opposite view.

Having considered all these arguments, I should prefer a permanent gonfalonier, because this would be much more beneficial for our city. And I would also like our city to have a supreme civil office of surpassing dignity, so that a very meritorious citizen in a republic can aspire to rise to it through legal means that are compatible with civic freedom [*per via delle legge e libertà*]. Thus, men who are very active and dedicate their lives to public affairs will be able to aim at an exalted position, which could be theirs if only they act outstandingly and work for their city; and without being tempted to seize tyrannical power [*alla tirannide*] and usurp that which belongs to others, they will realize that their meritorious deeds can receive due reward. And even if this is a prospect [*pasto*][66] that is likely to inspire [*infiammare*] only a few men, this stimulus is not therefore worthless, because in every well-ordered republic it is obvious that it is always a few able and virtuous citizens who exercise control; glorious deeds and great achievements have always been initiated and per-formed by a few men, because to be in charge of great enterprises and to be heads of government [*capi del governo*] in free cities, great and varied talents and virtues are required, and these are to be found in very few men. Such men should love their city; but so that they will work with more zeal, they need to have the spur of ambition, an appetite for greatness and for rising to a very high position in the state [*qualche sommo grado*]. And if they desire and work to achieve this, not through overriding the laws or by means of factions, but by being considered good and wise citizens and by benefitting their native city, who can doubt that such an ambition is praiseworthy and very beneficial? Anyone who is not motivated by such ambition suffers from a certain want of spirit and lacks the stimulus of glory; he will never be capable of performing great and noble deeds.

Therefore, in order to encourage this honourable ambition in men of great spirit and give them the opportunity to perform glorious deeds, it is very desirable to have such a high office available, which provides the chance of rising to the very highest position possible in a free city. Other men, who are less magnanimous and less talented, will be highly motivated by the prospect of attaining the other public offices of our city, which will be of sufficient importance to satisfy their more modest ambitions; but men of great appetite [*digestione*] will not be satisfied with such meagre dishes [*piccolo pasto*]. I conclude, then, that the gonfalonier should be permanent; and if his powers are limited in the ways described earlier,[67] this should remove any possible means and any temptation for him to seek to acquire greater authority or to become too powerful; for if citizens cannot hope for favours from him and have no reason to fear that he may harm them, it will be easy to make the laws that need to be made, without his approval being necessary, and to propose, discuss and deal with the ordinary affairs of state [*cose dello stato*]. Consequently, I do not see how he can become too powerful. Furthermore, the use of the right procedure and due care in electing the gonfalonier would make me confident that men who are suitable and of high quality will be elected. If this does not happen, the public office-holders or those to whom the appeals have been submitted will curb or punish them more effectively, perhaps, than has been possible in the past.

Now that the gonfalonier's powers and the kind of man suitable for this post have been discussed, we must consider what body should elect him. Not deviating from the position previously established, namely, that the people [*el populo*] should choose public officers and that office-holders should not be beholden to any individ-uals or groups, it follows that the Great Council [*(el) consiglio*] should make the choice. On the other hand, this office is exceedingly important, and there are very few men at any time who are fitted to hold it. The Great Council [*el populo*] knows who the meritorious and wise men are by what is said about them, which is adequate for filling all other public offices, but lacks the detailed knowledge and fine judgement required for considering and weighing exactly the qualities of candidates for such an important office. Therefore, I think that, when this office has to be filled, the inter-mediate body of which I shall speak soon,[68] in which all the wise and prudent men will sit, should choose (with a two-thirds majority required for each candidate) three citizens worthy of holding that office, whose names should then be passed to the

Great Council, and then within two or three days a secret ballot should take place; the man who receives the most votes will become permanent gonfalonier. If the candidates are considered in this way by shrewd men,[69] it is to be expected that the three ablest men in our city should be proposed. And even if it should happen that the Council [*el populo*] fails to choose the best of the three, this would not be as serious an error as would occur if the popular choice had to be made from many candidates. This procedure would preserve the principle that nobody should be beholden to individuals for a public office, because the Council [*(el) populo*] would make the final decision; moreover, because the preliminary choice of the three men would be made by a large body, there is no reason to fear that anyone would be proposed because of any factional manoeuvring. This method also has another important merit: since anyone who reaches this high office must be approved both by the Senate (so to speak)[70] and by the Council [*del populo*], a man who aspires to be appointed would have no reason to curry favour more with the Council [*(el) populo*] than with the Senate, or vice versa. Indeed, since there has to be general agreement,[71] such a man would avoid using any other means but good deeds and would act with integrity, so that afterwards, when he seeks high public office, everyone would approve of him.

A Senate Is Proposed

Since the two extreme points, the one and the many, that is, the gonfalonier and the Great Council, have been settled, we must now turn to the middle ground, to that body[72] that will have the function of coordinating them; it must be the guiding body [*el timone*] of our city and the controller of everything important. Since it has such a weighty role, it is essential that it should be composed of all the wisest men of the city and all those who are well suited to govern [*al governo*], so that important decisions will be made by knowledgeable and capable men. The following matters need to be discussed: what body should appoint them; how they should be appointed; how long they should hold office; what powers they need to have; what bodies should consult with them, and how this should take place.

The main elements of this body must be the Signoria, whose presence is essential to any such body, and the Colleges, which, since they were created in order to safeguard freedom, need to be present at these meetings. It is certainly desirable for them to have this honour; and if their quality or competence leaves something to be desired, with more experience of affairs they will improve. As well as these, there should be a group of the best citizens. Even if there are not very many who are deserving of inclusion because of their political [*dello stato*] knowledge and competence, nevertheless this group should be large, in order to preserve civic freedom [*per conservazione della libertà*], ensuring that such great power does not fall into a few hands. Moreover, in a free society [*uno vivere libero*] it is desirable to permit many men to participate in government [*dare parte a molti*], if this can be arranged without causing serious harm. Therefore, I am inclined to think that, including the Signoria and the Colleges, there should be about two hundred members. This was the practice in such ancient republics as Rome, Carthage, Athens and Sparta, in which that body which they called a 'senate' was composed of many members. In Venice, there are two hundred or more of those whom they call *pregati*, which is the same body.[73] And, as I have said, such a large body is essential, both for protecting freedom and also because a small body would not be appropriate in a popular regime [*in uno vivere libero*]. Even though it inevitably happens that in such a large assembly there will be many men who are ill equipped, this must be tolerated as being the lesser evil, especially since it is not really as harmful as it may seem; for when men who are wise and have a fine reputation discuss matters knowledgeably and perceptively, those who are less knowledgeable will tend to follow the lead of those who are more knowledgeable. And when six or eight of the leading citizens agree about a matter, it will rarely if ever happen that the rest do not follow their lead. Even when these outstanding men are unable to agree (as often happens in discussions), hearing the different arguments expounded and criticized will be such an education for the less able citizens that either they will understand matters or, at least, they will come close to doing so. Certain matters, which have already received some consideration in smaller bodies [*non al tutto acerbe ma cominciate già a maturarsi e digestirsi*], will often come to this body; it will not be necessary for all the details to be fully discussed there, but they should discuss matters sufficiently before making the final decision.

The most important point about the Senate, if it is to be really valuable, is that all citizens who are considered to be wise should be permanent members. It is not enough that most of them should be members, because it sometimes happens that one man will be more discerning than everyone else and will put forward a proposal that (even though it has been thought through only by him) will be approved by everyone when they have heard his arguments. In short, all the most important work of governing [*tutto 'l pondo del governo*] will really be carried out by very few men, which is what always happens in republics, in both ancient and modern times. Consequently, it is essential to hit on the best way of choosing them, so that their power becomes stable, for this is a matter of capital importance. I am not quite sure that it is desirable for them to hold office permanently, because I should like them to be under some pressure to act well, by holding, in the Great Council [*(el) populo*], frequent secret elections for these offices. This could be achieved by limiting their tenure of office to one year and requiring a two-thirds majority in order to be elected. But it is to be feared (as experience has shown) that the Council [*el populo*] would be very reluctant to re-elect the same men,[74] and the ambition of everyone to become members would cause great instability of membership (as has happened with the Council of Eighty),[75] and the Senate would cease to be an effective body. Therefore, it seems essential that the members should hold office permanently. But there is another possibility: the Council of Eighty could be elected in the present manner, and there could be a further eighty or a hundred members with permanent tenure of office (and these should be the leading and really outstanding citizens), who would always take part in meetings together with the Eighty and have the same powers. Thus, the principle that the leaders of the Senate should have permanent tenure would be preserved, and the others, who are less important,[76] would change from time to time, thus giving everyone a better chance of attaining office [*si darebbe . . . più pasto allo universale*],[77] but without harming the republic.

It would be difficult in the early stages to let the Great Council [*(el) populo*] elect these permanent members, because there is the danger that it might exclude some men who should not be excluded. Therefore, what should be done is that all those who have ever been gonfaloniers of justice,[78] or have been members of the Ten at least twice (because this body has for some time been open to a very large number of citizens), and those who have been ambassadors or general commissaries[79] elected by the Council of Eighty, shall all be permanent members of the Senate. Furthermore, since there are some citizens who would be worthy members, but who have not held any of these offices, there should be a further thirty members, to be elected by the Signoria and the Colleges and by these permanent members. Although this would result in a membership that is perhaps too large, it would be essential to put up with it for a while; however, for some time, those members who die need not be replaced, until the number is reduced to a hundred. After that, when a member dies, he should be replaced in the following way: the Senate (the members of the Signoria and the Council of Eighty and the permanent members) should elect by secret ballot thirty citizens for every vacancy and then choose the three who obtain the most votes (and each must receive at least two-thirds); then these three names should be passed to the Great Council, and the one who receives the most votes there would be elected to the vacant seat, in the same way that I described for electing the gonfalonier.

The functions of the Senate should be to ratify military contracts made by the Ten and to choose ambassadors and commissaries. (These offices should not be filled by the Great Council [*el populo*], because of their importance, and also because they require special skills and knowledge; and members of the Great Council [*el populo*] are not sufficiently discerning to know who is capable of undertaking them. Moreover, some of these posts require men of higher status than others, according to the special circumstances requiring these appointments and the duties that are entrusted to these officers, which the members of the Great Council [*el populo*] are unable to judge, because they do not always know the reasons for making these appointments and the secret negotiations that may be conducted.)[80] The Senate should also renew the appointments of the chancellors of the Palace[81] (which is not something the Great Council [*(el) populo*] should do), as well as examine measures that are proposed, before they are considered by the Council; it should also be responsible for the final passage of any fiscal laws; it should provide judges for the city, as will be explained later;[82] it should elect the gonfalonier and replace those of its members who die, as was explained earlier. It would also be desirable for the Ten of *Balìa* (even though they are elected by the Great Council) to be elected only from members of the Senate. Finally, the Senate should decide about affairs of state [*le cose dello stato*] and play a prominent part in legislation, in ways that will be explained shortly.[83]

In a republic, there are strict controls over the way that laws and decrees are made. Laws must first be proposed by the members of the Signoria, approved by the *fermatori*,[84] discussed again by the Signoria, passed by them and by the Colleges; then they must be passed by the Council of Eighty and, after so much sifting, finally come to the Great Council. There was, perhaps, a good reason for having such strict controls: since making laws is a matter of the greatest importance, which could at any time result in changes in the governmental structure and the institutions [*lo stato e li ordini*] of our city, there was a desire to block the plans of seditious or turbulent men, who do not hesitate to harm the welfare of others and who are always eager to subvert the constitution [*vedere . . . cose nuove*]. The history of the ancient republics gave added force to such considerations, for it is recorded that there were countless disturbances and revolutions [*infiniti moti*] in them, just because it was very easy for any seditious man to take the initiative in proposing new laws in popular assemblies [*al populo*]. On the other hand, the existing controls are so strict that they are harmful, because although it is not right that it should be so easy for anyone to propose new laws in large assemblies, it is also not right or beneficial for one man or a few individuals to be able to block proposals that may be considered desirable. With the present legislative procedure, and having a permanent gonfalonier, it is obvious that he is almost always able to block a measure, since six members of the Signoria very rarely unite to oppose him. Moreover, even if they were thus to unite, since the Signoria stays in office for such a short period,[85] and since it often happens that during their tenure there are changes of the Gonfaloniers of the Companies[86] and of the Twelve Goodmen,[87] which causes many problems, the gonfalonier, just by artfully playing for time, can block measures. Furthermore, even if the gonfalonier is not obstructive, it is almost always possible for a few citizens, if they know about matters in advance, to block measures in various ways in one of these small bodies. I do not myself believe that this complicated legislative procedure, which is under such strict control, derives from the free constitution [*dalla libertà*] of our city, but rather from the influence exercised by the oligarchy [*de' pochi*], who thought that they themselves could be deprived of authority by a single decree; not being sufficiently powerful to be able to take away from the popular bodies the right to pass laws, they wanted at least to make sure that, by introducing these controls, it would be impossible for any law to be passed against their will. This is a very serious evil, and a free society [*el vivere libero*] must overcome it.

There is another grave evil. When the Signoria, acting on the suggestion of a gonfalonier, wants to have a law passed, but is afraid that for some reason it will be hard to have it approved, it will contrive to initiate it and take it to the Council of Eighty in just one day. There will be little difficulty in getting it passed by the Colleges, whose members are almost always weak men, and then in reintroducing it quickly in the Council of Eighty where, even if there are a few men who are aware of its defects, there are not enough for it to be rejected; and its deficiencies cannot be made known outside this body, because it is not lawful to discuss these matters publicly, unless the Signoria permits it, and then only in favour of a measure. When it is approved by the Council of Eighty, getting the consent of the Great Council [*nel populo*] presents little difficulty, because it seldom knows more than it needs to know. To solve this problem, it was decreed long ago that every measure must be published a certain number of days before it was discussed by the Colleges. But there was a provision that the Signoria was entitled to dispense with this prior publication. All these practices are tyrannical in character, and such devices were introduced so that these men could ride roughshod over civic freedom whenever they wanted to [*fare alla palla della libertà della città*].[88]

To overcome all these evils, I would propose two procedures for making laws. The first is that they should be made in the same way and with the same controls that operate today, but with just two additional features. First, when a measure has been passed by the Colleges, before it can be considered by the intermediate body (which henceforth I shall call the Senate)[89] there must be a first reading of it, at least one day before it is discussed, and the Signoria must not have the power in any way to dispense with this. (The purpose of this first reading is that the Senate should not be caught napping, and that it should have sufficient time to examine it properly.) The other additional feature is that when a measure comes to the Senate, everyone (whether a member of the Colleges or a senator) should be entitled to speak in favour or to criticize it, just as he thinks fit. Such freedom of speech [*questa libertà*] would not be desirable in the Great Council, because it would cause so much confusion that proceedings would never be concluded; but in the Senate, whose primary function is to consider important matters and to guide [*timoneggiare*][90] our city, it is right that measures should always be thoroughly examined [*digerire*].[91] The person who took these powers away[92] did so in order that the councils would approve all measures, whether they were sound or not, because of exhaustion, and would decide matters without ever hearing what could be said against them. In a free city, it is essential that it should be easy to propose measures and to have them considered [*e venire in consulta*]; but then they must be examined and discussed rigorously, so that the decisions made about them are always well considered. This is how affairs should be conducted in a good republic. The present situation, however, is the exact opposite: proposing laws is difficult, and the process of discussing and passing them is easier,[93] in order to reach the decisions desired. These are all procedures devised by tyrants, who in reality take away our freedom, leaving only its name and certain forms of little importance; our city has only partially abolished those procedures [*quali forme*],[94] because the popular regime [*governo populare*] has not been established for very long.

The second procedure for law-making that I favour is that any member of the Signoria, without the consent of the others, should be able to propose in the Senate any law that seems good to him, but always with the proviso that it must be given a first reading, and that anybody should be entitled to criticize or support it. And if it is supported by three-quarters of the Senate, it should be passed on to the Great Council, and the member of the Signoria who proposed it should, in speaking in support of it, perform the function normally performed by the gonfalonier. Under this system, a useful measure could not be blocked by one man or a few men, for it would take just one member of the Signoria to be in favour of it to ensure that it is considered by a large assembly. On the other hand, initiating a measure in this way would not be so easy that it would happen very often, since it must go before the Senate, where it would require a three-quarters majority, whereas under the other system only a two-thirds majority is needed. Again, unimportant men [*uomini deboli*][95] would not initiate measures in this way, because much resolution would be needed to do it, and to be able to justify these measures and defend them from criticism or attacks. I would not want this second procedure to be used for finance measures, for which only the first procedure mentioned should be used. The reason for this is that permitting them to be passed by such a large body [that is, the Great

Council: *el lasciarsi questa larghezza*] could well result in disorder or injustice, because the matter is of keen interest and affects everyone to a notable extent; moreover, everyone is more disposed to prefer the measures that are the least hurtful to himself rather than those that he knows to be more reasonable and more beneficial to our city.

In discussing the ordinary affairs of state [*le cose . . . dello stato*], indeed in getting his own way concerning them, the gonfalonier Piero Soderini has displayed great determination. He has succeeded both because he has had excessive power (for the reasons already mentioned), and because of the shrewdness with which he has contrived to have matters considered in consultative meetings [*messe in consulta*] in ways advantageous to himself: sometimes he has wanted them considered by the Ten together with small consultative groups [*con le pratiche strette*]; sometimes in normal meetings of the Council of Eighty; sometimes in the Council of Eighty in its enlarged form [*con uno arroto di pratiche grande*]. He has chosen the procedure that he believed more likely to obtain support for his views. Again, when different opinions have been expressed, he has favoured that which he preferred; sometimes he has called for a simple 'yes' or 'no' vote, sometimes a vote by acclamation, sometimes a secret vote, and very important consequences have followed from using these different procedures. Thus, he has been cunning in knowing when to propose consideration of measures in smaller bodies, and when in larger ones, which is a very serious matter. There is a further problem: the practice of limiting discussion to members representing various city districts[96] is foolish and never results in useful discussions.

At any rate, I very much favour the Ten remaining in office in times both of war and of peace; it should deal with the affairs of our dominions [*le cose dello stato*] in the same way and with the same powers as it does today; but it should not be able to decide the matters that it must deal with today, without the intervention of the Senate. Moreover, the commissions given to ambassadors when they go abroad (which today are given by the Signoria and the Colleges) should be discussed and decided by the Senate. Even if these are not given very often, the authority of the Senate would require that every important matter (except those that require much secrecy) should be discussed and decided there. I think that, as need arises, the Signoria should consult the Senate and that the Ten should be entitled to do the same, even if the Signoria, which in any case would have to be present, does not want that done.

These consultations should take place in the following manner: the body that asks for advice should explain the matter and put forward a well-considered [*con qualche digestione*][97] proposal that they think is on the right lines, explaining the reasons for it. And it should be able to put forward one proposal or more than one, and not only all the members as a body but each of them separately should also be entitled to make any proposal that seems good to him, even if the other members are opposed to it. After this is done, any senator should be entitled to address the meeting, supporting or criticizing the measures under consideration, proposing the rejection of some elements, or the addition of new ones; and everyone should be able to do this. Afterwards, either at once or on another day (if the matter is very important), they should proceed to a secret vote, and the proposal that receives the most votes must be accepted. Because such frank public discussion is unusual, there would be reluctance to initiate it. Accordingly, someone could be nominated to speak, so that eventually speaking freely in public would become the custom. This procedure for discussing matters would result in the gonfalonier having no more authority than anyone else; and with this practice of speaking for and against proposals, matters would be fully discussed.

Apart from the affairs of our city being discussed more freely and efficaciously than in the past, there would be another desirable outcome: whereas now citizens have little opportunity to demonstrate their qualities in public, and those who speak little are often accounted wise, this continual display of their talents in arguing about proposals and measures would permit those who are more meritorious to become known. They would be distinguished from the rest, as gold is from lead, so that men's capacities would be known as a result of practical tests, not mere hearsay, which, as will be maintained, would be something very beneficial to our city.

Parliaments

In order to establish firmly this method of government [*modo di governo*], it is essential to maintain the law that prohibits the calling of parliament,[98] for this practice only has the effect of seriously undermining the popular regime [*el vivere populare*].[99] The practice of calling parliaments arose for the following reason. Since living in freedom [*con libertà*], with the people having much influence, is natural in our city, it was not possible to deal with important matters without the consent of the people; consequently, all those who at any time wanted to hold sway realized that, if they were to attain absolute power [*tenere la tirannide*], they could not completely eliminate free institutions [*la libertà*], but had to retain at least the semblance of them, which required the consent of the people and the assemblies for making laws and for conferring new powers. Because they realized that they could not obtain this consent through the established institutions [*per le vie ordinarie*], they devised this practice of calling the people into the town square with a show of force, in order to make them ratify publicly the measures proposed by themselves. This is really nothing else than using the terror induced by arms and military force to constrain the people to consent to everything that they propose, while pretending that whatever is done is done because all the citizens want it done and have approved it. Hence, in order to preserve free institutions [*la libertà*] effectively, it is essential that matters that have to be decided by popular bodies should be decided in a regular manner [*ordinariamente*] and by secret voting, and not to have any parliament, which is only a device for forcing the people to approve measures that they do not want.

THE LEGAL SYSTEM: REWARDS AND PUNISHMENTS

I should very much have liked to be able to end my piece at this point, for I have discussed fully what kind of troops should defend our city from external enemies, and which bodies and officers should control its internal affairs, namely, the Great Council, the Senate, the Signoria and the gonfalonier. But in any city it is inevitable that many misdeeds and crimes of every kind will be committed, which must be punished if it is to survive; indeed, ancient legislators maintained that republics were based on two main things, rewards and punishments. Therefore, it is necessary to consider in some detail how criminal cases should be dealt with, and which bodies should pass verdicts.

The institutions and procedures that I have discussed previously not only provide safeguards for our civic freedom [*la libertà*] and are a good way of governing the state [*governare lo stato*]; they also indicate in large measure the rewards for citizens who behave creditably and perform outstanding deeds. I mean the rewards that good men should want and expect in a republic, not those sought from princes or tyrants. To hold regular public office in one's city, of a kind that is appropriate to one's status, to be elected to important public posts and other offices, in accordance with one's talents and good conduct: these are the only rewards that a city should give to its citizens – not opportunities to become wealthy and to seize what belongs to others; not unconstitutional powers [*autorità estraordinarie*] and being able to distribute public offices as one pleases, or protect wrongdoers from the judges, all of which are characteristic features of a tyrannical regime. Instead, good and noble-minded citizens must be encouraged to seek those offices and positions that are compatible with a free society [*colla libertà*]. It should be enough for them to know that they are highly regarded and greatly respected by their fellow citizens – in short, to enjoy a good reputation and to acquire glory that may not be great but is assured.

These would be very striking outcomes of the form of government [*nel governo*] that I have recommended, because distributing the more important public offices less widely, and with more discrimination than has been the practice until now, must result in men of weight and reputation predominating. Moreover, facilitating public discussion of measures and proposals, and giving the freedom to criticize them as well as support them, would have the effect of distinguishing the able men from the others, so that capable and public-spirited men would easily acquire a fine reputation, which would not be based (as often happens today) solely on belonging to a noble family or having a distinguished father or ancestors, but on the excellence of one's deeds and the qualities that one actually possesses. Thus, a very fine man whose father was of low birth would not be accounted of little worth, just as a man of little worth whose father and family were distinguished would not be considered outstanding. Good deeds and abilities, then, would be rewarded in the ways that they should be in a republic, and consequently wickedness and ignorance would be dishonoured and despised. This desirable state of affairs would be the outcome of men being able to demonstrate their real qualities. Hence, when everyone appreciates this genuine well-being, men will desire, and be stimulated, to behave creditably and will want to possess the qualities that will enable them to obtain the high offices of state [*gradi grandi*] and to achieve great glory.

Certainly, I personally do not see how a greater reward can be offered to a man of noble spirit than being the head of a free city, not because he has intrigued to obtain power or has powerful relatives or has been favoured by a certain faction, but because of the high respect for his standing and the good reputation that he enjoys, resulting from his being recognized as a wise man and dedicated to his city. This position, which many men held in ancient republics (and, above all, Pericles in Athens), seems to me preferable to all the power or influence possessed by any tyrant: it is to know that one has a fine reputation and holds high office solely because of one's abilities and good qualities. Happy are the men who are moved by this ardent desire [*sentono questa fiamma*],[100] which can animate only those whose hearts are very noble! And happy are the republics that are full of such noble ambitions, because they always cause those things to flourish that lead men to these high public offices, namely, outstanding abilities and fine deeds, as well as a burning desire to perform great and noble deeds for the benefit of one's city, both in those men who want to rise to this exalted office and in those who already hold office. Their great power and standing are not incompatible with a free society [*alla libertà*], nor do they threaten it, because such pre-eminence is not achieved through sects or factions, or by means of the baser arts,[101] and such office-holders are beholden only to the Great Council [*(el) populo*] and their fellow citizens; if such a man were to cease to act well or effectively, they could remove him from power when they want to.[102] Indeed, this would be essential and very beneficial: because there are always few men capable of carrying out effectively such high duties, if there is not a genuine and widespread respect and regard for those in high office, they would be able to achieve little. Consequently, punishments and rewards are needed, for without them republics have a short and unhappy existence. May God grant that our own republic will be full of these noble ambitions and office-holders, and that all citizens will be animated by these noble desires. Then there would be fewer misdeeds, and there would be less need to have such a complex legal system, and crimes being punished with appropriate penalties, which I shall deal with at once.

In our city there are many bodies with authority over criminal cases: sometimes there is shared competence and jurisdiction, with the body that begins the case finishing it; but some have different functions and have authority over different types of case. The most important bodies are the Eight of Ward and the Defenders of the Laws.[103] Even though the Signoria has supreme authority, I do not include it in this category, because it was also created for other purposes, whereas the former bodies have special responsibilities for these matters; moreover, I have already discussed what authority the Signoria should have in criminal cases. We have to consider, then, whether the authority and power of the former bodies should be reduced or increased. Certainly, with regard to all criminal trials, except for political offences [*e' delitti dello stato*], the full powers that they have are undoubtedly desirable, because it is essential that the punishment of these offences should not pertain completely to assemblies, but should be undertaken by particular courts, which need to have full powers. For if they must act within the strict limits of the law [*co' termini di ragione*], hardly anyone would ever be punished, because it would not be possible to prove conclusively most charges. And if judicial verdicts always have to be in exact accordance with the penalties laid down by law, many problems would arise, because many offences that have the same penalty affixed to them by the statutes[104] (since legislators cannot take every circumstance into account) deserve somewhat different penalties, according to the different circumstances.

There is another problem: should these special bodies be authorized to judge political offences [*li errori apartenenti allo stato*]? This problem arises because it involves a fundamental principle — namely, in order to preserve a free city it is essential that citizens should have no reason to fear the powers exercised by any holder of public office. And giving these special bodies such powers violates this principle; six members of the Eight of Ward and seven Defenders of the Laws[105] could do much harm, because they have the right to execute citizens and to exile those whom they think deserve these penalties. Nevertheless, I think that these bodies should continue to have these powers, even with regard to political trials [*casi apartenenti allo stato*], so that straightforward cases need not be considered in the appeal courts and in assemblies. And the danger mentioned earlier does not exist in practice: since four of their members change every six months, there is no reason to fear that they will punish anyone in order to aggrandize themselves; nor should personal resentments harboured by any of their members lead them to harm citizens, because their decisions must be made with a two-thirds majority. Indeed, experience shows that these bodies tend to be very cautious in proceeding against citizens, and it is much more likely that a thousand citizens will go unpunished, or be punished very lightly, than that anyone will be punished excessively by these special bodies.

A remedy against this fear (although it is not necessary) would be to permit citizens to appeal against verdicts given against them in political trials [*per conto dello stato*]; I would not want to see appeals made to the Great Council, because this is a matter that requires much judgement and serious consideration. But if the death sentence is passed or someone is condemned as a rebel,[106] it would be preferable that appeals be heard by the Senate, with the Colleges not being present but only the Signoria. In all other political trials [*Con tutti altri*], if there is a lesser penalty imposed, forty or fifty members of the Senate could be chosen by lot to act as an appeal court, in order not to impose too great a burden on all the members; and for a sentence to be quashed a two-thirds majority should be required (otherwise the sentence should stand).

This suffices for the powers of the special judicial bodies. It is not enough to try to introduce a good system of justice. For the members of these bodies — because of affection for their relatives and friends, because they hesitate to offend or injure others and to stir up hostility against themselves, because of weakness and ignorance, and, sometimes, because of wickedness — often act so weakly and so slowly that our system of justice has obviously become very defective; indeed, justice could not be more shamefully or harmfully neglected, so that there has been a general increase in disorderly behaviour [*la licenzia*] and a readiness to harm others. In a few years, we have seen many excesses and violent acts, many unexampled breaches of our customary behaviour, which is naturally pacific, not aggressive. Our young men have become haughty, and swagger, with a marked insolence and audacity, which they use against those who are defenceless. It is common knowledge that our citizens are guilty of many thefts from houses outside the city and in the rural districts, committed against persons who are powerless and weak, and that holders of public offices have committed many wicked, cruel and oppressive acts outside the city on our poor subjects,[107] because they want only to increase their power by fair means or foul and lack any respect for God or their city or for human beings. This greatly damages the reputation of our city and leaves our subjects so discontented and, indeed, hostile, that if a strong enemy were to mount an attack on us it might well happen that the consequences would become obvious.[108] Furthermore, some citizens have boldly plotted or acted against the state [*contro allo stato*]. Although these activities have either been suspected or there has been pretty definite evidence of them,[109] because of the weakness of our judges, there has been a lack of firm action.

The realization that for many years there had been so many disorders resulted in the passing of the law of the *quarantia,* which was ill considered and had many defects, and indeed aroused very strong opposition, both from those who could not bear the prospect that their own crimes would be punished and also from those who feared that, because of this law, the gonfalonier, Piero Soderini (whose constitutional powers [*per lo ordinario*] already rendered him too powerful), would become very much more powerful. The latter reason caused so much opposition to this law concerning justice, promoted by him, that it was nearly not passed. Even though some of its features were ill considered, above all there were resentful fears that he wanted to make a law to enable him to punish the misdeeds of others, while leaving his own actions untouched, since there was no body to call his conduct to account [*e sanza superiore*]; he had usurped many powers that were unconstitutional [*fuora delle legge*] and contrary to the best traditions [*e buono vivere*] of our city. The principle of that law was good, but it did have some weaknesses. If these were to be corrected, it would be useful and beneficial.

What I would propose, then, with regard to any crimes committed by citizens (both political ones [*di stato*] and those of any other kind), is that after they have been denounced, either openly or secretly, to one of the competent bodies, and the case has not been concluded within a certain period (which should be about a month), it should be brought before a special tribunal [*uno ricorso o quarantia*], which I think should vary in character according to the type and gravity of the crime (as will be explained later); and at this tribunal the charge, together with all the details of the proceedings of the previous body, should be brought. The accused person could appear in person before this tribunal to defend himself, or else be represented by a lawyer, as he wishes, and the tribunal should have the power to conduct a new trial if it wishes, but it must reach a verdict within a month. The procedure for arriving at judgements, and handing them down in writing[110] (as in the *quarantia* courts), should moreover give all the members of the tribunal the opportunity to express their views openly, whether for or against the charge. If the accuser is known, he should press the charge openly; and the sentence that is passed should have a three-fifths majority (the voting to be secret). My view is that appeals against verdicts given in political trials [*delle cose dello stato*] should be heard before the whole Senate,[111] at which the Signoria should be present but not the members of the Colleges. For dealing with charges of misconduct by anyone holding public office, either in Florence or outside the city, I would recommend choosing by lot thirty men from the Senate and thirty from another body (which will be specified later).[112] For other criminal acts of any kind, there should be a tribunal of sixty citizens who are not themselves senators, but who should be elected by the Senate; they should be members for a year and receive an annual emolument of fifty ducats. They should not be disqualified from holding other public offices, but after serving for a year they should not be eligible for another term until two years have passed. The purpose of this different procedure is that political trials [*e' casi dello stato*], which are more important, should be conducted with more judgement and seriousness, and the same thing should happen eventually with trials of other kinds.

There would seem to be several grounds for criticizing this recommendation. The first criticism would be the ease and frequency with which appeals might be made, which could happen whenever three members of the Eight of Ward, or four of the Defenders of the Laws, disagree with the verdict of the majority of their colleagues; and it would be easy, through the judges, to harm or maltreat men of high social position, on the initiative of a madman or a wicked man who makes an anonymous denunciation. Again, there will be criticism of the written method of passing judgement (instead of using the oral procedure, without discussion and examination of cases). Finally, it will be claimed that I deem a three-fifths majority sufficient for a condemnation in such grave cases, which involve the death penalty, whereas according to the laws of our city a two-thirds majority is required in almost all other less serious cases. Nevertheless, I do not consider that these objections to my proposal and to its details are cogent; these features are essential, otherwise it will not be effective. Above all, it is evident that when appeals must be requested by the judicial body in the way stipulated by the old law, all the important men can avoid any problems, for someone who cannot influence three secret votes is certainly a weak man. Consequently, only those cases are sent to the appeal courts; and if this provision did not exist, the judicial body that sends them on would itself have sufficient courage to reach a guilty verdict. This provision was introduced because of fear of those powerful men whom the judicial body does not dare, or cannot agree, to condemn.

When accusations are made against men without even a shred of evidence, or are blatant lies, it is probable that the judicial body will dismiss them. And if their decision is appealed against, the appeal should be dismissed; this should be considered creditable rather than discreditable. Giving written judgements is essential in appeal bodies, for the same reason, because the fear that prevents the judicial body from delivering a verdict would also prevent the appeal body from giving its verdict fearlessly [*liberamente*]. And the long period of a month, the right to hear the appeal made in person by the accused, the ample discussion of it among themselves and the fact that they are men of high calibre would mean that the verdict will be delivered only after adequate discussion, especially since mercy is a natural characteristic of our city, our citizens usually showing a tendency to this rather than to severity. And except when fear or wild passions are aroused, which result in hasty decisions, affairs are usually conducted in a moderate and humane manner. I favour the introduction of verdicts with at least a three-fifths majority, because a two-thirds majority is so stringent that it often fails to be obtained; consequently, because they are very weary and bored, men resort to compromise solutions, which are unjust because the penalties are either too severe or too light. Therefore, I favour a slightly larger majority, but not one so large that it would lead to disorder and injustice. Moreover, this solution neither favours nor disadvantages an accused man, because with a three-fifths majority required he can equally be condemned or acquitted.

Having discussed cases involving private men and all the other holders of public offices, it remains for me to discuss whether a permanent gonfalonier should be subject to legal penalties during his term of office and, if so, of what kind. Other office-holders may be punished when they leave office, but this cannot be done in his case, since the end of his tenure of office coincides with the end of his life.[113] The dignity of his office and his prestige do not allow any such penalties, so that he cannot suffer continual criticism and undermining of his position. On the other hand, the welfare of our city would be enhanced by it, since he would not have excessive security. Bearing in mind both these fears, I would say that he should not be subject to any legal proceedings [*non avessi superiore alcuno*], except that any member of the Signoria should have the right to propose to the whole Senate (except for the Colleges) any punishment, whether it be removing him from office, financial penalties, executing him or anything else; and for this to succeed a two-thirds majority should be required. But members of the Signoria should not have the right to make any such proposal more than once during their term of office,[114] so that there would be no risk that this might happen very frequently.

CONCLUSION

I believe that the institutions and procedures that I have recommended would heal [*medicati*] many of the defects and evils of our society and of our system of government [*del vivere e del governo nostro*], because they would enable the various public offices to be distributed to the general advantage. The important affairs of state [*le cose . . . dello stato*] would be decided by the wisest and most prominent men of our city; the best citizens would have the status and powers that are appropriate, but not so much power as to endanger civic freedom [. . . *la libertà*], or arouse fears about it; and the increased ability to punish crimes would effectively deter men who are bad and want to seize either private property or public office. Even if all these measures would not result in a perfectly ordered republic, at least it would be more than merely moderately good. However, in order for it to be raised to a higher level, we should need to remedy the fundamental causes of our over-refined sensibilities and weak spirits, which cause men to be feeble and result in countless evils. It would be necessary to eliminate the excessive regard and esteem for wealth, because the craving for riches erodes the desire for true glory, prevents the cultivation of the virtues and results in countless seizures of what belongs to others, as well as many other dishonourable actions. Everybody is guilty of these evil desires and practices; they are very deeply rooted. Indeed, they are widespread not only in our own city but throughout the world; there is only a great desire to enrich oneself and to put wealth to self-indulgent uses or to evil ends. This corrupt way of living is certainly nothing new; it has existed for very many centuries, as is evidenced by the ancient writers who denounced the vices rampant in their own times.

There are, perhaps, some remedies that could alleviate these evils somewhat, but not enough to have a very marked effect on a malady [*malattia*] that is so universal, so old and so deeply rooted in the minds of men. To eliminate it altogether, Lycurgus's knife would be needed. In one day he eradicated from Sparta all wealth and sumptuousness; he put together all the property of all the inhabitants, then divided it equally among them; he prohibited the use of money and all the activities for which wealth is sought: sumptuous display, banquets, many servants, luxurious clothes and fine houses. It was certainly a most remarkable achievement, bringing about in one day in his city such moderation in living and such zeal for virtue and such low esteem for wealth, as well as the many fine and glorious activities he made flourish in it. Anyone who has the good fortune to reform his own republic so well is certainly very happy and glorious, and it was much happier to have reformed it in such a way that its institutions and laws should last for many centuries, so that, while that republic lived under them, it was usually so strong and powerful that it was the leading state in Greece; it was certainly always pre-eminent in glory and famous for its virtues in the eyes of foreign nations. It was easier for Lycurgus to achieve it than it was for Plato, Cicero and many learned and wise men to write about it. Indeed, it is not surprising that it was thought in his own times that he had benefited from advice received from the Delphic Apollo, and rightly so, because reforming a corrupt city and, moreover, reforming it in ways that were so meritorious, is a task for gods rather than for human beings.

We can only marvel at and praise such a remarkable achievement, but as for achieving it today, it is hardly possible for us to hope for it, or even to desire it. Therefore, to speak now of things that are in fact possible in our situation, I would say that the evil [*malattia*] is so deep-rooted that it cannot be eradicated. It would be necessary (as Lycurgus did) to prohibit the activities for the sake of which wealth is sought; and because of the softness of men one can only express these things in the broadest terms. I certainly believe that making our city well armed, and thus creating the chance for Florence to achieve glorious victories, giving public office to men of good reputation and conduct, making it easy to punish the crimes of anyone who follows evil paths: all these measures together would result in the rich being less esteemed than they are today. Moreover (something attempted many times but with little success), we should limit as much as possible sumptuous clothes and jewellery, which make the differences between rich and poor people so obvious and spur men on to seek wealth. Furthermore, since the normal ways of increasing wealth are usually insufficient for such purposes, men stoop to multifarious shameful and illegal methods of acquisition. These are incompatible with having a republic in which it is intended to remove the obsession with wealth; they are harmful in republics in which it is desired to keep the city rich, because they greatly impoverish it, instead enriching enormously other states [*nazione esterne*]. All these bad practices have no useful function at all, not even superficial ones, because they do not fulfil any reasonable needs, but only certain vain and empty urges – they satisfy desires that are to be expected in women rather than in men. Hence I would propose reducing dowries to moderate proportions, since these great expenses are harmful, both because of the reasons given earlier and because it is inimical to the maintenance of equality between relatives and noble families, and, finally, because this would greatly benefit men who are worthy but poor, who find it much harder to marry off their daughters[115] than men who are rich and unscrupulous.

In short, these are the measures that I think are necessary for reforming our city and the popular regime [*el vivere populare*]. With regard to the details of my proposals, I concede that many of them may be mistaken, but I am convinced that the general features, and the objectives to be pursued, have merit. Although our conduct does not deserve divine favour, may it please God one day to permit our republic to achieve (in this or in similar ways) good institutions and good government [*buono governo*]. If it were possible to see these things, and in our own times, I would gladly dedicate my life and all my energies to this task.

Finished 27 August 1512.[116] At Logroño.

Translator's Notes

1. The word 'popular' (*populare*) is always used in this piece in the sense of 'of, pertaining to, the people'.
2. The term *libertà* had two main senses: not being subject to any foreign power, or 'independence' (*indipendenza* and *indipendente* were not coined until the late sixteenth century); and not being subject to a *signore* or a 'tyrant', in other words, the civic equality and freedoms entailed by a republican form of government. See N. Rubinstein, 'Florentina Libertas', *Rinascimento,* 26 (1986), 3–26.
3. That is, the kings of Spain and France.
4. That is, in Italy.
5. That is, Italian rulers.
6. See the Conclusion.
7. Guicciardini seems to allude especially to the practice of forced loans.
8. A reference to Machiavelli's development of a civic militia.
9. They will be eager to return home as soon as possible, unlike mercenaries.
10. On 14 May 1509, by the armies of the League of Cambrai, between Vailà and Agnadello (it is sometimes called the battle of Agnadello).
11. Maximilian I (1459–1519).
12. Bartolomeo d'Alviano.
13. That is, the city of Venice itself would have fallen.
14. Cf. Augustine, *De civitate Dei* IV.4: 'Remove justice, and what are kingdoms but gangs of criminals on a large scale?': trans. H. Bettenson (Harmondsworth, 1972), p. 139. See also Guicciardini, *Ricordi,* C 48; *Dialogo del reggimento di Firenze,* in his *Opere,* ed. E. Lugnani Scarano (Turin, 1970), I, p. 464; also in English translation: *Dialogue on the Government of Florence,* ed. and trans. A. Brown (Cambridge, 1994), pp. 158–9.
15. That is, mercenaries.
16. See pp. 215, 224–30.
17. That is, military organization.
18. Instead of applying the laws impartially.
19. After the expulsion of Piero de' Medici and the rise of Girolamo Savonarola, the Great Council (Consiglio grande) was established in December 1494 as the sovereign body of Florence; it made all appointments to public offices and ratified bills. All Florentine citizens who met certain qualifications (e.g., were at least twenty-nine years of age, had paid their taxes) were entitled to be life members of this Council. Essentially, it was a body in which the middle class predominated. The quorum was 1,000, and it was originally intended that the number of members should not exceed 1,500; in fact, the number of members became much larger (3,374 in 1496, and 3,705 in 1508), and a special chamber

had to be built. Guicciardini often uses *el populo* (the people) to denote the Council, or its members; occasionally, he uses the slightly pejorative term *la multitudine* (the multitude). The Great Council was abolished after the return of the Medici, in September 1512.

20. This was a view that Guicciardini held firmly all his life. It was expressed in the first version of his *Ricordi* (composed, like this piece, while he was living in Spain). The final version (C 134), written in 1529–30, reads: 'All men are by nature more inclined to good than evil, and there are none who would not more gladly do right than wrong, other things being equal. Yet man's nature is so weak, and so frequent in the world are the occasions which invite one to evil doing, that men easily allow themselves to be driven away from what is good. For this reason wise legislators invented rewards and punishments simply to hold men firm in their natural inclinations, through hope and fear': Guicciardini, *Selected Writings,* ed. C. Grayson, trans. M. Grayson (Oxford, 1965), p. 35. See also Guicciardini, *Dialogo,* in his *Opere*, I, pp. 354–5, 437; *Dialogue,* pp. 53, 131–2.

21. See *CHRP,* pp. 453–534.

22. The Great Council was the most popular body.

23. Machiavelli's opinion was the same: see *Discorsi* I.47.58.

24. In 1505. See Guicciardini, *History of Florence,* ch. 26. He says (trans. Domandi, p. 255): 'the gonfalonier convened the Council and proposed the attack on Pisa; the motion was carried, with only 106 negative votes out of more than 1000'.

25. See, e.g., Aristotle, *Metaphysics* XII.10 (1076ª4), quoting *Iliad* II.204.

26. In 1502; the popular regime was established in 1494.

27. *Gonfaloniere* means 'standard-bearer' (and originally, in the late thirteenth century, the gonfalonier was a military officer). During the fourteenth and fifteenth centuries, the gonfalonier of justice presided over meetings of the Signoria, the highest Florentine political body (see n. 50) and was thus the republic's supreme civil officer. Like the other members of the Signoria, he held office for two months.

　　In August 1502, the *permanent* gonfaloniership of justice (a minimum age of fifty being stipulated) was instituted. The gonfalonier was given the right of presiding over any criminal trials. (This is mentioned in ch. 23 of Guicciardini's *History of Florence,* in which several other themes conspicuous in the present piece are treated.) Piero Soderini, who had recently been gonfalonier of justice, was elected to this new post and took office in November 1502.

28. This is the body that, later, Guicciardini calls a 'Senate'.

29. Guicciardini means that if a body like the Council of Eighty, or the 'Senate' that he proposes, did not exist, such decisions would be made either by the Great Council (to which he is alluding here) or by the Signoria, which in practice would mean by the gonfalonier.

30. The Council of Eighty (Consiglio degli Ottanta), which was also called 'the Eighty' (gli Ottanta), was instituted in December 1494 and shared legislative power with the Great Council (see n. 19). Its members (who had to be at least forty years old) were elected by the Great Council and held office for six months.

31. See pp. 218–24, esp. pp. 219–20.

32. That is, the bodies deriving their authority from the Great Council.

33. Punishment is the other thing.

34. The regime established in 1494, after the Medici family's fall from power.

35. The two-thirds majority.

36. *Sorte* means 'lot' or 'sortition' and also 'chance'.

37. If candidates are of exactly equal merit (which doubtless very rarely happens), it seems reasonable to decide between them by lot.

38. That is, would be held by nobles.

39. Of citizens competing for office.

40. The Ten of Liberty and Peace (before 1494, called the Dieci di Balìa). As its name implies, it was responsible for the conduct of war, procuring supplies and ammunition, making military contracts, etc.

41. The Eight of Ward (Otto di Guardia): initially responsible mainly for political offences, it later also became responsible for other criminal cases.
42. In 1512, there were sixteen captains in charge of military forces in various parts of the Florentine dominions, and the three cities mentioned were large and important.
43. Officials of the Tower were primarily concerned with public works of a civil and military character in Florence, and of a civil character in the countryside (*contado* and *distretto*).
44. In 1512, there were thirteen vicariates in the Florentine dominions, and each of them was subdivided into several mayoralties (*podesterie*): in 1494 there were sixty-four.
45. That is, the body that Guicciardini later calls the 'Senate'.
46. The *parte guelfa,* founded in the late thirteenth century to ensure the predominance of the Guelph party over the Ghibellines; later, it became an administrative body, and by the end of the fifteenth century it was mainly concerned with the defence of the Florentine countryside (*contado* and *distretto*).
47. There were two bodies having the name *conservadori.* First, the Defenders of the Laws (*conservadori delle leggi*), established in the early fifteenth century, whose function was essentially to ensure that the laws were obeyed; by the end of the century it had become the most important body concerned with the criminal law, except the Eight of Ward (see n. 41). There were ten Defenders (who had to be at least forty years of age), and they held office for six months. There were also Defenders of the Countryside and the Dominions (*conservadori del contado e del dominio*), 'whose function was to control and reduce public expenditure': E. Lugnani Scarano in her edition of the text, in Guicciardini, *Opere,* I, p. 266. In view of the context, she is surely right to interpret *conservadori* as referring to both of these bodies.
48. This was the most important element of the Merchants' Court, which had authority over all commercial disputes. These six members held office for four months and received a salary.
49. Members of the Signoria were disqualified for three years (from the end of their period in office) from holding any of the most important public offices (see n. 50); for their relatives in the male line, the disqualification was for one year. See G. Guidi, *Lotte, pensiero e istituzioni politiche nella repubblica fiorentina dal 1494 al 1512* (Florence, 1992), p. 622.
50. That is, the Priorates; the Signoria consisted of the eight priors (*priori* or *signori*) and the gonfalonier of justice, and the priors held office for two months. The Signoria was the most important governing body of Florence, being one of the so-called Tre Maggiori (Three Most Important Bodies); the other two were the Gonfaloniers of the Companies (see n. 86) and the Twelve Goodmen (see n. 87).
51. The Palazzo della Signoria, the seat of government; since the late sixteenth century, it has been called the Palazzo Vecchio. 'The members of the Signoria, the gonfalonier of justice, and their notary, resided in the Palace for the whole of their period of office, and they could not leave it except when accompanied by at least one of their number, and then only on official business': Guidi, *Lotte, pensiero e istituzioni politiche,* p. 622.
52. The last was done by the Great Council, the first two by the Ten of Liberty and Peace.
53. That is, the other members of the Signoria.
54. 'A special tribunal convened *ad hoc* to try important crimes against the state. As the name indicates, it consisted of about forty members, though they could be as few as twenty': M. Domandi's introduction to his translation of F. Guicciardini, *History of Florence* (New York, 1970), p. xlvi. The *quarantia* was frequently used in Venice.
55. See pp. 226–30.
56. The powers of the Signoria.
57. To act as ambassador or commissary.
58. As Machiavelli was sent on various missions, as L. Bonfigli notes in his edition of the text: Guicciardini, *Scritti scelti* (Florence, 1924), p. 68.
59. See pp. 221–3.
60. Guicciardini assumes that the possible intervention of the gonfalonier in such cases would effectively deter violence.
61. See pp. 226–30.

62. See pp. 212–15.
63. See pp. 226–30.
64. That is, a *permanent* gonfalonier who is not 'good'.
65. Literally, 'one provides food for more [men]'.
66. Literally, 'meal'.
67. See pp. 212–15.
68. The Senate.
69. The Senate 'should be composed of all the wisest men of the city'.
70. For the nature and functions of the Senate see the next section.
71. Guicciardini says *avervi a convenire ognuno* (literally, 'since everyone has to agree'), but, obviously, he is not saying that there must be unanimity. What is required is the agreement of the *majority* of the intermediate body (the Senate) to a man being one of the three proposed to the Great Council, followed by the agreement of the *majority* of the Great Council.
72. That is, the Senate.
73. That is, a Senate; *pregati* is the Tuscan form of the Venetian *pregadi* or *pregai* and of the Latin *rogati*. In Venice, the *Pregadi* were the Senators; they were 'requested' (*pregati*) by the doge to express their views to the Maggior Consiglio on the most important problems. See *Grande dizionario della lingua italiana* (Turin, 1961–), s.v.
74. Guicciardini's point is that the outstanding citizens should always be members of the Senate.
75. See n. 30.
76. That is, the members of the Eighty.
77. Literally, 'one would provide . . . more food for the people'. Food images are used in several passages: see, e.g., nn. 65–6, 91 and 97.
78. Before the institution of the permanent gonfalonier in 1502, gonfaloniers held office for only two months; hence, there would have been no lack of ex-gonfaloniers.
79. *Commissari* were men 'charged with representing the authority of the State, who were sent to a foreign State, or to a province or an army, in order to supervise the behaviour of officials or generals, to provide what was necessary for war, raising troops, etc.': *Grande dizionario,* s.v.
80. That is, with other states.
81. That is, the heads of the various sections of the Florentine civil service, working in the Palazzo della Signoria: the First Chancery (concerned largely with foreign affairs); the Second Chancery (concerned with the Florentine dominions); the Riformagioni and the Tratte: see P. Vettori, 'Memorandum to Cardinal de' Medici', in Chapter 14, nn. 22 and 25 respectively.
82. See pp. 226–30.
83. See pp. 221–4, 227–8, 230.
84. The *fermatori* were 'the eight officials charged with the drafting and revision of laws before they were presented to the assemblies': *Grande dizionario,* s.v.
85. For two months.
86. Since 1343, Florence had been divided into four districts (*quartieri*), which were sub-divided into four *gonfaloni;* consequently, there were sixteen gonfaloniers. They held office (unpaid) for four months and had a double function: they represented the views of the inhabitants of the various areas, and they participated (together with the Twelve Goodmen and the Signoria) in the most important political decisions.
87. This body was instituted in 1321, when the city was divided into sixths; each sixth had two representatives. Like the sixteen Gonfaloniers of Companies, they were not paid; they held office for three months. Two of the Goodmen acted as *fermatori* (see n. 84). Together, the Gonfaloniers of Companies and the Twelve Goodmen were called the Colleges (*collegi*).
88. More literally, to kick the civic freedoms around as if they were a ball.
89. The word 'senate' (rendering *senato*) occurred on p. 218. Now, Guicciardini has used *senato* again. In the intervening pages, he frequently used *questo consiglio* to denote the

body that he now says he will call 'the Senate'. I have translated *questo consiglio* as 'the Senate' instead of 'this body' in order to avoid vagueness or confusion.

90. Literally, 'to steer'. On p. 218, the same imagery is used; *timone*: 'guiding body'.
91. Literally, 'to digest'; another metaphor connected with food.
92. This is probably a reference to Piero Soderini, but Guicciardini may be alluding to Lorenzo de' Medici (see n. 94).
93. Guicciardini may seem to be contradicting what he said previously (see pp. 220–1), but there his argument was that the law-making procedure, although complicated, was designed to achieve the outcomes wanted by powerful men.
94. The words *quali forme* refer to the 'procedures devised by tyrants' (*[c]ose tutte trovate da' tiranni*). And Guicciardini means the practices prevalent during the Medici regime, when Florence was formally a republic but was in fact controlled by the Medici family. This tendency was especially marked during the hegemony of Lorenzo de' Medici (1469–92); indeed, in chapter 9 of Guicciardini's *History of Florence* (in which he reviews the life and career of Lorenzo), he says that Florence was then 'a city . . . free in name, but in fact tyrannized by one of its citizens': trans. Domandi, p. 71.
95. Literally, 'weak men'; cf. Machiavelli, *Discorsi* III.6, in which he says that revenge and conspiracies are not undertaken by such men.
96. Florence was divided into four districts or *quartieri;* see n. 86.
97. More literally, 'well-digested'; cf. n. 91.
98. This law was passed in August 1495.
99. And the republican institutions and procedures on which it is based.
100. Literally, 'feel this flame'.
101. Guicciardini was doubtless thinking of flattery, demagogy, etc.
102. This passage is unclear, and it is hardly possible to reconcile it with what Guicciardini says later. Earlier (p. 218), he emphasized that, in *practice,* it is almost impossible to get rid of a gonfalonier. In this paragraph, he is discussing what security of tenure a gonfalonier *should* have. Since Guicciardini stresses that political decisions should be made in a regular, constitutional way, through established institutions (e.g., see p. 224), the most natural interpretation of this passage would be that citizens could petition the Great Council to dismiss a gonfalonier, and the Council would do this if it considers such an action to be desirable.

 However, on p. 230 below, the Great Council and the citizens generally are not even mentioned. Guicciardini recommends that the Senate should take any decision to dismiss a gonfalonier (or punish him in any other way), that a two-thirds majority should be required and that the proposal of dismissal should be made by a member of the Signoria. In short, the procedure for dismissal recommended is much more stringent than that implied in the passage under discussion.
103. For the former see n. 41; for the latter see n. 47.
104. The printed editions read *stati;* but the manuscript (Florence, Archivio Guicciardini, Filza XV) has *stat^i* (= *statuti*).
105. Six out of eight, and seven out of ten, constituted the required majorities.
106. Citizens found guilty of rebellion incurred this penalty.
107. On the inhabitants of the territories subject to Florence.
108. The subject territories would rebel.
109. Guicciardini probably refers to the details of these plots and to the responsibility of individuals for them.
110. That is, the verdicts and the legal reasoning justifying them.
111. This differs from what Guicciardini says on p. 227, where he recommends that, when lesser penalties than death or confiscation of property are involved, forty or fifty senators should act as an appeal court.
112. Guicciardini does not in fact discuss this.
113. Except for a gonfalonier who chooses to resign.
114. This lasted two months.

115. Guicciardini had four daughters, and was very conscious of the problem of dowries. See also his *Ricordi:* A 142; B 166; C 106.
116. Roberto Palmarocchi, in his edition of the text, in F. Guicciardini, *Dialogo e discorsi del reggimento di Firenze* (Bari, 1932), p. 218, observes that at the beginning of the manuscript there is the following note in the author's hand, 'written in a different ink, and probably later: "In Spain in the year 1512 and I had almost finished it when I heard the news that the Medici had entered Florence."' Given the date in the text, this note is puzzling. Giuliano de' Medici did not enter Florence until 1 September, and Guicciardini heard about this (embarrassingly, from King Ferdinand) only on 25 September. Roberto Ridolfi, *The Life of Francesco Guicciardini* (London, 1967), p. 285, rightly remarks: 'when G[uicciardini] wrote [the note] at the head, without looking at the date written at the end, his memory failed him'.

Further Reading

Albertini, R. von, *Das florentinische Staatsbewusstsein im Übergang von der Republik zum Prinzipat* (Berne, 1955), pp. 95–8; also available in Italian translation: *Firenze dalla repubblica al principato: storia e coscienza politica* (Turin, 1970), pp. 91–3
Bondanella, P. E., *Francesco Guicciardini* (Boston, 1976), pp. 43–7
CHRP, pp. 435, 822
Gilbert, F., *Machiavelli and Guicciardini: Politics and History in Sixteenth-Century Florence* (Princeton, N.J., 1975), pp. 122–38
Guicciardini, Francesco, *Dialogo del reggimento di Firenze,* in Guicciardini, *Opere,* ed. E. Lugnani Scarano, 3 vols. (Turin, 1970–81), I, pp. 297–493; also available in English translation: *Dialogue on the Government of Florence,* ed. and trans. A. Brown (Cambridge, 1994)
  Storie fiorentine, in Guicciardini, *Opere,* ed. E. Lugnani Scarano, I, pp. 59–245; also available in English translation: *The History of Florence,* trans. M. Domandi (New York, 1970)
  Ricordi, ed. R. Spongano (Florence, 1951); also available in two English translations: *Maxims and Reflections of a Renaissance Statesman,* trans. M. Domandi, introd. N. Rubinstein (New York, 1965) [contains both the B and C series; the latter is the final version]; *Selected Writings,* ed. C. Grayson, trans. M. Grayson (Oxford, 1965), pp. 1–56 [contains only the C series]
Guidi, G., *Lotte, pensiero e istituzioni politiche nella repubblica fiorentina dal 1494 al 1512,* 3 vols. (Florence, 1992)
Pocock, J. G. A., *The Machiavellian Moment: Florentine Political Thought and the Atlantic Republican Tradition* (Princeton, N.J., 1975), pp. 122–38
Rubinstein, N., 'Guicciardini politico', in *Francesco Guicciardini 1483–1983: nel V centenario della nascita* (Florence, 1984), pp. 161–89 (esp. 167–9)
  'Italian Political Thought, 1450–1530', in J. H. Burns, ed., *The Cambridge History of Political Thought 1450–1700* (Cambridge, 1991), pp. 30–65 (60–1)

14

Paolo Vettori

RUSSELL PRICE

Introduction

Paolo Vettori (1477–1526) was the younger brother of the well-known Francesco Vettori (1474–1539).[1] Francesco was a close friend of Machiavelli, with whom he frequently corresponded while he was Florentine ambassador to the Holy See, after Machiavelli's dismissal from office. Paolo Vettori 'served an apprenticeship of two years from December 1492 to November 1494 in Niccolò Capponi's company of silk merchants. In November 1501 he matriculated in the silk guild on his own account.' And, with his other brother, Giovanni, Paolo apparently 'operated a furnace in which they smelted iron and probably also steel'.[2] At one time, he was captain of the papal galleys. He also held various political posts (he was a member of the Signoria in 1522) and was sent on several diplomatic missions, among others, to Milan and to France; it was while travelling from Rome to France to undertake one of these missions that he was taken ill, and died in Florence.

Like his brother, Francesco, Paolo was a friend of Machiavelli, who, in a letter to Francesco (written on 13 March 1513, just after his release from prison, where he had been held for a month on suspicion of being involved in an anti-Medici plot), expresses thanks to both brothers for having interceded on his behalf. Paolo Vettori had for some time been one of the leaders of the Medici faction in Florence. Although he had been fairly closely associated with Piero Soderini for some years, there is evidence that he was playing a double game. It is not altogether clear why he adhered to the Medici faction, but hope of personal gain was certainly not absent: his brother Francesco suggested that his financial difficulties were an important reason,[3] and Guicciardini also stressed his 'many debts'.[4] At any rate, he was one of the group of four men that went to the Palazzo della Signoria on 31 August 1512 and pressed Soderini to resign from his position as permanent gonfalonier.

Vettori's memorandum to Cardinal Giovanni de' Medici, in which he recommends the adoption of a princely framework of government in Florence, is undated, but it seems clear that it was written after the first three weeks of September 1512 (by which time the Medici family had been restored to effective control of Florence) and before the end of October 1512. In it, he refers to Niccolò Machiavelli and Biagio Buonaccorsi as being members of the Chancery, and they were both dismissed from office by a decree of 7 November. Much more important, a recurring theme in the piece is the impending departure from Florence of Cardinal de' Medici, and the possible consequences of this for Medici rule there. The cardinal left Florence for Bologna on 6 November. If the exact or approximate date of his departure was known to Vettori, he would hardly have waited to write his memorandum until a few days before the cardinal left, since Vettori recommended that he make various important decisions and arrangements before leaving. It is probable, therefore, that it was written during the first two weeks of October 1512.

The piece remained in manuscript until 1955, when it was published by Rudolf von Albertini (who discovered it in the Strozzi Papers in the State Archives, Florence). It bears the title 'Ricordi di Paolo Vettori al cardinale de' Medici sopra le cose di Firenze'; von Albertini notes that the manuscript is in Vettori's hand but the title is by Carlo Strozzi.

For the original text see Paolo Vettori, 'Ricordi al cardinale de' Medici sopra le cose di Firenze', in R. von Albertini, *Das florentinische Staatsbewusstsein im Übergang von der Republik zum Prinzipat* (Berne, 1955), pp. 345–7; also available in Italian translation: *Firenze dalla repubblica al principato: storia e coscienza politica* (Turin, 1970), pp. 357–9. I wish to express my great indebtedness to Paolo L. Rossi and Jill Kraye for commenting on my translation and suggesting many improvements, and to Alison Brown for valuable advice on many points.

Memorandum to Cardinal de' Medici[5] *about the Affairs of Florence*

Most Reverend Lord, since it is necessary for you to depart,[6] I wish respectfully to write down for you what occurs to me; if I have not written wisely, at least it is done in good faith, as I must, for the prosperity of this government [*questo Stato*] and of those who are linked with it.

Your ancestors, from Cosimo to Piero,[7] maintained power [*questo Stato*] more by skilful management [*industria*] than by force [*forza*]. But you need to use force more than skilful management, because you have more enemies here and not very much ability to satisfy them; therefore, since you cannot win them over again,[8] you will need to become so strong and secure that they will be afraid to attack you. The way to achieve this is to maintain the body of faithful armed men [*questa guardia*], and in order to be more in control of them, you must be able to pay them more easily. Therefore, I would recommend a decision in the *Balìa* that the office of the Ten[9] allocates all the funds needed for the upkeep of these forces and places these funds in the depository of the Signoria, so that they will be paid to the commissary who will have special responsibility for these forces. In this way, the payments would be made more easily and secretly. You should contrive to have spies within these forces and keep the soldiers well disposed towards you. But all these forces will not be sufficient, because this city is very large, and there are too many discontented citizens. Moreover, you cannot trust all the members of the *Balìa,* or all the information that they gather. Consequently, if all the previously mentioned forces are not supplemented by others, they will turn out to be very weak or useless.

You cannot have military forces that are more reliable, or more numerous, or that will cause more fear in the city or inspire greater trust in your family [*Casa*] than infantry troops, because you must realize that during the past ten years the city has been very prosperous, and therefore the memories of this period will give rise to much resentment or hostility.[10] On the other hand, your countryside and rural districts [*contado e distretto*] have been very far from prosperous, so that you should be able to win over their inhabitants, even if you cannot regain the allegiance of the citizens. And if you arm the inhabitants of the countryside, and win over those whom you arm by defending them from provincial administrators [*rettori di fuori*] and from public officers in Florence itself [*magistrati di dentro*] who oppress them, and if in fact you become their protector, within six months you will be more secure in Florence than if you were to have a Spanish army in Prato ready to help you. Here is the way to achieve this: before you leave, contrive to get the *Balìa* to decide to give as much authority to the Signoria for raising infantry and cavalry as the Nine[11] had, because the constables who will be chosen for that purpose will need no further approval and will be entitled to delegate that authority to the man they think most suitable; you will therefore be able to appoint a commissary favourable to you and who will obey you. The funds of the Signoria, given directly to their depositary, will be sufficient for paying these constables.

There is something else that you should decide before you leave: how Giuliano[12] should act and from whom he should seek advice, about both internal and foreign policy. And I must warn you frankly that if this matter is not dealt with properly, confusion and harm could well result; and including myself among all the others, you will find all these citizens to be ambitious and cautiously self-seeking [*rispettivi*]. Because of their ambition, it is hard to satisfy them, and because of their cautious self-seeking, they will give unsound advice. There will be very few who do not think first of saving themselves rather than you, and who are not concerned with being able to stay in Florence themselves, even if you should be driven out. Hence, the advice given by such men is not unbiased, and Giuliano will not realize this, because he is not yet well versed in the affairs of the city; if someone who perceives troubles that are merely brewing does not stay close to him and warn him about them in good time, your regime [*lo Stato vostro*] could come to such a pass that, even if it survives, it will be exceedingly weak. And if the situation were to be put right, fresh injuries would need to be done to the people. If such things are not done at once, they cannot be done later. All this is concerned with cautious self-seeking [*a' respecti*].

With regard to ambition, I wish to tell Your Most Reverend Lordship that, when you leave, that which keeps the citizens united in obedience will be removed, namely, your own personal authority and the respect it engenders. The discords will at once cause many problems for Giuliano, which he will not be able to overcome by himself, because he does not yet understand our affairs, and very serious troubles could result from this. Therefore, I would say that, before you leave, you must choose for Giuliano ten or twelve citizens, being careful to exclude any who are fair-weather supporters of your family. Giuliano should seek their advice on every matter, both at home and in the Palace,[13] both in secret and in public. Since it is possible that disagreements will arise among them, you need to choose from this number one or two, at the most, whom Giuliano, after previous consultations, can gather round him in order to discuss the proposals and opinions of everyone before making his decisions. If Your Most Reverend Lordship chooses the twelve men well, especially those two trusted advisers, and begins to control affairs in this way, all the ambitions, troubles and contentions, though they will not altogether cease, will at least remain hidden, so that men become accustomed to this way of doing things. For men complain and shout when they see that shouting gets them what they want; but when they realize that their shouting is ineffective and does not cause the decisions made to be changed, they quieten down and learn to accept what has been done.

Another matter that Your Most Reverend Lordship must decide is where you want affairs of state [*le cose di Stato*] to be handled. Dealing with all of them privately [*a casa*][14] would be too troublesome; if they are dealt with in the Palace, the Ten must deal with them, because the Signoria has always been the instrument [*il bastone*] and not the decision-making body of government [*il cervello dello Stato*]. Therefore, before you depart, you must reorganize the Chancery.[15]

In order that you may understand everything, in Lorenzo's day,[16] as far as I have been able to find out, the Chancery was organized as follows: Scala[17] attended to the letters of other rulers [*Signori di fuora*], which messer Marcello[18] does now; messer Cristofano[19] attended to correspondence about internal affairs, which Machiavelli[20] does now; ser Giovanni[21] dealt with the Riformagioni,[22] which ser Francesco[23] does now, and ser Simone of Staggia[24] the Tratte,[25] which is now the responsibility of ser Antonio Vespucci.[26] All these men have had their assistants. At the head of the Chancery of the Eight of Pratica and the Ten were messer Francesco Gaddi,[27] ser Alessandro Bracci[28] and ser Francesco, son of ser Barone;[29] and they had as assistants such men as ser Antonio della Valle,[30] ser Antonio of Colle,[31] Bernardo de' Ricci, ser Lorenzo Ficini,[32] ser Jacopo di Ruffino and Marco of Romena, and others that I have not discovered. But I certainly know that they had pairs of men, so that they could send them abroad together with ambassadors; and with regard to the latter, they began to establish permanent embassies in important places, like those of ser Antonio della Valle in Naples, ser Antonio of Colle in Rome and Bernardo de' Ricci in Milan. At present, the duties of the Chancery of the Ten and the Chancery of the Signoria are not entirely distinct, because messer Marcello deals with letters to and from the Ten, and Machiavelli dealt with letters about internal affairs, before he went to the Ordinanza.[33] Then, for the last four years, Biagio,[34] the assistant of messer Marcello, has served there; and there are three or four assistants who write letters.

Although the Chancery is organized in this way today, during the previous regime [*nello Stato passato*][35] it was organized differently. For in the Ten a post carrying a salary of 194 florins was left vacant; this money was put aside to pay a well-qualified man to help messer Marcello as an equal. Yet another post carrying the same salary was left vacant: this was used by the Ten for dealing with letters concerning internal affairs. These posts were not left unfilled in order to save the Comune money by economizing on their salaries, and in any case the Comune was sufficiently provided with staff. Your Most Reverend Lordship must think how the staff of these chanceries can be reduced at the present time. And if you want the affairs of state [*le faccende di Stato*] to be controlled by the Ten, Giuliano will need to meet with the Ten at least once a day and have with him some of those citizens chosen to advise him; and the replies to be given to ambassadors should be decided there, and everything else that he considers necessary. He should have a chancellor attached to the Ten who has much experience of internal and foreign affairs, and this man should also write on Giuliano's behalf to the ambassadors about those things that concern your own rule [*dello Stato vostro particulare*], not deviating in any way from what has been decided. Moreover, if you should remove an experienced or trusted man, that would be an excellent beginning for your rule [*per lo Stato vostro*], because it is essential that it should be seen as something ordered by you.

With regard to the funds required for everything, I shall not say anything; I shall leave Guidotto[36] to speak about it, or others who understand more about it than I do. I shall say only that it is essential to create a depository that has credit facilities, so that its credit can supplement money when necessary, and men can be reimbursed with promissory notes and not have to wait for money to come from the public treasurers every time.

Translator's Notes

1. Francesco Vettori's most important work was his *Sommario della Storia d'Italia dal 1511 al 1527*. See R. Devonshire Jones, *Francesco Vettori: Florentine Citizen and Medici Servant* (London, 1972).
2. Devonshire Jones, *Francesco Vettori*, p. 4.
3. Devonshire Jones, *Francesco Vettori*, p. 58.
4. Francesco Guicciardini, *History of Italy*, XI.4.
5. Cardinal Giovanni de' Medici (1475–1521), the second son of Lorenzo the Magnificent (he was created cardinal by Innocent VIII in 1492). He became Pope Leo X in March 1513.
6. Giovanni de' Medici was absent from Florence for more than two months. Pope Julius II had appointed him papal legate in Bologna and the Romagna in October 1511; and he was charged with recovering Ferrara. He left Florence on 6 November 1512, with papal and Florentine troops, and went to Bologna, where he remained until mid January 1513; he returned to Florence on 19 January. Pope Julius died on 20 February, and on 22 February Giovanni left for Rome, where he was elected pope on 11 March. The dates of his movements are recorded in Luca Landucci, *A Florentine Diary from 1450 to 1516,* ed. Iodoco Del Badia (London, 1927), pp. 263, 265, 266.
7. Cosimo de' Medici (1389–1464); Piero de' Medici (1471–1503). Vettori means the period between 1434 (when Cosimo returned from a year's exile in Padua) and 1494 (when Piero was driven from Florence), and he is referring to four men: Cosimo; his son, Piero (1416–69); Piero's son, Lorenzo the Magnificent (1449–92); and Lorenzo's eldest son, Piero.
8. As the Medici family had done between 1434 and 1494.
9. The Ten of Liberty and Peace (before 1494 called Dieci di Balìa). 'The Ten were responsible for conducting wars, procuring supplies and ammunition, hiring soldiers, and conducting diplomatic relations in times of war': M. Domandi's introduction to his translation of F. Guicciardini, *The History of Florence,* (New York, 1970), p. xlv.
10. Towards the Medici, who were absent from Florence between 1494 and 1512.
11. The Nine of Ordinanza and Milizia, the body concerned with military organization, founded in 1507.
12. Giuliano de' Medici, Duke of Nemours (1479–1516), third son of Lorenzo the Magnificent. After his brother, Giovanni (1475–1521), was elected Pope Leo X, in March 1513, he lived mostly in Rome.
13. The Palazzo della Signoria, the seat of government; it has been called the Palazzo Vecchio since the late sixteenth century.
14. That is, not through the established political institutions.
15. For the organization and work of the Chancery, see A. Brown, *Bartolomeo Scala, 1430–1497, Chancellor of Florence* (Princeton, N.J., 1979), pp. 135–92, and R. Black, *Benedetto Accolti and the Florentine Renaissance* (Princeton, N.J., 1985), pp. 115–83.
16. Lorenzo the Magnificent (see n. 7); in short, between 1469 (when Lorenzo's father, Piero, died) and 1492.
17. Bartolomeo Scala (1430–97), humanist and first chancellor of Florence, 1465–97. See Brown, *Bartolomeo Scala*. For his *Dialogue on Laws and Legal Judgements* see Chapter 12.
18. Marcello Virgilio Adriani (1464–1521), humanist and administrator. In 1494 he succeeded Angelo Poliziano in the chair of poetry and rhetoric at the University of Florence. After the death of Scala, in July 1497, Adriani was chosen to succeed him as first chancellor in February 1498 and served until his death.

19. Cristoforo Landino (1424–98), humanist and administrator. After early legal studies, he devoted himself to literature; he began to teach at the University of Florence in 1458 and obtained a chair there in 1471. From the early 1480s, he occupied high posts in the Chancery and became secretary of the Signoria, retiring in 1497 or 1498.

20. Niccolò Machiavelli (1469–1527), head of the Second Chancery and secretary to the Ten of Liberty and Peace, 1498–1512; head of the Nine of Milizia, 1507–12. Author of *The Prince, Discourses on Livy,* etc.

21. Giovanni Guidi (c. 1435–1515), son of Bartolomeo Guidi of Pratovecchio (c. 1400–77), who was head of the office of the Riformagioni from 1458 until 1477. Because of Bartolomeo's age, in 1471 Giovanni was appointed to help his father in his official duties, and on his father's death he was appointed in his place. He was head of the Riformagioni until 1494; he suffered hard times during the popular regime that was then established. (*ser* was the title of notaries.)

22. This office was concerned with drafting legislation and, after it was passed, transcribing it into the official books.

23. Francesco Ottaviani or Attaviani, born in Arezzo, was head of the office of the Riformagioni from 1499 until December 1514. It is not known whether he died or was dismissed; his successor was appointed on 11 January 1515.

24. Simone Grazzini, born in Staggia c. 1435, died after 1494. He became eligible to hold public office in Florence in 1459. He was head of the office of the Tratte from 1484 until 1494, when he was dismissed.

25. This office was concerned with elections to all public offices, with ensuring that candidates were of the correct age, that they were not disqualified from holding office for any reason, etc.

26. Vespucci was head of the office of the Tratte from 1498 until 1528, when he retired.

27. Francesco Gaddi (c. 1450–1504). After graduating in law, he entered public life in 1476; he held various important posts and undertook several missions in Italy and abroad. He was head of the Second Chancery, 1494–8.

28. Alessandro Braccesi or Bracci (1445–1503), scholar, poet and administrator. He was head of the Second Chancery for a brief period in 1498.

29. Francesco Baroni, also known as ser Ceccone (1451–1503), the son of ser Barone Baroni. He was appointed as head of the office of the Eight of Pratica in 1483; he was dismissed in November 1494.

30. Antonio della Valle (1449–1511) held various administrative posts during a long career. In 1509 he was notary of the Signoria, and in 1510 he was civil notary of the Council of Justice.

31. Antonio Guidotti of Colle, notary and clerk in the Chancery; he was entrusted with various missions (to Milan in 1499, to Siena in 1502).

32. He was also known as ser Luca Fabiani; Lorenzo Ficini was an adopted name. He was Bartolomeo Scala's assistant in the Chancery in the 1480s and 1490s. (I owe this information to Alison Brown.)

33. The Nine of Ordinanza and Milizia (see n. 11). The tense used here is different from that in the earlier reference to Machiavelli: the explanation is that when he was appointed to the Nine in January 1507, he retained his other posts as head of the Second Chancery and secretary to the Ten; to Vettori the new position doubtless seemed more important.

34. Biagio Buonaccorsi (1472–c. 1522), a junior colleague and close friend of Niccolò Machiavelli (with whom he corresponded frequently). He lost his administrative post (as did Machiavelli) in November 1512.

35. That is, between 1494 and 1512.

36. Almost certainly Leonardo Guidotti. He was elected a member of the Ten in September 1500. Previously, he had held various offices: he had been a member of the Eight of Pratica (in 1490), and one of the Defenders of the Laws (1493, 1499). According to H. C. Butters, *Governors and Government in Early Sixteenth-Century Florence 1502–1519* (Oxford, 1985), p. 247, at one time he held 'the office of depositary'. He is mentioned in

several letters written by Biagio Buonaccorsi to Machiavelli in 1502: see N. Machiavelli, *Lettere* (Milan, 1961), ed. F. Gaeta, pp. 78–80, 82, 84, 98, 104, 106. He may have still been alive in 1526 (*Lettere,* pp. 392, 394, 483, 488, 498); there are three mentions of 'Guidetto' and two of 'Guidotto', and Gaeta thinks Leonardo Guidotti is being referred to.

Further Reading

Albertini, R. von, *Das florentinische Staatsbewusstsein im Übergang von der Republik zum Prinzipat* (Berne, 1955) pp. 33–4; and Italian translation: *Firenze dalla repubblica al principato: storia e coscienza politica* (Turin, 1970), pp. 22–4.

CHRP, p. 431

Devonshire Jones, R., *Francesco Vettori: Florentine Citizen and Medici Servant* (London, 1972), pp. 78, 241

Pocock, J. G. A., *The Machiavellian Moment: Florentine Political Thought and the Atlantic Republican Tradition* (Princeton, N.J., 1975), pp. 147–8

Part V.
Political Theory in Northern Europe

15

Josse Clichtove

ALISON HOLCROFT

Introduction

Josse Clichtove (1472–1543) was a prominent humanist and theologian in early sixteenth-century France. Born in Flanders, he went to Paris around 1490. In Paris he was one of the early pupils of Jacques Lefèvre d'Étaples and, while still a student, collaborated with him on a number of influential textbooks. In the earlier part of his life Clichtove was known chiefly as a humanist; but, after his doctorate in theology in 1506, he moved more and more into theological studies and the editing of patristic writers. In the 1520s he became known as one of the chief opponents of Martin Luther.

On True Nobility (1512) was dedicated to a young French aristocrat, Jacques d'Amboise, who had been Clichtove's pupil in Paris for a number of years;[1] he was now, at his father's bidding, returning home to take up a military career.[2] The work was intended as a farewell present, a manual of the virtuous life for a young noble beginning his career in the world. Italian humanists of the fifteenth century had developed an idealized concept of nobility, dependent solely on virtue. Clichtove shares Aristotle's more pragmatic view that true nobility is greatly enhanced by certain external advantages, in particular noble birth. Clichtove's precepts for the noble life long outlived their intended reader: Jacques d'Amboise was killed in 1515.

For the Latin text of the passages translated here see the first edition of *De vera nobilitate* (Paris, 1512), ff. 3r–8r, 18v–19v. The work was reissued in an improved and extended second edition (Paris, 1520). This was followed by a French translation based on the first edition (Paris, 1529; Lyons, 1533, 1534 and 1535; Paris, 1540) and by a second eighteenth-century translation by the Abbot of Mery (Paris, 1761 and 1763).

On True Nobility: Selections

CHAPTER I

The Definition of Nobility and How Many Types There Are

Nobility is defined by the great writers of the past as the pre-eminence and honour that comes from high birth or some other factor. The word *nobilitas* is, in their view, derived from *noscibilitas,* that is, 'the quality of being well known', since it is easy for anyone to attract attention and become well known for the things in which he surpasses others.[3] In the *Politics,* Aristotle lists four types of nobility: nobility of wealth, nobility of birth, nobility based on virtue [*virtus*] and nobility derived from learning.[4]

There is also no reason why nobility should not sometimes be derived from the prestige of one's fatherland or birthplace. For a man's own honour and glory are much enhanced by the greatness of his country and its ancient grandeur. But these things are of little account, if he does not surpass others with respect to virtue, which, even on its own, makes a man truly noble. This is the point of the story told about Themistocles' reply to a man from Seriphos who claimed, in the course of an argument, that Themistocles' fame was due, not to his own qualities, but to the lustre of his fatherland. Themistocles replied, quite correctly: 'If you'd been born at Athens you'd still have been a nobody; but I'd have been famous even if I'd been born on little Seriphos.'[5] He meant by this that his reputation rested on the glory of his great achievements and not on the fact that he was an Athenian. The philosopher Anacharsis, according to Diogenes Laertius, gave an equally apposite reply to an Athenian who denigrated him for being a Scythian: 'I have nothing to be ashamed of in my homeland, but yours has plenty to be ashamed of in you!'[6]

I shall, however, pass over all the other sources of nobility and confine my discussion to the two types which correspond to the two basic elements of a human being, the body and the soul [*anima*]: nobility of birth and nobility based on virtue. Nobility of birth is that high distinction of birth based on ancestry. It is clear that this type of nobility can be referred to the condition and nature of the body, seeing that we acquire it at birth simply by being the children of our parents. By contrast, nobility based on virtue is that surpassing glory and honour which is acquired through moral rectitude and the virtue of one's rational soul [*animus*].[7] There can be no doubt that this pertains to the rational soul since it is the exclusive and special property of a rational soul which has been perfected by the continual practice of right actions. As Chrysostom says, the man who is truly glorious, great and noble, the man who can rightfully think himself the possessor of perfect nobility, is the man who disdains to be subservient to vice.[8] Apuleius refers to both sorts of nobility when he describes someone as a man made noble not by high birth but by his character and virtues.[9]

Furthermore, if these two forms of nobility are joined together, the result is a third type of nobility embracing both the first two forms: nobility of both birth and virtue, the combination of high birth and surpassing virtue in one and the same individual. It is the third form I intend to discuss. This is patently the absolute and perfect form since it incorporates both the other types into a complete concept of nobility. It is obvious that neither a body devoid of a soul nor a soul without a body is a complete human being. Rather, it is necessary for body and soul to come together in a single whole in order to make a whole human being. In the same way neither pre-eminence of birth without the addition of virtue nor virtue by itself, hidden away in obscure and humble circumstances, has the power to make a man wholly and unequivocally noble. True and perfect nobility comes from the combination of honourable birth and ancestry with the glorious radiance of virtue.

CHAPTER 2

The First Two Types of Nobility

The first two types of nobility differ greatly in value, and this difference is much the same as that between the body and the soul, to which, as I've already said, they correspond. For everyone agrees that the soul is greatly superior to the body. Similarly, the special properties and qualities of the soul are considered much superior to those which pertain only to the body. It is hardly surprising, then, if nobility based on virtue is more highly esteemed than nobility of birth.

In addition, noble birth depends on something external to ourselves, namely, our ancestry. By sheer accident of birth one man is born to high rank, another in humble circumstances. And so high birth is not a good which belongs to us; it belongs instead either to the ancestors who founded our family line or to nature, who bestowed such birth upon us. Ovid's Ulysses makes this point with a witty response to Ajax's loud-mouthed boasting about his noble lineage:

> As to family, ancestors and deeds we have not ourselves performed,
> We can hardly claim them as our own.[10]

And Seneca writes: 'The man who praises his own breeding, praises something that belongs to others.'[11] So also Apuleius: 'If you praise someone for being well-born, you are praising his parents.'[12] In contrast, nobility based on virtue is entirely our own. It is a good which we have acquired, not by inheritance, but by our own efforts.

Furthermore, noble families generally have origins that are themselves anything but noble, and their founders are for the most part totally undistinguished. What, I ask you, were the very first origins of Rome? It was set up by Romulus as a safe haven for a mob of fugitives who poured in from all over. These impoverished and humble refugees laid the foundations of Rome's greatness. Juvenal refers to this in his eighth *Satire:*

> Yet, if you look back to the earliest beginnings of your family,
> You trace your descent from a notorious haven for criminals and refugees;
> The founder of your family, whoever he may have been,
> Was either a shepherd or something I'd rather not name.[13]

Likewise, noble and ancient families often come to an end, when their last living descendants either die without offspring or are publicly disgraced and stripped of their noble title by extraneous circumstances. There is nothing extraordinary in this. Since nobility of birth is a fortuitous and external good, it is, like all the other goods of that sort, subject to change and instability. Nobility based on virtue, on the other hand, even if it has been acquired by a man's own efforts and lacks the support of noble ancestry, knows neither death nor decay and confers on him immortal glory and undying fame. Since such nobility is related to virtue and very close to it in nature, it remains glorious forever. Nor can the man who possesses nobility based on virtue be branded with any mark of dishonour. Virtue removes him from all possibility of shame and disgrace and renders him famous and celebrated in the highest heavens.

What about the fact that noble birth falls to the lot of good and evil men alike and makes no distinction between a righteous man and a corrupt one? Nobility of the rational soul, by contrast, can only belong to good men endowed with virtue. And just as those things which are peculiar to human beings are ranked more highly than those which human beings have in common with animals devoid of reason, so those things which belong to good men alone are obviously superior to those which are common to both good and bad men.

CHAPTER 3

Nobility Based on Virtue Surpasses Nobility of Birth

There is also the fact that a man does not deserve any praise or honour just for being nobly born. This point is made by Aristotle, who says that we should not be praised or blamed for those things which have been given us by nature.[14] As for the fact that the nobly born, like the wealthy, are rightfully deserving of honour, this comes about, not just in consideration of their birth or their riches, but because of the virtue which is associated, or thought to be associated (as it should be), with these things. For it is fitting that those who surpass other men in nobility, wealth or high office should also — if they are not lazy or feeble-minded — surpass them in virtue. It is for this reason that Aristotle, in the course of his discussion of magnanimity in Book IV of the *Ethics,* says:

Men who are well-born are considered worthy of honour, as are those who hold official positions or possess great wealth. For these things have their basis in excellence, and every good that excels is thereby worthy of greater honour. But in reality only the good man is truly honourable and those who combine wealth, noble descent and power with virtue are considered even more worthy of honour. Those, however, who possess such goods without also possessing virtue cannot rightly claim to be worthy of great honour. Nor can they be properly said to be magnanimous, for these other goods have no real existence unless virtue is also present.[15]

This is Aristotle's opinion.

By contrast, nobility derived from virtue renders a man supremely praiseworthy and honourable. Virtue is the only quality that deserves to be rewarded with praise and honour, since it cannot be acquired from elsewhere, but is gained by a man's own efforts, unremitting zeal and sheer hard work.

A further argument is that nobility based on virtue, without noble birth, is considered praiseworthy, and deservedly so. Would anyone refuse to applaud a man of great moral integrity and surpassing virtue just because he was of humble birth? To take the opposite case, noble birth alone, unaccompanied by virtue, is not merely undeserving of praise, but actually disgraceful. For a man tainted by vice merits no praise at all, even if he is nobly born. On the contrary, he should suffer severe censure and reproach for having failed to live up to the high moral standards set by his forebears — he has disgraced the distinguished family name with his shameful life and made a show of noble lineage to conceal his own lack of virtue. As Chrysostom says, noble birth and good family count for nothing unless we ourselves are good.[16] Therefore nobility based on virtue is more praiseworthy than noble birth and consequently preferable to it.

Nobility based on virtue without illustrious ancestry is certainly to be preferred to glorious ancestry without any pre-eminence in virtue. As Juvenal says:

I would rather you had Thersites for a father
And were yourself like Achilles and wielded the arms of Vulcan,
Than that you should have Achilles for your father and be like Thersites.[17]

Anything which is preferable to something else is also recognized as being superior to it.

Finally, noble birth is only praised in so far as it is associated with the prestige of virtue. If you take away virtue, there is nothing left to praise. So virtue – on account of which noble birth is praised – is more commendable than noble birth. Juvenal conveys this point indirectly when he uses the criteria by which one judges horses to revile people who take excessive pride in their ancestry:

Tell me, O scion of the Trojans, who thinks
A horse well bred, unless it's strong and swift? The answer's obvious:
We acclaim the breeding of the swift-footed horse which prances home to an easy win,
And glories in its victory before the roaring crowd. . . .
Do something yourself then, so we may admire you rather than your possessions. . . .
Respect for others is somewhat rare among those
Of high rank. But, speaking for myself, I'm unwilling
To see you resting on the laurels of your ancestors,
And doing nothing to gain a reputation of your own.
It's demeaning to clothe yourself in borrowed glory.[18]

CHAPTER 4

Nobility of Birth Has Its Origin in Virtue

It should also be noted that noble birth has its origins in nobility of virtue, which is its initial cause. It is clear that in ancient times, whenever any man surpassed all others in virtue, he received, as was proper, great acclaim and was deemed to have greater authority than other men. This reputation passed to his descendants, so that his sons and grandsons enjoyed leading positions because of their father's or grandfather's illustrious virtue. And so, those who were first termed 'noble' received that epithet on account of their virtue, and their children, as the offspring of such great and illustrious men, acquired the title of nobility from the fine deeds of their parents.

Philosophers say that a cause is greater than the effect which it produces. It is therefore absolutely clear that nobility based on virtue is prior to and more honourable than nobility of birth. Furthermore, according to Sallust, each thing is maintained by the same skills with which it was acquired in the first place.[19] And so, if men have earned the title of nobility by moral rectitude and virtue, their descendants will be truly noble and deserving of the title only if they too strive to attain virtue and imitate the characters of their forebears. If, on the other hand, they fall below the standards set by their fathers, then they are, in truth, ignoble, since they neither possess nor display in front of others the qualities on which nobility depends.

For the rest, I should not pass over one argument which demonstrates very clearly that nobility of the rational soul is superior to eminence of descent and bloodline. One of the defining characteristics of nobility based on virtue is that it does not lend itself to vice and moral corruption but rather opposes them outright as enemies. Nobility of birth, on the other hand, sometimes makes well-born men proud and insolent if they lack the virtue that would curb their arrogance. Such men generally despise those of low birth and hold them in contempt, as Juvenal explains in these lines:

> Plancus, you pride yourself on your descent from the noble Drusi, as if
> You yourself could take the credit for your nobility. . . .
> 'You others are lowly born', you say, 'the lowest of the low,
> And none of you can name his father's native land,
> But I trace my descent from Cecrops.' . . .
> But you are answered: 'You're nothing but your ancestors,
> No better than a sculptured bust!
> In fact, you're only superior to the sculpture in that
> Its head is marble, while yours breathes.'[20]

Aristotle agrees with this sentiment: 'Those who have noble birth, wealth and power without virtue become arrogant and overbearing. For it is difficult to handle prosperity and good fortune if you lack virtue. And so, since such men cannot handle their good fortune equably, they think themselves superior to others and despise them.'[21] Seneca agrees: 'If magnanimity is taken to excess, it makes a man menacing, proud, over-active, violent and inclined to rush to extremes in both word and deed without any consideration for what is right.'[22] (Noble birth, however, is one of the factors that go to make up magnanimity and paves the way for this virtue.)

It follows that, if noble birth stands alone, without the support of any embellishment of the rational soul, it does not (as I said already) render a man praiseworthy or confer lofty titles on him. Rather, as I have explained, noble birth takes its distinction and lustre from virtue, which is the foundation of true nobility. As the poet Juvenal noted:

> What does a long list of ancestors do for you, Ponticus? What advantage is it to be valued
>   for the antiquity of your breeding, and to exhibit the portraits
> Of your ancestors and statues of Aemiliani in their triumphal chariots? . . .
> What advantage do you gain from showing off your lengthy family tree, . . .
> With its branches containing famous generals keeping company with a dictator,
> If you conduct yourself badly before their eyes? What's the point
> Of the portraits of so many warriors, if you while the night away in gambling? . . .
> You must, first of all, show me the virtues of the soul.
> Have you earned the reputation of being a man of piety, one who clings to the principles of
>   justice in word and deed? [23]

And he also says:

> Who will call a man well-bred if he
> Is unworthy of his family and distinguished only
> By a famous name?[24]

Seneca says something similar: 'A hall full of ancestral portraits does not confer nobility. No one has lived his life in order to give us the glory for his deeds. We do not own the past. It is the rational soul alone that makes a man noble.'[25] Who then can truly claim noble birth? The man whom nature has endowed with virtue.

And so, if we were to consider two men, one of noble birth but a depraved criminal, and the other of lowly birth but endowed with outstanding virtue and loftiness of mind, who would not esteem the second more highly than the first?

Juvenal shows this in his contrast between the depravity of Catiline and the glorious fame of Cicero:

> Could anyone imagine a higher social station, Catiline,
> Than that to which you and Cethegus were born?
> Yet you planned an armed attack under cover of darkness, and arson for our homes and
>   temples. . . .
> But the consul is vigilant and suppresses your followers –
> A new man, from Arpinum, of low birth, and at Rome only
> A provincial of middling rank. He placed armed guards everywhere
> And worked tirelessly to protect the bewildered citizens.
> Civic office, within the walls of Rome, won for him
> Greater fame and renown than Octavius gained
> At Actium or on the plains of Thessaly
> With a blood-stained sword. But Rome hailed Cicero as her parent,
> Rome, which was still free, called him 'Father of his Country'.[26]

The same poet came to a similar conclusion when he compared the evil and depraved Nero with the venerable and learned Seneca – namely, that Seneca was much superior, even if he was of lowly birth:

> If the people could express their opinions freely, who would be so
> Morally corrupt as to doubt that Seneca should be preferred to Nero?
> To punish Nero fittingly you'd need more than a single ape,
> More than one serpent and more than one sack.[27]

Finally, if any species assumes the name of the genus to which it belongs, this is in itself proof that this species is more important than another which has failed to achieve the same distinction. This is like referring to man as a unique animal, not in order to separate human beings from other sorts of animals, but to make the point that man has first place among the animals. Or, to use another example, it is like referring to man as a mind, not with the intention of excluding the body from the human make-up, but in order to make the point that the mind is the most powerful part of a human being. In the same way, the nobility of the rational soul which springs from virtue has acquired the term nobility, the name of the genus to which it belongs, as its own private possession, to the exclusion of the other species based on birth. As Juvenal says:

> Even if all your halls are adorned with ancient
> Portraits, virtue and virtue alone is the true nobility.[28]

And Ovid agrees:

> Neither wealth nor famous ancestors
> But rather uprightness and character make men great.[29]

It is certainly not my intention to separate off noble birth as something completely foreign and extraneous to the concept of nobility, but rather to define nobility as resting primarily and principally on virtue and moral integrity. Therefore, it is, on many grounds, indisputable that nobility of the rational soul produced by virtue is greatly preferable to nobility of birth. Furthermore, from the comparison we have just made, it is absolutely clear that the third type of nobility, the one which embraces both good birth and good character, is superior to nobility of the rational soul by itself. For it is preferable to have more goods than fewer goods, and a double good is better than a single one: the compound good contains the simple good and adds some other good to it.

From this we can conclude that nobility of both birth and the rational soul is preferable to nobility of birth on its own. Certainly, as I've just shown, a combination of nobility of birth and of the rational soul is more complete than nobility of the rational soul alone. Furthermore, as I've demonstrated in a variety of ways, nobility of the rational soul is superior to nobility of birth. Therefore, the compound concept of nobility is superior to nobility of birth by itself. For if A is greater than B, and B is greater than C, then it follows that A is greater than C. Likewise, if one thing is nobler than a second thing, and that second thing is more noble than a third less noble thing, then it follows that the first thing is more noble than the third. . . .

CHAPTER 10

Noble Birth Needs the Addition of Virtue to Make It Perfect and Complete

It has been demonstrated more than adequately that noble birth is a good which depends on something else, namely, virtue. Noble birth is the faithful follower and close companion of virtue: it is the signpost which points to virtue. If virtue is present, then noble birth is a fine thing, much to be praised and honoured. But if virtue is absent, noble birth merely serves to make a man more reprehensible and more open to reproach for failing to display the qualities implied by his lineage. This can be further corroborated by evidence from the most authoritative sources. St Jerome writes in a letter: 'In God's eyes the only freedom is freedom from the tyranny of sin; in God's eyes the highest nobility is to be renowned for one's virtues.'[30] Chrysostom agrees: what is the use of noble birth to a man stained by vice? What disadvantage is there in lowly birth for a man of good character? The man who glories in his ancestry shows himself devoid of everything that is good.[31] And Bernard says, in a work addressed to Pope Eugenius III: 'The apostles were noble only in the freedom of their minds and the courage of their faith.'[32] Horace agrees:

> When you say it does not matter who a man's
> Father is, providing he is himself free-born,
> You speak the truth.[33]

But I've said more than is necessary on this point. Now let us return to our task.

It is absolutely clear from what has been said that, in order to survive close scrutiny, nobility based on ancestry and descent must dress itself in fine and beautiful clothing. In like manner, silver and marble are embellished with gold ornament. The embellishment which will prevent noble birth, bare and unadorned, from looking worthless is virtue. For virtue puts external and bodily goods, which are by nature indifferent, to the right use and is their finest ornament.

Besides, every station in life has its own special, appropriate virtues. Thus, a man of noble birth has different functions and responsibilities from a man of low condition. Likewise, a man who is a public figure has different responsibilities from a private citizen, and the duties of a man who holds public office differ from those of ordinary people. These diverse duties and responsibilities spring from diverse virtues, just as different fruits, all of them good and nutritious, come from different trees. It is obvious that nobility of birth has its own special virtues with which it may be perfected, enhanced, adorned and made worthy of admiration. For this reason, then, I shall go to some trouble to describe, one by one, the various virtues which are most appropriate for a man of noble birth. And I will take no less care in listing the shameful vices which pollute and defile noble birth. My aim in doing this, my dear Jacques, is that you may seize, embrace and cultivate the former and despise, shun and run away from the latter and, by so doing, enhance the nobility that nature gave you at birth with the nobility which you can win for yourself by dedication, hard work and an unremitting sense of purpose. In this way (which I will repeatedly recommend) you will become noble in each sense of the word – equally noble in birth and virtue. This is the purpose of my work, my goal and my intention. . . .

Translator's Notes

1. Jacques d'Amboise was the son of Jean d'Amboise, lieutenant-general of the duke of Orléans in Normandy. He had been placed in Clichtove's care by his uncle, Jacques d'Amboise, bishop of Clermont. See Josse Clichtove, *On True Nobility,* f. 46ʳ: 'I was chosen by your uncle, Jacques d'Amboise, the most reverend bishop of Clermont, a most excellent and worthy man, to be your tutor and to oversee your education in literature, the basics of grammar and moral philosophy . . .'.
2. Josse Clichtove, *On True Nobility* (Paris, 1512), f. 2ʳ: '. . . as you are now, at the wish of your parents, about to leave me and undergo military training . . .'.
3. The noun *noscibilitas* was unknown in classical Latin, although the adjective *noscibilis* appears in late antique writers such as Tertullian and Augustine. In the late 1440s the Venetian humanist Lauro Quirini traced the etymology of *nobilis* to the phrase *nosci abilis* (able to be known): see his treatise *On Nobility against Poggio,* in A. Rabil, trans., *Knowledge, Goodness and Power: The Debate over Nobility among Quattrocento Humanists* (Binghamton, N.Y., 1991), p. 159. Clichtove appears to have followed Niccolò Perotti, *Cornucopiae sive linguae latinae commentarii,* s.v. *nobilitas;* this work was first published in 1489 and reprinted in many editions.
4. Aristotle, *Politics* IV.4 (1291ᵇ28–9).
5. Cicero, *De senectute* III.8. Themistocles (c. 528–462 BC) was an Athenian statesman. Seriphos is one of the islands which make up the Cyclades in the Greek Archipelago.
6. Diogenes Laertius, *Lives of the Philosophers* I.104–5, in the Latin translation of Ambrogio Traversari (made in the 1430s). In the original Greek text Anacharsis (sixth century BC) makes his point positively: 'Granted that I have something to be ashamed of in my homeland . . .'. A few early printed editions of Traversari's translation offer the reading used here: e.g., Venice, 1475, and Brescia, 1485.
7. In Renaissance psychology, the rational or intellective soul (*animus*) was the element of the tripartite – vegetative, animal and rational – soul (*anima*) which belonged exclusively to human beings and which gave them their defining characteristic of rational thought; it was also the part of the soul which was immortal; see E. Kessler, 'The intellective soul', in *CHRP,* pp. 485–534. In terms of moral philosophy, the particular virtue associated with the rational soul was the consistent habit of choosing the virtuous option.
8. This passage and the other two attributed to John Chrysostom here appear to be loosely based on *De Lazaro* VI.6, which Clichtove probably knew through a Latin intermediary. In the revised second edition of 1520, all three quotations are placed together.

9. Apuleius, *Florida* IX.32, describes Hippias in this way: 'His family is unknown, but he is extremely famous; he came from humble circumstances, but he had a noble intellect and an outstanding memory; he had many, diverse fields of interest and many rivals.'

10. Ovid, *Metamorphoses* XIII.140–1.

11. Seneca, *Hercules Furens* 340–1.

12. Apuleius, *De deo Socratis* 23.175.

13. Juvenal, *Satires* VIII.272–5.

14. Aristotle, *Nicomachean Ethics* II.5 (1106ᵃ6–10). Clichtove uses Johannes Argyropulos's translation of the *Ethics*. This citation, however, actually comes not from the text but from Lefèvre d'Étaples' commentary; see, e.g., *Decem librorum Ethicorum Aristotelis ad Nicomachum ex traductione Ioannis Argyropili Bizantij, communi familiarique Iacobi Fabri Stapulensis commentario elucidati . . .* (Paris, 1510), f. 17ᵛ.

15. Aristotle, *Nicomachean Ethics* IV.3 (1124ᵃ21–9), in the Latin translation of Argyropulos.

16. See n. 8.

17. Juvenal, *Satires* VIII.269–71. Achilles, son of the Nereid Thetis, was the most famous of the Greek heroes of the Trojan War. Thersites was an ugly, foul-mouthed Greek of low birth, who made a speech abusing Agamemnon; see Homer, *Iliad* II.212–44.

18. Juvenal, *Satires* VIII.56–9, 68, 73–6.

19. Sallust makes this comment, in relation to power (*imperium*), in *De coniuratione Catilinae* 2.4–5.

20. Juvenal, *Satires* VIII.40–1, 44–6, 52–5; modern editions have 'Blandus' instead of 'Plancus'. The same lines appear in this form in Lefèvre d'Étaples' commentary on *Nicomachean Ethics* IV.3: see *Decem librorum Ethicorum Aristotelis*, f.41ʳ. According to Greek mythology, Cecrops was the first king of Athens.

21. Aristotle, *Nicomachean Ethics* IV.3 (1124ᵃ29–ᵇ2), in the Latin translation of Argyropulos.

22. Pseudo-Seneca, *De quattuor virtutibus cardinalibus* 7.1.

23. Juvenal, *Satires* VIII.1–3, 6, 8–10, 24–5. The Aemiliani were the two sons of the second century BC Roman military hero, Lucius Aemilius Paulus Macedonius. One of his sons, known as Publius Cornelius Scipio Aemilianus (185/4–129 BC), was adopted by P. Scipio (the son of Scipio Africanus the Elder, who defeated Hannibal). This Aemilianus was responsible for the final defeat and destruction of Carthage. He was awarded a triumph and acquired the title 'Africanus' in his own right; he is most commonly known as Scipio Africanus the Younger. Another son of Aemilius Paulus was adopted by the Fabii Maximi. Known as Fabius Maximus Aemilianus (c. 186–130 BC), he also enjoyed an illustrious career but was never a *triumphator.* There is a certain irony in Juvenal's reference to the Aemiliani: neither of them was the natural son of his noble family. A 'dictator' was a trustworthy citizen appointed to exercise sole power for limited periods at times of national emergency.

24. Juvenal, *Satires* VIII.30–2.

25. Seneca, *Epistulae* XLIV.5.

26. Juvenal, *Satires* VIII.231–3, 236–44. Catiline (d. 62 BC), who gave his name to the Catilinarian conspiracy, was, like his associate Cornelius Cethegus, a Roman aristocrat. Similarly, Octavius was adopted by his great-uncle Julius Caesar (taking on the name Gaius Julius Caesar Octavianus), and so counts as an aristocrat both by maternal descent and by adoption; under the name Augustus he was Roman emperor from 27 BC to AD 14. By contrast, Marcus Tullius Cicero (106–43 BC), who was consul in 63 BC, the year of the conspiracy, was a self-made man from a provincial family of no particular distinction.

27. Juvenal, *Satires* VIII.211–14. Nero was Roman emperor from AD 54 to 68; the Stoic philosopher and dramatist Seneca (d. AD 65) was one of his advisers but was forced by him to commit suicide for his alleged participation in a conspiracy. Juvenal refers here to the traditional Roman punishment for matricide (Nero had his mother Agrippina murdered in AD 59): convicted matricides were sewn up in a sack, together with an ape and a snake, and thrown into the Tiber.

28. Juvenal, *Satires* VIII.19–20.

29. Ovid, *Epistulae ex Ponto* I.9.39–40.
30. Jerome, *Epistulae* CXLVIII.21.
31. See n. 8.
32. Bernard of Clairvaux, *De consideratione* II.6.13. Eugenius III was pope from 1145 to 1153.
33. Horace, *Satires* I.6.7–8.

Further Reading

Ashworth, E. J., 'Renaissance man as logician: Josse Clichtove (1472–1543) on disputations', *History and Philosophy of Logic,* 7 (1986), 15–29

Chantraine, G., 'Josse Clichtove: témoin théologien de l'humanisme parisien', *Revue d'histoire ecclésiastique,* 66 (1971), 507–28

CHRP, pp. 166, 322, 348, 368–9, 443, 448, 479, 795, 814

Kraus, M. J., 'Patronage and reform in the France of the Préréforme: the case of Clichtove', *Canadian Journal of History,* 6 (1971), 45–68

Lohr, C. H., *Latin Aristotle Commentaries* (Florence, 1988–), II, p. 94

Massaut, J. P., *Josse Clichtove: l'humanisme et réforme du clergé,* 2 vols. (Paris, 1968)

Neuschel, K. B., *Word of Honor: Interpreting Noble Culture in Sixteenth-Century France* (Ithaca, N.Y., 1989)

Rabil, A., ed. and trans., *Knowledge, Goodness, and Power: The Debate over Nobility among Quattrocento Italian Humanists* (Binghamton, N.Y., 1991)

Schalk, E., *From Valor to Pedigree: Ideas of Nobility in France in the Sixteenth and Seventeenth Centuries* (Princeton, N.J., 1986), esp. p. 54

16

Guillaume Budé

NEIL KENNY

Introduction

Guillaume Budé (1467/8–1540) was widely considered to be the greatest French humanist of his day, rivalling even Erasmus in his European-wide fame. He composed *On the Education of the Prince* at some stage between 1515 and 1522, probably 1518–19. It was addressed to François I, who had become king in 1515 at the age of twenty. Since the king apparently did not know Latin, Budé resorted to composing in French for the first and almost last time (except for a 1522 summary of his 1515 treatise on antiquarian numismatics, *De asse*). *On the Education of the Prince* belongs to the popular genre of humanist advice-books for princes, to which Machiavelli, with *The Prince,* and Erasmus, with *The Education of a Christian Prince,* had recently contributed. As is customary in mirror-for-princes literature, Budé advises the ruler on how to acquire honour in his lifetime and fame after his death. He also supplies a radical justification of royal absolutism, free from any constitutional checks on the crown. Like several other northern humanists, he expresses sharp antipathy to war as a policy tool: it is only legitimate when conducted against infidels or (he implies) in self-defence. The list of princely attributes which will bring honour and fame is conventional: physical beauty, intellectual distinction and moral virtues. The Platonic notion of the philosopher-king is prominent, strongly informed by humanism, as one would expect from Budé: ideally the prince should have a good tutor, learn Greek and Latin, practise eloquence, and read history and treatises on 'political doctrine' so that he can model his behaviour on the best ancient examples. To show the way, Budé's text is studded with examples, sayings and commonplaces, drawn from the Bible, Plutarch, Aristotle, Suetonius, Homer, Pliny the Elder, Livy and so on.

De l'institution du prince was composed at some stage between 1515 and 1522. It was first printed posthumously in 1547. Three different editions appeared in that year. The present translation is based on the 1547 edition printed by Nicole Paris at the Abbey of l'Arrivour and edited by Jean de Luxembourg, abbot of Ivry (facsimile reprint: Farnborough, Hants, 1966); for the passages translated see pp. 20–4, 30–3, 36–7, 42–4, 82–4, 107–9, 136, 141–2. The chapter divisions, chapter titles and margin headings are not by Budé; they are probably by Jean de Luxembourg. On these and other changes made by him to the text, see M. Triwunatz (Trivunac), *Guillaume Budé's 'De l'institution du prince': Ein Beitrag zur Geschichte der Renaissancebewegung in Frankreich* (Erlangen, 1903), pp. 96–100. The original manuscript has been edited by C. Bontems in C. Bontems, L.-P. Raybaud and J.-P. Brancourt, *Le Prince dans la France des XVIe et XVIIe siècles* (Paris, 1965), pp. 77–139. The first twenty chapters of the Paris 1548 edition have been edited, with a German translation, by M. Marin (Ph.D. thesis, University of Cologne, 1982).

On the Education of the Prince: Selections

CHAPTER 3

The author discusses most fully the virtue of distributive justice, demonstrating that princes must prize it above all others as the virtue which, if they choose to practise it, upholds and enlarges their kingdom and makes their acts of generosity worthy of their majesty. If they do not practise this virtue, however, then they render these acts ineffective and turn them into the opposite of generosity.

. . . One part of justice is called distributive; it ensures that the distribution of honours and benefits is in accordance with the relative merit and knowledge of men who may be of use and service to the commonwealth and who may give advice and solace to the community when this is necessary or when there is need for it. And for this reason, kings have the most honour; they possess sovereign power and the right to bestow prerogatives; they extract more gain and money from the common people than anyone else, themselves deciding on the share that it is fair for them to take; and, unlike everyone else, they are certainly not subject to the laws or ordinances of their kingdom, if they choose not to be. For it must be assumed that they are so perfectly prudent, so outstandingly and supremely noble, so imbued and endowed with justice and equity that they need no rule or legal provision to restrain them through fear of punishments, fines (which we call financial penalties), seizure of their possessions, arrest or of any of the other punishments or constraints to obedience which their subjects must have. Kings should be governed only by divine law, which derives its authority not from men but from God, the sovereign legislator; in the eyes of this law, all men are equal, with no differences or pre-eminence among them so far as the obedience which they owe it is concerned. That is why the emperor says, in his written laws and imperial constitutions, that although he is not subject to civil laws, it is nonetheless a matter of honour for him and other princes to obey them.[1] To say that he wishes to subject himself voluntarily to the law is worthy of a king, as is the statement and affirmation of this intent in public, with a view to making his edicts, constitutions and ordinances venerable and authoritative. The reason for the state of affairs I have outlined is acutely, pertinently and fully discussed by the great and celebrated philosopher Aristotle in Book V of the *Nicomachean Ethics*. Here and elsewhere, that author has demonstrated better and more clearly than anyone else what justice properly speaking is, and from where royal authority and majesty derive. He shows that they issue from the outstanding virtue of certain kings to whom peoples voluntarily submitted themselves in times past, so as to be governed by them with justice.

But at this point one must observe and carefully consider the fact that kings implement in person, by their own decisions, that part of justice which we call distributive. They do this by extending to people honours, offices and other favours and benefits, as seems to them right and fitting. On the one hand, the authority and favour enjoyed by those who are beloved of great princes must be a powerful influence on this distributive justice, on the disposing of riches and honours. Given that these people are honoured so much that they are always present at the most secret and private dealings of those princes, they should therefore not be prevented from stating and explaining their informed reaction to the advancement of certain persons. On the other hand, however, I should like the prince (whom such advancement concerns more than any other person) to heed the words and judgement of the great and the good, to heed their views as to who merits such authority; and I should like favouritism and ambition to carry no weight in this matter. For when learned and virtuous men, to whom their commonwealth and country are much indebted, are given preferment and their rightful share of the benefits and honours which are to be distributed, in accordance with their endeavours and occupation, then generosity is joined to justice and assumes the nature of the latter. Whereas if things happen differently, then generosity assumes the name of the opposite of justice and becomes injustice. This vice, according to Aristotle, should be censured to the same extent that justice, which is so honourable, should be praised when practised in the proper way,[2] all the more so since there can be no vice more obvious and no evil more manifest than to defraud someone of the honour which is due to him of right. To do this is to harm both oneself and also the public resources, for which princes should care more than they do for their own pleasures.

And do not think that this distributive justice can only extend to secular princes (who sometimes abuse it, which is in itself a fine and excellent commendation of those who honour and prize it). At times there have also been some popes who have not discharged their responsibility for this justice or for its proper distribution among those who deserve to receive favours stemming from the pope's holiness and enjoy what they call benefices. Instead, these popes committed the great evil of giving these benefices to people who were unworthy of holding them. But when popes make mistakes, since they are men and the divine law has made them subject to human passions, it is for God alone to judge them, for they acknowledge no superior other than him. And according to the laws which we uphold now, popes are subject to no other powers. Indeed, it pleased God to grant them sovereign and complete sway, making them subject to the reprimand only of Our Lord. This means that the world is governed and goes round in accordance with their will and counsel, like a house which rests on a main pillar.

Nonetheless, God retains in his memory and views with some toleration the popes' acts of negligence, their faults and their absolute or dissolute ordinances, which are themselves subject to his ordinances, as he sees what will happen in the future through his divine providence. We cannot understand this providence, since it is too different from our own feeble intellect. But this does not mean that popes should be without fear or concern regarding providence. The reverential attitude towards popes in written law, in the answers supplied by prudent men, ancients and jurisconsults makes us consider them to be the representatives of the living, animate law which must have more force of justice than the law that is written on tablets or collected in books. Moreover, the opinion of the wise makes us believe with certainty that we must submit ourselves to this divine law and endure its verdict, however slow it is in coming. It will come at a time when verdicts are delivered with no acknowledgement of Roman dignity, majesty and holiness, when the degrees of status introduced into the world are transformed from prelacies and principalities into [divine] dispensations and manners of governing. It will come when the powers which are currently freed from human law find themselves fettered and restrained by the shackles of divine law.

Let me speak the truth about this matter, explaining it well and stating it clearly, saying what kind of vice is involved: it is reasonable to believe that when the high authority and holiness of our lord and pope, or the dignity of kings and of those who aspire to the monarchy, do not distribute justice with the distributive equity that should be observed, when they do not implement this justice properly in accordance with everyone's merit and good deeds, but instead sometimes elevate the wicked to the ruin of good people, then this abuse devolves on and impugns their majesty, conflicting with the duty of office. It damages their honour and reputation. It is just as if a witless young spendthrift, not yet old enough to be capable of good judgement, were to be given sovereign authority and jurisdiction for making legal judgements, against which no appeal was possible, and complete powers to arrange, give and revoke gifts, to bestow honours and strip them away, to elevate and demote, to make people capable and incapable, to introduce the new and abolish the old, and (in the words of the proverb, derived from Horace)[3] to change circular shapes into square ones, without attempting to determine what is fitting and what inappropriate, and with no assembly of advisers other than his undiluted will and pleasure. For the great princes and prelates discussed earlier are, if one properly understands the duty of their office, none other than the principal officers of the exchequer and the guardians of God's most vast treasures and riches. Their role is to perceive the nature of God's will, to arrange for and conduct its full execution, to provide things and multiply them, or to elevate everyone's authority according to the dictates of truth and rightful equity. If they are so mistaken as to fail in this, and if the misfortunes I have mentioned overcome them, because they have not acted with discernment or with awareness of the public good, then I can best compare them to a person who has a speck in his eye, preventing him from seeing the light which he would so much wish for. And if it happens that they understand and know what they should do and nevertheless do not do it, but rather attend more to their own private pleasure than to public equity and honour, then the speck blinds both eyes and is most difficult to remove; and no hand is sufficiently steady to want to undertake the cure, especially when the speck is deeply embedded and has not been treated from the outset.

For this reason, when they persist with such actions, God's sovereign justice sometimes deprives them of their riches and of the things which they hold dearest, so that they lose the use and pleasure of the virtue of generosity. This happens especially because, lacking judgement and discernment, they do not make the distinction between people of merit who should be chosen and selected and those who are unworthy of favours; so their acts of generosity, which they believe themselves to be performing well, are wasted because the recipients feel no gratitude. Another reason is that since these acts are performed without sense, proportion or good and virtuous advice, they are transformed into vices and are called rashness and wastefulness instead of generosity. A consequence of this is that great lords such as these, who believe their entourage includes good devoted servants who loyally advise them and give their views on the lords' affairs, often have flatterers, mockers, deceivers or people of little worth; full of incredible avarice, these people are busy seeking their own gain and are devoted to their own personal affairs, while being lavish with the wealth of others. They injure the reputation of their masters and lords, for whom they have neither reverence nor perfect affectionate love. And there is only one cause which makes them thus and creates this contempt. Knowing and having sure proof that the great benefits they receive from those masters derive not from circumspect and well-tempered affection but only from ignorance and lack of good sense, they despise both the gifts and the givers. And when a prince has such servants, they are like the Harpies who surrounded King Phineus of Arcadia and (according to poetical fictions)[4] ate his food in his presence, devoured everything they found – even what was being served up at his table – threw away what they could not consume, defiled it, soiled it with their nails and rendered it useless for others.

Let me return to my point, however: some of the ancients, who were worthy of praise, outstanding as much in their words as in their notable deeds, have given us many examples and precepts which deserve to be committed to perpetual memory. Yet some of them wrote none of this down, partly because it was not customary for the ancients to do so, and partly because few people have good ideas and a good imagination coupled with the ability to formulate these ideas well and write them down, fixing them in men's memories in such a way that readers will derive some pleasure from reading them and listeners from hearing them, and in such a way that their books contain much beautiful, strong, graceful eloquence, which is so delightful and agreeable that they continue to enjoy repute and high esteem for a long time. Nonetheless, some did have both excellent understanding and also the ability and industriousness necessary to write things down well and to communicate their ideas through abundant and beautiful words. Consequently, they have persuaded men – not only their contemporaries, but also knowledgeable and learned posterity – to delight in trusting what they wrote in their books and to apply their minds to it. For, as Cicero says in Book II[.3.7] of his *Tusculan Disputations,* reading without pleasure and delight is not something worth spending one's time on. And those who long to read the books of the philosophers, whether Plato or Aristotle, do so only because of the grace and eloquence of their works.

CHAPTER 5

In this chapter the author seeks to show how necessary it is for all princes to have knowledge of both Greek and Latin literature if they are to rule their kingdoms well.

[The kind of knowledge that enables everyone to govern himself and his family rightly and honourably] is needed more by those who are more powerful, and it is very much needed by those whose family and power are too vast to be numbered or exhaustively counted, such as great princes and monarchs, rulers of populous and opulent regions. The kings of France are like this; for their family and dominion extend as far as their territories and the boundaries of their countries. This is especially true when they are well revered and obeyed by their subjects. Such princes take care not only of their household servants or private officials but also of all who come under their jurisdiction and are answerable to them, and for whom the princes are held to be answerable before God and divine providence, which assigned these burdens to them and gave them great honours and prerogatives to enable them to fulfil their duty through the discharge of these responsibilities. Thus monarchs, to whom nature has given good sense, must understand that care, concern, charity and love of the people – qualities which maintain the public good and the country's honour – are wedded and coupled to their majesty by primeval law, just as reverence, worshipful awe and voluntary obedience must be directed by subjects towards those princes and their edicts. And for this reason Homer in his *Iliad* [II.243; X.3] often calls Agamemnon the people's shepherd; that king was always on the lookout for the safety and preservation of his people.

This concern is wedded to princes as a fundamental responsibility, one that can never be redeemed but rather was imposed when those honours were established and created. This was when the multitude of men and cities, gathered together by common accord, first let go of its freedom, depriving itself thereof, and giving up its communal and popular rights to place them in the hands and power of one man, making him the future father of a populous and innumerable family. They did this because they considered there to be more goodness, honour, understanding and virtue in a single man than in all the collective reasonings of a country. And that is why, on the basis of previous judgements in civil and canon law, sovereign rulers have made laws and decrees, both civil and canon; the court registry in which these are recorded is the ruler's mind; the laws are enclosed within the ruler's inner will, which is like a running well-spring of ordinances and edicts coming from the charity which was mentioned previously. And so there prevail pontifical bulls, prefaces to laws and ordinances, which are often written by kings in their letters patent, and public commands. Yet now we see certain people who govern the world abusing the first and oldest established practice, doing the opposite of what was done in the past. There must be reform of this prevalent abuse, which is in force in many regimes and which is a long way from the just equity that should be observed. It must be affirmed that those who persist in this fault have strayed from their duty and from the law by which monarchs have been instructed, whether in the spiritual or temporal realm.

The Sage says, in chapter 14[:28] of Proverbs: 'In the multitude of people is the king's glory.' And thus we read that the term of praise which Rome's good emperors desired and coveted above all others was 'father of the people', in exactly the same way that a town burgher is called father of his family because of his love for his children and servants, whom he governs and protects with great diligence and care. And today we can still see that ancient emperors called themselves protectors and fathers of the people: we need only look at the gold medals which depict the faces of Augustus, Nerva and Trajan. These were highly regarded, renowned princes, thanks to their outstanding wisdom and their upright virtues, which all the books are full of. And such moral matters are equally discussed in books by pagans, Jews and Christians, which teach us how to live well and honourably. Were it not for their instruction, for the precepts and encouragement which they have given us, then our human life, which in itself is highly inconstant and fraught with dangers and many difficulties, would be even fuller of many dark deeds and utterly devoid of any light.

At this point one should have faith in the most worthy testimony of Solomon, who says in chapter 3[:13–14] of his Proverbs (according to the Greek translation)[5] that the acquisition of wisdom is worth more than all the profit and benefit which can come to a man through dealing and trading in gold and silver, and that the fruits which derive from wisdom are more highly prized than pure unadulterated gold. Wisdom is greater in value than all worldly riches and plenty, and she cannot and should not be compared with anything that man can desire. For in her right hand, as Solomon says, she holds longevity, and the number of man's days; and in her left hand she holds riches and honour.[6] The right hand, which is the main limb, I interpret as signifying that she has the power to bestow life and eternal happiness; and I interpret the left hand as signifying temporal existence and transitory riches, which are to be prized less.

We can therefore conclude that through spiritual wisdom one gains an understanding of eternal riches and of life in the age to come; through worldly wisdom one obtains opulent riches and the glorious reputation which is the ultimate goal and limit of covetousness, the point at which desire is extinguished. It is towards this end that all the great kings and emperors of the past who wished to conquer and rule more lands have striven. This has been the aim not only of such princes, but also of all the worldly imaginations and intentions of the mind, of men's wiles, toils and cares, of branches of knowledge and ingenious discoveries, of all human diligence and studious reflection. None of these is turned away from the original goal sought by desire and covetousness until it has reached the outermost extremities of the domain of corruptible, transitory, perishable things, which by their very nature are subject to progressive decline. Those who adhere nowadays to the inspired philosophy transmitted to us from heaven and communicated by the oracle of wisdom and truth – in other words, humans whose trustworthy holiness and spirit of charity make them strive for eternity – when they see Christians whose hope has made them God's adoptive sons and heirs presumptive, they then acquire a new goal and hopeful expectation of the supreme good, which stretches out into perpetuity and further than the human mind can understand or look. This latter kind of longing is spiritual, and unlike us, the ancients and pagans did not have it. Yet they still wished and desired to perpetuate their memory in all areas, and indeed did so.

For the time being let me speak of temporal things, given that spiritual ones require a loftier exposition and a less accessible examination than I wish to undertake for the moment. It seems to me – going as much by what I have learnt from reading Greek and Latin books as by the disposition and the magnificent, resolute, high-minded valour which I can see and perceive in any man who has a virtuous heart and a well-directed will – that in the realm of the temporal the powers of our soul esteem and prize nothing as highly as honour in one's lifetime and a good, honourable reputation after death, as I mentioned earlier. For we see gentlemen and those with a noble and virtuous heart who, in their efforts to acquire and preserve these two things, not only disdain and scorn movable and landed property, spend and consume vast fortunes and wealth, but also place no value on life, shed blood, expose their limbs to all kinds of dangers and choose and desire to die in honour so as to ennoble the repute of their name and glorify their arms, rather than to live either in any shame or disgrace or even without having won great fame, great credit and a good reputation. After all, among people of the same condition, rank and occupation, each one wishes to hold the highest position and to place himself in every danger in order to reach it.

CHAPTER 7

The author now reveals the soul's function and what it should extend to. He then reveals the opinions of the philosophers on how knowledge should be attained and on which goods should be called goods in this world. He also shows into how many kinds these goods are divided.

[Superiority of the soul consists in learned eloquence and in elegant and graceful language.] And it also consists in that prudence which is called wisdom and the nature of which is such that it can only reside in a man if he is already clever and sharp, quick to learn, full of love for virtue and thus a sound judge of human and temporal matters. Those, however, who wish to know and learn need a good teacher whose manner instructs his disciples well and makes them eager and ready to pick up good learning. And it is right for such a teacher to be sought out with great vigilance and care, whatever the cost, by all who wish to have one, especially the great princes and rulers of the world. To them nothing can be expensive if it increases in some way their honour, which is their principal pearl. For it is quite certain that, if they are endowed with generosity by nature and have the means to exercise their generosity and great munificence, as well as people at whom to direct it, then all that remains to be known is who this teacher will be and where he is to be found, since great princes (such as you, Sire) and lesser ones should not be deterred by the cost.

As for my own view, Sire, it is that there are no preceptors more sound and authoritative than those whom I will discuss later. There are none more worthy, able and suitable to teach a ruler as holy, venerable and powerful as you, a ruler who is so thoroughly obeyed and so well endowed with goods provided by God and nature. I can assess these goods, having as much right as anyone to do so. For I have often turned my attention most diligently to this matter, focusing my thoughts and reflections on the formulation of my opinion of your fine figure, stature and mighty physique, of the attractive form of your body, the features of your face, as well as of the manner and way in which you listen, look about, speak, reply to those who address petitions, reports or other speeches to you, and of every posture and gesture which can be observed and examined in you when you are seated on your throne at a great assembly in order to deliver speeches on extremely important matters or to pronounce and give answers on affairs of state, or else when you are at table, whether eating your dinner or supper or else participating in the informal discussions and the other unaffected, spontaneous conversations which naturally arise there. And insofar as my poor understanding permits, I have perceived that all of these qualities of yours are too great to be captured by the eloquence of the most learned men and the eulogies of you which even those who are most well versed in literature might deliver.

CHAPTER 9

Having spoken of the goods of both body and soul, the author comes to discuss prudence, which is acquired through a knowledge of literature and history.

Now in order to fulfil, wholly or partly, your obligation [to God, the source of all goods] by making use of the aforementioned goods (internal as well as physical and external), by enjoying all the tempered power which you have annexed to your throne, together with your subjects' love and voluntary obedience, you need to acquire prudence through the erudition and learning in different languages that a prince as great as you can gain with honour. This will be made possible by your good judgement as well as by your ability to apprehend and understand promptly what you hear people say or what you read in books. Among other things, this learning will show you more fully that the exercise of absolute power (desired by some monarchs and sovereign princes who are not subject to any human authority) cannot coexist with those things which have been annexed to your sacred crown, and which have been given over, joined and pledged to it. The privilege of absolute power was obtained in contradiction to the Roman constitutions and to the practice of good emperors. It was neither approved at the council of the sages and the equity law advisers, nor was it recorded among the deeds and histories of Augustus, the much loved Titus, Trajan, Alexander the Roman Emperor,[7] or of others, whether emperors who govern in exemplary fashion and are renowned for their goodness, or kings who are well aware of their powers, rights and dues. By imitating these rulers, acting in the way described earlier, you will increase and improve upon the goods which nature has bestowed on you in full measure with an exceptional generosity which it does not often show to all its creatures, even to the persons of great lords and rulers.

Given that you possess all these qualities, I do not believe that you will find anyone wishing to be your tutor or master in order to advise you of what will, in his view, add to your great perfection. For you yourself are such a great and lofty master that all others are less than you, after God and the Holy Church, which is the mother of all Christians. You belong to this Church; you profess yourself to be its first son and act as such, in succession to your illustrious forefathers and ancestors, from whom you have inherited this role. Through their outstanding virtue, they acquired this commendation and title, which was then confirmed after their deaths by remaining for a long time in the possession of those who obtained that most famous and most feared crown. That crown can maintain its greatness and reputation over a long period only through the same virtues and methods which protected and enlarged it. For nature has arranged worldly things in such a way that the causes and methods which increase and preserve them are the same as those through which they were acquired.

Yet you *can* have a mighty mistress, who on her own is equivalent to many great tutors but nonetheless instructs with great contentment and kindness those who devote themselves to her learning. And the name of this mistress, whom you will have instead of masters, is history. Cicero, the father of Latin eloquence, called history a witness to the times, truth's light, memory's life, mistress of human life, antiquity's messenger.[8] And the Greek word for history denotes an enquiry and investigation into everything that has occurred and is worth remembering, so that it can be narrated in writing and reported as truthfully as possible. This is to enable people to judge and assess the present in the light of the past, to foresee the future and so be protected against rashness. Moreover, the examples and memorable deeds derive from virtues whose sparks nature kindles in noble hearts which have the goodwill and the disposition to imitate good and virtuous deeds.

Therefore, if it pleases you to listen to this mistress, not only will she provide you with recreation when you are tired of crowds, but in addition she will teach and enable you to acquire and preserve great honour and a magnificent reputation in your own lifetime throughout Christendom and as far as the fame of France extends. She will also give you the means to pass on after your death the worthy, honourable, joyful and praiseworthy virtue of your name and reign. For the tools of nature and fortune which are needed to achieve this are completely, fully and plentifully in your power, and you can wield them as you wish. I sincerely wish that you should understand, through the study and attention which you will devote to this, how to succeed; indeed, you have already begun to do so, with enormous pleasure. And in this way you will be able to enjoy not only the various parts of this present human life (as fittingly, moderately and fully as a mortal creature's condition can bear) but also the royal status and sovereign pre-eminence which represents the pinnacle of all happiness for such a creature.

As for me, I am sure — I am absolutely certain — that in all likelihood, by dint of the natural advantages which I discussed earlier and which you possess together with virtues, your future performance of deeds will provide writers and rhetoricians with most ample subject-matter for composing history, which will serve as an example worthy of imitation by your successors and by all other great princes. And in this way you will be acting like the good dealer and loyal agent of God in the Gospel,[9] whose story is often read out in church to refresh our memories: the talents which God placed in his hands he puts to use by multiplying them through trade, by giving them value through hard work, all in God's honour and for his sake.

Here then, Sire, are the great and excellent goods of body and soul which God has given and distributed to you by his grace, without stinting on those of nature: the organs of the physical senses, the parts of the body in their entirety (called instrumental and performative in philosophy), as well as the powers and capacities of the soul, with which you are endowed and adorned to the highest possible degree and as much as anyone I have ever known.

CHAPTER 20[10]

The author maintains that the might of kings is guided by God's will, unless it happens that they wish to resist his will and heed their own pleasures. Furthermore, the author teaches how they should conduct themselves when speaking both in public and in private. This way of speaking is swiftly divulged, because everyone observes everything that kings do and because everyone intends to imitate them, to follow them as closely as possible, rightly judging them to be worthier than other people.

And from what was said earlier it should be understood that almighty God holds and steers the rudder of the ship of kings and other princes (as the Sage testifies).[11] In other words, he guides their free will and, through divine inspiration which is beyond human knowledge, he directs them to the straight path of reason and of firm hope for salvation. Rather than it being down to them, he leads them to the straight and safe path.

The reason for this is because the world zealously beholds and examines the carriage and demeanour of kings, their temperament and all their deeds. It observes their behaviour both in prosperity and in adversity, because the actions or condition of their subjects depends on it; and everyone makes his own personal judgement of this behaviour. Yet sometimes it is spoken of and discussed in meetings and gatherings of the most upright people in their kingdoms, especially when there is reason to speak highly of it and converse honourably. And it is on this publicly voiced opinion and on the evidence of the king's reputation that historians of that country and also of others, assuming they have full freedom of speech, partly base their histories. For indeed the king of a country, and particularly of this one, is like the bull's eye used by those who shoot at butts: everyone wanting to win the prize seeks to hit the bull's eye or to get as close to it as he can.

So he must guard most vigilantly against any obvious fault which would create a bad impression or reveal a quality that could damage the esteem in which his reputation is held and the good opinion which everyone should have of him. For it must be understood that a prince's words are like oracles which are immediately recorded in the memory of everyone who desires to hear them and which are then broadcast by the mouth of the world, which has as many tongues as the cry which goes up when the trumpet of fame sounds.

For this reason, when the actions and words of kings are worth remembering, when they are performed and pronounced fittingly, at a stately gathering, in keeping with their status and majesty, with the authority of the law or of an unwritten ordinance, then they have considerable weight, prestige and repute among all honourable people. Similarly, kings are condemned if they utter any unseemly word that clashes with their calling and dignity. For such a word passes secretly and swiftly by means of the ears of the people, like a watchword among soldiers. And this is what creates different judgements, what makes some people withdraw the voluntary and unrestrained obedience or reverence that is a prince's due. If we examined closely the nature of dignity and royal majesty, such as that of France, we could safely state that the court of a king is the temple of honour and nobility, that his household is like the sanctuary of majesty, by which I mean governing majesty, and the dwelling-place of justice, which must always be open. Yet it must have porters and guards more vigilant than the dragon of the Hesperides;[12] and their commanders must be eagerly and supremely devoted to the public good and honour, as well as having the freedom to rebuke people. These two things are closely linked, if duties are performed faithfully, and they are barely compatible with making private and personal gain. Such gain is often a very powerful and much favoured element among those who manage the affairs of kingdoms; for it has been enjoyed virtually from time immemorial. . . .

CHAPTER 27[13]

The author discusses the qualities that were praiseworthy in Titus, son of Vespasian, stating that it is most fitting for a great prince to have somebody who is so devoted to his service that the prince is not afraid to tell that person the truth about everything, as and when the situation requires, exercising due and necessary prudence in doing so.

Suetonius, speaking of Titus,[14] relates how shortly before his death, with loud groans and sighs, he complained that death was casting him away before his life had run its natural course, and raising his eyes to heaven he said that he felt no guilt about any deed which he had committed in his life and which deserved repentance, with one exception, which he did not explain. After his death, however, some people imagined that he was repenting of adultery with the wife of a close relation of his. And although he never knew the Christian religion and teaching, nonetheless he never wished to practise violence, cruelty or tyranny, as many princes before him had done, and as would even his brother Domitian, who succeeded him and was classed among the malicious emperors because of his vices.[15] For Titus, that most excellent emperor, well understood that when the royal law called *lex regia* was proclaimed – when, that is, the people of Rome handed over to those princes who wanted to become monarchs the people's right and power to control the commonwealth and the distribution of all offices, honours and powers within it – the people did not intend through this transfer to divest itself entirely of such important rights or of its freedom, putting these entirely in the hands of those who wished to satisfy their own pleasures and will more than rightful justice and equity. Rather, the people intended to place all of this under the protection of someone who would rule well, with discerning authority and royal majesty, implementing the edicts and ordinances of both written and unwritten justice and equity, the records of which were held in the Senate at that time.

This interpretation seems reasonable to any man who examines properly the original foundation and establishment of monarchy, which could only take place with the agreement of subjects, without which those origins would not have been based on legitimate dominion but on unjust, unlawful seizure and usurpation. If this power was created by an agreement between two parties, it is essential for it to have and preserve the nature and substance of a contract based on trust. Consequently, there is a reciprocal obligation; it can be known only through a fear of God, which bestows the principles of wisdom. Yet sometimes force, the companion of dominion, is corruptly enticed into assuming more authority than it should; as a result, the order of things, that had previously been so carefully arranged, is abolished and destroyed.

According to Herodotus, whom people call the father of history, Artaxerxes, king of Persia, was more handsome, more shapely and better built in body and limb than any other man of his time, except that one of his hands was longer than the other.[16] Hence the nickname which the Greeks gave him: 'Macrocheir', which means Long Hand. This king was full of great clemency, infinite goodness and wonderful humanity, coupled with other royal virtues worthy of his majesty; indeed, having such a large number of virtues, he was held to possess outstanding physical beauty, greatness of mind and goodness of soul; for, as Virgil says, virtue is more becoming in a person who is beautiful than in one who lacks a handsome form.[17] Among the praiseworthy deeds of his which are recorded in books, and prized because of his great beauty, one was his devising of an ordinance and stratagem which deserve to be remembered and which give an idea of his peerless clemency and kindness. He did this because in Persia there was an extremely severe law and custom regarding great lords, provincial governors, war leaders and other people to whom important public business and affairs were delegated: if they committed mistakes and misdeeds, they were punished by death, even if these were committed without deceit or fraud on the part of the offenders. It was patently obvious that this was extremely harsh. Yet this ordinance also existed in the territories ruled by Carthage, as Livy says.[18] And it certainly had not been introduced without reason, as is clear to anyone who carefully considers the issue, the misfortunes that can be brought about by such mistakes, and their importance. In that kingdom of Persia, which was always the greatest of all kingdoms, the custom and the enactment of the law in such cases was for the offenders I mentioned to be first thrashed with rods and then beheaded.

Since King Artaxerxes wanted to preserve the authority of the legal system, he had no wish to revoke the ordinances of the kings who had preceded him; yet he also wanted to exercise the virtue of clemency. So, in order to temper the ordinance's rigour and harshness with equity and with gentle, royal humaneness, he decreed that in the case of those who had erred and lost some armies, as long as this was not due to enormous mistakes and total negligence on their part, then the sentence that had hitherto been customarily imposed by judges in accordance with the spirit and letter of the ordinance should be executed as follows: the offender would be stripped and his clothes whipped instead of him; and instead of having his head cut off, he would have his tiara felled by a sword — this tiara was a Persian-style hat, the name of which has remained with the crown-shaped tiara worn by our holy father in Rome.

The same king was once strongly urged by a gentleman of his household, whom he loved especially, to order the execution of an action that did not strike the king as being right or defensible in terms of justice. Since he neither wished to grant this request in any way, nor dared refuse it openly, given that this was one of his dearest and most devoted servants, and since he eventually saw that the man was persisting in his unjust request and that he, the king, would have to explain his final decision to him, Artaxerxes continued to lead him on with gentle answers and fine words, so as to turn his thoughts away from the pursuit of his request. Through his other servants he made secret enquiries to find out who was inducing the gentleman to beseech him so insistently and to put such an importunate request to him. Finally, he learned that the gentleman had been promised 30,000 Darics, that is, 30,000 gold coins minted in the age of the great king Darius. And when he had heard about the whole matter and the cause which induced the gentleman to pursue his unjust request so incessantly, he summoned him and told him that it grieved him to refuse him what he was asking for, but that this did not make his request any the more just or well founded and that he would indeed have been very willing to grant it if it had been in keeping with justice, which had more power over him than anything else. But in order to make the servant realize what goodwill and feelings of generosity he bore towards him, he gladly gave him 30,000 Darics in lieu of that which he could not decently do for him. For he would not be any the less wealthy for having made a gift of this sum to him, whereas if he had wanted to grant the servant what he was beseeching him for so insistently, then he would have been less respected by men: this blemish would have remained, and it could have damaged the esteem in which his reputation and good name were held. And so he would not have been behaving as a good king who should prize justice and equity in all matters more highly than any worldly riches. . . .

CHAPTER 33[19]

The author discusses the power of kings and how it can only have authority if it is in harmony with justice and equity. . . .

. . . After Pompey's death, Julius Caesar had arrived in Armenia to repel King Pharnaces, whose great pride and arrogance had led him to encroach upon the Roman Empire. Caesar then caught Pharnaces unawares at such an opportune moment that he defeated him instantaneously and drove him out of the province of Pontus, which he had previously occupied. And to point out the extreme rapidity of his victory, he wrote just these three words to the Senate: 'Veni, vidi, vici', which means: 'I came, I saw, I conquered.'[20]

He was so clement and humane . . . that when, after Pompey's death, he had gone to Africa and learned that Cato had taken his own life because he despaired of staging a recovery and of rallying together forces, seeing that the army led by Scipio and himself was weakened and torn apart and that there was no more resistance to Caesar within their party under the aegis of the Senate, backed by its name and authority, Caesar then declared: 'Ah Cato, I envy you and the reputation which you have won by ending your life in a way that will be remembered for ever and ever. For you, envious of my clemency and kindness, did not wish to suffer and wait and thereby benefit both yourself and me, giving me the honour of pardoning you and prolonging your life.'[21] Caesar said this because Cato, knowing Caesar's disposition, his kind and mild nature, had exhorted and persuaded the people in his party to address themselves to Caesar; he had given the same advice to his son. 'But as for me', Cato had said, 'I could not humble, bend and constrain my heart so far as to thank Caesar for having saved my life and to live the rest of my days thus indebted. For tyranny has now made him master of the empire; he has been made victorious not by lawful justice but by iniquitous fortune.'[22] Caesar was indeed more mindful of his own moral standards than of his anger or of the enormous power which he had acquired, and he did not harm Cato's son, although the latter did not desert his father until after his death. Caesar thereby displayed the unsurpassed, praiseworthy force of his humaneness, which stemmed from his great magnanimity. For cruelty and permanent vengeance often derive more from faint-heartedness and cowardice than from valour and great courage. And Caesar would have considered his name and his party to have acquired great honour and advantage if he had spared Cato's life, as he had already done and was to do subsequently with many other great people. For in this way he was pouring ignominy and shame on the cruel proscription ordered by his predecessor Sulla and on the triumvirate which was to follow him at the time of Augustus and Antony. In this respect, Augustus neither inherited his uncle's fine morals nor imitated his virtues; and for this he was roundly condemned.[23] Yet the justness of his subsequent reign up until his death effaced or blotted out the violence and cruelty of the triumvirate. . . .

Translator's Notes

1. The basic principle that the emperor is not bound by legislation was established by the third-century jurist Ulpian in his commentary on a piece of marriage legislation, the *lex Iulia et Papia Poppaea* (*Digest* I.3.31). The principle that the emperor should live in accordance with the laws is spelled out in the medieval gloss by Baldus de Ubaldis on an imperial law which was issued in 429 by Emperor Theodosius II and then extracted in Justinian's code (*Codex Iustinianus* I.14.4). I am very grateful to Andrew Lewis of University College London for supplying these references.
2. This assumption underlies Book V of Aristotle's *Nicomachean Ethics.*
3. Horace, *Epistles* I.1.100.
4. Apollonius of Rhodes, *Argonautica* II.187–93.
5. That is, the Septuagint as opposed to the Latin Vulgate.
6. Proverbs 3:16.
7. The Roman emperors: Augustus (63 BC–AD 14), Titus (39–81), Trajan (53/6–117) and Severus Alexander (208/9–235).
8. Cicero, *De oratore* II.9.36.
9. Matthew 25:14–21.
10. The chapters are numbered consecutively from 1 to 22; after chapter 22, however, the numbering reverts to 20. Thus, the present chapter, though numbered 20, is actually 23.
11. An allusion to Proverbs 21:1.
12. In mythology the Hesperides were guardians of a tree of golden apples given by Earth to Hera as a wedding present. The tree was guarded by the dragon Ladon.
13. In reality, chapter 30; see n. 10.
14. Suetonius, *The Lives of the Caesars* VIII: 'The Deified Titus' 10. For Titus see n. 7.
15. Domitian, Roman Emperor from 81 to 93, was notorious for the sensuality of his private life.
16. In fact, Herodotus says none of this. See instead Ammianus Marcellinus, *History* XXX.8.4, and Plutarch, *Life of Artaxerxes* 1. Artaxerxes I was king of Persia in the second half of the fifth century BC.
17. Virgil, *Aeneid* V.344.
18. Budé may be referring to the Carthaginian custom of crucifying unsuccessful generals: see Livy, *History of Rome* XXII.51.15, XXXVIII.48.13 and *Periocha* XVII.
19. In reality, chapter 36; see n. 10.
20. Suetonius, *Lives of the Caesars* I.37 ('The Deified Julius'). Pompey (106–48 BC), the rival of Julius Caesar (100–44 BC) for power in Rome, was stabbed to death upon his arrival in Egypt, after his defeat in the battle of Pharsalus. Pharnaces II (63–47 BC), an ally of Pompey, was defeated at Zela by Caesar in 47 BC.
21. Plutarch, *Life of Caesar* 54 and *Life of Cato the Younger* 72. Marcus Porcius Cato (95–46 BC) was an ally of Pompey against Caesar; in line with his adherence to Stoicism, he committed suicide in Utica after Pompey's defeat. Quintus Caecilius Metellus Pius Scipio (middle of the first century BC) was a general on Pompey's side at the battle of Pharsalus and afterwards commanded the forces against Caesar in the war in Africa.
22. Plutarch, *Life of Cato the Younger* 64.

23. Sulla (c. 138–78 BC), after being elected dictator in 82 BC, attacked his opponents by publishing proscription lists containing the names of Roman citizens who were declared outlaws and whose goods were to be confiscated. When Mark Antony (c. 83–30 BC) and the future Roman Emperor Augustus (see n. 7) were appointed triumvirs, along with Lepidus, in 43 BC, they revived the practice of proscription against their political and personal enemies. Augustus was the grand-nephew of Caesar and was adopted by him as his chief heir.

Further Reading

Bietenholtz, P. G., and Deutscher, T. B., eds., *Contemporaries of Erasmus: A Bibliographical Register of the Renaissance and Reformation,* 3 vols. (Toronto, 1985–7), I, pp. 212–17

Burns, J. H., ed., *The Cambridge History of Political Thought 1450–1700* (Cambridge, 1991), pp. 78, 666

CHRP, pp. 80, 83, 322, 443, 752, 811

Heath, M., 'The education of a Christian prince: Erasmus, Budé, Rabelais – and Ogier le Danois', in P. Ford and G. Jondorf, eds., *Humanism and Letters in the Age of François Ier* (Cambridge, 1996), pp. 41–54

La Garanderie, M.-M. de, *Christianisme et lettres profanes (1515–1535). Essai sur les mentalités des milieux intellectuels parisiens et sur la pensée de Guillaume Budé* (Lille, 1976)

'Guillaume Budé, a philosopher of culture', *Sixteenth-Century Journal,* 19 (1988), 379–87

McNeil, D. O., *Guillaume Budé and Humanism in the Reign of Francis I* (Geneva, 1975)

17

Reginald Pole

NICHOLAS WEBB

Introduction

Reginald Pole (1500–58) was born at Stourton Castle in Worcestershire. He was educated at the Sheen Charterhouse and Magdalen College, Oxford. In 1517 Henry VIII, his cousin, made him prebend of Salisbury, and soon afterwards he became dean of Wimborne and Exeter. During this period Pole came into contact with humanist scholars such as Thomas More. In 1521 the king sent him to the University of Padua to complete his education. He returned to England in 1527, but by 1530 his opposition to Henry's divorce from Catherine of Aragon made it prudent for him to leave the country once more. By 1532 he had settled again in Padua. Four years later he was created a cardinal, and in 1538 he acted as papal legate to Emperor Charles V and King François I. He established himself near Rome, in Viterbo, and developed cordial relations with Vittoria Colonna, Jacopo Sadoleto, Pietro Bembo and other notable figures of Italian intellectual life. He attended the Council of Trent from 1545 to 1546 and was nearly elected pope in 1549. A year after Henry's Catholic daughter Mary ascended the throne in 1553, Pole returned to England. In 1556 he succeeded Thomas Cranmer as archbishop of Canterbury. He died twelve hours after his kinswoman Queen Mary.

In 1536 Pole sent his *Defence of the Unity of the Church* to Henry VIII, in reply to the king's demand for a formal opinion on the royal supremacy. In this work Pole vehemently attacked both the king and his ecclesiastical policy, and warned of reprisals on the part of the emperor and king of France if he did not repent of his evil ways. The *Apology,* which is addressed to Charles V, is a defence of Pole's earlier treatise. In chapters 30–5, he criticizes Henry's chief counsellor, Thomas Cromwell, casting him as a disciple of the Florentine political thinker, Niccolò Machiavelli, whose *The Prince* had been published in 1532. The king's actions, particularly in relation to his divorce and remarriage to Anne Boleyn, are interpreted as direct expressions of Cromwell's Machiavellian politics. This is the earliest known condemnation of Machiavellianism (though it was not published until the eighteenth century). Many more were to follow. Challenging Machiavelli's willingness to adapt morality and, above all, religion to expediency, Pole appeals to absolute ethical and religious standards. He also warns subjects that Machiavellian beliefs are as harmful to them as to their rulers.

The *Apologia ad Carolum Quintum* was first published in Reginald Pole, *Epistolae,* ed. A. M. Quirini, 5 vols. (Brescia, 1744–57), I, pp. 66–171; for the chapters translated here, see pp. 136–52.

Apology: Selections

CHAPTER 30

I understood all these things much more clearly when I chanced upon that book which [Thomas] Cromwell had highly praised to me.[1] The book, which I saw after our conversation, was not sent by him, for I believe he regretted having exposed so much of his policies in my company. Having been alerted, however, to the nature of Cromwell's studies by those who knew about his secret leisure reading, I attempted to get my hands on this material, taking as much trouble to do so as those who undertake, with the greatest assiduity, to intercept messages in which the enemy's plans are revealed.

The book was, I discovered, written by an enemy of the human race. In it, all the enemy's plans are set out, along with the means whereby religion, piety and every natural inclination of virtue can be easily destroyed. I had scarcely begun to read the book, when I recognized the hand of Satan, even though it bore the name of a human author and was written in a discernibly human style. Those books which describe the right standard of living by means of which men are best able to live with God in grace, in peace and in harmony are said to be written by the hand of God, especially divine books which contain divine laws. In the same way, I shall never hesitate to say that those books which lead us so far down the path to ruin that they annihilate all true piety and divide human society against itself have been written by the hand of Satan. This is certainly the case with the book about which I am going to speak, even though it bears the name of a human author.

Not to keep you in suspense any longer, the book is inscribed with the name of Machiavelli, a certain Florentine, entirely unworthy to have been born in that noble city. But just as Satan's progeny are everywhere, intermingling with the sons of God, and will continue to exist until the time when he 'whose fan is in his hand will thoroughly cleanse his threshing-floor',[2] so this son of Satan, trained in all forms of wickedness in the midst of the many sons of God, was born in that noble city and has written things which stink of Satan's every wickedness. Among other works, he composed *The Prince* (for this is the title he has given to one of his books), in which he portrays for us such a prince, that, if Satan were to reign in the flesh and were to have a son, to whom he were to bequeath his sovereignty after his death, he would give him no other instructions than those found in this book.

Now mark this well, rulers, and listen carefully. This pertains above all to you and your sons, so that you do not permit them to swallow this most evil and pernicious doctrine; for this poison has been diffused throughout princely courts in the books of Machiavelli, which circulate almost everywhere. Listen then and pay attention. I call not only on you, but on every race, all nations and peoples. I urge you to listen, because this doctrine is a threat to the safety of everyone. He gives this poison to princes and their sons to drink not only in order to lead them to a ruinous end, but also to bring about your destruction, you who are the subjects of kings and princes. For it is the aim of his doctrine to act like a drug which causes princes to go mad, so that afterwards, just as wolves or tigers prey on sheep, or foxes on chickens, they will tear you to shreds, scatter your innards and destroy you.

To begin with, listen to his advice concerning religion. He persuades the prince that he should beware above all of appearing to neglect religion, which he wants to be a convenience and therefore something advantageous to the prince. Provided he knows how to use it correctly, nothing is more valuable than religion for procuring everything – whatever his heart desires. The prince secures this convenience because no one more easily deceives the people and the common throng of men than someone about whose piety they have conceived a measure of hope. For a prince, whether dealing with his own people or with foreigners, in all matters of state, treaties and alliances, what is most important is the reputation you have in religious matters: whether you are regarded as devout and as someone who respects the faith, or as someone who despises it. Extreme care must be taken that you do not appear to despise religion. Machiavelli wants this precept to be understood, however, in the following way: that unless you know how to change direction as the situation demands, your reputation as regards religion will not so much be served as damaged.[3] So, nothing is more ruinous than to observe religion sincerely and unswervingly, as religious books lay down, since religion can almost never adapt itself to human expediencies, and seldom can religion be seen in company with expediency. This is taught by means of several examples of people who wanted to observe religion and faith in all matters, as religion ordains. Some of these lost their life, others their power. Almost none escaped without receiving some injury. Amidst the deceitful stratagems devised by human ingenuity, no one can escape. A person who wants always to follow the truth and faith and religion can never live safe from assault. Nor does someone who openly neglects religion find himself in any better circumstances.

What then is to be done? Take the middle path, which practical wisdom recommends, so that you observe religion when expediency advises you to do so; and when it does not give this advice, do not be so scrupulous that you adhere strictly to religion, nor so rash that you reject it openly – this is especially damaging. Here Machiavelli demonstrates that pride of place is given above all to intelligence and practical wisdom. He concedes this splendid battleground to all counsellors of princes, for them to exercise their talents on, so that they continually invent specious arguments borrowed either from religion or from some other pretence of virtue (a point which Cromwell expounded on the basis of his own doctrine in his conversation with me, which I recounted a little earlier).[4] He thought that it was easy to extract arguments from the attendant circumstances which, so to speak, clothe each and every matter before it can acquire the name of virtue. These are by no means few in number, so not merely one but several can be applied to a deed, whatever it might be. He demonstrates and concludes that a person who is unable to lend some semblance of virtue to any desire whatever of a prince, along with some pretence of those things which contribute to the realization of virtue, is entirely unworthy to be summoned to his advisory councils.

As if he were frightened that he might perhaps be thought to have had certain religious rites in mind, when the opportunity presented itself to him, he expresses the same things which he says concerning religion with greater clarity when speaking about all the virtues which religion commands should be respected: piety, faith, justice, generosity and mercy. He says that to respect and possess these virtues is especially damaging to princes; but to have the appearance of possessing them and to be able to use them in their place, as expediency urges, is always advantageous.[5]

Finally, he sums up the general principle of his doctrine on instructing the prince by means of these two comparisons: he teaches the prince to act appropriately in the roles, first, of the lion and, then, of the fox.[6] He specifies these two animals, on which he fashions a model for the prince, because he prefers a principate founded on fear to one founded on love, on the grounds that it is more useful, safer and easier to handle. For this reason he assigns first place to the characteristics of the lion, on which he lays the foundation of the state. When that has been achieved, he entrusts the rest to the fox. In due course they can be used in turn: when guile, a vulpine trait, is able to achieve nothing, the force of the lion may show the way; where it appears that an open use of force is less effective, one may imitate the manner in which the fox enters burrows. This, he asserts, is the true way to protect an empire and a principate – the way which experience, the mistress of affairs, teaches.

The other type of policy, which is conducted according to virtue, is the one endorsed by learned men, who write much that is outstanding about those very virtues which pertain especially to the prince.[7] He does not deny that this policy is excellent – if it is found anywhere at all. If, however, it is not to be found, the more someone adapts himself to its pattern, the less useful it is to him, and the more his power diminishes rather than expands. There is almost no place whatever for the policy of virtue, especially when one lives among men teeming with lies and deceptions, who can never be ruled without duplicity. It is therefore best to subject the people to those same wiles which they will always be prepared to use, when the chance arises, against their prince. In fact, the prince will be more successful the more he knows how to pretend and dissemble. And in this let him take care to make a show of rejecting those virtues which the philosophers writing on this subject employ in order to make their books worthy of admiration. He should, however, hold religion, faith and justice in very high regard (and not pursue them grudgingly). As convenience permits, it will also be useful to exhibit these qualities through some action. Yet while it is admissible to employ them occasionally, he concludes that no one has ever benefitted from being committed to them and showing himself to be – or actually being – a determined practitioner of them. Therefore, he transforms the secret of holding on to power in complete security and happiness into the savagery of the lion and the wiles of the fox, in whose care he leaves the prince, as if he were within the most secure fortress, protected against all the hazards of fortune.[8]

CHAPTER 31

Observe, your majesty, I have set out the full extent of this man's doctrine and kingly art. What do you want now? For me to refute it? To show it to be harmful, the downfall of all those princes who learn it or may wish to follow it and the ruination of their subjects? Would I not be doing the greatest harm to you, in particular, and to other princes who profess the name of Christ and who follow his teaching if I were to judge it necessary to repeat the tenets of this impious doctrine in your company? And, in my view, there is nothing here that you and I do not see eye to eye on.

Keep this in mind above all: if the still tender minds of your sons were to soak up a doctrine of this sort, the regal spirits in their mind would be extinguished immediately, just as the vital spirits are immediately extinguished by a poison which has been diffused throughout the body. For what (to begin with the foundation of all life) is more kingly and more indicative of a noble nature than the love of truth, since God himself is called truth? Conversely, what is more base and more slavish than lies, duplicity and deceit? Is anyone prepared to see his own son delight in lies, deceit and duplicity? Is there anyone who would not rebuke this, who would not punish it, even in a servant, as conduct unworthy of a human being? And are the sons of kings to be educated in this way, so that they are able to pretend and dissemble about everything? Does this doctrine in its entirety teach anything other than deceit, duplicity, lying and life-long hypocrisy?

Yet what is more kingly and more divine than to benefit others? We know God best of all through the benefits he brings to us, and it is because of these that we especially honour and love him. Is there anyone who would not delight in a son in whom he saw this talent for doing good in all circumstances and a concern for bringing benefits to everyone? What if he should see a boy, with whom he was unacquainted, who relished doing good to others to the extent that he even undermined his own advantage in order to benefit others? Is there anyone, I ask you, who would not immediately recognize in this lad a kingly disposition? Even if he saw this spirit in the son of a servant, would he not call it noble, a nature to be admired and cherished? This book aims at nothing other than corrupting this disposition in princes and extinguishing it completely. It recommends that the prince should not refrain from shedding anyone's blood, nor from practising deceit or causing harm, and that he should always acquire things for himself and take them away from others.

I have not yet sufficiently described the potency and ferocity of this poison. If it is instilled in the minds of princes, it convinces them that piety and religion are to be respected when it is convenient and that they are to be ignored when it is inconvenient. This is the equivalent of teaching that you should believe no religion to be true, that there is no God, that divine providence has been driven from the world and its power and strength are irrelevant. The person who thinks in this way about religion, not from weakness, but from resolution of mind and judgement, argues that it can be observed or ignored at whim. He shows by that selfsame judgement of mind that there is no reason for accepting the will of God, as expressed in religion, but instead always subjects God's will to the convenience of man. For such a person, who thinks like this, there is no God.[9] How shall I argue against someone who maintains such things, when the pagans would never have put up with a person expressing such doubts? Thus, it is written in the histories of Athens that when a certain philosopher at the start of his book had merely stated: 'I cannot say whether or not God exists', he was instantly expelled from the city with the agreement of the public council.[10] And not only do we Christians allow men to write such things with impunity – things which destroy all divine piety – but we allow the student of such a master to rule, a student who expresses his master's precepts through his actions better than Plato expressed the precepts of his master Socrates, or the student of Christ, those of his lord and master. Look once again at the aim of this doctrine, and consider more carefully the purpose of the writer and where he is headed. Then we shall be better able to make a judgement on the student, inasmuch as he personifies his master.

Consider well whether this doctrine aims at anything other than the utter destruction of every regal quality and every nobility of nature – a prelude to extinguishing the spirit of God in us all. What else is he doing when he teaches that everything should be a matter of pretence and dissembling, when he advises that religion should be observed, not out of devotion, but from expediency, and recommends the same for all the rest of the virtues? Is this not to corrupt entirely that royal disposition which fosters the true, not the counterfeit, seeds of virtue? Is it not to remove the kingly as well as the priestly class from the scene? And, finally, is it not to condemn the rest of humanity, the very people who live in cities or in kingdoms and who are at the behest of such princes, to be thrown to the lions, so to speak, in arenas or amphitheatres? Is this not what he does when he entrusts to the force of the lion and the guile of the fox the government of the kingdom, which is also well supplied with tigers and bears? Has anyone ever decreed such a cruel fate for his fellow human beings, his own race? Can there be a clearer demonstration that these things were never written by the spirit of a man at all, but rather that the man holding the pen was taking dictation from that spirit who can never get his fill of human evil, who is never able to rejoice over the good and has therefore been made the enemy of God? And the more the name of religion is attached to all these crimes and impieties, is it not the more to his liking?

Indeed, if he achieves these things, it is an end beyond which his wickedness, though virtually boundless, does not seek to drag man. Nor can he have any greater guarantee that a human mind is dedicated entirely to him, captive and stripped of all the supports of grace and nature, than if he sees it to have descended so low that religion serves not for the sake of salvation, but rather as a trap to capture minions, as if they were mice to be tortured and destroyed. Such a person no longer sins out of weakness, nor can he receive absolution for his sins, since he recognizes no other role for religion, through which alone the soul can be restored, than as a snare for lesser mortals. Satan, possessing him thus duped and trapped, need look no further than this.

CHAPTER 32

You see, therefore, the prudence of this doctrine and where it leads. Although I have given a full account of it, I do not intend to refute it in detail. In fact, somehow or other, I have said more against it than I planned to do at the outset and than was necessary, especially for Christian princes and those who venerate the name of Christ, who cannot fail to see the impiety of this doctrine at first glance, and who, on seeing its wickedness, together with its impiety, cannot fail to loathe and revile it. What is even more despicable is that this doctrine is transmitted and disseminated not only in written form but also through its embodiment in students of it and their actions, bringing the greatest harm to the good and casting abuse on pure and holy teaching. I can scarcely bring myself to name the student who personifies his master in every respect, even as he employs this doctrine in full view of the world, and whose conduct, actions and deeds I have already shown to be cruel, inhuman, blasphemous, impious, lustful and foul.

What has he not tried to conceal under the appearance of religion? He wanted, first, to hide his lusts and desires under this veil. How hard he tried, right from the start, when bound by the law of God, to leave his wife and attach himself to his mistress, wishing to appear overcome by a great show of piety. Since, however, he could not successfully exploit those passages which he had extracted, like a stolen page, from the Book of the Law in order to cover up matters he was ashamed of, he realized that to adapt them he needed the help of those experienced in this art. Therefore, he ran, like a naked athlete, through all the literary gymnasia,[11] in order to purchase the assistance of those experienced in law. And he did this with every pretence of devoutness and modesty in order to show that in matters pertaining to ecclesiastical law and about which there could be some suspicion that he was motivated by his own desires, he relied not on his own judgement, but on that of the legal experts. Nevertheless, he was unwilling to try this until he had ascertained that the judgement of the Roman Church was at odds with his desire. He had always been accustomed to venerate the Church as a mother and to regard all her laws as sacrosanct, so as to conceal his rashness and lust, while leaving them undisturbed. This scheme therefore pleased him, and he secured for his own side as many of the opposing opinions of learned men as he could. Even though he harboured the bitterest enmities against the Roman pontiff and disregarded his authority in everything, he did not want to relinquish the title of 'Defender of the Faith', which the pope had given to him; and on all the impious decrees by means of which he overthrew the pope, he always affixed the name 'Defender'.[12] What, in the final analysis, did he accomplish in that tragicomedy without recourse to the appearance of religion? Once he had slipped from lust into cruelty and had made a true tragedy out of a mixed comedy through his indescribable savagery, in which he outdid all tyrants and impious men, no one could have better epitomized the precepts of his master — at any rate this precept, in which all the rest are encapsulated: that one may pander to one's cravings and longings under the pretext of religion. Herein lies the complete doctrine of Machiavelli and Cromwell.

It cannot, nevertheless, be denied that he has actually made a mistake in one matter and has deviated from their precepts. This is how it happened. When certain nobles whom he suspected on account of their virtue were absent from court in their own estates, he wanted to entice them to come to him. He saw, however, that this was going to be difficult because they, in turn, were suspicious of him on account of his cruelty and, furthermore, made their attitude clear. Therefore, unless some assurance were given, they had decided not to come when summoned. Seeing this, he very promptly sent an oath of assurance, in letters signed with the royal seal, showing a benevolent face towards them. As soon as they came, having convinced themselves that it was now safe, he had them killed.[13] But, up to this point, what he did is not opposed to the doctrine. On the contrary, his action conforms to the greatest extent with the art, for it lays down that a major benefit of feigned religion is that one is more easily able to deceive those whom one suspects and to do away with them. Therefore, in this matter, the student did not deviate from his master.

In what follows, however, he did so to a very great degree. When he had resolved on eliminating those now in his power and had openly declared this in a public meeting, one of the nobles immediately objected that he was not able to do this, since they had an oath of assurance. He replied without delay, as if astonished at the naïvety of the noble, who thought that an assurance prohibited him from removing those under suspicion. He said immediately that he was surprised and then added that he had given them an assurance simply to enable him to have in his power those who otherwise refused to come to him. 'And', he said, 'when I have enticed them by means of this device and have the suspects in my power, am I not obliged to exercise my legal right against them?' This reply was overheard by many, which clearly went against the rules of cunning. For Machiavelli writes that even if trust is not to be kept with those whom the prince suspects, nevertheless some artifice should always be devised by means of which it can be generally understood that it was the other side which did not keep its part of the bargain.[14] He says that this should not present any difficulty given the many circumstances which are involved in all oaths of assurance. The king, however, answered too quickly, before his teacher was able to supply the correct reply.

Nor would Cromwell have failed to have come up with a pretext in such a case of broken faith. Having deceived many, especially from among the common people, by the same means, he always used to claim that they were guilty of a capital crime because, after giving the assurance, they had conspired once again. Nevertheless, for all his cunning, he could not prevent the first person to have been deceived by this device from taking out of his breast-pocket, as he was dragged towards his death, an oath of assurance given by the king, pointing to it and exclaiming to the people: 'the king's good faith dies with me'. Let those who wish to remain alive, therefore, take care how they keep faith with their king from now on.

CHAPTER 33

Let us at last have done with this impious and abhorrent doctrine, about which more could be written, either in refutation or explanation. His deeds, far more than the arguments everyone has proposed, both refute it and reveal it for what it is – this man who does everything according to the rules of this doctrine, down to the last letter, and who, as far as possible, propounds its precepts and puts them into action. I have not said nearly enough about these matters, in proportion to the crime and to the magnitude of his impiety (which, I confess, transcend my competence). I trust, nevertheless, that I have sufficiently expounded these things, so that not only a person of sound mind, by the grace and merit of Christ, but also someone who has not been entirely deprived of the light of reason – who has one spark left of either genuine knowledge or love for his own kind – reading what I have written (in which if I have knowingly said something untrue, as God is my witness, I demand an avenger), must see the impiety of this doctrine, together with its crimes, and must oppose, hate and abhor the man (if this name should be given to someone who does everything to the detriment of humanity), as well as the doctrine. But if, as I hope, I have succeeded in this – for it has to do with my function and position at this time and, above all, it has to do with piety towards the Church – I am now going to do something which reveals not only the impiety of this doctrine, but also the remarkable stupidity, together with the impiety, of its author, who would no doubt prefer to be accused of impiety rather than stupidity. In fact, they can never be separated, because nothing is more blind and more dimwitted than impiety.

He shows this above all in his own book. What better demonstration is there of his crass stupidity than that, having discarded love for the prince as useless and false, he establishes his power on the basis of fear, as if it provides greater security and peace of mind? Nonetheless, he advises the prince to be careful not to provoke hatred, since hatred always follows fear, just as a shadow follows the body, especially in the case of someone who does nothing out of true and tangible virtue, but instead does everything out of a feigned virtue. Nor is it a single hatred which follows such a person, but a double or multiple one, derived both from vice-ridden actions themselves and from the pretence of virtue, which is the most prolific cause of hatred.[15]

But he is by no means unaware that if the pretence is recognized, it is impossible to avoid provoking hatred. Therefore, he strongly advises the prince to be careful never to be caught feigning virtue. But this, you most stupid and most impious of men, is not in the power of human beings to control. It is the responsibility of God, who knows all things and who reveals them when he wills. These are the words of his son: 'For there is nothing covered, that shall not be revealed;[16] a city set on a hill cannot be hid.'[17] Why is this so? Because, although the pretence of individuals may be covered up for a while, it is nevertheless difficult, if not impossible, for the prince: not only are all his actions and words observed, but so too are his sighs, groans and all his bodily gestures, which so often express what is in the soul. Nature herself says that nothing feigned lasts for long. And someone who reveals himself in one matter (and given the number of enterprises in which the prince is engaged, it would be exceedingly foolish to hope that this would not happen at least once) produces the same effect as if he had revealed everything else, since men judge all things relating to character and nature on the basis of one pretence. That very student who more than anyone has tried to use this cunning to cover up his vices with the feigned appearance of virtue can serve as an example of how impossible it is to do this, thereby revealing the very great foolishness of his teacher, who gives out precepts as if this were possible.

What means has he not tried in order to cover up his lust and, likewise, his other vices of avarice and cruelty, with a sham of religion? He has had, moreover, a very great opportunity to cover up his vices, because he began his youth with the highest praise for religion, piety and true virtue. He thus acquired that reputation for virtue which throughout his life has particularly enabled him to feign and to conceal his vices. But, in the final analysis, after adding to that appearance the advice of those who were held to be – and were – notably shrewd and skilled in simulating and dissimulating everything, what, I ask you, did he achieve? What, in the end, has he managed to hide? Is it the case that his retainers and those who live in his kingdom, where these crimes were acted out as if on the stage, do not see the impiety of his soul? Are they unaware of the pretence and trickery which virtually every foreign nation knows about? I cannot say whether some other more damning evidence is disclosed in his household than those facts I have recounted here. What I can say is that when I report the things which I have brought to public attention and which surpass all human wickedness, they are unknown to very few who have ever listened to the king. Indeed, right from the beginning of his dissembling with God and with everyone, I have constantly observed that the more he endeavoured to hide his lustful and criminal passions, the more divine providence exposed them all, to his extreme discredit. So that from its very onset, the flagrant dissembling of his lust, which he tried to cover up with the testimony of the divine law, was revealed.

CHAPTER 34

Has anyone ever worked harder to conceal the secret of his own soul? How many public declarations has he made in order to make it look as if he wanted to dispose of his wife not so much on account of his craving – though he was burning with lust – as on account of religion? Is there anything he did not do in order to protect his honour and to persuade people that he was motivated by religious scruple, which was his sole reason for seeking a divorce? He even sent representatives to all the universities of Christendom to test the views of good and devout and learned men, awaiting their verdict with a degree of patience that lust is never accustomed to show.[18] But surely he did not deceive these men? Surely he did not escape divine vengeance out of regard for him? This is his oracle, spoken through the prophet Ezekiel: 'Every man of the house of Israel that taketh his idols into his heart . . . and cometh to the prophet to enquire for himself of me; "I, the Lord, will answer him therein according to the multitude of his idols."'[19] Behold, here is God's first act of vengeance against a man who makes a pretence of religion, so that he reaps a reward which corresponds to his immoderate desire.

But do I now call that which he considers to be his greatest triumph the vengeance of God? No one ever showed himself to have heard anything with greater pleasure than when he was told that many learned men had given opinions which were in agreement with his will. When he heard this, he was most of all concerned that their written testimonials should be brought back to him. Later he exhibited them in public; and on account of these testimonials, he thought that he was able to dispose of his wife with honour and that he had handled the matter so successfully that his religious scruple, even in this deed, would be proved to God as well as to men.[20] Why then do I call this assent of learned men, compliant to the will of the enquirer, the vengeance of God? This is, in fact, what Scripture calls it, especially when the will of the enquirer was beforehand tainted with lust, which he was so incapable of dissembling that he constantly held the woman who corrupted him in his arms, for all to see. But here is what God says about such an assent: 'The iniquity of the prophet shall be even as the iniquity of him that seeketh unto him.'[21] What follows shows even more that this has resulted from vengeance against him, since Scripture does not hesitate to say about the false answer of the prophet to a feigned question: 'And if the prophet be deceived and speaketh a word, I, the Lord, have deceived that prophet.'[22] And these words contain the final judgement of God concerning his vengeance: 'I will set my face against that man, and will make him . . . a sign and a proverb, and I will cut him off from the midst of my people.'[23]

Whether this part of the vengeance is going to cling to him, so that he is a cautionary tale and a proverb among all nations, I leave to the judgement of the universities of all nations, which he approached in this matter through his representatives. The reason for their discussions, to be sure, usually arises from monstrous commands and from monstrous deeds which have been made public. But has any-thing more monstrous ever been heard of than that a ruler with an untarnished reputation for so many years of his reign, one whom nobody could charge with anything untoward and to whom it was permitted throughout his entire life to live in this same esteem among everyone – that this man should bring the scandalous charge of incest against *himself,* so that among the learned men of all nations he would be judged to have led an incestuous life for twenty years? But if an enemy of his had levelled such a charge against him, calling him incestuous, what could have been more insulting? He campaigned so earnestly, drawing on every favour and authority – and, when that did not suffice, resorting to bribery – and he desired so ardently to acquire the sort of judgements on his earlier life that no one stained by an infamous life had ever obtained, so that he could show off this testimony of virtue from upright men. And when they brought such testimonials to him with every honour, he showered them with every reward. As for those, however, who wished to maintain the honesty of his earlier life and to protect the honour of the marital bed, not only did he refuse to listen to them but he regarded them as his enemies. Could anyone have provided more ample material for human discourse, so that his name was turned into a proverb and an example? If one adds to these things his monstrous cruelty, monstrous avarice and impiety, which are known to virtually every Christian nation and which are now openly divulged by me, can the vengeance of God against him – revealed through the prophet, speaking on behalf of God, when he says: 'I will make him a sign and a proverb' – remain hidden now? Only the completion of this vengeance remains, so that he is cut off from the midst of the people.

Chapter 35

Yet the pupil of Machiavelli,[24] well versed in this new art of ruling, has seen to it that this will not now happen. When he realized that the security of the king was founded, not so much on the right of succession, which remained secure for him, as on the love of the people, he converted this foundation of love into one of fear. Now that love was utterly rejected as useless, false and opposed to many of the prince's desires, he established the seat of power in fear. All this conforms to the greatest extent with the precepts of the new art of ruling.[25]

Yet it never conforms with the experience of real life. Leaving aside my true case against him and turning, finally, to actual experience, a sphere in which he regards himself as superior to all others who have written according to the norms of reason: When, I ask, has he seen it to be the case or read it in history books that it is safer for a prince who has come to power with the love of his citizens to rule through fear rather than through love? This I know for certain (judging the matter according to real events, on which he above all relies, although this is a very deceptive way to make a judgement): the fate of no prince confirms this belief. Indeed, it happens very frequently that some ruler, having disregarded the love of the citizenry, descends to the point that he shows himself to be feared, as if this were a better way to preserve his power, and in this way greatly hastens his own downfall and transforms forever both his own lot and that of all the citizens from prosperity to misery. What then shall

I say about all this? Is impiety so blind that the man who claims to teach others prudence does not see what the collective wisdom of all ages confirms, what all reason and all experience consonant with reason proclaim and demonstrate daily by example?

But as regards Machiavelli, if what I heard when I was in Florence last winter (having taken a detour there from my journey) about the circumstances in which he wrote the book and his intention in writing it is true, then to some extent he can be excused for this blindness and ignorance. When the subject of his book had been raised, and I had reproached this impious blindness, his fellow citizens excused him, answering the charge with the same argument that Machiavelli himself had offered when they had previously confronted him. His reply had been that he followed not only his own judgement in the book, but also that of the person for whom he wrote it.[26] Since this person was known to have a tyrannical nature, he included those matters which could not fail to be particularly pleasing to someone of that sort. Nevertheless, he believed, as has everyone else who has written about the instruction of a king or prince and as experience itself teaches, that if the prince were to put these same precepts into practice, his rule would be brief. This is precisely what he longed for, since inwardly he burned with hatred towards the prince for whom he wrote. His sole purpose in the book was to write for a tyrant those things which are pleasing to tyrants, bringing about in this way, if he could, the tyrant's self-willed and swift downfall. On these grounds they excused the blindness of Machiavelli's mind.[27]

Cromwell, who has shown himself to be an actor in that tragedy which Machiavelli depicted solely through the written word, will see for himself whether he wishes to adduce these same arguments as an excuse for his own blindness. This much I know: someone whose every aim was to drag a prince guided by his advice down the path to ruin would never be able to devise a speedier method of leading him to destruction than that by which he has led his prince – the precepts, in other words, which are described in that book. He cannot be far away from ruin, especially now that he has been led to that steep precipice, a veritable Tarpeian Rock,[28] where everyone gazes upon him. He is now in a position to convince himself that all his subjects at home – men of every station – are very hostile to him. And unless he convinces himself of this, he is extremely foolish, for his impious avarice, his blasphemies, his murders of the best men of every rank proclaim it. From now on, those outside the kingdom, those who support religion, piety, nobility and virtue, must regard him with hatred as an enemy who lays waste to all piety and religion.

Translator's Notes

1. In the previous chapter, Pole had recounted a discussion which he had had with Cromwell at York Place, in which Cromwell had argued that the main role of a counsellor was to discover and obey the will of his prince, who was not subject to the constraints of ordinary morality. Cromwell's reading of Machiavelli's *The Prince* may well have been invented by Pole for the purposes of his invective.
2. Matthew 3:12; see also Luke 3:17.
3. See Machiavelli, *The Prince*, ed. Q. Skinner and R. Price (Cambridge, 1988), ch. 18.
4. See chapter 29 of the *Apology*, in Pole, *Epistolae*, I, pp. 133–6.

5. Here, and in the following paragraphs, Pole has in mind Machiavelli's *The Prince,* chs. 18–19.
6. Cf. Cicero, *De officiis* I.13.41.
7. For Machiavelli's views on the 'theories and speculations' of those who had written on this subject see *The Prince,* ch. 15.
8. See Machiavelli, *The Prince,* ch. 25.
9. Machiavelli never professes atheism; see, e.g., *The Prince,* p. 89 (ch. 26): 'you must play your part, for God does not want to do everything, in order not to deprive us of our freedom and the glory that belongs to us'.
10. The philosopher was Protagoras, a fifth-century BC sophist: see Cicero, *De natura deorum* I.23.63, and Diogenes Laertius, *Lives of the Philosophers* IX.51; in both these accounts Protagoras refers to 'the gods' rather than to 'God'.
11. That is, the universities. The term *gymnasium* (from the Greek word *gumnos* = naked) can mean both a centre for athletic activity and a school or college.
12. Henry married Catherine of Aragon, the widow of his elder brother, in 1509. He began his campaign to dissolve the marriage in 1527 by expressing doubts about the validity of the papal dispensation which had allowed him to defy the injunction of Leviticus 18:16 against an incestuous marriage to a brother's wife. The pope's unwillingness to grant Henry an annulment eventually led to the king being declared supreme head of the Church of England. On 23 May 1533, Henry's marriage to Catherine (the aunt of Emperor Charles V) was annulled by Archbishop Thomas Cranmer, and a few days later his marriage to his former mistress Anne Boleyn (which had taken place in January) was declared legal; Anne Boleyn was crowned queen on 1 June. Henry had been given the title 'Defender of the Faith' in 1521 by Pope Leo X in recognition of his *Asssertio septem sacramentorum,* directed against Martin Luther. Pole describes the events surrounding Henry's divorce in Book III of his *Defence of the Unity of the Church.*
13. Pole may have in mind the Doncaster meeting of 6 December 1536, during the 'Pilgrimage of Grace', at which the protesters, led by Robert Aske, were offered the guarantee of a free pardon by Henry. He subsequently executed Aske and over two hundred others. The king's behaviour was defended by Richard Morison in his *Lamentation* and *Remedy;* see D. S. Berkowitz, *Humanist Scholarship and Public Order: Two Tracts against the Pilgrimage of Grace by Sir Richard Morison* (Washington, D.C., 1984).
14. See Machiavelli, *The Prince,* ch. 18: 'How rulers should keep their promises'. There is a close parallel here with Cesare Borgia's treatment of the Orsini and Vitelli at Senigallia described in ch. 7 of *The Prince,* p. 25.
15. See Machiavelli, *The Prince,* chs. 17 ('Cruelty and mercifulness; and whether it is better to be loved or feared') and 19 ('How contempt and hatred should be avoided').
16. See Matthew 10:26; Mark 4:22; Luke 8:17.
17. Matthew 5:14.
18. The consultations began in earnest in 1529 at the suggestion of Thomas Cranmer: Oxford, Cambridge, Paris and Padua were among the king's supporters. The Spanish and the German universities, together with Naples were opposed to the divorce. Pole was commissioned to win over Paris to the king's side.
19. See Ezekiel 14:4 and 7.
20. See n. 12.
21. Ezekiel 14:10.
22. Ezekiel 14:9.
23. Ezekiel 14:8.
24. Pole returns here to Cromwell.
25. See Machiavelli, *The Prince,* ch. 17.
26. Machiavelli dedicated *The Prince* to Lorenzo de' Medici, duke of Urbino (1492–1519), the grandson of Lorenzo the Magnificent.
27. On the extent of Florentine republican ideas in Machiavelli's works, see G. Silvano, 'Florentine republicanism in the early sixteenth century', in G. Bock, Q. Skinner and M.

Viroli, eds., *Machiavelli and Republicanism* (Cambridge, 1990), pp. 40–70. On this passage from the *Apology* and its possible later influence, see P. S. Donaldson, *Machiavelli and the Mystery of State* (Cambridge, 1988), pp. 10, 88.

28. The Tarpeian Rock was a precipice, at the southwest corner of the Capitoline Hill in Rome, over which traitors and murderers were thrown.

Further Reading

CHRP, p. 444

Donaldson, P. S., *Machiavelli and Mystery of State* (Cambridge, 1988)

Fenlon, D., *Heresy and Obedience in Tridentine Italy: Cardinal Pole and the Counter-Reformation* (Cambridge, 1972)

McConica, J. K., *English Humanists and Reformation Politics under Henry VIII and Edward VI* (Oxford, 1965)

Pole, Reginald, *Defense of the Unity of the Church,* ed. and trans. J. G. Dwyer (Westminster, Md., 1965)

Raab, F., *The English Face of Machiavelli* (London, 1964)

Schenck, W., *Reginald Pole, Cardinal of England* (London, 1950)

Simoncelli, P., *Il caso Reginald Pole: eresia e santità nelle polemiche religiose del Cinquecento* (Rome, 1977)

Bibliography of Renaissance Political Philosophy Texts Available in English

Anthologies

Burns, J. H., and Izbicki, T. M., eds., *Conciliarism and Papalism 1511–1518: Almain, Cajetan, Mair,* trans. T. M. Izbicki (Cambridge, 1997)

Chambers, D., and Pullan, B., *Venice: A Documentary History 1450–1630* (Oxford, 1992)

Kohl, B., and Witt, R. G., eds., *The Earthly Republic: Italian Humanists on Government and Society* (Manchester, 1978)

Rabil, A., Jr., ed. and trans., *Knowledge, Goodness, and Power: The Debate over Nobility among Quattrocento Humanists* (Binghamton, N.Y., 1991)

Watkins, R. Neu, trans. and ed., *Humanism and Liberty: Writings on Freedom from Fifteenth-Century Florence* (Columbia, S.C., 1978)

Texts by Author

Alamanni, Lodovico, 'The making of a courtier', in A. Molho, ed., *Social and Economic Foundations of the Italian Renaissance* (New York, 1969), pp. 214–20

Alberti, Leon Battista, *The Albertis of Florence,* trans. G. Guarino (Lewisburg, Pa., 1971) *The Family in Renaissance Florence,* trans. R. Neu Watkins (Columbia, S.C., 1969)

Boccalini, Traiano, *I ragguagli di Parnaso: or Advertisements from Parnassus; in Two Centuries . . . ,* trans. Henry, Earl of Monmouth (London, 1656), pp. 175–6 (I.89); see also *Advertisements from Parnassus,* trans. N. N., 3 vols. (London, 1704), II, pp. 107–10; *Advices from Parnassus, in Two Centuries,* ed. J. Hughes (London, 1706), pp. 163–5

Bodin, Jean, *The Six Bookes of a Commonweale,* trans. R. Knolles (London, 1606; reprinted, with corrections, ed. K. D. McRae, Cambridge, 1962)

Botero, Giovanni, *The Reason of State,* trans. P. J. and D. P. Waley (London, 1965)

Bruni, Leonardo, *Dialogues,* in G. Griffiths, J. Hankins and D. Thompson, trans., *The Humanism of Leonardo Bruni: Selected Texts* (Binghamton, N.Y., 1987), pp. 63–84 *Panegyric to the City of Florence,* in B. Kohl and R. G. Witt, eds., *The Earthly Republic: Italian Humanists on Government and Society* (Manchester, 1978), pp. 121–75

[Brutus, Stephanus Junius], *Vindiciae contra tyrannos, or Concerning the Legitimate Power of a Prince over the People, and of the People over a Prince,* ed. and trans. G. Garnett (Cambridge, 1994)

Buonaccorso da Montemagno, *Treatise on Nobility,* in A. Rabil, Jr., ed. and trans., *Knowledge, Goodness, and Power: The Debate over Nobility among Quattrocento Humanists* (Binghamton, N.Y., 1991), pp. 24–52

Campanella, Tommaso, *La città del sole . . . The City of the Sun,* ed. and trans. D. J. Donno (Berkeley, Calif., 1981)

Contarini, Gasparo, *The Commonwealth and Government of Venice,* trans. L. Lewkenor (London, 1599)

Conversini da Ravenna, Giovanni, *Dragmalogia de eligibili vite genere,* ed. and trans. H. L. Eaker (Lewisburg, Pa., 1980)

Two Court Treatises, ed. and trans. B. Kohl and J. Day (Munich, 1987)

Elyot, Sir Thomas, *The Boke Named the Governor,* ed. S. Lehmberg (London, 1962)

Erasmus, Desiderius, *The Education of a Christian Prince* and *A Complaint of Peace,* in his *Literary and Educational Writings,* 5, ed. A. H. T. Levi, The Collected Works of Erasmus, 27 (Toronto, 1986) pp. 199–322

Gentillet, Innocent, *A Discourse upon the Means of Wel Governing and Maintaining the Good Peace . . . against Nicholas Machiavel* (London, 1602)

Guicciardini, Francesco, *Dialogue on the Government of Florence,* trans. A. Brown (Cambridge, 1994)

Maxims and Reflections of a Renaissance Statesman, trans. M. Domandi (New York, 1965)

Heywood, John, *Gentleness and Nobility,* ed. K. W. Cameron (Raleigh, N.C., 1941)

Hotman, François, *Francogallia,* ed. R. E. Giesey, trans. J. H. M. Salmon (Cambridge, 1972)

Landino, Cristoforo, *On True Nobility,* in A. Rabil, Jr., ed. and trans., *Knowledge, Goodness, and Power: The Debate over Nobility among Quattrocento Humanists* (Binghamton, N.Y., 1991), pp. 182–260

Lipsius, Justus, *Six Books of Politics or Civil Doctrine* (London, 1594)

Machiavelli, Niccolò, *The Discourses,* trans. L. J. Walker (Harmondsworth, 1970)

The Prince, ed. Q. Skinner and trans. R. Price (Cambridge, 1988)

Marsilius of Padua, *Defensor pacis,* in A. Gewirth, *Marsilius of Padua: The Defender of Peace,* 2 vols. (New York, 1956), vol. II

Writings on Empire: Defensor minor and De traslatione imperii, ed. C. J. Nederman (Cambridge, 1993)

More, Thomas, *Utopia,* ed. J. H. Hexter and E. Surtz, in *The Complete Works* (New Haven, Conn., 1963–), vol. IV

Osorio, Jeronimo, *A Discourse of Civil and Christian Nobility,* trans. W. Blandie (London, 1576)

Patrizi [of Siena], Francesco, *A Moral Methode of Civile Policie* (London, 1576)

Petrarch, *How a Ruler Ought to Govern His State,* in B. Kohl and R. G. Witt, eds., *The Earthly Republic: Italian Humanists on Government and Society* (Manchester, 1978), pp. 35–78

Poggio Bracciolini, *On Nobility,* in R. Neu Watkins, trans. and ed., *Humanism and Liberty: Writings on Freedom from Fifteenth-Century Florence* (Columbia, S.C., 1978), pp. 121–48, and in A. Rabil, Jr., ed. and trans., *Knowledge, Goodness, and Power: The Debate over Nobility among Quattrocento Humanists* (Binghamton, N.Y., 1991), pp. 53–89

Ponet, Thomas, *A Short Treatise of Politike Power* (Strasbourg, 1556); facsimile reprint in W. S. Hudson, *John Ponet (1516?–1556), Advocate of Limited Monarchy* (Chicago, 1942)

Ribadeneyra, Pedro de, *Religion and the Virtues of the Christian Prince against Machiavelli,* ed. and trans. G. A. Moore (Baltimore, Md., 1949)

Rinuccini, Alamanno, *Liberty,* in R. Neu Watkins, trans. and ed., *Humanism and Liberty: Writings on Freedom from Fifteenth-Century Florence* (Columbia, S.C., 1978), pp. 193–224

Savonarola, Girolamo, *Treatise on the Constitution and Government of the City of Florence,* in R. Neu Watkins, trans. and ed., *Humanism and Liberty: Writings on Freedom from Fifteenth-Century Florence* (Columbia, S.C., 1978), pp. 231–60

Smith, Sir Thomas, *The Commonwealth of England,* ed. L. Alston (Cambridge, 1906)

Starkey, Thomas, *A Dialogue between Reginald Pole and Thomas Lupset,* ed. K. M. Burton (London, 1948)

Vitoria, Francisco de, *On the American Indians,* in his *Political Writings,* ed. A. Pagden and J. N. H. Lawrance (Cambridge, 1991), pp. 231–92

Index Nominum

Index Rerum

abbot, 4
absolution, 11n, 17, 23, 29, 51, 279
absolutism, 36, 258
abstinence, 15
academy: Neapolitan, 69; Plato's, 107n; Roman, 88
acolytes, 194
Acropolis, 112n
action / activity, 90; hidden, 164; mental, 95, 97; virtuous, 141, 150, 156, 160
actors, 75
adoption, 256n, 273n
adulation, 71, 92
adultery, 95, 161, 164, 166, 185, 269
advantage: personal / private, 7, 90, 96, 136, 142, 144, 154, 156, 158, 168, 190, 206, 209, 223, 262, 268, 278; public, 90, 99, 136, 230
adversity, 72, 76, 82, 84, 95, 156, 158, 160, 169, 268
advice / adviser, 69, 73, 78–9, 90, 92, 95–8, 100, 109, 130, 136, 150–1, 153–5, 158, 164, 166, 168, 174, 223, 231, 240–1, 256n, 259–62, 266, 271, 276, 282, 285, 285n
aedile, 69–70, 110; curule, 186
aequitas, see equity
affability, 78–9, 81, 84, 94, 163
agency, human, 39
agriculture, 105n, 120
air, 101; Venetian, 120
alienation, 43
alliances, 213, 276
alms, 143
alphabet, written, 178, 191
ambassadors, 78, 182, 200, 213–14, 220, 223, 234n, 238, 241
ambition, 70, 89, 121, 140, 150, 190, 192, 202, 208–9, 217, 219, 226, 240, 260
anarchy, popular, 202, 208
ancestors, 90–1, 94–5, 100, 249–54, 266; portraits of, 91, 252–3
anchorite, 176, 195n
angel, 55, 58, 189; of the Lord, 55
anger, 51, 53, 72, 78, 84, 99, 159, 162–3, 271
animals, 84, 102, 151, 153, 155, 160, 170n, 178, 185, 190–1, 197n, 249, 253; skins, 120

annulment, 286n
anointing, 54, 64n
anxiety, 77, 101, 150
apologues, *see* fables
appeals, 180–1, 196n, 213, 227–9, 261
appetite, 150, 168–9, 190, 217
apostasy, 128
apostles, 11n, 27, 34n, 53, 58, 60, 254
Apostolic See, 10, 238
appropriateness, *see* decorum
aqueducts, 110
Arabs, 185, 189
archery, 75, 102, 268
architecture, 113n, 184, 196n
aristocracy, 9–10, 17, 19, 23, 37, 90, 92, 104n, 117–18, 125n, 128–9, 132, 135–7, 201, 256n
Aristotelian corpus: *De anima,* 128; *De caelo,* 128; *De generatione animalium,* 128; *De generatione et corruptione,* 128; *De partibus animalium,* 128; *History of Animals,* 87n, 128; *Metaphysics,* 11n, 44n, 49, 60n, 170n, 233n; *Nicomachean Ethics,* 12n, 44nn, 85n, 105n, 106nn, 107n, 109, 112nn, 145nn, 149, 170nn, 171nn, 196n, 256nn, 259, 272n; *Physics,* 128; *Politics,* 12nn, 44n, 59, 65n, 90, 104nn, 106n, 125n, 133n, 144nn, 247, 255n; *Problems,* 128; *Rhetoric,* 128
Aristotelianism, 46–8, 51, 105n
arms, 90, 101, 103, 121, 123, 138, 157, 189, 224, 231, 239, 250
army, *see* soldiers
arrogance, 72–3, 82, 98, 162–3, 167, 192, 202, 251–2, 271
Ascension Day, 121, 126n
asceticism, 66n
assemblies, popular, 161
Assumption of the Virgin, 27
astrology, 46, 192
astronomy, 46, 191
atheism, 278, 286n
Athenians, 131, 133n, 189, 248
atomism, 172n
attorneys, *see* lawyers
audacity, 167, 192, 227
Auditori delle sentenze, 122

301